MW01012849

UNCOMFORTABLE QUESTIONS FOR COMFORTABLE JEWS

By Rabbi Meir Kahane

Institute for Publication of the Writings of
Rabbi Meir Kahane
Jerusalem 2011

First Edition: 1987, Lyle Stuart Inc., Secaucus, N.J.
Corrected Edition: 2011, Institute for Publication of the Writings of
    Rabbi Meir Kahane
    P. O. Box 39020
    Jerusalem, Israel

Email: mrslkahan@yahoo.com

Contents

PART VI

OUTRAGE OF TYRANNY

PART VII

CONCLUSION

PART I

A SADLY NECESSARY PRELUDE

"And I will make thee unto this people a fortified, brazen wall and they shall fight against thee but they shall not prevail against thee. For I am with thee to save thee and deliver thee," saith the L-rd, "and I will deliver thee out of the hand of the wicked and I will redeem thee out of the hand of the terrible" (*Jeremiah* 15).

Chapter 1

The Hate

Old witch hunters never die; they return in the form of Israeli liberal-leftist news media people, intellectuals and politicians along with presidents of Jewish Establishment groups and rabbis in the United States.

For those too young to have even experienced the late United States Senator Joe McCarthy and his smearing of character and names of innocent people, for those below the age of 300 or so, who never lived in Salem or participated in the great hunt, "which is witch," regret not. McCarthy and the Salem witch hunters have returned in full regalia, but this time in the Jewish communities of Israel and the Exile.

As I step back and review the events that have occurred since 26,000 Israelis voted that I be their representative in the Knesset, I am overwhelmed by the sheer magnitude of the screeching hatred of the liberal intellectual mob. "Racist," "fascist," "madman," "pig" were among the kinder epithets thrown out by the liberal humanists and democrats of the Jewish state and their partisans in America. "Hitler," "Nazi" were the more relevant, juicier imprecations brought down on my head. And, of course, all from people who pride themselves on their culture, fair play, democratic tolerance and intellectual ability to discuss any and all issues scientifically, calmly, rationally. Their hatred is a poisonous, noxious thing.

In the time since my election to Israel's Knesset, I have seen hatred and defamation and lies and shrill, irrational, hysterical bile—all within the framework of a stupefying refusal to debate me on any of the issues at hand. I have seen Israel government television and radio rule that Meir Kahane, a Knesset member whom they utterly oppose, be, therefore, not permitted to appear on programs; to have his statements reported; to have his press conferences covered. I have seen yellow-journalism reporting and blatant, deliberate lies, all with intent to smear and defame. I have seen the armed forces, whose neutrality and non-political status must be assured in order to unify rather than drive yet another wedge in the fabric of the people, plan a campaign of hate and defamation against Meir Kahane, a Knesset member, forcing soldiers to attend lectures by leftists that drip hatred and poisonous venom. I have seen the official army radio devote an entire day to a non-stop attack on Meir Kahane, a Knesset member, including the damning of his "crime"—seeking to have Jewish Law obeyed in the Jewish State. I have seen the Knesset rules changed more in the space of a year than in the previous 36 of the state, all in order to limit, as much as possible, Meir Kahane, a Knesset member, from exercising his right to speak and to propose legislation. I have seen the Knesset pass a rule that allows the Speaker, on his initiative and without need to defend his action, to refuse to table any bill that he considers "racist," *when no definition of racism is provided.* I have seen the power used to ban as racist two bills by Meir Kahane that quoted the great Talmudic codifier, Maimonides, word for word! I have seen a bill presented giving a *political* committee of the Knesset the right to ban a party as "racist," with racism defined as "causing animosity between sections of the people"—a definition that could ban every party in Israel, every newspaper in Israel, every second person in Israel.

I have seen police arbitrarily either refuse to grant permits for our rallies or allow a counter-rally within 30 meters of ours, with a loud-speaker blaring and thousands of whistles drowning out the speech. I have seen unashamed and open appeals to physically prevent Meir Kahane, a Knesset member, from speaking, and I have seen hordes of leftist storm troopers physically assault Jews. I have seen Knesset members walk out as Meir Kahane, a Knesset member, rose to speak, thus justifying the walkout by Arabs, Communists and Third World states on Israeli speakers in the U.N. whom *they* consider to be racists because they are Zionists. I have seen liberal, progressive American Jewish Establishment groups join in the lies, the smears and the refusals to sit at the same table and debate issues with Meir Kahane, a Knesset member, thus justifying PLO "hardliners" who will not participate in discussions with Zionists. I have seen synagogues and temples who have hosted Arabs and Black anti-Semites refuse to allow Meir Kahane, a Knesset member, to speak. I have seen Jewish establishments in the United States pressure hotels and halls to cancel contracts for meetings by Meir Kahane, a Knesset member. I have seen Jewish Establishment groups in Canada and Great Britain ask their governments to refuse to allow Meir Kahane, a Knesset member, entry into their country—and they have succeeded. I have seen a joint effort by Israel and the United States to take away the U.S. citizenship of Meir Kahane, a Knesset member, despite the fact that other such Knesset members over the years never were so threatened. I have seen the President of Israel welcome to his residence Communists and pro-PLO Arabs and refuse to do the same for Meir Kahane, a Jewish Zionist Knesset member. I have seen the same president cheerfully attend a national convention of the Israeli Communist Party where a message from Arafat condemning Zionism was read, while refusing to participate in the national convention of the party of Meir Kahane, another Knesset member. I have seen the Prime Minister of Israel say that he does not consider Knesset member Meir Kahane to be part of the Jewish people, thus opening the doors to a host of religious Jews to offer similar exit visas to other Jews.

I have seen the blue-shirted uniformed and uninformed leftist youths of *Hashomer Hatzair* and *Hanoar Haoved*, faces twisted in unbelievable ugliness, mouths cursing, arms making obscene gestures even as they threw eggs and rocks at other Jews who backed Kahane. I have seen the season of hate and hypocrisy as those who foam at the mouth over "fanatics" who throw stones over the Sabbath threw rocks over "fascism," as those who worship at the altar of democracy attempted to break up a legal meeting and tried to stifle free speech, as those who blast the "rightists" for lack of respect for the law charged a platform which was granted by police permit, lawfully. I have seen murder in the eyes of the leftists, the "mixed multitude" which has infiltrated the Jewishness of the Jewish people and who pollute us with their sick self-hate and hatred of other Jews. I have heard a call *to murder Jews*, and not a Jewish leader or intellectual or newspaper or liberal humanist cried out! I have seen incitement to murder of Jews, open and hysterical; permission, *mobilization*, to shed Jewish blood. I have seen Jews walk over to me and say anxiously, with the gravest of concern: "Watch yourself, be careful."

I have seen the face of the real fascism and real cruelty and real hate and real vicious animalism, and it is important that you see it too. For it is the face of gentilized Hebrews who represent all that is foreign and antithetical to Judaism, and who are driven by a deep pathology to attempt to destroy the source of their existence.

Let there be no mistake. These are the haters, the primordial, visceral haters whose ugliness is a stench that comes from deep in the soul. These are the real fascists, the real killers. They hate and wish to destroy Kahane—but only as a symbol of that which is the target of their ultimate hate. They hate Kahane because they hate Judaism and Jews, and themselves. And there is nothing they will not do in order to wipe out that Kahanism they correctly see as true Judaism, a Judaism that brands their own lives as fraudulent, empty and truly un-Jewish. Concerning these did the rabbis say: "Greater is the hate that an ignoramus has for a scholar than that of a gentile for a Jew." Greater by far; far, far greater. And far more dangerous.

They hate the Sabbath and they hate the laws of Judaism and they hate the yeshivas and they hate the rabbis. And they hate being Jewish and they hate G-d and they hate Zionism and a Jewish state and the need to be different—and they hate Kahane for representing all of this. And they hate the bitter reality of hundreds of thousands supporting and marching for and believing in all the things that they hate, and so they are prepared to use any and all means to destroy the Jews of Jewishness. And the most frightening and dangerous thing is that, in all this ugliness, I have seen and recognized the face of Hatred and Murder Past.

Chapter 2

The Past Is Present

The mayor stood before the crowd and shouted: "Kill them while they are still small!"

No, not some Muslim Shiite fanatic mayor of an Iranian or south Lebanese village. The mayor was the very antithesis of that. He was Yitzhak Yaron of the predominantly leftist town of Givatayim, a Tel Aviv suburb founded by militant proletarians. He was a man of the left, a progressive, a humanist, a profound believer in freedom of expression. He was a man who opposed fanaticism and violence and fascism and hatred—and so, of course, he cried: "Kill them while they are still small."

"Them" were the members of the Kach movement of Meir Kahane. "Them" were gathered in the town of Givatayim for a legal rally, complete with police permit. "Them" were confronted by a group of blue-shirted leftist youths bused in especially for the occasion as Mayor Yaron, Assistant Cabinet Ministers Adi Amorai and Shoshana Arbali-Almozlino and Knesset members rushed up to the platform to attempt to physically stop the legal rally from proceeding. "Them" suddenly found themselves the target of eggs and stones from the leftist, obscenity-shouting mob, and here it was that the progressive-humanist-liberal shouted his immortal words: "Kill them while they are still small!"

That was Givatayim I, in August, 1985, and the obstinate Kach movement insisted on holding yet another rally there the following month. The police permit, granted the week before the rally, brought forth a crusade hardly seen in the country since the days of the Christian upholders of the faith come to liberate the Holy Land from the infidels.

Israel state radio and television all but turned over their facilities to Yaron and a whole host of freedom fighters and progressive humanists, all of whom took to the airwaves to cry: "Come to Givatayim and stop the rally!"

Stop the rally? The *legal* rally? The rally with a *police permit*?

"But, of course. "Law" is such a subjective thing in the hands of those who cry, "Kill them while they are still small!" It is most relative in the hands of progressives and those who create the world in their own image. For them political rights are sacred to all. *To all of whom they approve*. And they manifestly did NOT approve of Meir Kahane and Kach. Ergo, there was not only a right, but an *obligation* to stop them and, if at all possible, to indeed kill them while they were still small.

For that is what they came to do. They came by the thousands, mostly members of the kibbutzim, the leftist communal settlements. Hundreds of buses, thousands of people. They came armed. Armed with a hatred that captured their faces, a hatred that one could touch, worse—smell. And they came with rocks and with metal bars. They came in their humanism and their hatred of violence—to hate and to smash. Anyone with a Kach shirt was the target of murderous venom and brutal fists. Anyone who looked *religious* was beaten. It was indeed a religious crusade out of the Middle Ages. A crusade of the religion of secularism, whose high priests had commanded the faithful to go out to holy war.

As my car drove towards the platform it was surrounded by hundreds of them, cursing, shouting, pounding on the windows, attempting to turn the car over. And then a huge rock smashed the front windshield as the crowd went wild with anticipation. It was only the frantic intervention of the police and border patrol that saved four Jews from being lynched by the apostles of tolerance and coexistence.

And the next day, the newspaper *Al Hamishmar*, organ of the Mapam Marxist party, carried a gloating article under the heading: "How sweet to see a violent Left..." And thus spake Zara-Progressive: "It was a sight to gladden the soul to see the leaders of *Hashomer Hatzair* and *Hanoar Haoved* [two leftist youth groups] and just ordinary citizens upholders of law and order angrily throwing eggs and stones and brandishing clubs.

"To the holy cannon that sank the *Altalena* was now added the holy stone, the stone that smashed the windshield of Kahane's car."

The holy stone. And *the holy cannon that sank the Altalena*. Not one in 100 outside Israel knows what the progressive writer is talking about. But it is most important that everyone know about the *Altalena* and the "holy cannon" that sank it. For, indeed, without the one it is impossible to understand the "holy stone" in Givatayim. Because a direct link, an historical thread, runs from one to the other. For Givatayim is more than a place. It is a concept. It represents all the hate and capacity for murder that lie in the ideological bosoms of the

fascist left. And that is why Givatayim, the concept, becomes the symbol of what Jews can do to other Jews.

The sea turned red off the coast of Tel Aviv that bright, sunlit Tues-
day in 1948. It ran red with the blood of 20 Jews—murdered by Jews.
Twenty Jews from the ship *Altalena*. Twenty Jews murdered by the
ideological forefathers of Givatayim. It was June 22, 1948, and the
government of the State of Israel, led by the leftists of
Givatayim-the-Idea, did indeed murder 20 Jews in cold blood. The
ones who gave the orders and those who carried them out were, overwhelmingly, from the same groups that today so foam at the mouth
against "Kahanism," so eagerly plant the same seeds of blind hatred,
and so impatiently prepare to sow the same kind of murder of Jews.

The Jews who were murdered on that June, 1948, day were members of Menachem Begin's underground group, the Irgun Zvai Leumi.
They were on a ship that was the product of years of agonizing efforts
and which, together with its precious cargo of arms, was worth a small
fortune. The ship was called the *Altalena*, after the pseudonym of the
late Zionist leader, Zev Jabotinsky. It was an American military LST,
purchased as surplus by the Irgun's Hebrew Committee for a Free
Palestine, and commanded by a U.S. Navy veteran named Monroe
Fein. At Marseilles it had been loaded with 5000 Lee-Enfeld rifles,
five million rounds of ammunition, 250 Bren machine guns, 50 can-
nons, 1,000 grenades, 400 aerial bombs, nine tanks, 50 anti-tank guns,
tons of medical equipment and more than 900 trained soldiers.

The new Israeli provisional government, composed of leftists led by
David Ben Gurion and his Mapai Labor Party, was notified of the
arrival of the ship and agreed not only to its arrival, but to the dispo-
sition of the weapons—80 percent to the regular army and 20 percent
to the Irgun, which would then disband and become part of the army.
The ship and its arms were a godsend to a tiny state that was attacked
by seven Arab armies, that was rapidly running out of weapons and
whose Jerusalem was under siege, surrounded by bands of hostile
Arabs. But the hate, the *psychopathic hate* of the leftists—driven by
the need to crush any opposition that threatened their grip on
power—overcame reason, logic, and love of Jews and state.

Menachem Begin, the "Kahane" of his time, was on board and the
leftists determined to liquidate him and crush for all time the Irgun
and its potential for taking power from the spiritual Bolsheviks.

As the ship lay at anchor off Tel Aviv's Frishman Street, David
Ben Gurion, darling of the Hadassah and UJA set, together with the
army's Chief of Staff Yigal Yadin and a man named Yitzhak Rabin

—later to become Prime Minister and Defense Minister of the State of Israel—gave orders to fire on Jews. To murder them.

Here are the words of Navy Commander Monroe Fein: "The ship continued to receive heavy firing from the shore for a period of about one and a half hours. Some of the heavy machine guns ashore were using armor-piercing ammunition which passed right through steel bulkheads of the ship. This fact began to cause numerous casualties. We had no doctor on board and some of our casualties were very seriously wounded. We contacted the army command and requested a cease-fire in order to allow us to remove the wounded men from the ship. We arranged that we would use our own LCVP for this purpose....

"During this time one of them [the wounded] died. One hour and a half later, and after repeated requests, there was still no sign of any boat. At this time, we were suddenly taken under fire by a large gun which was located on the coast to the north of the city. This gun fired three shots, all of which passed over the ship and exploded in the water beyond....

"During this time I conferred with the commander-in-chief of the Irgun and told him that if the gunfire should hit the ship, the ship, the cargo and possibly a good many lives would be lost and that he should at all costs maintain the cease-fire order until there could be further negotiations. This he agreed to do, but as he himself came up to talk on the radio to the headquarters ashore, the heavy gun resumed firing.

"As soon as the gun started a second time, I struck the flag as a sign of surrender. We again inquired of the Palmach commander whether the cease-fire order was in effect and the reply came that the cease-fire order was in effect but that he had been 'unable to contact all fronts.' Within a few seconds after this message was received, there was a direct hit on the ship which started a large fire in the cargo hold. The ship's crew made immediate and valiant efforts to put out this fire, but because of the nature of the cargo it proved beyond our capacity and I ordered all men aboard to prepare to abandon the ship.

"The first thought all of us had was to remove the wounded men. There was no panic. Everyone behaved in an extremely calm and heroic manner. As the men began jumping off the ship and swimming towards the shore, those of us still on board saw that they were being shot at continuously from rifles and machine-guns on the beach. I rushed to the bridge and began waving a white flag and shouting to stop the fire on the men who were swimming for their lives. At the same time another man hoisted a large piece of white canvas on the halyard, but these efforts were of little avail, as the firing continued."

(From the book *Days of Fire*, by Shmuel Katz, W.H. Allen, London, 1968.)

The sea turned red off the coast of Tel Aviv that day. It ran red with blood, Jewish blood, Jewish blood shed by Jews—in *cold* blood. Twenty Jews died that day, some shot as they swam to safety. It remained for Ben Gurion to add the obscene to the criminal. Addressing the Provisional State Council, the interim Parliament, the following day, he declared: "Blessed be the cannon that blew up the ship. It should be enshrined in the Third Temple of the Jewish people."

Obscene? Of course, but hardly as obscene as the gleeful remembrance of it—37 years later!—by a descendant of the fascist left who, naked of all decency and Jewishness, chortled not only over the murder of 20 fellow Jews in 1948 but over the desire to murder more, less than four decades later.

This is the reality of the Hellenized, gentilized Hebrews who took their East European socialism and hunger for power and cruelly set about the job of murdering Jews. And it was hardly the first such horror. There is more.

The same Ben Gurion, head not only of Labor but of the *Yishuv*, the Jewish community in *Eretz Yisrael* (known then as "Palestine"), addressed the Histadrut Convention in Tel Aviv on November 22, 1944. The Histadrut was the ingenious Labor monopoly-conglomerate-industry owner, trade union and political power all in one. The Histadrut was the economic barrel of the gun from which came leftist political power. And on that November day, Ben Gurion was furious and frightened. The Irgun and the Fighters for the Freedom of Israel, whom he derisively called the "Stern Gang," had made some incredibly daring attacks on the British, gaining the hearts and support of tens of thousands of Jews in the land. They were the heirs of the hated Jabotinsky movement (of which we will hear more a bit later), and posed a threat to the minds, hearts and political-economic power which Ben Gurion was determined never to lose, at any price. And so he spoke to his leftist comrades and Hellenists and declared war on Jews. He announced the start of a crusade that has become known as "The Season," the hunting season, the season of hunting down Jews. And thus spake the leader of the ethical, moralist, democratic, gentilized Hebrews:

"The time for action has arrived. Words have no influence—they are blank bullets. We have decided to vomit them out of our midst. Let those words, 'vomit them out of our midst,' not be empty phrases. The terrorists are not influenced by phrases.... The gangs are now waiting what will come out of this convention. The demand to vomit them out of our midst must be translated into a language of deeds by every one of us.... We must suppress in our hearts every personal feeling—let them not preach piety to us. Let every boy or girl be taught by our Youth Organizations that if the gangs come asking money of their fathers and mothers, he or she [the children] must immediately notify the proper authority. And if they don't know any other address, let them go to the [British] police....

"Since the British government and police are intent on exterminating the terror, we are collaborating with them—to that extent.... Without helping the British government and without its help we shall not uproot this contagious disease. I repudiate the kindness which was justified in other times. In our circumstances this is a twisted kindness, a kindness of fools.... There is no neutrality between us and terrorism. Either terrorist gangs or an organized Jewry—there is no escape from the alternative."

The leftist moralists did more than speak. They did, indeed, act in the spirit of their sickness. Special units of the Haganah, the "defense" organization, were set up to kidnap Irgun soldiers. One of the heads of these special units of Jewish shame was the man who later became Jerusalem's mayor, Teddy Kollek, yet another darling of the "Jewt" (Jewish jet) set. Jews of the Irgun and Sternists were taken to kibbutzim where they were tortured in an effort to extract information from them. One youngster, 17-year-old Yedidya Siegal, died as a result of the torture. Sympathizers with the Irgun were fired from jobs and youngsters were thrown out of school. It was Hellenistic totalitarianism at its most obscene. And they are the same; the same who, today, shout of Jewish values and morality, even as their faces are twisted in a hate that goes back to "The Season."

And there is more.

The American Jewish leadership is famous for its liberalism and dedication to free speech (and they are endlessly prepared to so inform anyone who inquires about it). Indeed, many are the Arabs, leftists and other "lovers of Zion" who have found shelter under the umbrella of Jewish Establishment liberalism and ideological largesse. But as with all things in this finite world, the liberal umbrella is certainly not unlimited. And the perimeter of its limits coincides, not too remarkably, precisely with that of liberal sympathy. And so the same Jewish leader who revels in the euphoria of tolerance and democracy and free expression for all who do not endanger his views and his calm, contented existence, becomes a raging, braying beast as he rushes to prevent the "fascist" and the "fanatic" from speaking, writing and—if possible—existing.

The year was 1935. Zionist leader Zev Jabotinsky was arriving in America from Europe. Zev Jabotinsky was what the genteel, gentile press would describe as "controversial and militant." Zev Jabotinsky was described by the snarling Jewish internal press as a fascist, Hitlerite demagogue and murderer. Needless to say, not one in a hundred of the American Jewish leaders, flunkies or writers had ever heard Jabotinsky speak or read a single essay of his. No matter. The Jewish Establishment, from time immemorial, possessed sensitive antennae capable of instantly recognizing one who was dangerous to its grip on power. This, in turn, led to a conditioned reflex: the use of every weapon of hate, calumny, filth and lie to disparage, crush and destroy him.

And so, Jabotinsky came to America to speak to Jews. To explain the disastrous policy of official Zionist cooperation with the British and of "self-restraint" (read pacifism) against murderous Arab attacks. To cry out for a militant policy and demand that the Zionist movement openly declare that its goal was an independent Jewish State (incredibly, Weizmann and Ben Gurion refused because of fear of British reaction), to appeal for understanding of his cry for emergency Jewish evacuation from Europe before the terrible flood of fire and holocaust. The "libercrites," the liberal hypocrites, who sin as Zimri and demand the reward of Phineas, began a campaign of defamation, smear and threats, whose purpose was to prevent as many Jews as possible from going to hear Jabotinsky.

Not a single Jewish leader, of course, dared to deal with the issues. Instead, every possible Jewish force was marshaled to fling as much filth as possible. The first big gun to be wheeled out was Albert Einstein, genius of physics, whose Theory of Relativity was most profoundly proven as he proceeded to demonstrate that genius in physics and asininity in political and ideological thinking are, indeed, most relative.

Einstein warned the American Student Zionist Federation, known as *Avukah*, "against the sirens of Jabotinsky and his Revisionist followers who are as much a danger to our youth as Hitler-ism is to German youth." No less! An impressively cool and well-reasoned statement from the genius of logical physics.

The libercrites were of course delighted at this blend of hatred and nonsense and got Einstein to issue a statement to *The New York Times* which accused Jabotinsky and his movement of seeking "to exploit the people and deprive them of their rights. The state of mind fed by Revisionism is the most serious obstacle in the way of our peaceful and friendly cooperation with the Arab people who are racially our kin." Indeed. And, indeed, a remarkably familiar theme.

The students, as expected, were used by the Establishment as the main thrust of the lance against Jabotinsky. *The Avukah Bulletin* of November 1934 accused Jabotinsky's movement of fascinating sins, "from murder and the use of knives in Poland and Palestine...." Of course, youth is unfortunately volatile and most unstable, and a rebellious Manhattan chapter of *Avukah* went against the party line and organized a Jabotinsky lecture. This outrageous display of liberal independence and affirmation of the right of Jewish expression was immediately punished by the feudal barons who ran (run!) the docile Jewish community. The chapter and its chairman, Isadore Solkoff, were expelled. The national president of *Avukah*, Selig S. Harris, a young man who understood quite well that one gets ahead by pleasing the barons, wrote a letter of explanation (March 20, 1935), saying:

"Free speech is all very nice but I think that Fascism by its very nature denies itself the right to ask of Democracy free speech."

Ah, how quaintly clever the liberal totalitarian mind. Having stated the axiom that "fascism" has no right to demand freedom of democracy, all that remains is to describe anyone whom we oppose as being a "fascist!"

In the monthly *Opinion*, the official magazine of the American Jewish Congress, published by James Waterman-Wise (son of Dr. Stephen Wise, doyen of American Zionism), an article appeared entitled, "Vladmir Jabotinsky—An Appraisal." It was somewhat less than that. Objective critics might have called it a piece of character assassination worthy of the talents of liberal-humanist intellectuals. He was merely called "a man-hater, a reactionary, militarist, vainglorious demagogue" whose Revisionist group destroys the Jewish youth of Poland so that "their minds became distorted with a hatred for all that is idealistic in Zionism, and they became a bastard organization which sends brown-shirted soldiers to Zionist Congresses."

And with the propaganda ground laid out (241 Reform rabbis signed an anti-Jabotinsky ad on January 27, 1935), more practical means were now begun to ruin the Jabotinsky visit. The Jabotinsky Reception Committee, a group of individuals from various Jewish groups, now became the target of the libercrite feudal barons. *Opinion* called on its members to resign and the Revisionist organ, *Our Voice*, sadly wrote that, "In certain out-of-town places, methods of coercion have been employed—threats have been made to deprive physicians of their patients, storekeepers and professions of part of their clientele."

And, of course, the Pope of American Zionism, Stephen Wise—the man who during the Holocaust years refused to jeopardize his master-dog relation with Franklin Roosevelt by leading militant demonstrations to demand the bombing of the extermination camps and the rail lines leading to them—now joined in the chorus of baying liberal hounds. In a speech in March, 1935, at New York's Carnegie Hall, Wise declared that "under the leadership of Mr. Jabotinsky, Revisionism is a menace to the security of the people of Israel and dangerous to the future of Zionism ... a peril to the Jewish people and to the dearest and holiest hope of the Jewish people."

Wise blasted Revisionism, saying that it was "becoming a species of fascism in Yiddish or in Hebrew (neither of which Wise, the "rabbi," could speak), adding, "If Revisionism prevails, we shall within a few years have fascistic labor armies *more Germanico* in Palestine." He attacked Jabotinsky for aspiring for an "Arabless Palestine" (and what strange echoes of the Wise man redound through the ages) as well as for a philosophy of militarism when the whole tradition of the Jewish people is against militarism" (thus effectively excommunicating the Maccabees, Bar Kochba, King David, the Judges and, of course, Moses, who failed to petition the Egyptian he saw smiting the Jew). And then Wise added: "Democracy and liberalism are almost as precious to me as the life of Jewish people." Of course, Wise was less than straightforward. Democracy and liberalism were *much more important* to him than the Jewish people and he said it best when he declared:

"A fascist and undemocratic Jewish State in Palestine would to me be an abomination to be destroyed."

No other reply could surpass Jabotinsky's. He quietly said: "Dr. Wise has one great quality: he says what he thinks. But he has a great defect: he does not think...."

But America remained a veritable sea of Jewish tolerance compared to the European and Eretz Yisrael leftists, born to gentilization and nurtured in the psychopathic hate of the Exile. The leftist-haters, already blooded by their murder of the Jew, Dehan (patience, dear reader, we will come to that in good time), organized a broad umbrella group against Jabotinsky and the Revisionists, which incited to hate, attacks and worse. In a statement in the summer of 1934 the coalition, made up of the Socialist leftists, *Poalei Zion, Hashomer Hatzair, Hapoel, Hechalutz* and the General Zionists of Yitzhak Grinbaum, stated: "Whoever is still concerned about the fate of Zionism must shake himself clear of the Revisionist past. No intercourse whatever with Revisionism. Let our motto be: 'Expel the Revisionist gangs from

Jewish life!'" Yet another leaflet, this one from the leftist *Hechalutz* group, was a vicious personal slander and character assassination of Jabotinsky, describing him as a "bloodthirsty beast" and "a man with a dark past." *Shades of our days!*

Jabotinsky's followers, knowing full well the nature of the Jewish leftist beast, pleaded with him to hire a bodyguard. He adamantly refused and only after determined badgering did he agree—for two weeks—to have a husky Jew named Kuliawy protect him.

The Zionist left in Europe determined to stop Jabotinsky in every way possible. Gangs of leftist humanists, dedicated to proletarian brotherhood and love of Arabs, attempted to physically disrupt Jabotinsky's speeches and to attack him. In the summer of 1933, an angry mob, incited by the leftist groups and Jewish news media, stoned him as he went to the lecture hall in the Polish city of Brest Litowsk. In Kovno (Kaunas), capital of Lithuania, a coalition of leftists composed of *Poalei Zion*, the *Bund, Folspartei* and Communists attacked Jabotinsky's car as it arrived at the hall where he was to speak. About thirty meters from the entrance, rocks began to fly and suddenly a large stone smashed the windshield of Jabotinsky's car, injuring the driver. Jabotinsky walked the remaining distance, surrounded by members of his *Betar* youth organization who protected him from the howling mob that shouted: "Murderer! Stop him! Here he is; stop him!" During the lecture the wild mob threw a hail of rocks on the iron roof of the hall.

The "democratic character" of the leftist-liberal-humanists rose to the surface during the Eighteenth Zionist Congress in 1933, a congress in which, Jabotinsky's biographer, Joseph B. Schechtman, writes, Jabotinsky "felt almost physically affected by the cold, intense hatred and scorn surrounding him and his colleagues in the Revisionist delegation. The entire atmosphere was permeated by a deliberate tendency to isolate and humiliate the Jabotinsky-led Revisionist faction." (*Fighter and Prophet*, Thomas Yoseloff, London (1961).)

The humiliation and baring of leftist-humanist-democratic fangs came about at this "congress" controlled by Labor, when in the election of a *Praesidium*, the tradition of including all the parties was broken when Labor stated that "there is in this hall a party, together with which Eretz Yisrael Labor refuses to sit on the Praesidium." Jabotinsky and the Revisionists were excluded.

When the first Revisionist speaker rose to address the convention, the Labor Zionists set a precedent for the Arabs and Third World U.N. states, by demonstratively walking out. But the depths of Zionist totalitarian realism were seen in the "debate" over the murder of Labor Zionist leader Chaim Arlosoroff that year.

Arlosoroff had been murdered while walking on the Tel Aviv sand dunes and, despite the fact that Arabs had been attacking Jews regularly during that period, the leftists erupted in a hysterical charge that the Revisionists were the murderers. Three Jabotinsky followers were arrested by the British and after a long and desperate campaign by Jabotinsky, aided by the late Chief Rabbi Avraham Kook, all were acquitted. All during that terrible summer of 1933, the liberal-leftist-humanists, committed to ethical qualities such as "innocent until proven guilty," embarked on an unbelievable witch hunt. Jabotinsky followers were attacked, vilified, thrown out of work. And at the convention, the Laborites pushed through a resolution which condemned, in barely-concealed innuendos, the Revisionists for "tendencies that are contrary to the fundamental principles of Jewish ethics," and which called "to eradicate from the Zionist movement any elements who are guilty or responsible for such tendencies."

When Jabotinsky sought to present a statement of declaration opposed to the official one, the Praesidium ruled that only such declarations could be read as it considered "admissible"! No discussion was allowed. It was a precedent that, some 50 years later, the Knesset of Israel would cheerily adapt.

The ugly face of the totalitarians of the left. A face and hands that did not stop even at the murder of those they politically opposed. And there are those who remember Jacob de Haan.

Jacob de Haan was a troubled man, torn and tossed by a stormy soul. Born in Holland, the son of a cantor, he fled his Jewishness and, as with so many young Jewish intellectuals, sought meaning against his rootlessness in the secular religions of socialism and anarchism (even for a while, flirting with Christianity). His divorce from Judaism appeared complete when he married a non-Jewish doctor. None of this, however, gave him the solace he so needed and his agony grew even as rumors of his homosexuality began to be heard. They were denied, but persisted.

And then, through a process that none will ever be able to define, he returned to his people and became an observant Jew. More, Zionism became a beacon to him and in 1918 he left his family and went to the Land of Israel where, again, he began a search for a tranquility that always eluded him. The religious community of the Land was divided between those who accepted Zionism and, within its context, sought to build a religious Jewish state, and the anti-Zionist observant Jews who saw the secular Zionist movement as a threat to Judaism and who condemned as a sin against G-d the effort to create a Jewish state without waiting for the Messianic era.

De Haan was attracted to the religious anti-Zionist movement and offered them a writing and publicity talent they badly needed. He began sending anti-Zionist reports to the general, non-Jewish press and even pro-Arab memoranda to international and British Mandatory agencies. But when he began to establish ties with the Arabs, including the Hashemite family of the Hejaz and later Jordan, he won the undying enmity of Zionist leaders and organizations. Threats were made on his life, threats that he ignored. He underestimated his enemies. As his bitterly unpopular views burgeoned into closer ties with the opponents of a Jewish Zionism, a decision was made to eliminate him. In the early evening hours of June 30, 1934, as Jacob de Haan left a small synagogue near Jerusalem's Shaarei Zedek Hospital, two men gunned him down. That was the first Jewish political murder in the Land of Israel in modern times.

But the murderers of the Jew were more than Jews. They were members of the official defense organization, Haganah, and one of the killers was a top Haganah Jerusalem official, Avraham Tahomi. More to the point, however, is the fact that the order to assassinate a Jew, a decision of monumental gravity, was given by the Haganah political high command in Jerusalem, headed by a man who would later become the second President of the State of Israel, Yitzhak Ben Tzvi, and his wife, the poetess Rahel Yanait. No matter how obnoxious or abhorrent de Haan's views may have been, the coldly planned murder of a Jew by the official leftist leadership of the Jewish community was an outrage of monumental proportions, and the fact *that not one in ten thousand Jews has ever heard of the incident* is testimony to the power of the established Jewish authorities and their news media to prevent and bury ugly truth when they so desire. It remains only to contrast the planned, calculated murder of De Haan by the highest echelons of the left, with the murder of a Peace Now activist, Emil Grunzweig, in Jerusalem in 1983. Oceans could not hold the flood of words, articles and moral outbursts by the left after the latter incident, despite the fact that the accused killer was an individual, with no membership in any organization, who took the action solely of his own volition. None of that prevented the leftist-dominated news media from embarking on an orgy of witch-hunting and Jewish flagellation not seen since the previous year's exhibition of Jewish masochism over the Christian massacre of Moslems in Beirut.

Let history record that the first brutal Jewish political murder in the Land of Israel of modern times was coldly and politically planned by the top leadership of the left and that one of the planners is immortalized today after having been elected president of the Jewish State. Woe unto the political tyrants who honor murderers of Jews for surely that guarantees the repeating of the process every time yet another Jew threatens their narrow interests.

There is hardly a Jew in Israel who doubts that the Israeli authorities are totally capable of political murder should they feel so threatened, should they perceive Meir Kahane as achieving mass political strength. That is the reason why at every rally there are Jews who nervously whisper, "*Shmore al atzmicha* (Watch yourself)."

And if the history of the Jewish left reeks of *physical* liquidation of those whom they perceive to be threats to their political power, let it be known that the worst of their crimes was the *spiritual* holocaust perpetrated upon the Jews of Arab lands, who poured into the country beginning in 1948. How little the average Jew outside of Israel knows about *that!* How important it is that he learn about the unholy tragedy that took place in the Holy Land even as the spiritual murderers boasted of their "ingathering of the Exiles."

The humanists and progressives, the leftists of Israel, unabashedly set themselves up as the high priests of ethics, democracy and other such sugar and spice and everything nice. These are the cloaks in which they sanctimoniously garb themselves in their war against Kahane.

One stands in utter awe, almost compelled to salute the sheer arrogance of people who speak of morality, Jewish values and democracy after what they did to the Sephardic Jews, those who came to Israel from the Arab countries of the Middle East and North Africa. The very same parties, groups, in many cases individuals, who deliberately and ruthlessly destroyed hundreds of thousands of these Jews in order to insure their political and ideological hegemony, today have the gall to condemn "Kahanism" in the name of morality, democracy and Jewish (sic) values!

The tragedy is, of course, that thanks to the stranglehold that Jewish leaders in both Israel and the Exile have on Jewish news media, the real story is simply not known. Indeed, thanks to the Establishment feudal barony, the story of the emigration of Jews from Arab countries to Israel has become a legend of magic carpet, pure and noble, and one of the truly great fund-raising tools for the United Jewish Appeal and Israel Bonds. The truth is quite different. The truth is mirrored in a youngster called Mordechai.

I first met him in what passes for the dining room in the Jerusalem police detention center. He looked to be no more than ten (I was to learn later that he was 14), tiny, thin with large, sad—such sad—eyes staring out of the pinched little face. He sat among the others, some his age, most older than he, a weak little smile on his face as the shouts for food rose from his table.

He was there awaiting removal to an "institution." He had been involved in various minor crimes and the authorities felt that he needed the discipline of an institution. Home for Mordechai was one of the "distressed neighborhoods" in Jerusalem (as they are known here). Home was a two-and-a-half room flat occupied by a father who drank a great deal and regularly engaged in loud and angry arguments with the mother. She was the main crutch for the family, working as well as keeping house for the six children, two of whom were no longer home, serving jail sentences in Ramle and Tel Mond prisons, respectively. A sister, 17, had just had an abortion, the indirect compliment of an Arab she met in a Zion Square disco one night.

And home was the Jerusalem neighborhood, a former Arab area that had been settled after the 1948 war by new immigrants, mostly from North Africa. It regularly produced more than its share of criminals for Israel's prison system, and drugs and violence were a regular part of its life.

Little Mordechai, who did not know it, was already doomed to a hopeless life of crime and violence, of prisons and arrests. He would acquire a broken heart even as he would break the hearts of others. Mordechai was going to an institution, the next stage in his descent to crime and hopelessness. In the institution, Mordechai would meet dozens of other Mordechais, each with his own need to show toughness and strength—the main measure of value in that society. He would learn more about crime than he knew before; would either submit to physical and mental degradations or endure regular beatings; would be in the hands of "counselors," the majority of whom were both unqualified and uninterested in helping the children; would be punished for offenses, run away and be returned. He would "graduate"—a child no longer, but rather a twisted youth, hurt and ready to hurt back, whose values would forever be shaped by the fundamental rule, "Get as much as possible without being caught."

There were tens of graduates of the institutions with me when I sat in the Ramle maximum security prison, courtesy of an "administrative arrest," yet another strange manifestation of "democracy," liberal-humanist-leftist style.

(For those who are unfamiliar with an "administrative arrest," it is an order signed by the Defense Minister which allows a person to be jailed for six months at a time without benefit of trial and without being informed of the charges. Clearly another example of "democratic Jewish values," as conceived by the Israel secular humanists who so oppose "Kahanism.")

The prisoners in Ramle and those of every other prison in Israel are eager testifiers to the criminal educational system through which they are passed. They are the Mordechais, ten, fifteen years afterwards. If the "institution" is the elementary school in the system, then Mordechai will inevitably be arrested and sent to the secondary school—the Tel Mond prison for youth, a hotbed of sadism and homosexuality. It has an unmatched record in the number of its graduates who continue on to the prison "universities" of Ramle, Beersheva, Shata and Damon. Mordechai's cot already awaits him.

Mordechai, his home, his neighborhood, are more than specific entities. They are concepts that symbolize hundreds of thousands of Israelis living in thousands of homes in hundreds of urban neighborhoods, development towns and *moshavim* (villages) in the Jewish state. For Mordechai is one of the huge number of Sephardic Jews who represent the greatest failure of, *the greatest crime* of and the greatest danger to the State of Israel.

In Mordechai is the example, *par excellence*, of the bankruptcy of secular Zionism, a political (and often socio-economic) ideology whose dream was to make the Jewish people a "normal" nation. Looked at from one aspect, the effort was a rousing success. If one measures normalcy in terms of all the social evils that beset every gentile nation, then secular Zionism succeeded brilliantly. Israel today is a state with a rampant drug problem; a spiraling crime rate with ever-increasing "hard" offenses such as murder, severe assault and rape; vandalism and extortion by school children against property and fellow students; an alarmingly large number of prostitutes; hard-core pornography and one of the highest rates of children born out of wedlock and abortions in the world.

The overwhelming majority of the criminals, prostitutes, drug pushers and drug addicts are Sephardic Jews. They are the victims of secular Zionism's "normalcy." They are the results of what can only be called the criminally deliberate efforts by the secular Zionist leaders (overwhelmingly European, socialist, progressive and anti-tradition) to secularize more than 700,000 Jewish immigrants from Arab lands.

When pointing to Mordechai, the ones who made him so invariably cite "poverty" as the culprit. Clearly, it is easier to seize upon that than to have to face up to one's own crimes, an admission that carries with it an excruciating realization that one's personal philosophy and beliefs are failures. For it is certainly poverty that created Mordechai and all the others like him. But not the material poverty that the socialists and politicians and the left so eagerly indict and that the neighborhood activists see as the cause of their plight.

The slum dwellers in Jerusalem surely lived in worse housing and under more frightful material conditions in Yemen, Morocco, Libya and Kurdistan. But one would have to strain his research to discover Jewish murder, rape and prostitution in those lands. In the slums of the Meah Shearim religious quarter one also finds tiny, cramped apartments populated by large families woefully in need of material items. For some reason, drugs, prostitution and criminals do not come from that poverty. No, those who created Mordechai and those whose secularism created the State of Mordechai would prefer to blame material poverty, but the reality lies elsewhere.

The bitter truth is that Mordechai and a hundred thousand like him are victims of a spiritual and values poverty. *And it is a poverty that was deliberately created for reasons of political power.*

It is beyond dispute that the Sephardic Jews who poured into Israel beginning in 1948 were overwhelmingly religious Jews. Close to 2,000 years of exile and a millennium under Moslem rule could not shake the deep religious faith of these Jews. Neither discrimination, nor persecution, nor persistent and often desperate poverty shook their belief in and practice of Judaism. Adherence to their faith created the high moral standards, the tightly-knit families and firm values that precluded moral and social degeneracy. It also, of course, kept them Zionists, in the real and original sense of the term—Jews who looked upon the return to Zion as a religious destiny, and who daily prayed for the opportunity to fulfill it.

History will record the heartbreaking truth that what the Moslems could not do in a thousand years, the secular Zionist Establishment in the Jewish State was able to accomplish in less than 25. Hundreds of thousands of Sephardic Jews who came to Israel wealthy in values and tradition, deeply Jewish and Zionist, were turned into spiritual paupers as the result of a deliberate policy of the secular Labor government of the new state.

The founders of political Zionism were overwhelmingly secularist, Western-oriented and determined to create a "new" Hebrew nation, free of antiquated religious ties. As the Jewish settlement in the land grew through the 1920s and 30s, the Zionist leader tended to be more and more a laborite, a socialist, as the workers' Parties gained in strength. They, in classic socialist terms, were at best negative to religion, and it was they who controlled the government and life in the new state.

It was a pitifully small country, with barely 600,000 Jews on the day of independence, and it had not only been created to gather in the exiles, but needed those exiles in order to survive. And the exiles came. Not from America or Canada or South Africa or Australia or Western Europe. Aside from remnants of the survivors of Hitler's Holocaust, the overwhelming majority of the immigrants were Sephardic Jews, impelled by a Zionism that needed neither Herzl nor Ben-Gurion for legitimacy. This was the Zionism that had preceded the secularists and socialists by some 1800 years, carried by religious Jews who, three times daily, prayed to Heaven: "And may our eyes behold Thy return to Zion in mercy...."

By the hundreds of thousands they returned to Zion, propelled by a naive belief that their arrival in Eretz Yisrael—the Land of Israel—meant their arrival in a Jewish State. It was hardly that, for the political, secular Zionists rather intended a *State of Jews*, and the difference was enormous. Indeed, that difference was so clear to the leaders of Israel that they understood exactly the danger that the Sephardic immigrants posed to the secular State of Jews which they sought to build.

In reality, there were two dangers. Here were masses of Jews whose birthrate was much higher than that of the "enlightened" Europeans, pouring into an Israel that was pledged to equality and democracy. These people represented everything that contradicted what the progressive secularists sought. They were religious, the Israeli leaders were not. They would seek a society that was traditional, the Israeli leaders wanted a modern, secular state. They would expect religious law—the same that they had followed for centuries in the Exile—to, naturally, shape the state in Eretz Yisrael. This was anathema to the European-born leaders of Israel, not only the Marxist and other socialists, but also the middle-class liberals and intelligentsia.

On the other hand, these new immigrants posed a distinct threat to the political hegemony of Labor. Here was a huge bloc of citizens. For whom would they vote? It was more than reasonable to assume that eventually they would follow one or another of the religious parties, or a nationalist one. The thought was a nightmarish one to the Israeli leaders who had already taken steps to deal with more minor threats in the past.

Thus, for example, in the terrible pre-holocaust 1930s, with European Jewry desperate to escape to Eretz Yisrael (then the British-ruled "Palestine"), legal migration was limited to the number of entry certificates issued by the British. These certificates—which meant life to the recipients—were given to the heads of the Jewish *Yishuv* (community) in Eretz Yisrael to distribute as they saw fit. These leaders, essentially the same as those who later took control of the new state, blatantly discriminated against religious Jewry. The Agudat Israel party in Poland, religious Jewry's largest and one that could easily claim the allegiance of almost half of Polish Jewry, was limited to six percent of the certificates. The right-wing Revisionists and Betar groups, the deadly political enemies of the socialist groups, were treated even more brutally, with certificates almost never finding their way into their hands. If the secular laborites did not plot the destruction of the nationalist and religious Jewry, their deliberate policy of blocking their entry to the Land of Israel resulted in precisely that.

During the war years, the same determined policy to defeat—by any means—any religious growth in the land, was manifested in the case of what has come to be known as "The Children of Teheran." These were youngsters from all over Eastern Europe who had escaped the Nazi terror and had been gathered up by the Jewish Agency (the representatives of the Jewish community in Eretz Yisrael). They were taken to Teheran, capital of Iran, where they lived in a special center. Overwhelmingly religious, they were subjected to pressure, coercion and other efforts to rid them of their religious convictions and practices. The efforts were largely successful, since it is difficult for children, some as young as eight and nine, to withstand constant derision, punishment and other forms of adult pressure. Now in 1948, faced with a far greater danger to their views and political power, the secular, socialist Zionists brutally embarked on essentially the same solution.

A deliberate, ruthless campaign to spiritually destroy Sephardic Jews through the brutal use of governmental force and coercion, in manners so reminiscent of totalitarian, police states, was planned and launched by the same leftists and "progressives" who today bellow and belch forth their orchestrated attacks on Kahanism." Those who today din into our ears the cries of "morality, Jewish values and democracy" were guilty of the crudest and most ruthless campaign of spiritual genocide against fellow Jews.

The newly arrived immigrants were awed by the immense change in their lives wrought by their sudden removal from Moslem lands to modern societies, so different in every way—politically, economically, religiously, culturally, socially. They were placed in transit camps that were physically controlled by the leftist officials of the ruling Mapai and Mapam secular-socialist parties. There, their lives were scrupulously dominated by these officials, who barred almost all contact between the newly arrived immigrants and religious and nationalist representatives of Israeli groups. Police were literally brought in to enforce the isolation of the Sephardic Jews in order to ensure the spiritual genocide that aimed at destroying the centuries-old religious- national way of life of these hundreds of thousands of immigrants, who threatened the political hegemony of the secular left.

The key weapon was employment, or the threat of withholding work from those immigrants who did not cooperate with the authorities. And so, those who sought employment were asked: "Are you a member of the Histadrut?" Those who were not were simply not given jobs. Those who did join, under the crude pressure and extortion, found themselves locked into a political-economic-social complex which demanded that they vote a certain way if they wished to retain their jobs. And the threat of no employment was also a part of a brutal blackmail and extortion used against families who sought to send their children to state religious schools. Jobs were withheld from fathers, and towns were told that employment and funds for needed services would be allocated on the basis of their school enrollments. Religious schools and teachers were often the target of physical violence by government-paid hoodlums. Let those who today, in Israel, speak of "religious coercion" know what religious genocide means.

Time and space simply do not suffice here to detail the specific tragedies that occurred (such a thing should be produced for public enlightenment in detailed book form). But who can overlook the brutal deception of Youth Aliyah, which brought tens of thousands of young Sephardic Jews to the Land of Israel? Almost all were religious and their families were convinced that they would be placed in a religious environment. Instead, they were sent to irreligious and anti-religious institutions and frameworks, such as kibbutzim of the Marxist Hashomer Hatzair, where short shrift was made of their millennia-old religious traditions. Saddest of all, in this connection, was the spiritual destruction of thousands of Yemenite children, unanimously religious, who naively arrived in the Land with their *payot* (earlocks) and *Shabbat* (Sabbath) and were quickly shorn of both.

And all the time, the left totalitarians kept their grip on the private lives of the Sephardic Jews. Cultural and social life was given over to secular, anti-religious counselors whose job was to "transform" at least the younger Sephardim. And all this with a "philosophy" that justified spiritual genocide by rationalizing: "Religion was needed for the Exile. Here in Israel one can be a Jew without it."

The bottom line, the great lesson to be learned from the spiritual destruction of Jews in Israel, is that it was a deliberate, cynical, ruthless effort by hypocrites who revel in attacking others for their lack of "morality, ethics, Jewish values and democracy." It is they, the leftists and progressives of Israel, the liberals and humanists, who are so riddled with hate of Judaism, who are so ensnared in their lust for power, that they stop at nothing. If the rabbis tell us that "one who condemns speaks of his own blemish," the proof is blatantly clear for all to see in the State of Israel. Brutal politicians, gripped by a totalitarian mentality, coldly and ruthlessly set about to use every weapon of rightist and leftist fascism to destroy people.

Within twenty years, no one could doubt the success of the secularist. Hundreds of thousands of young Sephardim, conditioned by their modern "enlightened" Ashkenazi teachers, counselors, media and leaders to look upon the religion of their parents—and their parents themselves—as "primitive," dropped their Judaism. Aboard the new Jewish ship of state, they jettisoned the spiritual baggage of ages. Overboard went the Sabbath, *kashrut*, prayers, study, laws and obligations. "This year we are free men; this year in Jerusalem." The secular Zionists had won. But though the triumphant politicians did not realize it, the Jewish people and the Jewish state had been dealt a fatal blow. All—including those who had designed the spiritual genocide—would soon pay a bitter price. The spirit-snatchers believed that they could rob the Sephardi of his Judaism and leave him with "Jewishness" or Zionism. No greater mistake could have been imagined.

Those who destroyed the Jewish spirit of the Sephardic Jews left only a body that demanded satisfaction of its hunger. Without Judaism, gone were all the religious values of holiness and awe of Heaven, abstention from material excess, spiritual discipline, respect for property, horror of shedding the blood of a fellow Jew, the sanctity of marriage, man's purpose and joy in life to love a wife and raise a family faithful to G-d, Divine reward and punishment.

In place of all this, the secular Zionists could give nothing except "normalcy." And normal the Sephardim became. The void in their lives was filled by materialism and the need for money to satisfy desires. The movies, magazines, television, newspapers and songs that became the normal fare of the "normal" secular state pandered to and inflamed those material desires.

Life's goal became one of avoiding as much pain as possible and achieving as much pleasure as one could. Values centered totally about money and the cost of an automobile, refrigerator, television set and clothing. Yesterday's luxury items became today's necessities.

One's status was determined no longer by Torah knowledge or piety, but by money and possessions. Dreams of a fancy automobile, good-looking women, clothing and trips to Europe were fueled and fed by the culture of the "normal" secular state.

Everything foreign, and especially American, became an object of envy and emulation. American jeans, American songs, American products, American movie and TV stars—and most of all, America itself. The dream was of being able to emigrate from an Israel that meant poverty, taxes, annual army service, inflation and war. The vision was of becoming rich in America. The values of Torah having been destroyed, the secular leaders of Israel watched as the Sephardic Jews hastened to replace them with those of Dizengoff Street. And that, only until the glorious day when they might reach the Promised Land of Times Square and Beverly Hills.

Irony of ironies! "In the manner that a man measures, so is he measured." Divine punishment was grimly humorous. The punishment of the destroyers of Judaism became the precise consequence of their own actions. They believed that they could destroy Judaism and create a new "Hebrew," with pride in Jewishness and Zionism. The reality was the new "normal" Israeli they created who did not care a fig about Judaism *or Zionism*. Too late did the spirit-snatchers realize that, eventually, there is no meaningful logical pride in being "Jewish" without Judaism. To their dismay, they came to understand Zionism can only survive on the basis of Judaism.

Of course, the "new" Sephardim did not become "Zionists." After all, in this they were merely following the disintegration of the Ashkenazi children of the secular Zionist leadership, who had been spiritually destroyed even earlier. If the Ashkenazi product walked about proclaiming, "I am an Israeli, not a Jew," what could one demand from the Sephardi?

Logically speaking, what was this ideal of "Jewishness" in the hands of the secularists? Religion had no place in it. What was left was "nationalism." Who really cared about that? What in the end was so different about a pretty girl if she was Jewish, Swedish, French or Arab? Zionism—Jewish nationalism shorn of religion—could not explain to the young Israeli why he should not marry a *shiksa* or remain in a Hebrew-speaking Spain or Greece with its heavy economic and military burden of insecurity, when he could live the good "normal" life in the West.

The contentment and inner peace of Judaism for the Sephardi had been replaced by "normal" dissatisfaction and desire. Their effects were seen in the angry and sullen resentment of a wife who was not as beautiful as the American actress; of the small flat which did not match the magnificent homes shown in the previous night's American television movie; in the frustration of repressed and unrequited desires.

Husbands and wives quarreled bitterly; both became unfaithful. Escape was found in drinking and drugs. Children demanded things parents could not afford. Envy and coveting, desire and yearning for material things, led to breakdown of family and social life. Conversation became obsessed with money and possessions.

Desire remains unrequited for just so long. Yearning and coveting eventually lead to active steps towards acquisition. Burglaries, robberies, auto thefts. And sin begets sin, so that the crimes begin to assume an ever more violent form. Beatings, muggings, extortion accompanied by bombings. And sin begat more sin so that violence escalated and was joined by brutality. Brutal robberies of elderly people in their homes; brutal tortures and terror by school children against fellow students; an explosion of rape and murder, every month, every week, every few days.

How much Jewish murder was there in Iraq? Rape in Jewish Yemen? Brutal extortion of the elderly in Morocco? Let the secular Zionists who decry and deplore and rage against crime know who planted the seeds. *And who are the worst of the criminals.*

And know that if, today, on Jerusalem walls there can be painted swastikas and horrifying messages aimed at Ashkenazi Jews, the source of the evil is the same. If a potential Ashkenazi-Sephardi communal confrontation looms and shocking hatred lies just beneath the surface, the spiritual destruction of Sephardic Jewry is the major cause.

Those who took from the Sephardic Jews their Judaism robbed them too of their self-esteem, pride, sense of identity and reason for being. The Sephardim arrived in Israel, products of Arab underdeveloped countries. They lagged behind European Jews in secular, scientific areas of knowledge. What they did have, with pride and expertise, was religion, with all its values and practices. It was this that made them second to no other Jew. When that was taken from them, they were stripped naked and left as "backward people," lagging behind the "enlightened" Ashkenazim.

From the proud communities whose antecedents lay in the great Torah centers and scholars of the past, they became "primitives," in need of Ashkenazi enlightenment. It destroyed their self-esteem and bred feelings of inferiority, self-doubt and self-hate. And he who hates himself cannot but hate others.

And thus, so many fill the prisons and welfare centers, sit on the iron railings and waste their days and lives, escape through drugs and drink. Their women are the streetwalkers of Tel Aviv and they live with Arabs in the orange groves of the coastal plain. Their families are split asunder and a sense of deep bitterness and anger rests in them.

It is a bitterness that is a ticking time bomb, whose moment of explosive truth arrives in the wake of social, economic and political crises in Israel. The descendants of communities that produced Maimonides, Nachmanides, the Rif, Rabi Yosef Karo and an army of scholars—see them today in the prisons of Ramle and Shata. The Jews of our time underwent two terrible holocausts. The one was launched by gentiles and was a physical genocide. The other is less readily recognized; it was the Jewish attack on the spirit of Judaism that pounded within the hearts of hundreds of thousands of Jews from Arab lands. It is a crime for which we all pay today but whose ultimate cost will be frightening.

Secular Zionists sought to destroy the "old" religious Jew and create a new Sephardic one in their own image. Let them look well at the image they created. It is secularism by practice. No greater proof of the colossal failure and bankruptcy of secular Zionism can be found than in the fruits of its own works. They destroyed Judaism—and with it, any semblance of Zionism, any proud sense of uniqueness. They destroyed any hope of a Jewish State and did not realize that with it would also go the State of Jews. The deliberate destruction of the magnificent Sephardic Judaism is a crime that will pound and tingle all the ears of future generations that shall hear of it. And how many Western Walls, and how many tears of penitence, and how much beating of the breast will it take to begin to wipe away the terrible stain?

For 37 years, many waited for someone to reach the Knesset and say these things, to give unto the hypocrites of humanism and enlightenment as they gave unto others. I have arrived.

Chapter 3

The Bulldozers of Hate

That is the background. That is the record of the people and parties who screech in hate against Kahane. And it is that background and that record that help so much to explain the sickness of soul and the capacity of these people today. Those who killed and trampled on Jews yesterday are clearly capable of repeating it today in their una-dulterated, blind, psychopathic hatred of Kahane and of what has come to be called "Kahanism." Not the slightest effort to reason; not the slightest attempt to debate; not the slightest willingness to meet and intellectually discuss the very real issues. Hate, only hate. And *murder*, in the eyes and in the souls of the haters. The hate and murder that come from a long left-liberal-humanist tradition. The hate and murder that blind and block all reason, logic, normalcy. The hate and murder that turn man into a savage beast, lusting and yearning to lash out and kill.

The hate and murder that lays bare the sheer hypocrisy of "demo-crats" who call for the shutting of mouths and the utter fraud of "hu-manists" calling for physical violence against those they oppose. The naked contradiction of soul of liberals who call for the end of rights and freedoms for those they consider dangerous to *their* views.

And so, the Kach Movement prepares for its annual convention. It applies for a hall in Jerusalem's Convention Center, owned by the Jewish Agency, the public body set up to coordinate Zionist activities between Israel and Jews in the Exile. Arye Dulzin, the chairman of the Jewish Agency, a corpulent, wealthy Mexican Jew, refuses the application. He bitterly differs with Kach's policies. He will not allow the public hall to be rented by a Zionist Political party that sits in the Knesset. The night before the scheduled convention, the Communist Party has the hall for a concert featuring a Soviet Moslem singer. No doubt a radical Zionist.

The court forces the Jewish Agency to rent the hall. That, it turns out, is the easy part. The second half of the problem, the storm troop-ers of the left, is not so easily disposed of.

Large ads appear in all the papers. They read: "There is no place for Kach in our country." Peace Now and a host of other leftist groups, including one called *Ma'ane*—an umbrella group formed to fight Kahane—openly proclaim their intention to stop the convention; thousands of leftists are bused in from kibbutzim and other cities. A large PLO flag is carried as well as banners against Kahane, Kach and "racism." Leftist and Arab Knesset members speak; Teddy Kollek brays. The message is the same: Stop the "fascists."

As Kahane arrives, the leftists grow mad with rage. The police succeed in getting Kahane through the crowd into the hall but Kach members are attacked and physically beaten. The police, after an hour of indifference, now give the Border Patrol, the tough special police force known for its sympathy to Kahane, orders to push the leftists back. In a letter to the Histadrut paper, *Davar*, one of the leaders of the anti-Kahane crusade, veteran leftist Dov Yirmiya, writes: "I am a criminal; I broke the law when I burst the barriers near Convention Center to stop the arch-racist. I broke the law and am proud of it."

Gideon Rafael, former director-general of the Foreign Ministry writes in *the Jerusalem Post*, calling for mass violation of the law in order to stop Kahane. He says: "A human wall of non-violent but steadfast resisters can make the slogan 'Kahane shall not pass' an irresistible reality, a wall that stands firm even if confronted by baton-wielding mounted police." And Rafael exemplifies the babbling and dangerous "progressive democrat" as he continues: "It is unthinkable that the political authority responsible for the police would permit it to trample down nonviolent defenders of Israel's democracy." Translation: Since we have decided that Kahane is dangerous, we expect the political minister who runs the police to give orders to them to allow us to break the law and prevent Kahane from speaking.

A leaflet at a Kahane rally, issued by the Israeli Socialist left, is headed: "He has no right to speak!" Its operative sentence reads: "Preventing Kahane and his associates from their racist incitement is a remarkable example of civic action and no factor, government or other, has the right to stop us."

Young children are mobilized by the leftists to come to Kahane rallies with whistles and to shout him down. Leftist writer Teddy Preuss, writing in the newspaper *Davar*, says: "In view of the apathy of the Knesset, citizen organization is the last barrier to fascism. By organization, I mean the taking of steps more practical than whistles. How the mounted police will behave is not difficult to imagine, but this is the danger that the supporters of democracy must take upon themselves."

The call is to smash the law and destroy the opposition. All this I have seen. The twisted faces, the obscene gestures, the curses, the hate. The face of those who want a civil war. Once again, the face of The Season.

How important, how terribly important it is for all to know them, as they truly were, as they truly are. No one can even begin to understand their awesome sickness of soul and thus learn to discount their vicious lies and wild, savage defamation, unless he really knows their past, their awful crimes, their terrible readiness to stop at nothing to crush those who stand in their way.

And those in the Exile. The Jewish leaders, the feudal barons of the Exile. How *they* hate and fear Kahane and move heaven and earth to silence him there. How they frantically use their awesome money and power that has created such a feudal empire, to attempt to prevent Kahane from appearing before Jews. They who control Jewish public funds and dispense to only those institutions they see as acceptable (read docile and accepting). Through the weapons of fear and monetary blackmail, they rule unfettered, never elected by the community, never questioned by the bleating flocks. Benevolent despots, they move patronizingly among their fawning serfs, dispensing favors and honors, sure of both their own power as well as of the timidity, apathy, fear and docility of the serfs. But when a rebel rises up and when he dares to cry out the truth of their nakedness, their ugliness, their threat to the very existence of the sheep, the flocks, the Jews—then the fangs are bared, the ugliness revealed. Then the fascists arise!

They are frozen at the thought of Kahane describing their own Establishment's emptiness, of their having sat quietly by during the Holocaust, of their apathy concerning Soviet Jewry, of their policies of "the melting pot" and interfaith and all the rest that led to the spiritual destruction of hundreds of thousands of Jewish youth.

They are terrified at having Jews asked by Kahane the simple question: Do you agree that Arabs have the right to democratically, peacefully, quietly and non-violently become the majority in Israel and vote the Jewish state out of existence? They shudder at Kahane describing the weekly murders of Jews in Israel; the incredible assimilation and growth of intermarriage in Israel between Jews and Arabs; the clear, logical, painfully obvious fact that Arabs in Israel do not want to live in a Jewish state and will do everything possible to make sure that their national anthem will not be the "Hatikva" that speaks of "the soul of a Jew yearning." They resent Kahane's laying out of the basic contradiction between western democracy and a Jewish state.

Above all, their blood chills at the Kahane message to his Jewish audience: *Who elected your Jewish leaders?* Who elected the feudal barons who control Jewish funds, allocate Jewish moneys, run the community as their fiefdom? They, who are so bankrupt, can never allow Kahane to tell the Jewish community: *Your Jewish leaders are bankrupt!*

And, so they must attempt to silence Kahane, and the methods they use do not matter. You ask: If Kahane is so insane and so wrong, why not debate him and, before millions of people, destroy him once and for all? A magnificent question. Why *not* debate Kahane and destroy him intellectually? But of course, they can never debate Kahane; he will destroy them. And so, when Kahane comes to any Jewish city and demands a debate or meeting, they run in terror. Of course they tell the news media that their reason is that they do not wish to "legitimatize" Kahane. But the truth is clear. The same ones who will meet with Arabs because "one must meet with those with whom we differ"; the ones who, if Farrakhan wrote and asked for a meeting to "dialogue," would fall all over themselves—these can never meet with Kahane. For the Arabs and Farrakhan are really not threats to the Jewish feudal barons. Kahane is. He rips away their pretensions. He tells the sheep: Look at your shepherds, your murderers.

And so, in Los Angeles, one Rabbi Harold Schulweis, famous in the San Fernando Valley, esteemed by the masses as a "scholar," has had an Arab Knesset member speak in his temple. The Arab won fame for his desire to fly to the PLO conference in Amman (against Israeli law); but he is welcomed. Kahane, despite a barrage of advertisements in the local L.A. press, is *verboten* in the castle of the Baron of Schulweis. Not one temple in the Valley (or on the mountain) will have Kahane. Not one Jewish leader will speak with Kahane on the issues.

But that is only the beginning. The Jewish establishment bulldozer attempts to insure that the Jewish community will not hear Kahane at all.

Let me tell you a story. A story about the feudal barons, the fat, the powerful, the frightened—in Houston, Texas.

Houston, Texas, a powerful land, a powerful state, rolling in wealth and arrogance; as Heine said, "as the Christian, so the Jew." The arrogant Jewish feudal barons are suddenly shaken as they hear that "Kahane is coming." The local Kach chapter, under Dr. Richard Rolnick, a physician at the Baylor College of Medicine, has a signed, paid-for contract with the Marriott Astrodome Hotel to have Kahane speak. Rolnick sits down with the *Jewish Herald-Voice*, the local paper, and they work out with him an advertisement. It is paid for, set to go into that week's paper. The democratic way of life is proceeding smoothly in Houston, Texas.

Enter the Jewish barons. The Greater Houston Jewish Federation and the American Jewish Committee now contact the Marriott. The usual is said: "You could lose Jewish business," "Possible violence." The Marriott understands the facts of life. It cancels a signed contract. That same day, the Jewish paper which was so happy to take the ad suddenly contacts Rolnick. It cannot. The bulldozer of fascism has crushed the little people.

Rolnick finds another hotel, the Astro Village. Its owners, not Jewish, do not give into pressure. Ellen Cohen of the American Jewish Committee tries the same tactics: "You may lose Jewish business." The answer: "We have no Jewish business." "There could be violence." "We can handle violence." When the newspapers contact the embarrassed Jewish barons, they are forced to admit that they did contact the hotels, but only to make clear to them that Rabbi Meir Kahane of the Knesset in Israel is not the local rabbi, Moshe Cahana (that is how he spells his name) of Houston!

The lies are so grotesque that even the newsmen laugh. By now it emerges that the Israeli Consulate sent a man down to the local Jewish paper to make sure that no ad would appear. Rolnick has the facts on tape. Needless to say the two Jewish merchants who originally were eager to sell tickets for the speech suddenly call and say they don't agree with Kahane.

The feudal barons are terrified of Kahane. The thought of the Knesset member being heard by Jews is so nightmarish to them for the sublimely simple reason that they know that once Kahane has an opportunity to meet and speak with Jews, the ugly and false image that has been so perfidiously constructed will melt away as snow in the warm spring sun.

The fat, the powerful, the frightened. Kahane frightens them more than any Jew since the rise of Israel. For he speaks of a total change in society. Not merely a political one, but the total redoing of society. The remaking of Israel into a Jewish state. The permanent remaking of values in Jewish ones, the creation of a new and permanent generation of Jews. The promise that the feudal barons, the Hellenists, the mixed multitude, the Hebrew-speaking gentiles in Israel and the foreigners in Jewish Establishment clothing in the Exile will be forever thrown out of power.

That is the greatest of all fears, and as we see that fear oozing out of their pores, the vicious smell of their natural reaction, fascism, fills the air and the nostrils. They will stop at nothing. They have in the past murdered, bodies and souls. Why not the same now, when their very kingdom is at stake?

The haters who comprise the power structure have poisoned millions of Jews, have injected them with their poisonous hate. Millions who have never heard Kahane speak, have never read a book of his, have never had the slightest contact with him or his views, hate and despise him. They are victims of the haters with their immense power over the news media, their intense *supporters* within that news media. If in centuries past, Alexander Pope could write of a social gathering as a place where "with every word a reputation dies," can one imagine the awesome power of a political machine-television-radio-newspaper conglomerate that can destroy a reputation in the minds of *tens of millions* with every broadcast or telecast or issue?

The average person is the daily victim of the awesome power of a political-economic machine that controls communications, that shapes him, that directs him, that makes him. He is the victim, he is the lamb led to intellectual slaughter. The feudal barons of Israel and the Jewish Establishment leaders in the United States and other parts of the Exile control the Jewish community in a way that is almost breathtaking in its awesomeness. They use this power to put into motion their drive to smear, defame and destroy Kahane in the eyes of the Jew and gentile alike. And their most powerful of weapons, the one they count most upon to assure their control of the mind and pocketbook of the Jew who lives outside of Israel, is their knowledge of *his psychological dependence on Israel*.

Not one in a thousand western Jews will ever willingly go on *aliya*, emigrate to Israel. But millions of Jews *need* a Jewish state, *need to believe in it*. For most western Jews believe in nothing that is Jewish, except Israel. For millions, it is Israel that is the cornerstone and totality of their "Jewishness."

They are not observant Jews and therefore Judaism for them is, at best, the Reform and Conservatism that allows them to play with Judaism as much or as little as they care to. They do not really believe in the G-d of the Jews, but lacking the courage to state their atheism, they create a G-d, a comfortable G-d in their own image, cut to garment center proportions. What, then, can give them practical and concrete expression of their "Jewishness?" What can give them the identity they so desperately need and seek? Why, only Israel.

It is Israel that can make the Jew feel strong in the face of gentile contempt for Jewish "weakness." It is Israel that makes him its partner in swift vengeance against Arab armies and terrorists so that a Six Day War finds the Jew of Cleveland or Chicago basking in the reflected sun of gentile awe. It is Israel that allows him to see a Jewish tank, a Jewish gun, a Jewish jet—all things that in his heart of hearts, even the most liberal and progressive Jew secretly loves.

And it is Israel that is his insurance policy against the anti-Semitism he may publicly pooh-pooh, but which in his secret chambers he deeply worries about.

He loves this Israel, and his check to the UJA or Israel Bonds is a cheap enough price to pay for the vicarious benefits it gives him. And this being so, he is willing, indeed, eager, to hear only good about the Jewish State. He does not want to visit Israel and hear about the real problems. He does not really want to visit the real Israel; his is the world of the tourist that has about as much connection and relevance to the real state of the Jewish State as does the Statue of Liberty to the reality of United States economic, social and political problems.

He knows nothing about the real, critical problems and less about the political machine that is the power in Israel. He knows nothing and *does not want to know!* He wants to celebrate and be happy when he comes to Israel or attends lectures about Israel in his temple or community center. He wants to feel good and wants to listen to people who will make him feel good. Israel is his vicarious escape into the world of pride and strength and he is not about to be disillusioned.

But such a person does not love Israel. He loves only himself. Those who love someone or something do not run from the terrible realities that afflict the one they love. They seek to look, diagnose and cure. That is why this is written. To give concrete form to the words of the rabbis:

"All love that does not have with it criticism, is not real love." He who truly loves Israel, the Jewish state, lives there and says the difficult things that will not only make it better, but will help it to survive. The difficult and so-uncomfortable things! Things like: A Jewish state, a Zionist state, stands in stark contradiction to western democracy.

PART II

A *JEWISH* STATE VERSUS WESTERN DEMOCRACY

Chapter 4

Jewish Terror

Jewish terror awakens at the terrible thought—and subconscious realization—that western democracy is simply incompatible with Zionism and its central idea of a Jewish State.

What is Zionism, after all, if not the movement to create a Jewish State? And, indeed, the modern idea of political Zionism found its ultimate expression in a book by its founder, Theodore Herzl, that was the catalyst that led to the creation of the modern-day Zionism movement. It was titled *The Jewish State.*

And a flood of Zionist leaders and thinkers expressed this central thought:

"I do not bring you a new idea but an ancient one.... This idea is the establishment of the Jewish State" (Herzl, *The Solution of the Jewish Question*, 1896).

"We need a home like all nations, to live in our historic land...." (M. Lilienblum, *The Future of Our People*).

"The Jewish people is sitting on a volcano and this situation will continue to exist until a terrible catastrophe occurs and drives us toward a solution of the Jewish question—towards the only and specific solution offered to us by Zionism—the rehabilitation of Israel in its historical land" (Chaim Weizmann, 1903).

"In order for us to succeed... we need a home of free men in which we can create in accordance with our own spirit and with our own forces, without being dependent on strangers from outside *or within* and in which we can create without inhibition or hindrance; we need that land where alone this people was free a*nd its own master* and in which alone it could be free *and its own master*; we need Zion" (Martin Buber, *Zion and Youth*, 1918).

And this concept, "a Jewish State," we made the focus of the central and moving paragraph of Israel's Declaration of Independence which declared: "We hereby proclaim the establishment of a JEWISH STATE in the Land of Israel."

What in the world does this "Jewish State" mean? What is its minimal and fundamental definition, the one that every Zionist—religious or not, rightist or leftist, whatever his political, social and economic hue—will agree upon? Why surely it is the definition of a Jewish State as one *with a majority of Jews*. Of course this is the most basic and bottom-line definition possible.

Only a state with a majority of Jews guarantees all the things that Zionism and Zionists dreamed of, worked for, demanded. Only a state with a majority of Jews guarantees Jewish sovereignty, and independence. Only a state with a majority of Jews guarantees that the Jew will be captain of his ship, master of his fate, free from dependency on and prostration before strangers.

Only a state with a majority of Jews will insure that never again will we enjoy such dubious benefits as Crusades and Inquisitions and pogroms and holocausts—small and very large. Only a state in which the Jew controls his destiny will free him from both gentile Church *and* State, from both the intolerance of the non-Jew as well as his humiliating "tolerance." A Jewish majority *is* a Jewish State and a Jewish State is the repudiation of the ghetto, the Exile, humiliation, degradation, weakness and the shame of raising our eyes unto the stranger, "from the gentile shall come forth our salvation...."

Anything less than a Jewish majority is not a Jewish State. Surely Brooklyn has many, many Jews but it is not a Jewish State for it. It is not a sovereign, independent one, and this is what Zionism and its founding fathers understood and fought for: a Land of Israel with a majority of Jews in it. A Jewish State.

This being so, what is one to do with western democracy? What is one supposed to do with a concept that demands that anyone, regardless of religion or national background, has the right to sit quietly and peacefully, have as many babies as possible, and become the majority? The question, simply put, the question that explodes terror in the hearts of the Jew is: *Do the Arabs in Israel have a right to quietly, peacefully, democratically, equally and liberally become the majority?*

Let me put it more agonizingly. Let me increase Jewish terror. Not only is there a clear intellectual, ideological and philosophical contradiction between Zionism and western democracy, but the Declaration of Independence of Israel, in a mindboggling example of schizophrenia, proceeds to institutionalize the contradiction unto all generations. The Declaration does not only passingly mention a "Jewish State." It fairly *wallows* in it. Paragraph after paragraph speaks of *the Jewish people, Jewish* history, *Jewish* rights. *Jewishness* permeates the very fiber of the document. Consider:

"The Land of Israel was the birthplace of the *Jewish* people. Here their spiritual, religious and political identity was shaped. Here they first attained to statehood....

"After being forcibly exiled from their land, the people kept faith with it throughout their dispersion and never ceased to pray and hope for their return to it and for the restoration in it of their political freedom.

"Impelled by this historic and traditional attachment, *Jews* strove in every successive generation to re-establish themselves *in their ancient homeland....*

"In the year 5657 (1879), at the summons of the spiritual father of the *Jewish State*, Theodore Herzl, the first Zionist Congress convened and proclaimed *the right of the Jewish people to national rebirth in its own country.*

"This right was recognized in the Balfour Declaration of the 2nd November, 1917, and re-affirmed in the mandate of the League of the Nations which, in particular, gave international sanction to the historic connection between *the Jewish people* and *Eretz Yisrael* and to *the right of the Jewish people to rebuild its national home....*

"The catastrophe which recently befell *the Jewish people* —the massacre of millions of Jews in Europe—was another clear demonstration of the urgency of solving the problem of its homelessness by re-establishing in *Eretz Yisrael the Jewish State* which would open the gates of the homeland wide to every Jew and confer upon *the Jewish people the status of a fully privileged member of the Comity of Nations.*

"On the 29th November, 1947, the United Nations General Assembly passed a resolution calling for the establishment of a *Jewish State in Eretz Yisrael*, the General Assembly required the inhabitants of Eretz Yisrael to take such steps as were necessary on their part for the implementation of that resolution. This recognition by the United

Nations of *the right of the Jewish people to establish their state is irrevocable.*

"This right is the natural right of the Jewish people to be masters of their own fate, like all other nations, in their own sovereign state...."

And, of course, the moving and fundamental sentence in the Declaration of Independence, indeed, the "declaration" itself:

"Accordingly, we ... hereby declare the establishment of a JEWISH STATE in the Land of Israel, to be known as the State of Israel."

Is there, *could* there be, a clearer and more uncompromising definition of the identity of Israel as a Zionist, Jewish State? Here is a clear and unmistakable pronouncement of Israel as a Jewish State created for the Jewish people in which the Jews can be masters of their own fate. And this cannot be unless that sovereign Jewish State has a majority of Jews. Only that guarantees their being "masters of their own fate." This is a Jewish State. This is Zionism.

Consider now the inexplicable schizophrenia of this remarkable Declaration and the even more remarkable people who wrote it. Having poignantly described Jewish suffering and the awesome Holocaust as a consequence of the lack of a state of their own, having ringingly declared "never again" by asserting the establishment of a Jewish home in their own sovereign state where they will never have to rely on others or be the prey of the majority, having clearly and explicitly declared "a Jewish State in the Land of Israel," a state with a majority of Jews, the Declaration of Independence, the model of exquisite schizophrenia, goes on to pledge, promise and guarantee "equal *political* and social rights to all its citizens regardless of religion or nationality." It goes on to appeal to the Arab inhabitants to "participate in the upbuilding of the state on the basis *of full and equal citizenship and due representation in all its provisional and permanent institutions."*

Is there, *could* there be, a clearer and more uncompromising definition of Israel as a democracy? Here is a clear and unmistakable no-nonsense definition of a democratic state in the best traditions of the West. It is also a firm, no-nonsense model of confused, bewildered, mad contradiction and intellectual fraud.

All hail to the bewildered of the Mosaic faith. Having firmly declared the need for a state in which the Jew is master and sovereign, the most bewildering of G-d's creatures—Homo *Judaica—just* as firmly pledges to the Arabs their democratic rights to equality and their due representation (if a fifth of the population, a fifth of representation; if a third, a third; if the majority ...) to peacefully and democratically put an end to the Jewish State in which the Jews are masters and sovereign. The schizophrenic framers of the schizophrenic document have their feet planted firmly between heaven and earth, between Zionism and western democracy. The question, of course, is: which paragraph do you read?

If, under the first paragraph, Israel is created as a "Jewish State" with a guaranteed Jewish majority and if, under the second paragraph, all its citizens, Jews and non-Jews, have equal political rights, do the Arabs have the equal political right to become a majority, elect a Knesset with an Arab majority and change the country from "Israel" to "Palestine"? Do they have a right to then change the country's present Law of Return (to which we will return, for a fascinating inspection of Israeli democracy), which guarantees free entry into the country and automatic citizenship only *to Jews*? Do they have a right to amend that law and have it now apply to Arabs under the well-known Arab axiom that what is good for the Jewish goose is no less for the Moslem gander? Will all who wish to help in the development of the ancient homeland now be privileged to contribute to the United Arab Appeal or United Palestine Appeal or Arab National Fund or invest in Palestine Bonds?

Under paragraph two, above, of the Declaration of Independence, the "democratic" paragraph, of course the answer to all the above is a resounding *yes*. Of course, any advocate of and believer in western democracy would agree that the Arabs have an absolute and inalienable right to the same political aspirations as the Jews and should their birthrate produce enough Arabs to produce an Arab majority within the State of Israel, they have the right (and from their point of view, the obligation) to create a state that would no longer be known as the Jewish State.

On the other hand, what would the Zionist—the one who advocates and fights for a Jewish State in Israel—say to all the above? Why, in response to all these questions, his would be a resounding *no*. No, they have no right to become a majority and eliminate the Jewish State through babies instead of bullets. No, they have no right to change an "Israel" to a "Palestine." No, there is no way that Israel should commit suicide as it pays homage to western democracy.

Clearly a contradiction, as basic as possible, and the creators of the State and those who drafted the Declaration of Independence of Israel knew it. But terror gripped the founding fathers in 1948 just as it grips the leaders of today. Sheer, basic terror. Terror at having to choose between Zionism and western democracy after all the years of safe self-delusion, of successful flight from terrible reality.

Dishonesty being the sad hallmark of so many liberal intellectuals and politicians, the Declaration of Independence of Israel, conceived and born through the fraudulent midwives of liberal Hellenism, is thus able to issue a stamp to fight "racism." The stamp piously and loudly includes a sentence from the "democratic" paragraph of the Declaration, guaranteeing equal political rights to the Arabs. Of necessity, it avoids all reference to the other paragraphs dedicated to a Jewish State created to guarantee the concept of "never again," and which, of necessity, will never allow western democracy.

The Declaration of Independence of Israel is a schizophrenic document precisely because those who drafted it and breathed life into it were schizophrenics. They—and those who followed them to this very day, as Jewish leaders—are Jews and Zionists who are rooted in concepts that are un-Jewish and un-Zionistic. For decades they were able to deceive themselves and the average Jew and proclaim that Judaism *was* western democracy and western humanism and western equality and western integration. The bald lie could never be met until history created the objective conditions that made the contradiction clear and unmistakable, a painful truth, risen ironically, only with the establishment and development of the Jewish State that is the central aim of Zionism.

For years, Jews and their leaders were able to deceive themselves and everyone else except the Arabs with a breathtaking contempt for Arabs that sounded amazingly like some paternalistic, colonialist high commissioner marching to a Kiplingesque tune of noblesse-oblige. How many cabinet ministers (and prime ministers) and how many guided tour guides and how many speakers at UJA, Jewish National Fund, Israel Bonds and other meetings patted themselves glowingly on their Jewish-Israeli back as they described how much they had done for the (backward) Arabs. "Their villages had no electricity—and we lit them up. They had no sanitary facilities—we gave them indoor toilets. They were illiterate—we not only gave them education but thousands learn in our universities."

Was there ever greater contempt for Arabs? Was there ever greater blindness by Jews? The words sound like some grotesque echo of a British imperialist in Kenya shaking his head in puzzlement and asking: "What do the natives want? We came here and found a jungle and turned it into a garden...." The answer of the "natives" was, of course: "True, but it was OUR jungle and now it is YOUR garden." And, of course, that is exactly the answer of the Arab to the absurd and paternalistic contempt of the schizophrenic Jew: "True. You came

and found a desert and turned it into green fields. But it was OUR
desert and the green fields are now yours."

Is there an honest person alive who believes that one can buy the
Arab's national pride with an indoor toilet? Is there anyone with a
minimal intelligence who does not understand that it is precisely the
educated Arab, the university graduate of whom the schizophrenics
boast, who is the most dangerous of all Arabs? That the head of the
PLO-supporting Progressive List in the Knesset, Muhamad Miarai, is
a graduate of Hebrew University? That revolution never comes from
the numb and the dumb but precisely from the educated? That Israel,
with its own schizophrenic hands, is creating the new leadership of
the PLO?

Is there anyone who does not understand that the Arab is not a fool,
and that you cannot create a modern, educated, rising generation and
tell them that they can have everything except the right to rule in what
they consider their own country? Is there no one who grasps the elementary fact that a country which is defined as a Jewish State *cannot*
be anything except a foreign concept for the non-Jewish Arab? Is
there no one who cannot perceive that on Israel's Independence Day,
the Arab does not rush into the street to celebrate his defeat? Is there
no one to admit that when the Arab, equal citizen of Israel, sings the
words of his national anthem—"Hatikva (The Hope)"—he does not
swell with deep pride at the words "the soul of a Jew yearning," and
tears of happiness do not run down his cheeks as he emotes "the hope
of two thousand years," since his forefathers really did not mourn the
absence of the Jews each year, raising their eyes into the heavens and
imploring G-d: When will the Jews come home?

In the famous letter from Queen Victoria to her prime minister,
Lord Salisbury, the monarch, who epitomized British imperial rule,
laid down the qualities needed in a viceroy of India. These qualities
were vital, she said, "if we are to go peaceably and happily in India
and be liked and loved by high and low—as well as respected as we
ought to be—and not trying to trample on the people and continually
remind them and make them feel they are a conquered people. They
must, of course, feel that we are masters, but it should be done kindly
and not offensively, as alas is so often the case."

A more delightful example of blind naiveté and utter contempt for
a conquered people would be hard to find, or so I would have believed
if not for the Children of Israel who—in their awesome terror at having to face Jewish-Arab reality—outdo the Queen most regally. Jews,
both the Israeli politicians who decree it as the political line and those
other Jews who hopelessly plunge into it in lemming-like craving for

suicide-through-love, walk a path of scorn, disdain and utter contempt for the Arabs of Israel.

Because they desperately fear to look at the reality of Arab hostility, the two-legged lemmings of the Mosaic faith proclaim that the root of the Jewish-Arab problem is, firstly, a lack of social and economic equality, but even more important, because there is no contact between Jews and Arabs, there is a "lack of understanding." *A lack of understanding.* We must, therefore, rush to break down "stereotyping, fear and suspicion," as Arabs and Jews work together, play together, create together. And so the liberal vision of happy and equal Jews and Arabs spending summers together in a camp, visiting each other's homes, laughing at each other's jokes in a cafe. Break down the barriers and peace and tranquility will reign as we put an end to the "lack of understanding."

If I were an Arab I would fairly shake the walls with my disgust and anger. *This* is the problem and *this* the solution? The fact that Jews and Arabs do not "understand" each other? That there is no social contact?

The truth is that the Arab understands the Jew and the State of Israel very well. And that is precisely what makes him hate it and oppose it. The Arab understands very well that his ultimate complaint, anger and inability to accept the State of Israel, is the fact that it is a Jewish State and is so defined officially in the Declaration of Independence. The Arab knows all too well that there exists in Israel the basic Law of Return that grants automatic citizenship to Jews and not to Arabs. The Arab knows that everything about the state—its anthem, its heroes, its language, its religion, its aspirations—is all Jewish, and he is not. The Arab has nothing but contempt for the liberal who holds him in such contempt by thinking that all the Arab wants is equal economic conditions and social intercourse. No, one does not buy an Arab's national pride with an indoor toilet or a summer camp. And if all the liberal Jews had a trace of the national pride that the Arabs possess, they would understand that not by bread alone does the Arab live. They would understand that the Arab understands the Jew precisely and they would realize that what bothers the Arab is *Zionism, per se*; the existence of a Jewish State that, by definition, makes him less than equal. What does the Arab want? A "Palestine" in place of Israel in which he will create groups through which the Jewish minority can be helped to be soothed and "understood."

The refusal to respect the Arab and face the truth of his eternal hope for an Arab Palestinian state in place of the Jewish-Zionist Israel is the hallmark of the Jewish liberal-leftist and makes us a people in

immediate need of a national couch. And it is this indigenous contempt of the left-liberal, growing out of his materialist concept of man
which leads to the pathetic question: Are all Arabs *bad* Arabs? Are
there no good Arabs?

The utter contempt for the Arab that is at the very root of the question! Are there no good Arabs? What does the liberal Jew who asks
that inanity mean by a "good" Arab? Why, of course, an Arab who
will gladly and happily accept the fact that Jews live in what he
believes is *his*, the Arab's, land in order to benefit from the economic
advances the Jews will give him. An Arab who will trade in his
national pride and heritage for a higher standard of living, who cares
more about a refrigerator than "Palestine." An Arab who will give up
the struggle for "his" land because Jews are decent, liberal, humane
people who will "help" him, and because Jews are sad sufferers of
persecution who need a homeland of their own. An Arab who, because
Jews hate war and bloodshed, and because the Hadassah and Reform
rabbis preach the glories of beating swords into ploughshares, will
agree to an "Israel" in his "Palestine." In the mind of the good
liberal-left Jew, the good Arab is the one who will become a Semitic
Quisling, and, like some modern-day Esau, trade what he sees as his
birthright for a mess of Zionist lentils.

Are there no good Arabs? Of course there are. They are *all* good
Arabs. But let the liberals, who assume that one can buy Arabs as one
buys condominiums, understand very clearly just what a good Arab
really is. A good Arab is one who wants to live in what he believes
is *his* homeland, who wants an *Arab* State, who wants an *Arab* Knesset, who wants *Arab* sovereignty. In a word, a good Arab is remarkably similar to a good Jew and his desire to live in a Jewish State is
about equal to the Jew's wanting to live in Syria.

It is precisely Jews with national pride who can understand the
reality of Arab pride. It is only good Jews who can define a good
Arab. It is only good Jews who can understand a good Arab. Indeed,
that is why Kahane understands the Arabs. And that is why the Arabs
so very well understand Kahane. And that is why neither Arabs nor
Kahane understand Jews.

There will be no remedy for the Jewish liberal, the two-legged lemming of Mosaic persuasion, until he rids himself of the contradiction,
the immutable contradiction, between a Zionism with its call for a
Jewish State and between Western democracy. The liberal Jew must
purge himself of his contradictions, his schizophrenia, and above all,
of his terror at the thought of having to do just that. He must throw
away his contempt for human beings, in this case Arabs. He must

learn that which the Arabs and normal Jews already know. The problem of the Arabs of Israel is not material and economic. It is not a lack of understanding that can be solved by having Jewish and Arab children meet and having Jewish girls get together with Arab men at Haifa's Arab-Jewish center or the assimilation cesspool of Nvei Shalom. *There is no misunderstanding on the part of the Arabs.* They understand the problem perfectly. And they have understood it from the earliest days of Zionism.

In 1921, the Arab writer Izzat Darwazeh wrote an article in the Haifa Arabic paper *El Karmel*, replying to a speech by Zionist leader Nahum Sokolow calling for good will and understanding between Arabs and Jews. Wrote Darwazeh:

> "They (the Zionist leaders) keep dinning the word 'misunderstanding' into our ears. I don't know what they mean. Do they mean that we don't understand their true aspirations and intentions, and that if we understood we would hold out our hand to them? ... Are they trying to tell us that flooding the country with an overwhelming Jewish majority is nothing to frighten the Arab nation in Palestine? ... Won't Mr. Sokolow tell us of which rights the Arabs in the Land of Israel will not be deprived by Zionist political fulfillment? ...
>
> "You must return to the unadulterated truth, and you will see that Palestine was a purely Arab country before you ever settled in it and after you left it.... Let the leaders of the Zionist movement... find for their nation some uninhabited country."

And in 1974, the Lebanese newspaper *El Muhrar* replied to the then prime minister's advisor on Arab Affairs, Shmuel Toledano (a Jewish lemming of extraordinary suicidal tendencies), and wrote:

> "Even if there was an opportunity to integrate the Arabs into Israeli society, this would not solve the problem since man does not live by bread alone and he has other needs—among them, to live in peace in his own state."

Indeed, and that is precisely the question. Is the Jew prepared to allow the Arab the democratic right to have his own state? If the Arab, through peaceful and democratic methods, becomes the majority, will the Jew agree that he has the basic, fundamental, western democratic right to change Israel into *his* Arab state? Do the Arabs have a *right* to become a majority in Israel? The question is hardly an academic one. It is a very, very real problem.

Pity the poor schizophrenic Jewish leaders, liberal, Hellenist. Pity them for the terror that the question raises in their soul-seared hearts. The dichotomy that is at the very basis of their existence finds the obvious answer more horrifying than the question. And only that can explain the truly magnificent madness that surrounds them in their struggle against both Kahane and the United Nations, a struggle which is so clearly contradictory that one can only mutely stand in pity of them.

On November 10, 1975, the United Nations General Assembly passed Resolution Number 3379. Simply stated, it equated Zionism with racism. Needless to say, Jews were outraged. Then Israeli U.N. Ambassador Chaim Herzog frothed at the mouth; Jewish groups from "A" (American Jewish Committee) to "Z" (Zionist Organization of America) poured forth their wrath on the nations who knew Israel and Zionism not, and temple rabbis now had material for yet another month of sermons. The common denominator beneath all the anger was the firm, absolute denial that Zionism could ever be considered racism, and self-righteousness joined with sublime ignorance in battle with the anti-Zionists and anti-Semites of the United Nations.

How droll. For it is the same indignant Jews—indignant that anyone could ever dare to paint Zionism as "racism"—who are in the process of doing exactly that, proving to their enemies that they are, indeed, correct. What did Solomon, the wisest of men, say? "He diggeth a pit into which he shall fall and rolleth a stone which shall return upon him." The rolling stones of Israel....

The very same infuriated, fuming Jews of indignation who have spent the last two years in unbridled attempts to paint Meir Kahane a racist for declaring that Zionism, a Jewish State and Judaism are incompatible with western democracy and that there must be a legal and political differentiation between Jew and non-Jew so that Israel should remain a Jewish State, these same Jews proceed by this very obsession down the mad road of "proving" that Zionism is "racism."

For "Kahanism" IS Zionism. Kahane declares that the Jewish people have returned to the Land of Israel to create a Jewish State, and that is exactly what Zionism says. Kahane says that a Jewish State can only be one with a majority of Jews and that that alone will guarantee us sovereignty and mastery over our destiny, and that is precisely what Zionism declares. Kahane states that we must take steps to insure that Jews will always be a majority and will always control the State of Israel, and that is absolutely what Zionism is committed to.

And that is why the most basic law in Israel, the one that was passed immediately upon independence, was the Law of Return that guarantees *every Jew* the automatic right to enter the country and acquire citizenship. *Every Jew*, not every gentile. The worm in the apple begins to rear its ugly head as it stares us fully in the mouth and asks: Only *Jews*? This is democracy? This is equality? *Only Jews?* This is racism!

Let us leave the worm turning for a while and go on to another definition.

What is *a Jew*? The answer is clearly found in a definition that differs from that of almost any other people. When one asks to define a Frenchman or a Pole or a German, the answer is, one who is a citizen of France or Poland or Germany. Thus one can be of Greek national origin or Chinese; one can be Buddhist or Catholic; the acquisition of citizenship papers of the *country*, Germany, will make that person a "German," with all the rights of any other German.

Not so the Jew. A Jew is a *religio-national*, and is defined by religious criteria; and one who wishes to become a *Jew* must undergo a religious process.

It is not the piece of the land that determines whether the citizen of Israel, the Jewish State, is a Jew. It is membership in the *Jewish People*, and that can be acquired only by birth or religious conversion.

And when Israel was created as a *Jewish* State, it was this Jewishness that became the prime concern and yardstick of belonging. Totally unlike an America where your Jewishness or non-Jewishness makes not the slightest difference, where your national origin becomes irrelevant to the fact that you were born in the country or acquired enough residence in the country to make you an American. Totally different from anything that the western liberal, democratic world knows. And so, the worm wiggles again. This definition of a *"Jew"* that Zionism accepts and bases its state on—*this is equality? This is democracy? This is racism!!!*

What will President Herzog and the Knesset and all the alphabet Jewish groups say to all this? Why, they will rise in great indignation and proclaim, "No, *this is not racism; this is how the Jew is defined.* The Jew is different from other people. He is not defined in the usual, western manner and we cannot create Jews from that which they are not."

And they would continue, "No, what we do in Israel by giving Jews and denying non-Jews automatic citizenship is not racism, *it is self-preservation.* If we wish to create a *Jewish* state then we must guarantee that it will have a majority of Jews. We must, in a word, sacrifice equality and democracy for our own national interest, our own national existence."

How remarkably similar to Kahane!

Of course, I fully agree. And, of course, Zionism is not racism, because racism means the absolute and permanent relegation of one race or people or color to a position of inferiority, whereas Judaism decrees that all who wish to convert properly and according to *halacha* may, indeed, do so and thus become *Jewish* and equal to every other Jew and quality under the Law of Return that applies to Jews. Judaism, Zionism, proclaim not the racism of the Jews, but his *havdala*, his separation and difference, a status that is not biological but ideological. And the moment that the non-Jew adopts the ideology and becomes Jewish, the *havdala* drops away.

But if Zionism is not racism, it certainly is not democratic and it can never be so. For it is *not democratic* to demand that one become a Jew to benefit from the Law of Return. And it is certainly not democratic to define Israel as the Jewish State with the implication that one cannot allow non-Jews to become a majority. And this is the real tragedy and dilemma for the poor secular Herzogs and Zionists and A-Z Establishment types. They would dearly love to present Zionism as the paragon of democracy and equality. They cannot.

I suggest to the Israeli schizophrenics to be extremely careful. For it you define what Meir Kahane says as "racist," and then ban it, you will legitimize the U.N. resolution that delegitimizes Zionism. For what I say is Zionism, true and logical. I call for a Jewish State with political rights only for Jews as the logical extension of the Law of Return of Zionism. The latter discriminates against non-Jews, not for racist reasons, but for sane self-preservation, and I do the same. But it takes courage to go all the way. I attempt to guarantee that the aim of Zionism, a Jewish State, a state with a majority of Jews, will not be destroyed. I attempt to put an end to the insanity of a State of Israel, defined in its Declaration of Independence as *"the Jewish State,"* granting the Arabs the opportunity to destroy Zionism. Kahane is the purest and most honest of Zionists and the law that attempts to smear him will destroy Zionism itself and Israel.

Knesset of Israel, U.S. Jewish leaders of the dwarf persuasion, the rabbis warn us: "Wise men, heed your words." Knesset of Israel, American Jewish leaders of the dwarf persuasion, remember, the same admonition holds true for fools.

Zionism. Western democracy. One is east and the other west and the twain do not meet. The terribly uncomfortable question remains to haunt the thoughts and lives of comfortable Jews who will remain from this day and forever increasingly uncomfortable. Democratic, liberal, humanist, Zionist: Do the Arabs have the *right* to become the majority in Israel, through democratic, peaceful means? Again, the question is hardly an academic one. It is all too terribly real, for Zionism's enemy—an Arab majority—grows not only bolder but much closer.

Chapter 5

Demography, Democracy and Demagoguery

The Histadrut—the giant labor union and industrial conglomerate of the left in Israel—publishes a regular branch paper in Jerusalem called *Ba'Moetza*. Its March-April 1986 issue carried a story under the banner headline:

THE JEWISH-ARAB CIRCLE CONDEMNS JEWISH KAHANISM

Clearly, the democratic forces of the left in Jerusalem were joining the progressive circles of the Jewish State in firmly taking a firm, no-nonsense stand against the reactionary forces who preyed on Jewish fears of growing Arab danger. How curious, therefore, to note that on page one of the very same issue, the progressive labor union of Shimon Peres carried a story under the remarkable heading:

IN THE YEAR 2010 THERE WILL BE MORE ARABS THAN JEWS IN JERUSALEM

The story did, indeed, describe the sharp rise in the Arab population of Jerusalem and then stated: *"There is no doubt that these figures must trouble the government."*

Fascinating is the complex mind of the complex Jew. Fascinating. And most fascinating is the amazing hypocrisy and even more astonishing utter lack of awareness of it by the selective Jewish leftists and liberals in Israel. Surely, there is something awe-inspiring about a people who can, in the very same issue of their paper, decry "Kahanism" that warns against the danger of Arab population growth which could destroy the Jewish State from within, and then says that such a possibility must worry the government! Surely there is something malignantly ill with a soul that can swear to the Arabs that they are equal to Jews and then become hysterical over the possibility that these "equal" individuals may become the majority.

But, of course, the hypocrisy and demagoguery that surround the Arab demographic threat are not limited to the Histadrut. The government of Israel—which searches as with candles in the night for every opportunity to swear its fealty to the principle of absolute equality of Arabs in Israel, while lashing out at the "racist" attitudes of those who speak of the contradiction between Zionism and western democracy—bares its awesome hypocrisy regularly, and seemingly without the slightest awareness of perfidy.

On June 19, 1985, Labor party Knesset Member Aharon Nahmias (also Vice-Speaker of the Knesset), presented a motion in Parliament to urgently debate the problem of Jews leaving the Galilee and the danger of an Arab majority in the sensitive northern region that borders on Lebanon, the Golan Heights and Samaria. Warning that some 16,000 Jews had left the Galilee in 1984, Nahmias spoke of the Galilee's "emptying of its Jewish inhabitants."

The democratic Knesset of Israel, poised on the verge of passing an anti-racist bill aimed at those who would place Jews and Arabs on different footing, for some reason suddenly became alarmed at the "danger" of Arab *citizens of Israel* becoming a majority, and it was agreed that the motion should indeed be debated in the Interior Committee. There, "racism" continued its incredible march in the democratic Knesset as Zohar Gindel, Director of the Labor Ministry's Development Towns Advisory Bureau, told the committee (May 22, 1986) that in December 1985, the Arabs in the Galilee outnumbered the Jews (355,000 to 352,000) and that "the situation was worsening."

"Worsening"? What Israeli Arab, told that he was an equal citizen, exactly like the Jew, would not rise up in anger at a Knesset Committee listening to a government official speaking of Arab growth as a situation that was "worsening"? And what democrat would not be appalled by the conclusion of the democratic, racism-hating Knesset Committee (July 14, 1986) that "settlement of the Galilee and the increase of its *Jewish* population are a national objective of the government."

Truly the fraud and perfidy of the Israeli government would be comical if not so sad.

And yet, this was as nothing compared to the panic that broke out among the progressives and democrats of the government in the wake of a study released by Professor Roberto Bacchi, head of the Hebrew

University's Statistics Department. The study (April, 1986) warned of the dire effects of the demographic problem of Israel, which sees the Arab birthrate threatening to make them an ever-growing number of the population.

The academician never did bother to explain why he, a liberal, an enlightened professor, was worried about certain Israeli citizens becoming a majority merely because they were Arab, but the Knesset went into action and the problem was debated in the House in May, 1986. And thus spoke Moshe Katzav, the Minister of Labor of the democratic "equal rights to all Arabs" State of Israel:

"Since 1965, the rate of growth has been much smaller among Jews than non-Jews in the Israeli population. While between 1952-1964, the annual growth of Jews average 3.7% as opposed to 3.8% for non-Jews, between 1965-1978 the Jewish rate dropped to 2.4% and the non-Jews rose to 4%. Since 1979, this trend has sharpened in a most serious manner. The annual growth average among Jews is only 1.8%."

That the facts and figures are frightening is indisputable. But only if you agree with Kahane that Jews and non-Jews are *not* equal in a Jewish State which seeks to insure that *Jews* should be the majority. But if you consider this "Kahanism" to be racist, why be alarmed if a certain kind of equal Israeli citizen, i.e., Arab, grows at a larger rate than another kind of equal Israeli citizen, i.e., Jew?

It was not long before the cabinet itself debated the critical issue, and on May 11, 1986, issued the following declaration:

"1) The government is troubled by the demographic trends in Israel and the Diaspora and is especially concerned over the slowing of the population growth in the State of Israel."

Clearly, the government—true to form—was less than honest. It was not concerned over the slow "population" growth, it was troubled by the slowdown of *the Jewish* population growth. And, indeed, in its second paragraph, it bit the Jewish bullet:

"The government decided to adopt a wide and coordinated demographic policy that will strive to guarantee an acceptable level *of Jewish* population growth."

There is little doubt that this resolution is one that will go down in the annals of western democracy, and which brought cheering Arabs into the streets of their state.

Of course the problem is serious. It is catastrophic. In an article on Passover Eve, 1986, *Davar* editor Hana Zemer, citing the incredible fact that, despite the vastly larger number of Jews in the country the number of young Arab and Jewish youngsters below the age of 14 is now the same, warns of the demographic threat to the existence of Israel. A feeling of helplessness and depression sweeps the land. The army magazine, *BaMachane* (November 17, 1982), writes: "The Arabs of Israel are the world leaders in rate of population growth, and in its wake there grows and is felt a deep danger that is almost impossible to deal with."

In a thoughtful letter to the newspaper *Ha'aretz* (June 30, 1986), Dov Friedlander goes over the various demographic schemes and gloomily admits: "There can never be a solution of demographic policy to the problem of a large and growing Arab population;" And the article in *Yediot Aharonot* (May 15, 1986) headed: "Significant Rise in the Number of Non-Jews in Tel Aviv," merely points out the obvious fact that every city in Israel is seeing a large increase of non-Jews as Jews flee.

The problem has been obvious for years to all those who wished to see. Clearly, few have. All are ripped apart by their dedication to Western democratic values and have not the courage to choose between those and Zionism. Thus, some look away with a silent prayer that somehow they will wake up one day and the problem will have disappeared. Others simply *lie* about the situation and the facts. The worst of these offenders are the right-wing parties—especially Tchiya, right wing secular nationalists.

For years, unable to respond to Kach arguments, Tchiya leaders, notably Geula Cohen and Yuval N'eman, have spread the blatant falsehood that the Arabs of the territories are leaving. As a lie it was a clever one, because they *were* leaving. The trouble was that they were not leaving *permanently* and the right-wingers knew it.

Arabs were leaving to work in the oil states, in Saudi Arabia and around the Persian Gulf. But they were sending their checks back to their families and had every intention of returning. Indeed, by 1984 the newspaper *Ha'aretz* (June 26) carried a front page story headline:

SECURITY SOURCES: SIGNS OF A RETURN OF ARABS TO THE
WEST BANK AND GAZA

The story began: "In the wake of the Iran-Iraq war and the economic pressures in the oil states, the past few months have seen a change in the balance of people leaving and coming into the West Bank. Many residents there cancelled plans to go out to the Gulf States to seek work and a movement has been seen of returnees who have been left unemployed there."

On August 17, 1984, *Ma'ariv* ran a story that began:

"On the Jordan bridges there has been recorded, in the past months, an increase of 30-40% of those entering from Jordan, mostly residents of Judea and Samaria who work in the oil states of the Persian Gulf.

"In the Civil Administration (Israeli) it is believed that part of the 2500 who return daily will remain in their cities and towns because of layoffs in the Gulf States and Jordan. Not a few have stated that this time they have returned for good 'because we did not find a better place than our homeland.'"

And sure enough, on April 17, 1986, *Yediot Aharonot* carried a wire service report that stated:

"The Arab states in the Persian Gulf and Saudi Arabia have decided to expel from their borders 1.5 million foreign workers, especially Palestinian and Shiite Lebanese. Those expelled will return to their countries no later than 1987."

So much for political fraud. So much for the myth of Arabs "leaving."

The real truth lies in the fact that the Galilee in Israel today has a majority of Arabs, and Jews are afraid to drive at night through Arab villages there. Jewish cars are stoned on the Acre-Safed road and as far back as March 14, 1980, the headline in a *Ma'ariv* story about one Jewish settlement in the midst of a sea of Arabs in the Galilee read simply:

53 JEWS AMONG 40,000 ARABS

Ironically, the demographic danger underlines the greatest weakness of the nationalist, secular groups. A party like right-wing Tchiya, unable to muster the courage to call for Arab expulsion and yet committed to the annexation of the territories, is forced to propose a "democratic" solution under which Arabs would have the option of choosing either Jordanian or Israeli citizenship. The question, *the so-obvious question*, is: What if they choose *Israeli* citizenship? Obviously all that Israel lacks today is another million or so Arab citizens. Perhaps we should note the news item that appeared in the Israeli press (August 30, 1984):

"A member of the Jordanian Parliament is seeking Israeli citizenship. Friends in Jerusalem explained last night that it is only natural that a Jerusalem-born individual would seek to guard his right to live in the city whenever he wished to."

And in an interview with the leftist magazine *Koteret Rashit* (November 13, 1985), Dr. Sari Nuseiba, professor at Bir Zeit University and son of a former Jordanian cabinet minister (from Jerusalem) Anwar Nuseiba, repeated his statement, in an article in the Arab weekly *Al-Maukaf*, that he seeks Israeli annexation of the territories and the granting of citizenship to Arabs there. His goal is obvious: A huge Arab minority, and soon a majority, to end Israel, legally, peacefully and, above all, democratically.

This was clearly the point being made by Dr. Tahar Cnaan, Jordanian Minister for Affairs of the "Conquered Land" (sic), when in December, 1985, he called for "the correct use of the Arab demographic issue in the conquered areas in Palestine, in order to cause cracks in the Zionist entity."

Given this obvious, naked demographic threat to a Jewish State, the pathetic calls of the Jewish leftists and liberals to give up the territories grow louder:

"If we do not give up the 'occupied territories' we will become a bi-national state and then a minority of Jews. Only if we give up Judea-Samaria and Gaza will we be able to keep Israel as a democratic, Jewish State." The call of the wild left.

Thus speak the democratic, liberal moralists. Did they ever consider what the Arabs inside Israel (pre-1967) think about the liberal desire to keep Israel a "Jewish" State? About the call to get rid of land in order to get rid of Arabs? What joy and brotherhood this means for the Arab who is told—daily—by the liberal, leftist hypocrite that he, the Arab, is equal to the Jew and that the struggle is against the racism of "Kahanism"?

And who of any remote touch of sanity would take us back to the horror and danger of extermination of 1967 when, with the same borders envisaged by the leftists (for anything less than that would not even earn a passing yawn from the most "moderate" of Arabs), Israel's existence hung by a thread? Who is prepared to bring the enemy back to within 15 miles of the sea, their artillery and missiles looking down from the Samarian hills into the lights of Tel Aviv and the coastal cities? Who agrees with the mad hatters of the Left on a step that can only be characterized as an irrational attempt to commit suicide lest we be killed?

But the main point is, of course, that this mad move will save Israel nothing more than a handful of years before the same inevitable population deluge. The Arab birthrate danger continues in all its terror *within the State of Israel*, just as within the territories. The Arab population explosion in Israel means that in 15 or 20 years we face the same danger of an Arab majority. And these Arabs are all citizens. And they are all educated. And they all hate the fact that they—Arabs—are forced to live in *a Jewish state*.

The simple, if unnerving, question for Jewish democrats is: If G-d grants us peace and there will be no war with the Arabs; if Arafat becomes a born-again penitent crying out to the Arabs of Israel, "Make love not war"; if that is *exactly* what the Arabs make each night, love not war, *how many Arabs will there be in Israel in ten years?* How many equal rights Arab citizens of Israel will there be? How many equal rights Arab citizens will sit in the Knesset of the democratic State of Israel in 10 years? How many equal rights Arab citizens will sit on the sensitive Committee on Foreign Affairs and Security in 10 years, to hear a top-secret report from the Chief of Staff? Better still, for all the barricade climbers for democracy and equal rights, perhaps *the Chief of Staff* will be an Arab? Fascinating. And how many Arabs will there be in 15 years? And how long before they are a quarter, a third, a majority? Most uncomfortable questions for a shrinking number of comfortable Jews.

The Arabs inside Israel who are rapidly becoming radicalized as they free themselves from the bonds of the corrupt village chiefs and learn in the Israeli schools and from their Jewish leftist friends about Marxism and democracy, will grow and grow and demand more of the national cake. If they have 20% of the population and then 25% and then one-third, they will not only sit in the Knesset with a massive bloc, but they will join with the leftists in an attempt to form a coalition government, even as they demonstrate for Arab cabinet ministers and vice-ministers and director-generals of those ministries.

Above all, in the democratic state of Israel where laws passed *by the left* favor Jewish immigrants, bar Arabs from owning state land and which commit the state to be a Jewish one, there will be an explosion of violence as the Galilee and the Triangle become the Northern Ireland of Israel. And liberal western Jews who give to the UJA, who swear by their temple rabbis, who denounce Kahane and who love Israel and democracy, will sit by their television sets each night watching Jewish soldiers and police shooting at rioting Arabs who burn cars, throw stones and shoot back at the security forces. Is that what we want? No, but that is precisely what we will get.

And how many troops will be needed in case of a war, just to remain in the rear, to watch over the Arabs, the loyal Arabs? And what an immense Fifth Column will be a generation of young, educated, radical Arabs—so utterly different from their frightened, cowed, uneducated fathers? And what will they do, knowing that their fellow Arab armies are fighting the Jewish one in order to end the Zionist state and create a "Palestine"? Of course, they will do nothing. Of course they will sit quietly perhaps even volunteering to fight the Palestinian and Arab "enemy." Of course ...

In the face of all this, the two-legged lemmings of the Mosaic faith have no answers. None. Consider this almost unbelievable excerpt from a Knesset session (December 2, 1985).

The speaker was Knesset Member Nachman Raz of the Labor party and chairman of the Knesset Committee on Education, speaking about the problem of keeping the territories of Judea-Samaria-Gaza:

RAZ: "If all the people in the territories who live under our rule enjoy the same rights as we do, then you have a democratic problem. They can become the majority. If not, there is no democracy.... The solution is simply not to rule over them and not over the territories in which they reside."

At this point, Knesset Member Geula Cohen asked: "And what will be within the *State* of Israel?"

RAZ: "In the State of Israel they will have equal rights."

COHEN: "When they are a majority?"

RAZ: "They will not be a majority. *When they reach the point of threatening our status as the majority, we will begin to think about it.*"

The Chairman of the Knesset Committee on Education. G-d help Israeli education.

Had the above appeared in a satire or farce, it would have, indeed, been comical. But it was a deadly serious exchange in the Knesset by a man who is one of the foremost opponents of. Kahane's "racist" plan to forestall an Arab majority by transferring them out of the country. His mind is truly the knife of logic:

1) They will never be the majority.

2) When they start threatening to be the majority, *then we will begin to think about it*.

Yes, two thousand years of exile leave their trace on the bewildered, confused, mind-wandering Jew.

And yet, the very same insanity—is there a more apt word?—occurred two nights after my appearance on the ABC television show, "Nightline." This time the guest was Prime Minister Shimon Peres and when the host Ted Koppel mentioned that I had been on two nights earlier and had posed both the problem of Arab majority and the solution of removal from the country, he then asked the Prime Minister what *his* solution was. The answer, after a number of irrelevant sentences, was: *as of now, we have none.*

As of now? And when will the Prime Minister begin looking for one? Perhaps when they reach the Razian point of "threatening our status as the majority"? And when is that? When they become a third of the country? Forty percent? How typical, this ghetto mentality of waiting until the knife is on the throat to say: Perhaps the time to do something has come.

How best to end the chapter? How best to emphasize the danger and the madness of the present Jewish leadership?

Perhaps it would be to point out that not only do Israeli Arabs have many babies, *but we pay them for each one*. Every month, for every Arab baby (as with every Jewish one, for we are democrats and non-racists), the Arab receives a check from the National Insurance Institute. He receives a subsidy for each and every one of his children. One child is good for one check; two for two, ten for ten checks and twenty brings a book of checks. Indeed, one of the most exciting moments for any tourist is a suggested visit to the main post office in Jerusalem (as one example) on the day of the month when the checks are issued and there to watch the huge lines of Arabs waiting to cash them. If one is polite, he will surely be able to ask how many checks his friendly Arab is holding. He can then double his contribution to the United Jewish Appeal.

Is it any wonder that, from far-away Cairo, PLO chief Yasir Arafat—through an interview in the paper *Al Ahbar* (May 1986)—called for Palestinian women to increase their rate of child-birth? Arafat in a parody of the Biblical injunction "be fruitful and multiply and fill the conquered land," told the newspaper that the thing that most concerned the Israeli establishment was the high Arab birth rate. This is "a biological Palestinian bomb in the conquered land," he said.

True. Too true. And the answer? I, of course have mine. What is yours, opponent of Kahanism? A most uncomfortable question to an increasingly less comfortable Jew.

Chapter 6

Arabs with "Jewish" Heads

Not far from the Jewish town of Ma'alot in the upper Galilee, stands the Arab village of Mi'ilya. Jewish Ma'alot, of course, became tragically world-famous some years ago when its school was seized by Arab terrorists and more than twenty children died as Israeli soldiers stormed the building. Arab Mi'ilya is not as well known, no Jews ever having seized and murdered its children. Nevertheless, it is more than important that Jews who visit the Wall and Masada and the kibbutz and the Dead Sea get a glimpse of the Galilee Arab village—and some of its inhabitants. For few tourists who see Jerusalem of Gold ever see Israel of Reality. Worse, precious few Israelis do.

Mi'ilya is a prosperous village. Construction goes on constantly as the Arabs there build homes or add rooms to their present ones. Nearly every family has a vehicle and many are new ones. It is a Christian Arab village, for the most part, hence according to existing Jewish mythology, "moderate." Many of its inhabitants possess a higher education. In short, it is the very model of the modern, progressive Israeli Arab village, which, thanks to liberal, humane, progressive Jews, will produce "good" Arabs.

And so, meet Salim. Salim lives in Mi'ilya and does quite well, thank you. He is an attorney, as are his wife and his brother, all three sharing an office in the Jewish city of Nahariya. He speaks Hebrew fluently (being a graduate of Hebrew University) and, in his jeans, no one could possibly know that he is not an Israeli Jew. But when asked by the Israeli weekly *Newsview* (October 16, 1984) to describe himself, this is what the Christian, educated, prosperous attorney, beneficiary of Jewish liberalism and coexistence, had to say:

"First of all I'm a Palestinian. Then I'm an Arab. Last, I'm a Christian. I also happen to live in Israel but I don't feel I'm an Israeli citizen. I can't be a real citizen of Israel as long as it's a Jewish State which discriminates against non-Jews. The Law of Return says any Jew anywhere in the world has a right to settle in this country. Yet my own people who once lived here are refugees in Lebanon and the Gulf, and don't have the right."

A word of explanation is more than in order. The Law of Return. Every progressive, liberal Jew knows that the struggle against Kahanism, racism, must be fought unto the death. Kahanism, we are told by every Jewish leader from Chaim Herzog, Israeli President, to Conference of Jewish Presidents, is the very antithesis of Zionism, which is democracy and liberalism and humanism from the top of its ideology to the tip of its philosophy. And the Law of Return is the very heart of the democratic, liberal, humanist, Zionist state, that is, the very antithesis of racist Kahanism. And just what does this Law of Return, the law that sets down the rules for immigration and the right to live in Israel, say? Just what does a truly Zionist law passed by David Ben Gurion, of blessed memory, set down?

THE LAW OF RETURN (1950)

1. Every Jew is entitled to immigrate to the Land.

2. An immigration permit shall be given to every Jew who expresses his desire to settle in Israel.

Every Jew. Any Jew. The Law of Return of the State of Israel. Passed by the Labor Zionist government of David Ben Gurion. Every Jew. Any Jew.

Question: If David Ben Gurion had *not* passed such a law; if the State of Israel did not have such a law and *Meir Kahane* proposed precisely such a law—word for word—what would the Labor Zionist party of David Ben Gurion have said? What would the President of Israel, the Prime Minister, the Knesset Speaker, the news media, the intellectuals, B'nai B'rith, the American Jewish Committee and *The New York Times* have said? *Need I tell you?*

But let us return to Salim and his complaint that in a Jewish State Arabs cannot be first-class citizens, that a Jewish state cannot be fully truly democratic to all its citizens. Not true? *But it is true.* And just as important is the fact that, unlike Jews who flee as from the devil from the awful, painful reality of the contradiction, Salim faces it and gives his answer—Salim's choice:

"We're against Arabs participating in Israeli elections because this legitimizes the Jewish State." And, again: "We could accept a West Bank state only as far as a first step to the liberation of the Galilee."

Liberation of the Galilee? Surely, our educated, enlightened Christian Arab, the beneficiary of the Jewish largesse and darling of the United Jewish Appeal and Hadassah women, must be joking. *The*

Galilee? Of course, all progressive Jews join with him in deploring Israeli occupation of areas that do not belong to her, such as the West Bank (Judea-Samaria) and Gaza, the Biblical areas where Jewish ancestors lived and created their own Jewish states. But to speak of the liberation of the *Galilee?* An area that is part of the State of Israel, that is *Jewish?* How can Salim say such a thing?

Easily. For Salim does not believe that the Galilee is "Jewish." For Salim, like countless other Israeli Arabs who live in Israel, does not believe that "Israel" should be Jewish. He does not believe that Israel should *be.* And this is what he says, in the same interview:

"We are against Arabs participating in Israeli elections because this legitimizes the Jewish State."

To liberate the Galilee is an obvious thing to Salim, who remembers that until 1948, the Galilee was overwhelmingly Arab and that its entire western part was originally given by the United Nations Partition Plan of 1947 to the projected Arab state. In the war that followed, the Jews overran the entire Galilee and tens of thousands of Arabs fled the country. Salim is, of course, also interested in "liberating" Hebron and Shchem and Jericho and Bethlehem and all of the Judea-Samaria-Gaza- Golan territories that Jewish lemmings of the leftist persuasion call "occupied." But Salim, living in the Galilee, is not interested in moving to any Palestinian state that might be set up in those "occupied lands." He intends to stay in "occupied Galilee," and fight to liberate that, so that it too can join the ever-larger "Palestine" that will know no peace until it liberates *all* of Israel.

And Salim is hardly alone in his hope for Galilee liberation.

July 2, 1979, was a typically beautiful Jerusalem day. Not a cloud in the sky, warm breezes wafting through the late afternoon air and 6,000 Israeli citizens gathered in front of their Parliament, the Knesset. Six thousand citizens, come in a hundred buses from the Galilee to their center of government. Six thousand citizens; from the Galilee; *Arabs.* They had come, in one of the largest Knesset demonstrations ever, to protest the "Judaizing" of the Galilee, and their posters, bold and harsh, told the story:

"With blood and spirit we will liberate the Galilee." "The Galilee to the Arabs, Jews out."

No, Salim is not alone; the overwhelming majority of Israeli Arabs agree. *All* would rather live in their Arab Palestine than in Jewish Israel. Too many are convinced that it is just a matter of time before they *will* be living in Palestine without having to move from the Galilee.

And so Salim, the new Israeli Arab of Israel, is not any longer afraid to openly say to a reporter in Israel that which the vast majority of Arabs in the Jewish state passionately think in their hearts:

"We Palestinians of the Galilee are basically all in the same boat. We all felt the same during the *katyusha* [rocket] attacks [from Lebanon of the Galilee]. The Jews in Ma'alot went into their shelters and we went up on the roof to watch. No rockets fell on Mi'ilya or Tarshiha (the Arab town twinned with Jewish Ma'alot). The *katyushas* raised our morale. I felt the man firing them from the other side of the border was my brother fighting for his land. When Israel invaded Lebanon and the PLO lost its position there, all of us were shocked and depressed."

I can imagine that the ordinary Jew, simple and naive, a captive of the absurd and deceitful Jewish Establishment propaganda concerning Jewish-Arab coexistence in Israel, in reading Salim's words, is also shocked and depressed. I am too, I am shocked and depressed that any Jew is shocked and depressed. I am shocked and depressed that any Jew is so blind and obtuse and ignorant of Arab national pride that he should be shocked and depressed upon reading Salim's words. They are so logical, so obvious, so self-explanatory. They are the words of an Arab who has no need for "understanding." He understands perfectly. He understands that Zionism believes in a *Jewish* State in which the Jew rules and that he wishes a Palestinian state in which the *Arab* rules. Even if he were not an attorney with an LLB from Hebrew University he would understand that. It is only the two-legged lemmings of the Mosaic persuasion who persist in fleeing in terror from the terrible (for them) reality.

The average Jew has not the slightest idea of what is happening today inside Arab Israel. One can pray at the Wall, climb Masada, gorge himself at the King David Hotel, walk tourist row in Jerusalem and Tel Aviv, swim in the Dead Sea—but have not the slightest understanding of what Israel is, what volcanic eruptions are stirring beneath its surface, what terrible clashes and contradictions stand between the Jew and Arab. But if the ignorance of the Jew of the Exile is a tragedy, then the one who lives in Israel and *refuses* to understand is more than a tragic figure. He is a criminal who will bring down disaster on his own children and, of course, on everyone else.

Salim is, in the end, more than a person. He is a concept. He represents the thinking of the Arab in Israel. The one who can never be a Zionist because he is not a Jew. The one who can never desire a Jewish State that makes him, *de facto*, unequal to the Jewish citizen.

Ten minutes from the bustling Jewish city of Kfar Saba on the coastal plain of the Jewish State, stands the Israeli town of Taibe. It is an *Arab* town, whose living standards are—to quote any proud UJA fund-raiser or Israeli cabinet minister—higher than those of the average Arab town in the Arab world. And in August, 1984, with the lights burning (courtesy of the Jewish state) and the plumbing working to perfection in both kitchen and water cooler closets (courtesy of the Jewish state), Taibe held a Festival of Palestinian Tradition, created and produced and executed by Arab intellectuals and artists (courtesy of the Jewish state). The entire production was under the chairmanship of one Salah Barnasi, once one of the leaders of the Israeli Arab organization, Al-Ard (The Land) which refused to recognize "the authority of the State of Israel over the territory which it rules." This was, of course, in 1959, *before* the "occupied lands" of 1967.

And as the festival moved on, a speaker rose and cried: "They wanted us to forget. They wanted us to forget. We dare not forget; long live the revolution, long live the PLO" (*Hadashot*, August 23, 1984). The crowd, excited, moved toward the platform, fists in the air, many with the PLO "V" for victory sign. Ten minutes from Kfar Saba, which in turn is twenty minutes from Tel Aviv.

On July 24, 1982, the same town was the scene of a rally. According to the *Jerusalem Post* (July 25) "scores of youths chanted, 'Zionists go home, the land of Palestine is ours and free.' The paper added: "One of the speakers at the rally, Anayat Burgul, a biology student at Bar Ilan University (an Israeli university founded and funded by religious Jews from the United States), said: 'Palestinians in Israel and everywhere else have no leadership but the PLO.'" Other slogans heard at the rally were: "With blood and power we shall reclaim Palestine," and "Begin, Begin, *katyushas* will fall again on Kiryat Shmona (the Jewish town in the Galilee)."

No, there is no end to the suspicion that a large section of Jewish people is in need of a national couch. How else explain the fact that in the Knesset, Arab member Muhamad Miari rose (October 15, 1985) to deny the right of the Jewish people to Israel? I quote from the Knesset minutes:

Miari: The State of Israel is *not* the state of the Jewish people but of the citizens who live there as citizens of the State of Israel. I said this, we have said it, and we shall continue to struggle for this."

There could be no clearer challenge to the State of Israel as a Zionist, Jewish State, created by the Jewish people for the Jewish people. The Arab claim (a cunningly temporary one) that it belongs only to its citizens who live there, is meant to pave the way for a time when the State of Israel will have a majority of *Arabs* who will then have the legal right, under this definition, to undo all the Zionist laws that give preference to the Jews, especially in terms of immigration. Miari was paving a legal way for the realization of the statement by an Israeli Arab teacher, N'ama Saud of the Israeli Arab village of Araba, to the Israeli newspaper *Ma'ariv* (May 28, 1976):

"Now we are a minority. The state is democratic. Who says that in the year 2000 we will still be a minority? Today I accept the fact that this is a Jewish State with an Arab minority. When we will be the majority, I will not accept a Jewish state with an Arab majority."

It could not have been put more bluntly. More clearly. And for those still tied to the illusion that at least the Druze accept the permanent fact of Israel as *Jewish* State, in that very same Knesset session (October 15, 1985), Druze Knesset Member Zaydan Atshi said: "The State of Israel belongs to those who live in it." There they sit, in the Jewish Knesset of the Jewish State, openly denying the Jewishness of that state. I hardly blame them. I understand them. I will never understand the Jew.

But there is more to this psychoanalyst's delight. In the same Knesset sits Tewfik Zayad, the Communist Party's mayor of Nazareth. Zayad is also a poet, the author of an artistic paean of praise to the Egyptian tanks that crushed the bodies of the Israeli soldiers during the Yom Kippur War. A Knesset committee took the "bold" step of declaring his poem "incompatible with the oath taken by a Knesset member pledging allegiance to the State of Israel." Naturally, no penalty was imposed.

Zayad, as early as 1976, waved high the banner of democracy and proportional quotas in the best tradition of Jewish liberals of the American Jewish Committee or B'nai B'rith persuasion and said that, as a minority, constituting (then) 15 percent of Israel's population, the Arabs should be allotted three ministerial cabinet posts, 18 Knesset seats and a proportionate number of senior posts in the various ministries (*Jerusalem Post*, May 2, 1976). Breathes there a democrat with soul so dead who would not agree? Breathes there a normal Jew with brain so unwarped who would not cry out: "Never!"?

Not for nothing did Zayad and the other Arab Knesset members rise up in anger over a proposed bill by Knesset member Pinhas Goldstein in March 1984, proclaiming "Hatikva" the official national anthem of Israel and making it a crime to insult it. Knesset member Zayad called Goldstein's bill "racist" and he and the heads of the Arab town councils demanded a new anthem that would be "acceptable" to Arabs and which would recognize the Jewish-Arab "partnership" in the country.

What was bothering the Arabs of Israel, the Jewish State? *Just that.* "Hatikva." An anthem whose words breathe Jewishness and which sets the tone of Israel as Jewish State. "Hatikva," written in the early days of modern Zionism, is a Jewish anthem:

As long as deep in the heart
the soul of a Jew yearns,
And towards the East
an eye looks to Zion—
Our hope is not yet lost,
the hope of 2,000 years—
To be a free people in our land,
The land of Zion and Jerusalem.

Said Asad Aziaza, council head of the Israeli Arab village of Duburiya:

"I cannot ask an Arab child in school to stand at attention and sing 'the soul of a Jew yearns.' I am not against a national anthem but it must apply to all its citizens of the state—including Arabs."

Aziaza's solution? Instead of the "soul of a *Jew* yearns," let it read, "the soul of an *Israeli* yearns." Such a change, of course, is exactly what all Arabs in Israel want: A state which is not a Jewish one, not one that belongs to the Jewish people including those who live outside the country, but an "Israeli" one, that belongs only to those who live there—Jews and Arabs; an "Israel" which is acceptable until the first opportunity to turn it into "Palestine."

And that, of course, is precisely what Miari has in mind when he tells the *Jerusalem Post* (August 8, 1984) that he wants "changes in the national anthem and all national symbols to accommodate Arab feelings."

One, of course, cannot but sympathize with any Arab who—quite understandably—finds it difficult to sing of a "Jewish soul." The solution, however, is hardly the dismantling of the Jewishness of Israel. The answer is for the uncomfortable Arab to move to a country which sings of an *Arab* soul that yearns, and where he will be comfortably at home. As positive and ideologically confident are the Arabs of Israel, so are its gentilized Jews confused, schizophrenic and warped by guilt and depression. Jewish liberals, leftists and intellectuals, those who make up the gentilized Hebrews of the land, clearly feel the utter contradiction between their sterile, secular Zionism and their western, gentilized liberal values. Thus, Uzi Benzamin, a member of the editorial staff of the newspaper *Ha'aretz*, wrote a piece for the Jewish Telegraphic Agency on June 10, 1976, in which he painfully brought out the problem and reached a conclusion which speaks volumes for himself and the Hellenists he represents:

"Israel was created to enable the Jews to have their own independent state where they would implement the Zionist vision of a restoration of sovereign national life. But relations between the Arab inhabitants and the Jews living in and immigrating to Israel were never sufficiently defined and clarified....

"The real problem, after all, is rooted in the very definition of the State as a Jewish country which allows the Arab minority to have its own life. Relations between the Jewish majority and the Arab minority cannot be described in the same terms as relations between the Anglophone Canadians and their French minority (and even they have quite severe problems). Relations between Jews and Arabs are complicated because the majority represents a unique entity that embodies a religion and a nationhood while the minority belongs to a larger, supra-national entity which exists, in different national forms, along the borders of Israel.

"A new definition of the Israeli nation is needed.... *The Jewish people, as a whole, must ask itself whether the existence of a Jewish independent state is an important value which deserves a personal sacrifice.*"

One can only hope that every Jew who reads the words of Benzamin, a bitter and irrational hater of Meir Kahane, understands what the Hellenist is saying. For if he does, he will finally begin to grasp who the enemy of the Jewish people and of a Jewish State really is.

A new definition of the Israeli "nation" is needed. Benzamin is afraid to state clearly what that definition is for him—a state which is no longer defined as "Jewish" and which will no longer insist on Jewish majority and sovereignty. But he also deliberately uses a counterfeit concept, "Israeli nation," when no such concept exists. There is no *Israeli* nation. There is only an Israeli *State* which belongs to *the Jewish nation.*

Indeed, under Judaism, the country was called the Land of Israel because it belonged to the People of Israel and logically the new Jewish State that arose in 1948 should have been called *Judea* because it belongs to the people of Judea, *the Jews. Benzamin, a guilt-ridden Hellenist, wants a change. He needs a change.* He wishes to see the end of a Jewish State and comes a step away from saying it:

"The Jewish people must ask itself whether the existence of a Jewish independent State is an important value which deserves a personal sacrifice."

The outrage and the obscenity of this confused Israeli! For 2,000 years his ancestors made personal and national sacrifices for that greatest of Jewish values—a Jewish independent state— and this product of western Hellenism, riven by guilt and self-hate, dares to suggest that the dream of 2,000 years, the sublime Jewish value of a Jewish State, be abandoned.

Benzamin, having been *given* a state by Jews who were Zionists and who gave of themselves for *a Jewish* state, now takes this land that cost so *much Jewish* blood, blood of Jews who fought for Jewish sovereignty, and blithely decides that it is time to change it to a non-Jewish Israel in order to save himself from the problems and terror of Zionism. More than they are confused, the Hellenists of the left are also moral and intellectual cowards. For if Benzamin sees the problem as he does, and if the contradiction with democracy troubles him, let him leave and find a democratic country for himself where he can live in his kind of western state without the mental agonies that beset him in Israel.

Benzamin wishes to see the self-destruction of the Jewish State because in his twisted and pain-wracked soul he wishes to see the end of the Jewish *people*. What is needed is not a new definition of Israel but the passing of the generation of the desert of Uzi Benzamin, with their slave mentality, and the rise of a new Jewish generation, proud, free and cleaving to Judaism and nation.

This is the real struggle. The battle of the Jew against the Hellenist. On the one hand, the Jew who sees himself as part of a Jewish nation which is special and different and unique, with the ultimate of values; the Jew who sees the State of Israel as meaningful because it is part of the *Land* of Israel, a unique land for a special, chosen people, a Jewish state for a *Jewish people*. And on the other hand the Hellenist, who is stripped of all specific Jewish values, wracked by tortuous conflict between his accidental Jewishness and his chosen gentilization, driven by guilt and self-hate and dreaming of escape from his hideous hump-Judaism. The struggle between these two is the real struggle, a war, far transcending that between the Jews and the Arabs.

It is a war seen in novels such as the one by leftist Yoella Har-Shefi, *Beyond the Gunsights: One Arab Family in the Promised Land*. Naturally, as in a host of movies, plays and books by the disturbed, leftist Israeli Hellenists, the hero is an Arab. Naturally, there is love and intermarriage between an Arab and a Jewish female. Consider the deathless words of Maya, the Jewish girlfriend of the Arab hero: "He is our hope, our bridge to the Arab world. If we turn our backs on him we are destroying our future." And, of course, the main point of the author is stated by her *alter ego* in the novel:

"I think that all our discomfort about the Arab citizens stems from the fact that the State of Israel is actually a bi-national state though it refuses to admit this.... The Jewish state will be faithful to Jewish values as I understand them if its Jewish citizens do not have a preferred status over its non-Jewish citizens."

Clearly, neither Maya nor her creator, Ms. Har-Shefi, understands "Jewish values." Indeed, one wonders why liberals, universalists and humanists bother with such racist concepts as "Jewish" values rather than dropping such tribalistic nonsense and speaking instead of "human" ones. Surely, these would be much more easily accepted by their non-Jewish lovers and husbands.

The awesome realization of the contradictions between Zionism and western democratic and liberal values was grasped by some Jewish Hellenists even before the creation of the State. And, indeed, many of them were therefore opposed to the creation of a Jewish State during and immediately after the Holocaust. It is fascinating to see the extent of the effect of the Exile on the Jew.

Thus, Albert Einstein, whose stepping out of his four ells of physics revealed the stupendous limitations of genius, wrote: "I should much rather see a reasonable agreement with the Arabs on the basis of living together than the creation of a Jewish State" (*Out of My Later Years*, 1950). The physicist's dream of a Jewish Lebanon was, thankfully, rejected by normal Jews but was pushed by men like the philosopher Martin Buber (whose brilliant device of writing things that no one could understand led to his elevation as a great thinker), and the former President of Hebrew University, Judah Magnes. They, in a sense, joined with the self-haters of anti-Zionism (Julius Rosenwald, Elmer Berger, Alfred Lilienthal and most of the Reform Jewish movement), whose views were symbolized by Congressman Julius Kahn of California. In a petition (March 5, 1919) published in *The New York Times* and signed by a number of well known Jews, including the *Times* publisher himself, Adolph S. Ochs, Kahn stated:

"A Jewish State involves fundamental limitations as to race and religion, else the term 'Jewish' means nothing. 'The rights of other creeds and races will be respected under Jewish dominance' is the assurance of Zionism, but the keynotes of democracy are neither condescension nor tolerance, but justice and equality."

The latter-day apostle of anti-Zionism, Elmer Berger, put it rather similarly in a speech at Ohio's Heidelberg College on January 19, 1971:

"By definition, the State of Israel's Zionist 'Jewish people' nationality base cannot accommodate any number of 'non-Jewish people,' nationals who might, in normal democratic procedures, threaten the 'Jewish character' of the state."

The anti-Zionists of pre-World War Israel, and even afterwards, were people intensely afflicted with the *Galut* complex of "what will the gentile say?" The fascinating thing is that today they have been joined by the "proud" new Israeli-born Hellenist in calling for the same thing: An Israel that will not be "Jewish," and that will reject the concept of a State for the Jewish people, with sovereignty and political power limited to Jews.

And yet, in a way, there is even more madness involved in those Israelis who remain Zionists, who insist on a Jewish State and who then emerge with some of the most astounding statements seen outside of a freshman class in logic. Blissfully and blithely traveling through life's minefields, they see nothing particularly dangerous in the environment. Thus, in a debate in the monthly *Counterpoint* (April 1986), Dr. Yosef Ginat, assistant to Ezer Weizman, and clearly his master's faithful voice, states: "There is nothing wrong with an Arab voting for a Zionist party. We want to see Israeli Arabs who are proud to be Arabs and proud to be Israelis. There is no contradiction between the two." Deathless prose; breathless logic. Reminding us of the cheerful words of former Advisor on Arab affairs to Menachem Begin, Binyamin Gur-Arye, who stated in 1980: "There is no radicalization of the Arabs in Israel..." Or of former Defense Minister and top leader of Likud, Moshe Arens: "One of the great achievements of the State of Israel has been the equal rights of its Arab citizens. But we are still far from complete integration in Israeli society when the young Arab from the village will feel himself Israeli when he also walks in the street of Tel Aviv. That is the challenge that all citizens of Israel—Jews and Arabs alike—are called upon to meet" (*Ha'aretz*, January 10, 1981).

One can only shake one's head in wonderment.

And one cannot but shake one's head in rage at the deliberate efforts by Jewish Establishment and news media groups to bury the almost daily proof of Israeli Arab hate of the Jewish State and desire to see its end arrive quickly. The Jew who reads the "official" Jewish press or who is a member of an Established Jewish group is simply abysmally ignorant of the reality of this Arab hostility. He is a victim of the deliberate policy of ignoring the increasingly implacable hostility and struggle against Israel that is taking place today among the Arabs of Israel. He is a captive of people who are in turn prisoners of their own liberal ideology and thought and who have neither the honesty nor the courage to admit that they are wrong. No greater theological fundamentalists exist than the liberal, progressive types. Their blind need to believe the platitudes of "Jewish-Arab coexistence" and "a Jewish, democratic Israel with full rights for the Arab minority" makes it impossible for them to want to see the reality of Arabs who hate a Jewish State with *its Jewish majority* since they reject the paternalism of tolerance for themselves *as a minority*. *They* want to be the majority; they want an *Arab* state; they want an opportunity to beam and write platitudes about coexistence with the *Jewish minority*.

In February, 1985, the representative of the Lebanese Christians stationed in Israel was due to speak in the lecture hall of the Law School at Hebrew University on Mount Scopus. Hundreds of Israeli Arab students gathered and fought pitched battles with the security guards and police. The climax of the evening was watching the Arab students, citizens of Israel, progressive and educated—by liberal Jewish standards moral debtors to the Jews for all they have been given by generous, merciful matrons in Great Neck and socialist-liberal cabinet ministers in Jerusalem—rising to sing the PLO anthem, "Baladi":

> Homeland, homeland,
> Fatah is the Revolution against oppression.
> Palestine, land of our ancestors
> I must return.
> Fatah is the Revolution which will prevail.
>
> And Al Assifa the hope of my homeland.
> Palestine, my homeland
> I have no greater love, purpose or future.
> I shall march to you
> With a determination that shall slap
> Injustice in the face.
>
> Palestine, my homeland,
> My only hope we must regain for you
> The dignity of your dispersed people
> Rallying under the banner of sacred struggle.
>
> Palestine, my homeland,
> Your people shall never die
> Nor shall they remain silent
> And Al Assifa will keep its finger always on the trigger.

And so, the news item that appeared in the Israeli paper *Ma'ariv* (May 26, 1986) becomes perfectly understandable:

"The hostile terror organization in Judea-Samaria-Gaza rests on supply sources *within the Arabs of Israel*, senior army officials yesterday told Chief of Staff Moshe Levi."

Surprise? Hardly. Will the two-legged lemmings of Mosaic faith learn anything from it? Hardly.

The poor Jew, the one who sits vaccinated against logic by Reform rabbis' temple speeches and isolated from sanity by hopeless liberal Jewish leaders, never sees an item such as the one that appeared in the Israeli papers (October 30, 1984). It was a story by the Israeli wire service *Itim*:

"Songs of hate and provocation among which 'Abu Amar' (Arafat) is called, together with 'his brave fighters to Palestine, to cut off the heads of the cursed Zionists' are now heard at many weddings and celebrations in the villages of the Galilee.

"*Itim* writer-reporter, Arye Meir, writes that as these songs are sung, the audience cheers the singer and no one protests or attempts to stop the singing.

"Two days ago, in a wedding in one of the western Galilee villages, a female folk singer appeared and sang a song that included: 'Oh, Mother, give me the rifle so I can liquidate the Zionists standing at the top of the hill.' In the past, there were isolated incidents of this kind but now they are heard openly and with high frequency. When it is not possible to get a singer, tapes are used."

The truth is that the "phenomenon" is hardly a new one. The newspaper *Yediot Aharonot,* back on May 4, 1977, reported on a wedding in the Lower Galilee village of Rumana in which the crowd cheered a song that included the lines "we will slaughter the children of the Zionists," "we will trample with our feet their Torah." And in January, 1986, the same *Itim* reporter, Ayre Meir, reported that Nazareth, the Arab "capital" of Israel, had become the center for the distribution of anti-Israel cassettes and video tapes.

Only an imbecile, a knave or one totally lacking in his own national self-respect would be dismayed. The incredible thing would be if the Arabs of Israel did *not* react this way. Only abnormal people enjoy living in a state that belongs in law and in practice to another people. Normal men and women—the Arabs—seethe in anger and only the pitiful liberal lemmings of the Mosaic faith see nothing and understand less.

For years we were besieged by people who triumphantly "proved" Israeli Arab loyalty to Israel by pointing to the very few Arabs who were involved in terrorism. Needless to say, such people could easily have "proven" the loyalty of Frenchmen to the Nazi occupation since hardly a few thousand of the 40 million Frenchmen were involved with the anti-Nazi underground. The fact is that it takes courage to rise up and act against a government, against police authority. The reason why so few Frenchmen took armed action against the Nazis was not their support of them; it was their fear of them. The very same holds true for the Israeli Arabs. The overwhelming majority, for the time being, may be too frightened of Israeli security forces to act against the Jewish State, but they certainly do *hate* it.

But things are changing. In March, 1986, seven Israeli Arabs from the town of Kfar Kassem, just east of Petach Tikva, were arrested on charges of planting bombs in the Tel Aviv Central Bus Station and other places in Bnei Brak and Petach Tikva. In April, 1986, ten Arabs, including residents of Baka-Al-Gharbiya, one of Israel's largest Arab towns, were arrested and charged with murdering a 19-year-old Israeli soldier, Moshe Tamam. Tamam had been picked up while hitchhiking near the Israeli city of Netanya, kidnapped by the Israeli Arabs, tortured horribly and murdered. An interesting note is that one of the 12 Israeli citizens chosen to light a torch at Jerusalem's Western Wall on Independence Day was the mayor of Baka-Al-Gharbiya, chosen for the honor because of his town's reputation for loyalty to Israel.

Every day, in little and not such little ways, the Arabs of Israel assert themselves and their hostility to the Jewish State. As far back as June, 1979, the Ford Foundation-funded Arab-Jewish Center at Haifa University unveiled the results of a poll taken among Israeli Arabs. It revealed that fully 50% of the Arabs asked had the courage to admit that Israel—as a Jewish State—had no right to exist. Fully 64% believed that Zionism was racism and no less than 59% said Israel should be rolled back to the 1947 borders of the U.N. Partition Plan. Naturally, an overwhelming majority said that the Law of Return was racist and should be abolished.

Since then "progress" has been made. While the Arabs living in the Jewish State have usually defined themselves as "Israeli Arabs," by December, 1985, 68% were prepared to openly state that they were "Palestinians."

And, of course, the key to seeing the whole picture is the knowledge that untold numbers of Arabs are afraid to say what they *really* think.

Is it any wonder that at the funeral of Israeli-born Rashed Hussein of the PLO, held at his Israeli village of Musmus, thousands of Israeli Arabs turned out to hear Knesset member Twefik Zayad say:

"We shall never give in until the goal that Rashed Hussein and his friends advocated, fought for and struggled for, is fulfilled." Rashed Hussein and his friends? What friends? Why, the PLO, of course. And what do they fight for, and what is their goal? The Palestine Covenant, the Bible of the PLO, make it eminently clear: the elimination of the Jewish State and in its place the creation of a Palestine Arab one. That is what Knesset Member Zayad wants. That is what every Arab in Israel would like to see.

Whatever else the Arab is, he is not a fool. He knows of the incompatibility between a Jewish State and an Arab one. More, he knows that a Jewish State cannot be a democratic one, in the western sense of the word, a concept that gives all people, regardless of nationality, exactly equal rights. Democracies are not modified by adjectives. There is no *Jewish* or *Arab* democracy. There is *democracy. Or a Jewish State. Or an Arab one.*

The Arab Israeli writer, Anton Shamas, wrote in the Jerusalem weekly, *Kol Ha'ir* (September 13, 1985): "The Declaration of Independence that still has a reputation as a liberal document, is, in my eyes, the AIDS of a Jewish State in the Land of Israel. A Jewish State, uni-national, carries within itself, by definition, the seeds of disaster: the collapse of the immunity system of every state—democracy."

The Arab, with nothing to lose, understands perfectly. The Jew, trembling as with the ague, sees this knife of logic, this absolute truth, and flees in panic. It will not avail him. One can run away but the problem remains and grows. Malignancy, when dealt with early, is curable. Too late, it means death.

PART III

IN SEARCH OF A
NATIONAL COUCH

If all the waters were ink and all the trees were quills, they would not suffice to record the daily tragedies and madnesses that take place within the Jewish State. Things of which the Jew outside the country, the "Zionist," the one who is "well versed" in Israel affairs, the tourist who has seen the Wall and Masada and the Dead Sea and the live bar at the King David Hotel, has never heard.

Here are some of the news events of which we doubt you have heard, incidents that occurred within the Jewish State. They are dedicated to all the fighters for coexistence and absolute Arab-Jewish equality who grace the liberal Jewish communities. Here are the incidents that show so clearly the tragedy towards which the Jewish State is being directed and driven by Jewish leaders, inside and outside the country; by its self-righteous moralists and "humanitarians"; by the gentilized Hebrews and Jews who, by their confusion of mind and cowardice of heart as they persist in refusal to choose Jewishness over gentilization, are the silent partners in the regular campaign of terror and murders of Jews that take place today in Israel. By their mercy for fools, their compassion for the wicked, they murder the innocent and destroy the dream—the dream of a Jewish State.

Chapter 7

The Dream

"The hope is not yet lost—the hope of two thousand years; to be a free people in our land..." (From the Israeli national anthem, *Hatikva*).

The following item appeared as a letter to the editor in the Histadrut Labor newspaper *Davar* (June 30, 1986):

"On June 19, we were waiting on line to see the doctor, some 30 of us. An argument broke out between a young woman, elegantly dressed and obviously well off, and an elderly man. He quietly explained to her that it was his turn to see the doctor. She began screaming at him and among the other gems, said: 'I am an Arab; this land is mine and who needs you Jews here? Go back where you came from.'

"A large crowd gathered from all the departments—and, now, pay attention: An Arab woman stands between perhaps 100 Jews in a Jewish institution waiting to see a Jewish doctor and shouts. Then she slapped the elderly Jew. He wished to hit her back but could not reach her. She gave him a hard blow and sent him flying. He lost consciousness, blood flowed from his head, and he was given oxygen and taken by ambulance to the hospital. But no one touched the Arab woman! What would have happened if this had been a Jewish woman among Arabs?

"The police came and she shouted, 'I am not afraid of anyone, not you or the police.'"

For two thousand years, the Jew—in every one of the four corners of the earth—would pause three times daily, lift his head unto heaven, face the Land of Israel and say, "And may our eyes behold Thy return to Zion in Mercy." It was a national dream, a national hope, a yearning that filled the Jew's soul. Someday he, too, would be able to come home. Someday, he would leave the Exile with its fear and terror and death and live in his land, strong and secure, with none to make him afraid. And how was it expressed in the *Yiddish* song of yearning?

A Jewish kingdom, gentlemen—
Can you understand it?
A kingdom of sheer brilliance
A kingdom of kings alone....

"A kingdom of kings alone...." In his ghetto, in his poverty-ridden *shtetl-village*, in his fragile island surrounded by hostile waves of Christians or Moslems, the poor Jewish tradesman who drank deeply each day of the dregs of humiliations and poverty dreamed of a kingdom of kings. The Land of Israel. A Jewish State.

And then, in the year 5708—1948 by the gentile calendar he had lived under for so long—the dream was realized. A Jewish State was declared in the Land of Israel. A Jewish State! No more fear, no more terror in the streets! A Jewish State! Free and proud and a kingdom of Kings!

Hardly.

The following news item did not appear in the local Brooklyn, Bronx, Boston, Philadelphia, Miami, Syrian or Soviet papers:

"In the *Halisa* section of Haifa, a mixed Jewish-Arab neighborhood, there has been renewed, after a period of quiet, harassment of (Jewish) elderly, young women and religious Jews, by young Arabs.

"Moshe G., a resident of Halisa, said that young Arabs, some from the neighborhood and others who work in the stores and factories there, gather at bus stops and harass the elderly and especially the religious among them, insulting them and making fun of their clothing. At times they throw stones at the elderly and use other means of frightening them, especially in the alleyways and the hallways. They make advances to the passing young girls and often make indecent proposals.

"Moshe G. said that the young Arabs have cast their terror on the neighborhood and said that it was a disgrace that in a neighborhood that until recently was mostly Jewish with new immigrants and religious Jews, bit by bit a group of Arab toughs take over and nothing is done to remove them. Because of this, he said, Jews are leaving the neighborhood" (*Davar*, June 30, 1986).

No, not Brooklyn and not Syria and not Leningrad. Halisa, in Haifa, where a few months ago earlier Arabs broke into a synagogue and burned it and Torah scrolls. This is the dream of Zion?

The phenomenon of the South Bronx and Brownsville, Brooklyn and Mattapan-Dorchester, Boston and Detroit, the phenomenon of Jews fleeing neighborhoods and those who remain living in fear, is repeated daily in Israel, land of the Jewish brave. Tel Aviv. Jewel of

Zionism, the first all-Jewish city of modern times. City of pioneers and Jewish culture, symbol of the rise of the new Jew and new Jewish state.

Not exactly. In *Shchunat Shapira*, in the south of Tel Aviv, hundreds of Jewish families are fleeing the neighborhood because of fear. Fear of Arabs, many from Gaza, who come in nightly; many of them now live there, terrifying the residents. And as the Jews flee, their places are taken by Arabs, who find themselves Jewish prostitutes and introduce hard drugs into the neighborhood. *Yediot Aharonot* (January 8, 1985) described the situation:

"'The situation is serious,' says Aharon Baruchim, 62, who has lived in the neighborhood for 50 years. 'In every fifth home now live Arabs. We are afraid to go out at night. I do not let my wife come home at a late hour. They walk the streets at night, some drunk, others drugged and we live in fear.'"

Baruchim tells how the Arabs first moved into deserted houses and then made life so miserable for the nearby Jews that the latter fled, their places being taken by other Arabs, and so on. The reality of widespread sexual perversion among Arabs—a fact so abhorrent to liberals that they revert to their natural reaction, denying the police statistics while covering their intellectual retreat with defamation and name-calling—is ever-present among the normal, sane people of Shaira who have to live with reality.

"Dahlia Hallavish, mother of seven, says that she fears for her children: 'I do not allow my children to wander about at night, alone. I fear that someone will seduce my child.'"

The newspaper account continues, quoting a 77-year-old resident: "We lock ourselves in our homes from eight in the evening. We lock the doors with two and three bolts. Once, we would sit in the street on the sidewalk until ten p.m. Today, that is finished. Each one locks himself in his house." No less than 500 families have fled Shapira in the last two years. South Tel Aviv, like neighboring Jaffa, is becoming Arab with all the security and assimilation risks that are involved.

It is not new. It is only getting worse. For years, Jews in Israeli authority refused to deal with the obvious issue. Thus, the July 27, 1979, issue of *Ma'ariv* headlined a story:

YOUTH STABBED WITH A POLE IN CLASH BETWEEN JEWS AND ARABS

The story describes an attack on a group of young Jewish teenagers, 16 to 17 in age, by some 20 Arabs, working and living illegally in the Bitzaron section of Tel Aviv. One of the teenagers, Yaakov Avrian, was stabbed in the back with a sharp pole. What was more important was what two residents of Bitzaron, said:

"Our children are afraid to go out and play. During the day Arabs come and chase them from their playgrounds. At night they are afraid that they will attack them and assault the girls. Not long ago, a girl of 16 was assaulted and went into shock. The family wants to leave the neighborhood. The Arabs work in almost all the large and small factories in the area and most sleep here without a permit. They wander about, cursing the Jews and deliberately playing their radios loudly to anger and disturb us."

Of course the police do nothing. It is the *nature* of police throughout the world to try to do as little as possible and to discourage complaints. It is also easier to avoid having to deal with difficult Arabs and instead deal with elderly Jews. Of course there is a law that forbids Arabs from the territories from staying inside the "Green Line" of the Jewish State beyond one a.m. The law is a farce because it is simply not enforced. Why not? There is a deliberate governmental policy of "letting the Arabs sit quietly so as not to cause problems." And so the fear grows as the attacks on Jews grow, especially the sexual assaults on both Jewish females and young Jewish boys. No matter how it may anger the Jewish liberal who rarely allows facts to get in the way of his prejudices, the percentage of Arab sexual crimes is staggering. Not only rape of Jewish women but perversion against young Jewish children of both sexes. The cases are widely prevalent (the local Haifa area paper, *Heyd Hakrayot*, in July, 1984 was told by the spokesman for the Haifa police, David Frankel, that "the problem has become widespread lately"). Consider this example that carries with it yet another illustration of Jewish madness.

A young Arab from Yafia village was charged with sexually harassing a young married woman as she took her child to kindergarten by uncovering his sexual organ and masturbating in front of her. Naturally, the woman—a product of the new, proud Hebrew race—failed to report the act, out of fear. But when the Arab appeared in front of her home and repeated the act, police were finally called in. The wire service *Itim* reported on November 5, 1984, the following remarkable result. The judge, Reuven Ben Horin of Haifa court, in a splendid example of tolerance and understanding (one did not get the reaction of the victim), fined the Arab the equivalent of $100 and gave him a suspended sentence. More to the point was the judge's comment:

"We all know the strict rules among certain sectors of the Arab community, in all that is involved between men and women before marriage. It is also known that in many cases, because of these rules and limitations, *men of positive character* will do acts that they would not have done had the approach of Arab society been more progressive." The judge found that the public interest would not be damaged if the Arab was allowed to go free.

This is the tragedy that rides the Israeli horse of the Apocalypse today. Jewish women and children are victims of Arabs "of positive character" who are sexually twisted, and the only punishment that could conceivably prevent the outbreak of sexual terror against Jewish women that is taking place today in Israel is a swift and harsh one, until the Arabs are removed to their own society. If not, the same abomination of Arabs at Israel's beaches or at the swimming pools in the Valley of Jezreel, where they sexually harass and terrorize Jewish women regularly, will continue and worsen. (It was there, on August 24, 1980, that *Yediot Aharonot* reported a massive fight between Jews and Arabs, with the Arabs shouting "*Itbach-al Yahud* (Slaughter the Jews.)" And there will always be a "progressive" judge who will "understand" the Arabs of basically "positive character" in a way he would never do in the case of Jews.

Until then we will continue to read such headlines as the one concerning the woman soldier Dafna Karmon, murdered by Israeli Arabs: "The accused forced the girl into the car, ripped off her clothing, raped and stabbed her" (*Ma'ariv*, July 12, 1984). Until then we will continue to read of sexual assaults on children aged eight by Arabs in the Gilo section of Jerusalem (*Hadashot*, June 27, 1985). Until then we will read about such Arabs as Rusan Luka, who was found guilty on June 10, 1985, of raping Jewish boys. One child testified that the Arab said to him: "Come, boy, let's work. Pull down your pants."

But the pathetic guilt-ridden Jewish liberal will hasten to defend the Arabs by bleating: "Aren't there Jews who commit such acts also?" The answer is, yes, but the more pertinent points are:

1) The percentage *of Arab* sexual acts is incredibly higher than that of the Jews. What did the Talmud say? "Ten parts of immorality came down to earth and nine were taken by Arabia" (*Kiddushin* 49).

2) If Jews do it, who needs to add to the horror by having Arabs do it too?

3) A major part of the reason for Arab sexual assaults on Jews is their nationalism, their hatred of Jews and their feeling that this is how they attack the Jewish people and state. To quote a Hebrew University professor (*Jerusalem Post*, February, 1977): "For many of the Arab students, the best way to ____the Jewish State is to ____a Jewish woman."

The truth is that the dream of a state in which Jews would be free from fear and insecurities has turned into a nightmare, and the myth of the Supersabra may go down well at UJA dinners but its ring grows more hollow from year to year in an Israel where—because of the two-legged lemmings of Mosaic persuasion—the Arabs have succeeded in instilling fear into the Jew.

On January 30, 1985, the newspaper *Ha'aretz* carried the following front-page news item:

"Children of the Carmel in Haifa show a deep fear of Arabs. The immediate association in most cases is that of a kidnapper of children, a murderer, a terrorist and criminal." The question arises: What kind of soldiers will these children be, when the Arab enemy becomes so psychologically frightening to them?

But it is hardly only children. Following a series of attacks and murders by Arabs on hitchhikers and taxi drivers, *Yediot Aharonot* came out with a full-page story headline: "Fear on the Highways."

The story began: "Avi Reiss (23), a student, stood for a long hour at the exit from Jerusalem waiting for a hitch. Sadly he said: 'This is not new. It has been this way for months now, ever since they have been kidnapping and murdering soldiers and drivers who gave them hitches. Now, I, an officer in the reserves, have to suffer'" (January 29, 1986).

The day before, Moshe Cohen, who stopped to pick up a hitchhiking Arab, was stabbed brutally, and Miri Levi, a physical education teacher, was stabbed but miraculously fought off her Arab assailant.

A taxi driver from Ramle—a Georgian Jew in the country a few years—was found murdered in his cab in the Arab section of the city of Lydda. The week before, another taxi driver who picked up two Arabs was stabbed near Latrun, and yet another driver from Beersheba had an Arab's knife miss his heart by centimeters.

The result? Fear. Not of general crime but of a particular kind—of Arabs in Israel trying to murder Jews—*because they are Jews*. Like before the dream.

Fear, Jewish fear. In the words of the head of the Jerusalem taxi association, Shem Tov Shem Tov:

"Our boys are just afraid of going out at night..." (*Ha'aretz*, January 5, 1986). Israel. The Hope. Israel. Land of milk and honey. And Fear.

Fear. Jewish fear within the Jewish state because of Jewish spiritual madness and, again, fear of doing what must be done to save Jewish lives. Fear. So that the newspaper *Hadashot*, a mass-circulation cheap secularist sheet that mirrors everything that is gentilized and un-Jewish about Israel, carries a full page of photos of Jewish victims of Arab attacks. It is an eminently *partial* list, and does not record many other Israelis murdered by Arabs *inside Israel*. The caption:

"Your fear. Eighteen similar incidents. Kidnapping, mutilation, a corpse. A side road, a pit, a cave. Suddenly there grows awful fear... and perhaps the greatest fear is the thought, for a moment, that you are the next victim."

The victory of the Arabs over the Jewish State begins with the destruction of the Zionist dream of a state free from fear. The Jewish victims of Arab murder stare at us from the pages, faces and names the "nice" liberal Jew—so busy with Arab-Jewish coexistence—never knew or saw just a sample of:

Yosef Eliyahu and Leah Almakayas, murdered in their car. They were school teachers in the town of Afula (July 21, 1985).

Meir Ben Yair and Michal Cohen, murdered near the town of Bet Shemesh (June 30, 1985).

David Caspi, murdered in his cab in Jerusalem (April 20, 1985).

Zecharya Karni, a watchman in the hospital in Kfar Saba, murdered (body found on February 2, 1985).

Ron Levi and Revital Seri, shot in the head in a forest near Jerusalem. Levi was an active member of Peace Now (Oct. 22, 1984).

But perhaps the most terrible—the children. Dani Katz, 15, from a comfortable upper-middle class family in the exclusive Haifa suburb of Dania. Disappeared. His body was found in a cave. Investigation revealed that he had been raped and murdered. The murderers were Israeli Arabs who worked in the supermarket near his home (December 8, 1983).

And Nava Elimelech. Eight years old. Her dissected body was found on the beach near her Bat Yam home. The then Chief of Staff, Rafael Eytan, revealed that she had been murdered by Arabs as an initiation into the PLO.

Every one of the murdered was murdered by Arabs. And as the pall of fear grew, the thing that most concerned the Minister of the Interior, Dr. Yosef Burg, was:

"We must do everything to insure that the personal tragedy of families does not become the tragedy of a part of the citizens of Israel. We must not create an atmosphere that threatens coexistence between Arabs and Jews in Israel" (December 14, 1983). Madness. Worse—an insane policy that guarantees the continued murder of Jews inside the Jewish State to which we returned "'to be free people in our land." Jews, who by virtue of ghetto mentality and westernized assimilation, become accomplices in the murder of fellow-Jews.

And another kind of fear. Fear for Jews who disappear. *Disappear?*

What have we here—Texas? We speak of a tiny Jewish State, with tiny amounts of territory. Where did 125 citizens vanish in 1985? How is it that the police report that fully 10 percent of all missing Jews disappear and are not found again? (*Yated Ne'eman*, May 20, 1986).

Consider the case of Ayala Alfasi, age 21 at the time she disappeared on October 10, 1982, from her home in Jaffa. Her frantic family received a phone call from her in which she was able to blurt out only that she was in Gaza and to please save her; then the phone went dead. An Arab from *Gaza*, serving a prison term in Beersheba prison, returned from a 48-hour holiday to say that he had heard that the girl was being held in a brothel in Gaza. Is she? Has anyone really looked? How many others may be in Arab cities or villages in the territories or carried away into Jordan? Where is Rachel Albaladas of Holon? On July 15, 1983, the then 16-year-old girl left her Tel Aviv place of employment to buy things for her employer. Since then, she has never been seen. Hundreds, thousands of young Jewish girls become involved with Arabs. The latter have money in their pocket and the young girls are carried away by the excitement. Many become involved with them—with drugs, prostitution. Where do so many of these girls disappear? Who cares?

Fear. And the most humiliating of all: fear felt by soldiers standing at night on the highways and hitching rides. Fear by Jewish soldiers, in the Jewish State, of standing on Jewish highways! And the liberal Jew of "coexistence" who comes to tour Israel with the American Jewish Congress or Hadassah sees nothing, hears nothing, knows nothing. And babbles on anyhow. But it exists—and we know it. Fear felt by soldiers because of the incredible murder of Jewish soldiers by Arabs within the Jewish Land!

Soldier Moshe Levi, murdered three kilometers from his home in Petach Tikva, suburb of Tel Aviv. His body was mutilated and burned (December 5, 1985).

Soldier David Palzan, choked and murdered. His body was found near the Negev kibbutz, Kissufim (June 10, 1985).

Akiva Shaltiel, soldier who phoned his father to say that he was five kilometers from his home in Rosh Ha'ayin, near Petach Tikva. His body was found April 4, 1985.

Soldier David Manos, disappeared November 11, 1984. As part of the obscene policy of attempting to deny that terrorists are necessarily to blame, the police spread outrageous rumors that he had been seen in a homosexual bar after his disappearance. His body was found two years later. Investigation revealed that he had been murdered by Arabs the night of his disappearance.

Woman soldier, Hadas Kedmi, disappeared after being seen hitching a ride in Haifa. Her body was found 12 days later (December 11, 1984). She had been gang raped for days.

Soldier Moshe Tamam, disappeared after hitching a ride near Netanya. His mutilated body was found on August 10, 1984.

Soldier David Bukra's mutilated body was found in pieces on December 31, 1983, seven months after disappearing near the Megido crossroads.

Woman soldier Dafna Karmon, raped and murdered. Her body was found near Damon prison, Haifa, July 4, 1982.

Soldier Avi Brumberg, picked up and murdered in a car. His body was thrown out near Pardes Chana, June 28, 1980.

This is just a sample. These Jewish soldiers were murdered, raped, mutilated by Arabs—many of them Israeli Arabs, citizens of Israel. But the most humiliating aspect of the murders is the fear that Jews in Israel have allowed to envelop the army of the Jewish State. And the most humiliating of the humiliations is the reaction of the Israeli defense forces. Instead of an angry and ruthless effort to root out Arab terror, on December 12, 1984, the IDF issued a directive under the heading, "Hitching rides—women soldiers:

"In light of the increase in criminal (sic) activities recently, herein is enclosed an obligatory order:

"1. An absolute prohibition to hitch rides (for women soldiers)."

On March 17, 1985, the newspaper *Ma'ariv* carried the following headline:

EVERY WOMAN SOLDIER WHO WILL HITCH RIDES AT NIGHT
WILL BE ARRESTED

A magnificent response to Arab terror. Truly in the footsteps of the Maccabees. Not even the courage to make the highways safe for Jewish soldiers by acting against Arabs and not even the courage to clearly state that the problem was Arab terrorism (instead of the disgusting cover of *"criminal activities"*).

On June 10, 1985, an IDF directive to male soldiers was issued, declaring:

"1. A soldier shall not wait for a ride except in an official station.

"2. A soldier shall not hitch a ride after dark.

"3. There is an absolute prohibition against getting into a car belonging to local Arabs (!), those from the territories, UN or foreign diplomats."

And the head of the IDF manpower department, General Matan Vilnai, issued the following directive on May 11, 1986:

"Soldier and (Woman) Soldier:

"I turn to you to remind you of the dangers threatening you on the roads and how to act ..." To be a free people ...

There then follows a list of soldiers murdered by Arabs and suggestions on how to avoid getting killed. All in all, it is a document that is a primary source for sociologists wishing to study the bankruptcy of secular Zionism. Having lost all spiritual and Jewish meaning, the minimum expectation we might have had from the gentilized Hebrews was at least a state where Jews would be free from fear. But no, not even that. The army document warning soldiers to be careful when standing on their own Jewish roads in their own Jewish state is glaring evidence of the totality of bankruptcy in the Israel of secular Zionism.

And the refusal by the governments of Israel to take the obvious steps—removal from the state of the Arab menace, fifth column and internal subversion—is part of a far wider sickness. It is a disease that causes frightened, timid, gentilized Hebrews, stricken with the suicidal curse of false and perverted democracy, to hobble and destroy their own security forces and their effectiveness as the one wall of defense against the Arab flood that threatens to sweep over and drown us.

The newspaper *Yediot Aharonot* carried what is described as "a monologue with a high-ranking army officer" after the infamous Kahan report that ripped apart the IDF after the massacre of "Palestinians" by Christians in Beirut. The story itself was headlined:

THEY HAVE TURNED THE ARMY INTO A PUNCHING BAG

The gist of the story was the bitter complaint of the army officer concerning the efforts to impose perverted "morality" on the security forces. Let every Jew—liberal or normal—read, weep and think:

"I know how many efforts we dedicated (in Lebanon) to keep from harming civilians. I state categorically that the army had tens of casualties, if not more, only because of the order not to harm civilians. In general, during a war, one first softens a target with artillery in order to prevent casualties among your soldiers. Here, they forbade us lest we hit civilians. From the time we entered Lebanon we adhered strictly to orders not to fire on targets when there was a civilian center. We would hand out flyers, warn them by loudspeakers. If not for that, we could have advanced more swiftly, to crush the terrorist strongholds and, most important, save ourselves tens of our own casualties.

"The terrorists knew this and they entered civilian centers. We could do nothing because of the stubborn orders of Raful [Chief of Staff Rafael Eytan] and [General] Amos Yaaron not to fire even when we were positive that terrorists had penetrated a certain area. Where is the red line that determines for a commander which is more important—to preserve the lives of his soldiers or to save civilians, part of whom are aiding the terrorists? It appears to me that the Israeli commanders long since crossed this red line in favor of preserving the lives of foreign civilians even at the cost of casualties among our soldiers."

A poignant and bitter indictment by an army commander—hobbled by civilian politicians who in turn were targets of leftist propaganda in Israel's sick news media, that never let up for a day in their self-hating campaign to force Israel to eat of their own vomit of guilt. They are accessories to murder; they are the direct cause of an insane, almost unbelievable policy of military madness, that led to the death—the murder—of tens of Jewish soldiers.

The irony is that Chief of Staff Eytan, roundly condemned by leftists as a brutal "hawk," also collapsed before the Hellenist onslaught, and gave "stubborn orders" not to shell terrorist bases in civilian areas lest we, Heaven forbid, cause Arab civilian casualties. Far better that our own boys die.

Too few recall Eytan's statement (September 25, 1982) after the Sabra and Shatila massacre:

"We feel the pain of our enemies. Our moral values arouse within us a feeling of responsibility and determination not to ignore the slaughter that happened in our midst. There is no doubt that the tragedy has cast a shadow over our accomplishments because of the obligation that is instilled in our people for the values of human life." What an incredible moral position! Had the Chief-of-Staff of the United States Army made a similar statement concerning the bombing of German civilians in World War II, no doubt all ethical Jews would have cheered.

We feel the pain of "our enemies," the "Palestinians" who live and dream of the day they will destroy Israel? From these ranks come forth the PLO who support, nurture and give of their children to ter_orists who murder us. *We feel their pain?* We are mad!

And irony of ironies—the man who paid the highest price of the Kahan commission, Defense Minister Ariel Sharon, the villain and arch-murderer of "innocent Palestinians" himself wrote the following nonsense in an Op-Ed piece in the *New York Times* (August 29, 1982):

"No army in the history of modern warfare ever took such pains to prevent civilian casualties as did the Israel Defense Forces. Indeed, most of the losses suffered—some 350 dead and 2,000 wounded [as of that date—MK]—resulted from the rule we imposed on ourselves to avoid harming noncombatants. In Hebrew we call this *tohar haneshek* (the moral conduct of war) [literally, "purity of arms"—MK]. We are proud our soldiers followed this Jewish [!] doctrine scrupulously, despite the heavy costs we incurred in warning civilians we were coming, in attacking only predetermined PLO positions and in bombing and shelling buildings only when they served as PLO strongholds."

The sanctimonious pieties emerging from Sharon are made worse by the knowledge that he does not believe a word he says and that this "moral" policy of murder of Israeli soldiers was forced on him by the merciless leftist propaganda and the weak and vacillating Menachem Begin, who was already approaching the end of his psychological political tether. The murder of Israeli soldiers cries out to the heavens and justifies any soldier's refusal to serve in any army whose commanders and leaders do not place his life over those of enemy civilians.

The life of one Jewish soldiers was worth more than those of all the Arabs—soldiers, terrorists or civilians—in Lebanon, and how one longs for the days of normalcy of World War II, when gentiles of the United States and British air forces, knowing that their own people would die unless the German back and morale were shattered, bombed German cities—with their civilians—mercilessly. They knew that they were fighting a war. A war against forces that, if they won, would plunge them and the world into a nightmare. The gentiles never invented a madness called "purity of arms." Arms are not pure. Arms are used to kill the enemy. Anyone thinking otherwise should not go to war in the first place.

And what an arrogant unfolding of ignorance on the part of Sharon! There is as much intellectual honesty in General Sharon lecturing on "Jewish doctrine" as there is in a Hassidic rabbi pontificating on military strategy. "Purity of arms" a Jewish doctrine? Yet another part of the fraud of gentilized Jews who twist, corrupt, counterfeit authentic Judaism. If one would know what "Jewish doctrine" on war is, let the truth be heard:

"When you go to war against your enemies" (Deuteronomy 20). "Said the Holy One, Blessed Be He: Go against them as enemies. Just as they do not have mercy upon you, have no mercy on them" (Midrash Tanhuma, Shoftim 15). Or:

"If you have mercy on them they will go to war against you. It is similar to a shepherd, tending his sheep in the forest, who found a sickly baby wolf. He had pity on it and nursed it from the goats. When his employer saw it he said: Kill him; have no pity on him lest he cause disaster to the flocks. But the shepherd did not listen to him. When the wolf grew he would see a sheep and kill it, a goat and eat it. Said the employer: Did I not tell you not to have pity on it? So did Moses tell Israel: If you have pity on them, those that shall remain on them shall be as thorns in your eyes and as thistles in your sides and they shall harass you in the land wherein you dwell." (Midrash Dvarim Zuta). Or:

"Harass the Midianites and smite them, for they harass you" (Numbers 15). From here the rabbis learned: "If one comes to slay you, slay him first" (Midrash Bamidbar Raba, Pinchas).

What an astounding difference between the morality of true Judaism and the perverted ethic of the schizophrenic Jews, conceived in gentilized concept and born in an admixture of a Hellenism they trumpet as "Judaism." Neither Judaism nor normalcy countenance the deliberate sacrificing of your soldiers' lives in order to save the enemy who is not in uniform.

But, of course, Israeli is *not* Judaism. Its beginnings and the fount from which it draws its values are supremely un-Jewish. And so, in a clash with terrorists in southern Lebanon in July, 1986, soldier Arye Tubul was killed. The terrorists hid behind three youngsters. The officer in charge prevented the soldiers from firing. Tubul was killed. Murdered. By the terrorists. And by ...

And who still recalls Israeli General Yekutiel Adam, murdered by a 12-year-old youngster in Lebanon? And the killing in 1969 of soldier Hanan Sampson in the Jordan Valley as he and other soldiers approached a cave before which was sitting a woman nursing her child who told them that there were no terrorists there. As they turned away, the terrorists burst from the cave, shooting and killing Sampson.

"Purity of weapons." We are "better" than they. And so we remain better. Deader—but better. Warping Judaism, twisting normal logic and common sense and self-preservation, because of a sick legacy of the ghetto and the Exile, a sad need to be loved that leads us to die and thus prove to the gentile how moral we really are. So he can love us—posthumously.

In the Jerusalem corridor today stands a settlement called Ramat Raziel. In the East Talpiot section of Jerusalem (as well as in half a dozen other Israeli cities), people live on a street called "Raziel Street." Raziel is a hero in Israel, lionized by leaders, with a stamp issued in his honor. Who was he? What great things did he do that led to his becoming a national hero? Listen.

It was the Ides of May, 1937, and the Arab pogroms that had been sweeping throughout Eretz Yisrael grew in fury and in scope. Under the religious urging of the Mufti, Haj-Amin el Husseini, Arab gangs burned Jewish fields, murdered Jewish men and brutally raped Jewish women. Terror, in the real sense of the word, swept the Jewish Yishuv.

The *Vaad Leumi* (National Assembly), elected representatives of the Jews of Eretz Yisrael, debated the terror with passion. A minority led by the Revisionists and supported by parts of the Mizrachi and the General Zionists political parties, demanded counter-action. The majority led by Chaim Weizmann and David Ben Gurion cleaved to the concept of *havlaga* (self-restraint) which was based on the idea of *tohar haneshek*. The Jew was better than the Arab; the Jew would not sink to his level. And so, the policy of the Jewish community was just that. No counter-terror—rather, restraint, gritted teeth, every day another burial of a Jew. The Jew would not sink to the Arab level, he would sink six feet below it.

Within the ranks of the unofficial defense group of the Jews, the Haganah, the debate raged as well. A new group, Haganah Bet, was violently opposed to the official policy and demanded that Jews teach the Arabs a lesson. From this group there broke off a smaller one determined that there had already been too much talk. It called itself the Irgun Zvai Leumi, and after many inner problems, its leader became David Raziel.

Raziel, a disciple of Betar and its founder Zev Jabotinsky, was a religious Jew from Jerusalem. His father was a Hebrew scholar, and David himself studied in Yeshivat Merkaz Harav, of the late Chief Rabbi Kook. He watched with bitterness and frustration as Arab attacks grew and Jewish passivity kept pace with it. On May 10, members of the settlement Bet Yosef in the eastern Emek Yizrael were attacked on their way to work. The barley field in Tel Amal was set on fire by Arab gangs. And then, on May 19, on Strauss Street, in the heart of Jerusalem, a Jew was shot down. The Jews of the capital were furious but the official leadership kept them in line with a stiff demand to "observe moral discipline." But this time, the die was cast.

In a little room which served as the modest headquarters of the Irgun in Jerusalem, David Raziel sat with a member of his tiny group. Carefully, he outlined the plan. The man nodded in understanding. Raziel reached beneath his shirt and took out a revolver, his personal one. Without a word he handed it to the Irgunist. The latter rose, shook Raziel's hand, and walked out.

That morning, at 5:30 a.m., an Arab walking past the Menora Club on Bezalel Street was shot dead. The Irgun had broken *havlaga*; it had determined to avenge Jewish blood with that of the Arab.

The Jewish Establishment, led by the Laborites, reacted with unparalleled fury. The Histadrut paper, *Davar*, in a front page editorial fumed: "The Yishuv has an obligation to openly declare its bitterness against this obscene action. Only a totally irresponsible gang lacking all public and moral responsibility could do what it did."

Not 24 hours later, the Arab gangs, apparently assured by the official Jewish reaction and considering the Irgun attack to be a one-shot affair, murdered another Jew. He was Avraham Zindani, shot down in cold blood near Lydda. On June 3, Arabs threw a bomb at a Jewish bus going from Meah Shearim to Givat Shaul. By a miracle it did not explode. Meanwhile, throughout the country, murder, rapes and burning of Jewish fields grew. The Arab appetite grew, too, in direct relation to the official Jewish policy of self-restraint. And David Raziel, knowing this, was preparing for the formal breaking of that policy.

November 16, 1937, marked that day. It became known as Black Sunday to the Arabs and Mufti. A group of Jews had been attacked in the Old City and now, after months of training and preparation, Raziel's men struck. That day, two Arabs walking on Gaza Street in the Rechavia section of Jerusalem were shot down. One was killed and the other wounded. Half an hour later, two Arabs were shot down in the new Bet Yisrael section. That morning an Arab bus in Romema was attacked by automatic weapon fire, with two Arabs killed.

But there was more. To show that the Irgun was now capable of striking throughout the country, that same day a bomb was thrown into an Arab cafe near the Armon movie house in Haifa, and two Arabs were shot down in the Wadi Niskas area. The official Jews frothed at the mouth and the Arabs began, for the first time, to walk the streets with trepidation.

The Irgun, small and penniless, hounded by the British authorities and by fellow Jews, slowly built its strength as the Arab terror spread. Had the Haganah and the official Jewish leadership done what the Irgun wished, terror of an unprecedented scale would have stricken the Arabs into cowering silence. But with the Irgun perceived, still, as a small group with no official support, the Arabs continued to discount it and to escalate their murder of Jews. Under the prodding of the Mufti, and the Moslem Supreme Council and Higher Committee, gangs began to turn Eretz Yisrael into a country of the pogroms that it was meant to stop. Raziel, moving from house to house to escape arrest and Jewish reaction, was slowly building his anti-terror machine. It now struck, to the terror of the Arabs and the anger of the Jews.

On July 6, 1938, time bombs were put in milk cans and placed in the Arab market place in Haifa by an Irgun member dressed as an Arab porter. In the explosion that followed, 21 Arabs were killed and 52 wounded. Terror spread throughout the Arabs of Haifa, among the most vicious of the enemies of Zionism.

The attack was in reaction to the murder of two Jews the previous day in Jerusalem, and the Arabs of Jerusalem were not to be spared. A bomb thrown into a crowd of Arabs on David Street in the Old City killed two and wounded four. Two days later, the Irgun threw a bomb into a crowd of Arabs waiting near the bus terminal near Jaffa Gate; three were killed and 19 injured. A week later, on a Friday, as Arabs left their mosque at the foot of David Street in the Old City, an electronically detonated mine went off killing 10 Arabs and wounding 30.

Official Jewish reaction bordered on the hysterical. The *Ichud* group, made up of intellectuals such as Dr. Judah Magnes of Hebrew University, Martin Buber and others, condemned the Jewish "terrorists" in language they had never used for the Arab gangs. Ben Gurion, Weizmann and other Jewish leaders called upon Jews to "wipe out the cancer from our midst." The Irgunists were libeled as "murderers, fascists and extremists," who were going against the elected majority of Jews. They were henceforth to be known as *porshim* (those who split from the community).

It had little effect on David Raziel. On July 25, 1938, a 30-kilogram explosive went off in the Arab marketplace in Haifa. Hidden in a barrel of sour pickles, it killed at least 35 Arabs and wounded 70 more. The Arabs were terrified; the Jews were hysterical. Raziel was content.

One month later, the Irgun switched to Jaffa, a nest of the worst gangs of Arab vipers in the country. An Irgun member, once again dressed as an Arab porter, placed a bomb in the Arab Dir-a-Salach marketplace. The official version listed 21 Arabs dead and 35 wounded. In reality many more went to Islamic heaven.

February 27, 1939, proved to be yet another "Black Day" for the Arabs as the Irgun, sensing the impending collapse of Arab terror in the face of Jewish vengeance, attacked three cities. In Haifa, two powerful explosions went off, one at the ticket window of the railroad station in East Haifa and the other at the Arab marketplace. At least 27 Arabs were killed. Half an hour later, in Jerusalem, three Arabs were killed and six wounded in an Irgun explosion on David Street, while another died after being attacked on an Arab bus passing Mahane Yehuda.

Finally, in Tel Aviv attacks on Arabs near the power station in the north and in the Salama district in the south killed three more.

There is more, but the lesson is clear. David Raziel was a terrorist, a murderer who went against everything that was "Jewish." Today, one may visit a settlement due west of Jerusalem named Ramat Raziel and live on Raziel Street in East Talpiot in Jerusalem. One may hear talks on the glory of Raziel and see mementos of him at the Herut headquarters on King George Street in Tel Aviv and may look up paeans of praise of him from the speeches of Yitzhak Shamir, Menachem Begin and Moshe Arens.

"If one comes to slay you, slay him first!" This is Judaism, this is what should be a light unto the feet of the Israeli Defense Forces. Instead, thanks to the gentilized concepts of the gentilized Hebrews, their hearts and minds have been hobbled by perverted mercy. The Mercy of Fools.

And this is the beginning of the destruction of the Israeli army, of the security forces, of security, of, G-d forbid, the state. It is this madness that gives rise to a Kahan Commission which sees Jews creating a little Yom Kippur to atone for the sins of Christians who killed Moslems because Moslems killed Christians. It is this inexplicable Jewish madness that sees a Kibbutz Maagan Michael—which would never dream of fasting on Yom Kippur or on the traditional national day of Jewish mourning, Tisha B'av—proclaim a 24-hour fast for the Palestinians who would destroy us and who were killed by Christian Phalangists.

This was the ad the suddenly "ultra-Orthodox" leftists placed in the Israeli papers September 24, 1983:

> As a protest over the slaughter in the Beirut refugee camps, the participants will take turns standing outside the entrances to their homes. . . .

No African tom-toms ever resounded louder than the beating of Jewish kibbutz breasts.

It is this madness that sees a supposedly normal people rip apart its Security Service over two Arab terrorist jackals who came to massacre Jews and who did murder a woman soldier. The truly ill Israelis who destroyed their Security Services and their spirit have systematically been destroying the armed forces in Lebanon and the Border Police, the tough, special elite forces who put terror into Arab hearts and who now have been emasculated by arrests and trials for "unnecessary force"—as if the saving of Israel from cruel and vicious Arabs can be accomplished by "nice" means. It is this madness that sees Knesset members call for the heads of Jews who have given years of their lives to the state and their people, because they have "lynched Palestine fighters."

And this madness that decried the killing of terrorists is inexorably linked to more insanity. Had the terrorists been captured and kept alive, they would have been tried, found guilty and given—at the most—life imprisonment, for the Mad Hatters of Hellenism refuse to implement the death decree for terrorists, no matter how heinous their crimes.

(As a temporary aside and as a mini-madness adjunct to the major one, know that on December 9, 1975, the newspaper *Hadashot* reported that Nehemia Perlman, the military prosecutor of terrorists who had murdered a Jew, Aharon Avidar, in Ramallah, received a sentence (suspended) of 14 days in military prison because during the trial he told the court that it had an option by law of sentencing the murderers to death. He was convicted of "violating orders.")

No terrorists are given the death sentence. They remain alive to sit in prisons where they receive Red Cross packages and benefits that Jewish criminals do not get, while waiting for their comrades to kidnap a Jewish soldier so they will be exchanged for him. As happened in 1985 in the awesomely insane exchange of no less than *1150 Arab terrorists*, including vicious murderers, for three Israeli soldiers. And Jewish madness being a complex thing, coming in stages and layers, not only were 1150 terrorists freed, but 600 were allowed to remain in the Land of Israel. One can visit one of the murderers in his large supermarket in Shchem, or one can go to Mina Bar Yosef, widow of Moshe Bar Yosef murdered by terrorists at the foot of Jerusalem's Mount of Olives, where he was buried. In a petition to the High Court of Israel, the widow protested that the murderers of her husband were freed and allowed to go back to their village of Silwan, at the foot of the Mount of Olives. On her visit to her husband's grave she can look into their homes. She asked that they be deported. Her petition was denied. Naturally.

Consider, therefore, what would have happened to the terrorists who hijacked the bus in 1984, had they not been killed. They would have received life sentences for murdering the woman soldier and been freed the following year in the Great Exchange. They would have been freed along with these Palestinian "freedom fighters," who were indeed freed:

• The murderers of six young Jews in Hebron in 1980.

• The murderers of 19-year-old yeshiva student Aharon Gross in Hebron.

• The murderer of paratrooper Eli Lupo.

- The two terrorists who attacked Jews in the middle of Jerusalem's King George Street in 1984, murdering one.
- The murders of Uriel and Hadassa Barak.
- The murderers of David Rosenfeld, director of the Herodion site.
- The terrorists who placed a booby-trapped refrigerator in Jerusalem's Zion Square, killing 16 people.
- The murders of soldier Avi Brumberg and soldier David Shamir.
- Kozo Okamoto who murdered 25 people at Ben Gurion Air port.

Madness and part of a greater insanity that sees Israeli soldiers not only refusing to serve in Lebanon but, now, in the "occupied territories" of Judea-Samaria-Gaza as well. The war in Lebanon was lost. But not on the battlefield. It was lost at home as, for the first time in Israeli's history, as Jewish soldiers fought and died, Peace Now and other leftists demonstrated against the war in Israeli cities. Soldiers could watch at night on television as their fellow citizens protested their "aggression" in Lebanon. Little wonder that the Arab Lebanese paper *Al Mustaqbal*, on the eve of the Israeli ignominious retreat from Lebanon (after the death of 650 soldiers), published a cartoon showing a smiling, "V"-waving, confident Israeli soldier entering Lebanon in 1982, and alongside, the same soldier, bandaged, tattered, limping out of the same country in 1985. Little wonder that *Ma'ariv* carried a cartoon by international cartoonist Raanan Lurie showing an Israeli soldier in the sea rushing to the shore as he shouts for help, pursued by two sharks. The smaller is labeled "Lebanese terror." The larger is labeled "Israeli public opinion."

But of course it was not "Israeli public opinion" that was against a war that in its four days smashed the PLO and cut through to Beirut wherein were trapped, like frightened sweating animals, the terrorist leaders. A war that could have, in three more days, physically liquidated the terrorists and their leaders. A war which, instead, saw Israel allowing them to leave with their weapons in one hand and the other raised in "V" for victory. A war that saw defeat snatched from the jaws of victory primarily because of the small handful of leftists who control state radio and television, and the communications industry. (And indeed, the worst of Menachem Begin's sins and disappointments for the Jewish people was his failure to sweep the leftists out of control of the state TV and radio that brainwashes an entire country day and night.) It was a war that saw the kibbutzim (only three percent of the population but with huge funds and resources) able to truck in tens of thousands of their people to a Tel Aviv rally that their cohorts in the news media could soon multiply into a gathering of 400,000 (!) people.

On October 6, 1984, Peter Kobi became the *hundredth* (official) reserve soldier to refuse to serve in Lebanon. Many more followed. The army tried to keep the plague under wraps but it was a disease and symptom of a dangerous malady in the Israeli body politic. Today, more and more soldiers refuse to serve in the "occupied lands." And tomorrow?

The State of Israel is being Vietnamized, but the difference between the process in American and in the Jewish State is vast. If the forces in America that helped to defeat the United States and wreck the armed forces were wrong, it was a mistake that was 8,000 miles away and barely threatened America's existence. But the insane forces of Peace Now and *Yesh Gvul* (There Is a Limit), which supported those who refused to serve in Lebanon and today finance trials of those refusing to serve in the "occupied territories," will destroy the very State of Israel if they are permitted to poison the minds of young Israelis.

Madness. The madness of which the Bible spoke at the very birth of the Jewish nation.

"The L-rd will smite thee with madness and with blindness and with astonishment of heart" (Deuteronomy 28).

The question that fairly cries out for an answer is sure: What is the source of the madness that sees a people and state rip itself apart with its own hands? What is the answer to the puzzle of Jewish lemmingism, the mad national drive to suicide? Surely it can only be the Divine Biblical curse.

We have become a people cursed with madness of soul and mind, with the blindness that gropes in the darkness of insanity, and the Divine punishment we so disdained and mocked has begun its terrible course.

The beating of breasts, the setting up of a thousand private Israeli Wailing Walls because of the killing of the two terrorists who seized a bus with tens of terrified Jewish passengers and were prepared to murder all of them, is a stupefying, breathtaking example of mass insanity that must be the intense subject of investigation by dozens of experts in abnormal psychology. No one can exceed the Jew in heights and in lows. No one can reach the enormous levels of greatness and holiness of the people of Israel and none can sink to the record depths of the people of Abraham, Isaac and Jacob. If to climb the heights of holiness and sanctity is to go beyond "normalcy" and the norms of the rest of humanity—that is surely greatness. But to sink below all the rest in a stupefying exhibition of national suicide is to wave, for all to see, the awesome sickness of the Jewish product of millennia of Exile, of a ghetto people riddled with all the neuroses, guilt feelings and self-hatred that are a necessary by-product of the Jew's wanderings.

And the fact that he has come home to his own state changes nothing. The removal of the Jew from the Exile has absolutely nothing to do with the removal of the Exile from the Jew. And never was there a sicker Jewish society, in terms of self-hate and madness and blindness of heart and mind, than this one, which so arrogantly—just a few decades ago—boasted of the new, proud Hebrew society that had taken over from the weak, decadent Jewish one of the Exile.

A tasteless joke, a mirthless jest. This is a country that is so riddled with guilt and sin, so unsure of its basic beliefs, that its race to self-destruction becomes a subconscious crusade. At first glance, the incredible wailing over the two Arab terrorists falls merely into the misguided mercies concerning which the Ramban in explaining the commandment, "Thou shalt devour thine enemies, have no mercy upon them" (Deuteronomy 7:15), declares: "For through the mercy of fools, all justice is lost." Ah, magnificent phrase by the halachic master, a delicious decree of Jewish morality. "The mercy of fools!"

But there is far more than this in the present disturbed state of the Jewish State, in the present psychotic state of the State of Israel. Mirrored in this wailing over the "rights" of terrorist swine is the deep psychopathic tendency of large sections of Israel to take up Arab positions on almost every issue. It is the movies that portray the Arab as the oppressed human and the Jew as the oppressor. It is the hysterical-obsessive need to march on Shabbat with Arabs in Wadi Ara, an area known for its bloodthirsty Arabs who would wring the neck of every Jewish male and do much worse to his woman. It is the book that is put out by the wife of Israel Radio's "interpreter" of Arab affairs glorifying a leading Arab terrorist and recounting his visit to their home and their meetings with him in England. It is the kibbutz members rebuilding homes of Arab families whose members had been apprehended as members of terrorist gangs that had attacked Jews; homes which had been destroyed by the IDF. It is the Chief of Staff stating that the "Arabs are not the enemy" (thus revealing for the first time that for the past 40 years Israel has been fighting the Chinese). All of these are inherent aspects of the same moral-spiritual sickness that now has led to the sacking of the head of Security Services, a man who has dedicated his life to his country, and the hasty granting of a "pardon" to him and three other Jewish heroes.

What we have here is part of a moral and mortal disease of national dimensions—a loss of belief in the most fundamental and basic tenets of national faith. It is a loss of faith that is so terrible to its victim because he must either own up to it, drop it, change his life entirely, move over to the enemy camp or live an agonizing lie that gives neither sleep to his eye nor rest to his lids.

Hundreds of thousands of Israeli Jews—almost all secular, educated Ashkenazim, direct descendants of Zionism—fear, in their heart of hearts, that they are thieves who have no right to be in the country. With G-d playing no part in his life or calculations and the Divine Promise of the Jews to the land irrelevant, the secular Jew is riven with guilt over his inability to explain away, to others and to himself, Arab arguments that the land is really theirs and was stolen from them by the Zionists. The fact that Jews "once lived there" is simply not enough for him to answer the Arab, who asks: But I have lived here for hundreds of years, why did you take over my country, "Palestine," and make it a Jewish State, "Israel"?

And so, driven by these awe-inspiring feelings of guilt (the degree of which few but the Jew can attain), he walks in a permanent state of depressive-guilt, which is only augmented by his moral cowardice.

For if he is, indeed, a thief as he so darkly fears, should he not stand up and tell the Arab: Here is my kibbutz—your land—I return it to you? But the secular Israeli Hellenist is not even an honest thief. He lacks the courage to return what his brooding soul tells him Jews stole. And thus, he continues to brood and writhe in guilt and self-hatred over his cowardice and he desperately attempts to soothe his aching conscience by supporting the Arabs on every possible issue. He hopes, prays (to whom he knows not) to win from them some crumbs of forgiveness for both his robbery and his cowardice. He is prepared to destroy himself and his state in order to win Arab penance and absolution for his imagined sins.

And side by side with this sick thought is another: That time is on the side of the Arabs and that ultimately they will win the struggle. The terrible thought of an Arab victory, and its accompanying bloodbath against the Jews, drives the spiritually disturbed Jew to stand by the side of the Arab on issue after issue in the desperate hope that, should the Arabs emerge victorious, he the "good" Jew, the "moral and ethical" Jew, the one who fought Kahane and the rightwing fascists of all kinds, can shout: I was your friend: I supported your legitimate rights; I was a good Jew.

To understand what is happening in Israel one cannot analyze things logically, but psychologically. And what is happening is the penetration of a madness and blindness that is Divine punishment, measure for measure. Those who threw off Judaism and the yoke of Heaven are stricken with an empty soul and madness, and blindness of heart and mind. Zionism without Judaism in Israel is an empty vessel leaving those who drink from its dregs empty, guilt-ridden and sick with the ague of self-hate. That is why a people that was once blessed as "a people wise and understanding" can reach the point where it tears itself apart over two Arabs who came to kill Jews. That is why the country daily rides its own various horses of the Apocalypse.

A final word. A final word to assure that the false moralists and ethical frauds are not only not allowed to continue their assumption of the mantle of righteousness, but will be branded as the accessories to murder—murder of fellow Jews—that they really are.

In December, 1983, a number 18 bus, driving down a Jerusalem street, had a bomb go off under one of its seats. Six Jews were killed. In the aftermath, a young, 20-year-old woman named Rina Pollak wrote a poem. Rina is the only daughter of her family. Today. She was not always the only daughter. In fact, until the bomb exploded on that bus, she was one of three daughters to her father and mother. Unfortunately, two of the six Jews who were murdered on that bus were sisters. Rina's sisters, aged 15 and 16. And so, a few weeks later Rina wrote a poem. It is commended to all the mentally lame, blind and halting Jews of gentilized morality and respectability who fight unto the intellectual death any thought of removing the Arabs from the land:

> You get up in the morning, and it is like any other morning;
> You go to work, and the work is like all other.
> You ride the bus and it is like all other buses,
> You return in the afternoon and suddenly you hear that
> you no longer have two sisters.
> And to lose two sisters is not like just any other day.
> You walk and you cry and breathe with difficulty and wonder;
> Why did G-d suddenly take from you two sisters?
> So small, and you cannot understand.
> How is it that you get up in the morning and by
> the afternoon you no longer have sisters who lived with you
> for fifteen years until now and not be with you
> for many years afterwards?
> You get up in the morning and the morning is not like other mornings
> You go to work and the work fails to lessen the greatness of the loss,
> You ride the bus and the bus is already gone.
> You return home in the afternoon and must grasp that you no
> longer have two sisters.
> I sit and try to think where my mind will lead me to two dead sisters

To continue a life, painful, filled with tears and fears,
thoughts and pains,
Or to hover above with two small sisters taken by terrorists;
Or to wait for another bus that takes innocent children to
a different world.

Every Arab who remained in the land to murder a Jew, to place a bomb that took a Jewish life, to stab a Jew and take from him his life, was able to do so because of Jews who refused to remove him. Those Jews are accessories to murder. Those Jews are partners in the murder of fellow Jews. Their hands are stained with blood and on their breasts will forever be branded the scarlet mark of Cain. "And the mercies of the wicked are cruel" (Proverbs 12).

One wishes to weep. To weep at a miracle of G-d given to us and turned by us into a travesty, a dream of strength and pride become an incredible parody of the Exile. Who would have believed it? Who would have believed that the day would come when the Arabs of Hebron, the descendants of the bloody murderers of Jews in 1929, would today drive and walk and stroll without fear in Tel Aviv while Jewish tour guides warn fearful Jews against going to visit the graves of the Patriarchs in Hebron?

The dream. The dream of a people huddled for two millennia in an Exile of fear, dreaming of the pride and strength and glory of a Jewish national home of their own. "To be a free people in our own land." A dream twisted by the gentilized disciples of Hellenism, whose mercy of fools allows the murderers to remain within us and the fear to enter our hearts.

Leftist columnist Tuvia Mendelson, writing in the Histadrut paper *Davar*, produced a piece under the heading: "Home Before Darkness" (November 13, 1985).

In it he describes leaving a meeting in the Beit Hakerem section, in the heart of Jerusalem. The meeting finishes quite late. Outside, all is silence and very dark. The Jerusalem municipality, to save money, dims and shuts many lights after midnight. Tuvia Mendelson, progressive extraordinaire, fighter for equal Arab rights and bitter opponent of Kahanism, goes out to his car. He cannot find it in the dark. He wanders from auto to auto, his nervousness and fear growing with every passing moment. He writes:

"With nervousness comes tension and with tension—fear. And the fear remains after I found the car and after I succeeded with no little effort to push the key into the keyhole and open the door. And also after I started the car and began to drive...."

"While driving I locked the doors. I closed the windows securely. I tried to remember if I had my identity card or other papers through which my body could be identified [!]. I was panic-stricken to think that I was driving without a jack and if, G-d forbid, there would be a flat tire I would not be able to change it. I was covered with cold sweat.... When I got home I could not fall asleep. I heard sounds. Footsteps. Someone on the porch. Someone on the roof...." Incredible. The dream of Zion. But the madness within the madness is Mendelson's conclusion. The next day he angrily phoned the municipality. *To demand that the lights not be dimmed at night.* This of course is the problem. Tuvia in cuckooland.

The people of Israel. The dream. In search of a national couch.

Chapter 8

The Temple Mount Is...

It was the unforgettable, majestic, glorious day in June, 1967, as Jewish soldiers crashed through the walls of Jerusalem's old city. Redeeming, reclaiming, liberating the ancient streets and alleyways; racing towards the Wall, scaling it and then—the electrifying words of the Commander, Motta Gur: "The Temple Mount is in our hands! The Temple Mount is in our hands!"

There was not a Jewish heart that did not pound with a sense of Divine, historic moment. There was not a Jewish spine, so straight and proud after two millennia of being supine, that did not shiver in a sense of awe. There was not a Jew, though the most extreme of scoffers, who, at that moment, did not see G-d!

"The Temple Mount is in our hands!" Jerusalem of Gold, of holiness, of David; Zion, out of which the L-rd roared and uttered his voice. The Temple Mount, from which the trumpet of the Holy One, Blessed Be He, blasted. "When our feet stood within thy gates, O Jerusalem"—we wept with tears of disbelief. For the Temple Mount was in our hands. "As the mountains are round about Jerusalem, so the L-rd is round about His people"—and we knew it to be true. For the Temple Mount was in our hands. "Ye that stand in the courts of the House of our G-d, praise the L-rd!" And we believed. For the Temple Mount was in our hands!

Let me quote from a letter that appeared in the March 21st, 1979, issue of *Ma'ariv*, Israel's largest newspaper. It was written by a rabbinical student at Yeshivat Merkaz Harav and is obligatory reading for all those who, for Zion's sake, will not be silent:

"It was the *Shabbat*, when many Jews come to visit the Old City of Jerusalem.... Suddenly, after leaving one of the gates near the Temple Mount, the rioting began. Tens of Arabs, throwing stones and carrying knives and broken bottles, came at us. A storekeeper leaped upon me and I joined the others fleeing, as my hand bled profusely, eyeglasses left behind.

"How could it happen in the State of Israel today? Arab police are responsible for the safety of the East Jerusalem region. 'Autonomy' already exists when Arab police see Arabs throwing stones and nothing is done to arrest them. One who was arrested was a yeshiva student who kept calm and tried to help others. Before my very eyes, the police leaped upon him like wild beasts. This can serve to show us what we can expect in the future under 'autonomy.'"

Jerusalem. Where in 1967, electric shocks of ecstasy, a national thrill of incredulity, swept the Jewish people throughout the world, as Israeli Jewish troops smashed into the Old City, sweeping terrified Arabs before them as chaff in the wind. Jerusalem, City of David, Jerusalem of the Temple Mount and Western Wall and Holy of Holies and Zion, was, once again, in Jewish hands—all of it, *Jewish*. By the tens of thousands, Jews streamed through the alleyways of the Old City where just a few days before the Arabs had ruled and no Jew dared step. Now, the Arab—awed, shattered—groveled before the Jew whom he saw as being blessed by G-d and His miracles. Fear gripped the Arab in Jerusalem just as pride and confidence and certainty were the Jewish cloak in the wake of the awesome war of Six Days.

Jerusalem. Where, by 1986, less than 20 years later, Jews fear to go to the Wall by way of the Damascus Gate, as Jews are stabbed and shot in the same marketplace and streets where a short time earlier they walked as Jewish giants on the earth. As night falls, only a handful of foolhardy Jews risk walking through what the Israelis allow to be called, still, the Moslem Quarter. No Harlem ever held greater fears for the Jew than parts of his own capital city. Nothing more underlines the obscenity of Jewish fears in their own capital than the picture report that appeared in the Jerusalem weekly, *Kol Ha'ir* (August 4, 1984).

Three pictures; all taken in the Old City of Jerusalem. The first shows a *Hassidic* Jew, surrounded by Arab youngsters, two of whom have snatched his hat from his head. The photo shows a policeman standing calmly by with obviously no intentions of intervening. He is, like the vast majority of police in the Old City, an Arab.

The second picture shows the Jew, watching helplessly as the Arabs taunt him. The Arab policeman has, by now, disappeared. The third shows a large rock being thrown by an Arab youth at the Jew. It hit him in the head. Another day of Jewish pride in Jerusalem, Zion. The tragedy of Jewish glory turned into humiliation and fear by a Jewish policy that defies any normal logic and understanding.

Jerusalem, where the Jewish students on Mount Zion sign a petition of desperation, detailing not only sexual and criminal assaults on them by Arabs, but the cynical indifference and lack of any law enforcement by the local police—Arabs.

"We, the undersigned to this petition, are demanding security for our lives and property. For the past ten years there have been thousands of incidents such as those outlined in this petition: stabbings, rapes, attempted rapes, molestings, obscenities through indecent exposure, burglaries, vandalism...." And the police do nothing. And Jerusalem becomes Arab autonomy. The tragedy of a Jewish policy that defies any normal logic and understanding.

A Jewish policy? Say, rather a policy of Jews that was conceived in un-Jewishness and born in gentilized fear and timidity, a policy whose apex of humiliation is the desecration of Judaism's holiest site—The Temple Mount. The very moment of glorious Jewish victory in 1967 was the beginning of a flight to shame.

It began immediately after the greatest Jewish victory and miracle in 2500 years. The terrified and cowering Arabs of East Jerusalem were approached by Defense Minister Moshe Dayan. Not enough that the Israeli government of 1967 committed the worst of mistakes by not driving out the Arabs who hated Israel and had tried to wipe her out. Not enough that in their fear of "world opinion," of what the Vatican and Islam might say, orders were given by the Israeli army to the liberators of the Old City not to use artillery to shell Arab positions lest they damage a single holy Moslem or Christian place (and how many Jewish soldiers died because of that policy!). The fearful and timid leaders of Israel immediately approached the heads of the Moslem community to assure them that the Temple Mount—the holiest of holiest of Jewish places—would remain in their hands. Jews were forbidden to enter there to pray, on their holiest site, a site stolen from them by invading Moslems who desecrated Judaism by building two mosques there. (And can one imagine the reaction of Moslems if Jews, conquering Mecca, built, on the holiest site of Islam—a synagogue?)

When in 1967, on the Fast of Tisha B'Av, the national day of mourning for the Jews, the anniversary of the destruction of both Temples, Army Chief Rabbi Shlomo Goren and 50 Jews went to pray on the Temple Mount, Defense Minister Moshe Dayan ordered the commander of the Central Command to prevent any further action that might incite the Moslems: "Honored Rabbi," said the general, "if you will go up to the Mount again, I will be compelled to remove you by force." The following day the Ministerial Committee in charge of the holy places met and unanimously forbade Jewish prayer that had been set for the following Shabbat. That was the beginning of a humiliating Jewish policy that stunned no one more than the Moslems who could not believe the manifestation of Jewish madness they had just seen.

From that day, the government of Israel, in a remarkable exhibition of masochism, has paved the way for a total change in Moslem attitude. From a frightened, cowering population, they turned into a confident, arrogant, dangerous one. From people who feared the Jewish conqueror, they became throwers of stones, knife stabbers, and grenade and bomb throwers. Most of all, the Temple Mount became once again *theirs*, this time returned to them by two-legged lemmings of the Mosaic persuasion—and they grow ever more passionately convinced that time is on their side.

The government, police, courts have all had a hand in the shameful, tragic Jewish descent into humiliation. Already on April 15, 1969, responding to an *order nisi* against Police Minister Shlomo Hillel (who later went on to become Knesset Speaker), the State Attorney explained that Jews should not be allowed to pray on the Temple Mount because "premature prayer" (sic) by Jews there would raise grave security and international political problems. The years that followed saw police again and again forcibly remove Jews attempting to pray on their holy site. Moslems watched in growing amazement, and growing arrogance and boldness, as the Jew who wished to enter as a *tourist* with camera and jeans was freely allowed access but the same son of Abraham entering with prayer shawl and prayer book was banned!

(In the years when American synagogues sold tickets for pews at High Holiday services, a rueful joke told of the Jew rushing up to the door without a ticket and telling the guard that he only wished to tell something to someone inside. Said the guard: "Fine, but if I catch you praying, I'll throw you out." The joke is alive and well today on the Temple Mount.)

Then, in 1976, a lower Jerusalem court, through Judge Ruth Or, ruled that Jews have a right to pray on the Temple Mount, but Police Chief Hillel blithely announced that he would continue to bar Jews. (This contempt for law is apparently endemic with Hillel as, nearly ten years later, in his capacity as Speaker of the Knesset, he announced that he would refuse to table certain bills by Knesset Member Meir Kahane, despite a High Court order to do so.)

The government hastily appealed the lower court order and on July 1, 1976, the Jerusalem District Court overruled Judge Or in a fascinating display of ghettoism. The court ruled that Jews who attempted to pray "demonstratively" (sic) on the Temple Mount were guilty of behavior "likely to cause a breach of the peace." Jews had an unquestionable right to pray on the Temple Mount, but public order, ruled the court, overrules that right of prayer.

The decision was mindboggling, the product of thinking most Jews assumed had disappeared with the Warsaw Ghetto revolt. To state that Jews had a right to pray on their holiest site and then to declare that this should be prevented because of fear of Arab rioting, was a paean to the *shtetl* of Minsk, Pinsk or Casablanca. But not even this was enough for the Israeli government, which wished to remove the decision that Jews have a theoretical "right" to pray on the Temple Mount and an appeal was taken to the Supreme Court. Meantime, Interior Minister Dr. Joseph Burg (himself a leader of the National Religious Party) declared that "the law will be kept." (Translation: Jews will not be allowed to pray on their holiest site.)

The astonished Arabs saw that the Jews, far from meting out to them the punishment that they deserved and that they had given to the Jews when they ruled the Old City, were allowing them to retain all the power and authority that they would use later to demand total autonomy and independence. The Temple Mount served as the most glaring example of the fact that, despite Jewish protestations to the contrary, the land taken in 1967 was not liberated but "conquered." The Jews had come not as returnees to their own borders, but as an occupation army. One who loses his property and then unexpectedly finds it does not allow it to remain in the possession of another. He leaps upon it joyfully and cries out: "It is mine!"

The Arabs correctly understood Jewish "concessions" to be the product, not of goodness and grace, but of timidity and fear. And so, from a cowering Arab, the Jews produced a sneering, openly hating, stick bearing, stone throwing, grenade tossing thing—a time bomb waiting to explode.

The newspapers described some of the events. In 1979, as a number of yeshiva students came up to the gate of the Temple Mount to pray (in front of and not on the Mount itself), they were showered with rocks. Soldiers hid behind cars because they had orders not to shoot, lest *The New York Times* and *Time* magazine feature them on their front pages. The head of the Central Command, General Moshe Levi, watched the mob. Levi, a member of the leftist Hashomer Hatzair kibbutz, was later to become Chief of Staff and won undying something-or-other with his statement during a speech in Tel Aviv (May 25, 1986): "To say that the Arabs are the enemy is simplistic and dangerous. For me the Arabs are not the enemy." When the Jew excels, he outdoes all others—especially in madness.

I return to the newspaper account of the Arab riot in 1979:

"'Only in this state could such a picture emerge,' a police officer said angrily, yesterday, at the sight of the commander of the Central Command, Moshe Levi, and the head of the police central region, who entered the Temple Mount to meet face-to-face with angry Arab youths.

"The general walked over and asked them why they were holding sticks in their hands [!]. But during the entire conversation not one of them backed down and not one dropped his stick. 'This is the real autonomy,' muttered the same officer."

Meanwhile, in 1980, the Knesset passed a new "Jerusalem Law" which declared in paragraph (3):

"The holy places shall be protected from any desecration or attack on anything likely to damage the rights of all members of religions to access to the holy places or their feelings concerning them."

This paragraph which clearly—to all but those who would refuse to see—outlined the absolute right of Jews to access to their holy places, now seemed to guarantee that the High Supreme Court of Israel would order the government to allow Jews, on their holiest site, the same right of prayer that they allowed Moslems who had stolen the site. But no, the *ghetto-shtetl* syndrome remained part of the Israeli genetic code, proving once again that it is far easier to remove the Jew from the Exile than the Exile from within the Jew. On October 30, 1981, the High Court of Israel ruled on the issue. The following is the UPI wire service report:

"Jerusalem (UPI)—The Supreme Court today upheld the right of Israeli police to keep Jewish worshippers from praying on the Temple Mount because it creates a threat to public order, Israel radio said."

A threat to public order. The Arabs might riot. Ah, if Meir Kahane were Prime Minister and the Arabs knew that the police had orders and full backing to use as much force as they desired to keep public order—is there one normal person who believes that there would be an Arab threat to public order?

Since then, the Arabs have systematically destroyed every vestige of Jewish presence on the Temple Mount, destroying valuable archaeological evidence. A memorial to the Arabs killed at Sabra and Shatila is even placed on the Jewish holy site. The Temple Mount is on our hands! ...

The lemmingism of the Israeli government is incredible! Who can count the ways?

In February, 1985, the Mufti of Jerusalem, Sheikh Sa'ad a-din Alamei, told the French news agency:

"Any Moslem who will give up one inch of Palestinian land will lose, without benefit of appeal, every attachment to Islam."

The Mufti, by declaring a ban on any Moslem who sold land or houses to Jews, was clearly guilty of sedition against the Jewish state. On February 26, 1985, I wrote to the Chief of Police asking that criminal proceedings be opened against the Mufti and personally filed a criminal charge with the police commander of Jerusalem's Old City. In my complaint I noted that if a Jew were to hand out flyers calling on Jews not to buy from the Arabs of the Old City because they were enemies of Israel and pro-PLO, he would be arrested for sedition (indeed, a few months later, that is precisely what happened). On March 13, 1985, the office of the Chief of Police sent me the following reply:

"Your complaint has been investigated and it is clear that the material of the investigation does not indicate a criminal offense. Because of this, the police will not investigate the complaint."

The successor to the other Mufti who in the twenties and thirties led pogroms against the Jews of the Holy Land and who in 1942 met with Hitler to discuss the "final solution" for the Jews there, should have been given a Nobel Prize for extraordinary ability to keep from bursting into hysterical laughter. And, indeed, the Moslem religious leader has good reason to believe that Jews are mentally limited.

When the PLO conference was held in Amman, Jordan, in November 1984, one of the telegrams sent to Arafat was from the Jerusalem Mufti. It read: "From Al-Aksa mosque (on the Temple Mount) we emphasize our support of your Council and renew our oath of loyalty to the man of struggle Yasir Arafat.... Continue forward on your path, we are with you."

When the Sephardic Chief Rabbi of Israel in January 1986, called for a synagogue in the southeast part of the Temple Mount, Mufti Alamei declared: "Over the bodies of a million Moslems."

The Israeli reaction? Timid and fearful silence, lest the Arabs, Moslems and world react. And so, a mentally unbalanced Jew, Alan Goodman, shoots and kills two Arabs on the Temple Mount declaring that he wishes to liberate the spot and "become king of the Jews." Some thirteen years earlier, a Christian, Dennis Michael Rohan, set fire to the Al Aksa mosque. The Israeli court declared the Christian not criminally liable by reason of insanity. Yet Goodman, clearly unbalanced, received a life sentence plus two terms of 20 years. Once upon a time, in the Exile, the Jews would decide every major step by the proposition: What will the gentiles say? Then they created Israel, where Jews would be sovereign and free.... Laugh not, but rather weep for generations.

Jerusalem. Where the Palestinian autonomy and eventual state is being built. Jerusalem, which mirrors so much of the other desecration that fills the land.

The Temple Mount is not in our hands. East Jerusalem is not in our hands. Judea and Samaria and Gaza and the Golan are not in our hands. The Biblical Eretz Yisrael which we liberated through G-d's decree in 1967 is not in our hands.

"On Mount Zion which is desolate, there the foxes walk ..." (Lamentations 5).

The Temple Mount is in their hands, the foxes, the cunning Arab foxes. And the words of Motta Gur ring hollowly—and it is we who are to blame. We, who took a miracle and disdained it. We, who took holiness and profaned it. We, who were given a Zion, a Jerusalem, a Temple Mount—and gave it over to the jackal-foxes.

What we see today is a mini-renewal of Arab rioting, murder and pogrom of the twenties and thirties. Then, the Arab mobs surged into the streets shouting, "*Addowlah ma'anah* (The government is with us)!" They meant the British Mandatory occupation government. Today, the Arabs know that the Jewish "occupation" government, because of its fear of world opinion, has given strict orders to soldiers not to shoot. In that sense it has opened the door to Arab boldness and contempt and attacks on Jews. In that sense the Jewish government of occupation is also "with" them. The Arabs have smashed the dam of fear and it will spill over. If Jews are attacked on their way to the Wall, and if a Jew is seriously hurt, or, G-d forbid, murdered, and if the residents of the Jewish Quarter are in increasing danger—know that it is the Jews who are to blame.

He who controls the Temple Mount will control Jerusalem. And he who controls Jerusalem will control the Holy Land. And the desecration of the Land and of G-d is inconceivable. One shakes his head in utter incomprehension when reading the words uttered by Menachem Begin in 1977:

"If I become the Prime Minister, I will open the Temple Mount to Jews. I will not fear the reactions of the Christian and Moslems."

Begin became the Prime Minister. The Temple Mount is still in Arab hands.

Chapter 9

Artists, Intellectuals and Imbeciles

I have never, ever been afraid of the Arabs; it is the Jews who terrify me. The ultimate danger to Jews has never been the gentile; it is the Jews who have always been their own worst enemy. And no Arab state or combination thereof can ever bring Israel to its knees. To accomplish that, they must look to the enemy within, the Jews of self-hate, of cancerous guilt, the lemmings of Suicide Now. To our bitter regret, there is no lack of these; the enemy is indeed within the gates, within the walls.

And so, a quick tour of Jewish cuckooland—the bastion of the liberal-left in Israel, the fortress of the guilt-ridden and self-haters, the modern Samsons who yearn for death and to take us with them.

Tzalach Ta'amri is a senior PLO military official. He was the one who created the young Fatah (military wing of the PLO) branches and was commander of the PLO in the battle with Israeli forces in Karama, Jordan. He was one of the military commanders of the terrorists in Lebanon, where he was captured by the Israeli army. There, he was placed in the infamous prisoner camp, Antzar, infamous because the terrorists under his command daily insulted, threw excrement and food at Israeli soldiers, attempted to attack them and escape—all with Israeli guards under frustrating and humiliating shackles not to use force against them, lest international opinion cry out.

Ta'amri, senior terrorist official, hater of Israel, is handsome, intelligent and so much cleverer than Israelis that he automatically becomes the target for all the Israeli guilt and sickness of soul. Little wonder that a book glorifying him has just been completed by Aharon

Barnea, the official commentator on Arab affairs for Israel State Radio, and his wife. Barnea, a leftist whose love affair with the Arab world is worthy of a place in the psychological classics, interviewed the Arab, and was stricken by him. Naturally. Here was the Arab, totally convinced of the justice of his cause, versus the Israeli, not sure of his right to be in Israel, of his Jewishness, of his very identity. It was simply no match. Suffice it to say that Barnea intervened with the military authorities to allow the PLO leader to tour Israel: kibbutzim, Barnea's home in fashionable, wealthy Ramat Hasharon and—Yad V'Shem, the Holocaust Memorial Center.

Naturally, the terrorist became a penitent. Naturally, the Arab whose victory over Israel would repeat the Holocaust was deeply affected by the original one.

Amos Oz, kibbutznik, writer and idol of Jane Fonda, met the Arab lion, who by now had become a must for all the intellectual and artistic lemmings of the gentilized Hebrew "in" crowd. Said Oz: "I am invited to many cocktail parties but I do not go. But if there is ever a Palestinian state and you are its ambassador, I promise to come to the party you give." Poor Amos, he makes a poor prophet. On the day there is a Palestinian state, the PLO terrorist will try very hard to make sure he will never have the opportunity to be an ambassador to a state he wishes to destroy.

Prizes for not laughing should have been showered upon him, too, as he was released from Antzar, thanks to his Israeli friends who saw in him all the justice, heroism and nationalism they lack. He was last heard of in May 1986, when, having returned as senior commander of the PLO in Jordan, he was expelled by Hussein as being too dangerous to the country. I would clearly be ready to exchange a sane Hussein for two mad Jewish Israeli Barneas (*Monsieur et Madame*), who will always be able to tell their children how proud they should be of having sat on the lap of a terrorist in their home in Ramat Hasharon. Who knows? He may return there, for that is certainly what the Arab plans to do.

The national Mafia of Israeli lemmings has already leaped upon this book. Yehoshua Sobol, playwright of the Theater of the Jewish Suicidal, announced immediately that he would make a play out of the book. Sobol is the major playwright for the Haifa Theatre, and both the theater and the playwright have made permanent places for themselves in the Hall of Fame of Jewish Cuckooland.

Indeed, Israeli plays and movies have become a sea of Jewish masochism, whose themes repetitively proclaim and describe the ugly Jew, the Nazi-Jew, the oppressed Arab, love between an Arab and

Jewish woman in a world of bigotry, ridicule of and hatred for Judaism. It is almost impossible to plumb the depths of this Jewish self-hatred, a disease that infects countless young Israeli Jews and that shatters their belief in Zionism, the army, the justice of their cause. Sobol and the Haifa Theatre are among the generals in this army of Jewish masochism and self-hate. They are a disease, a Black Plague of Jewish hatred of Jews.

In the spring of 1986, the Haifa Theatre travelled to Chicago where they presented the two Sobol plays, *Ghetto* and *Soul of a Jew*. For a brief understanding of *Ghetto*, the words of *Yediot Aharonot* writer, Noah Klieger, a Holocaust survivor, are pertinent (May 29, 1986):

"In Chicago and Washington they raved about *Ghetto* and *Soul of a Jew*. They raved about *Ghetto*, frightening and horrifying, whose main aim is, apparently, to prove that even in the shadow of death the Jews do not stop being ugly, corrupt, informers and egotists. They raved about unlikeable Jews who arouse among non-Jews the feeling that it was not so terrible that the number of such disgusting characters was lessened. It is no surprise that they enjoy it when a Jewish writer through a Jewish theater presents a plan that confirms what they think anyway." (It may be added, that the obscene play was presented on the eve of Israel's annual Day of Remembrance of the Holocaust.)

The other play, *Soul of a Jew*, concerns Otto Weininger, one of the sickest characters in Viennese Jewry of the 1920s, a man who became a household word as a prototype of *selbsthass* (self-hatred). A brilliant and deeply disturbed person, he hated his Jewishness and himself, finally committing suicide at a young age. The play, perfect as a mirror-image for Sobol, is a non-stop Jewish anti-Semitic flood. One particular passage shows more than anything else the deep disturbance within Sobol's soul and mind that so symbolizes the secular Israeli artist and intellectual.

In the scene, Weininger, naked, is being massaged by a woman, and he speaks:

"Oh L-rd, G-d of our times, the woman and Jewess of all times, blessed are you and our name who gives man sex; L-rd, G-d of sex, strengthen my spirit with sex, strengthen my body with sex, bless my deeds with sex."

(Here, Sobol satirizes the sacred prayer for the dead, *Eyl Malei Rachamim*, which has in it the words "*hamtzei menucha nechona* (grant perfect repose)", and changes the word "*menucha*, (repose or rest)", to "*tnucha*," so that the meaning becomes "grant a perfect (sexual) body position ..." It is this sick vomit that is produced in Israel, presented in Israel and then exported to Chicago and Washington and

Edinburgh (where it opened the famous Edinburgh Festival in 1983), as well as Broadway in 1987.

And it was in Chicago that the gentilized Hebrews of Israel met with members of the Chicago Jewish community. Having begun their tour on the right foot by opening on the holiday of Passover, the meeting with the Chicago Jews was an eye-opener, if a shocking one, for the lovers of Zion who attended. A letter from Professor A. I. Weinzweig, professor of Mathematics at the University of Illinois, who was present at the meeting, was published in the *Jerusalem Post*, July 10, 1986. In it he speaks of the anger of a Jewish Holocaust survivor over a scene in the play which portrays the humaneness of a SS officer who caught a Jew with a gun, took it away from him and allowed him to go. The letter reads in part:

"The German lady said that the portrayal of the SS man was not *true*—as no SS man who had caught a Jew with a gun would simply have taken the gun away and released the Jew, as happened in the play. [Doron] Tavori, who played the SS man, answered, saying that he was born in Israel and his parents were born in Israel and he knew nothing of the Holocaust [a sad commentary on Israeli education], that he did not want to portray the Nazis as monsters, but wanted to show that they were also men of culture, that inside all of us is a little Nazi. This touched off a storm of protest in the audience.

"People demanded to know if Tavori was comparing Israel with Nazi Germany, and he answered: 'Look at Germany in the early days of Hitler and compare it to Israel today.'

"The moderator, no doubt to change the subject, asked another member of the cast a question. [This was Yusuf AbuVarda, an Israeli Arab.] He proceeded to answer by stating that he was not a Jew, that he was born and grew up in Haifa but was a Palestinian. Here was an individual, born and educated in Israel, travelling abroad as part of an Israeli theatre troupe and stating that he is a Palestinian, not an Israeli. He then proceeded to argue that Israel today is very much like Nazi Germany.

"Later that week there appeared in the local papers an interview with Tavori in which he stated that the Haifa Theatre tries to represent the cause of the Palestinians and he added, with obvious approval, that they are regarded as the PLO representatives in Israel.

"On Saturday evening, May 10, we attended a reception for the Haifa Theatre troupe. The hostess apologized, explaining that this had been planned long in advance of the incident in the theatre. In discussion ... members of the troupe ...complained about the fact that the Chicago Jewish community did not support them. I pointed out that by opening on *Pesach* (Passover) they alienated the community. They then asserted their right to open on any day they chose."

There is no end to the long list of masochistic and self-hating Israeli plays and movies that denigrate, attack and defame the army, Judaism and Zionism. The Arab's greatest allies are the Israeli artist, theater and news media. At the end of 1985, the play *Efraim Returns to the Army* was banned because it compared the Israeli rule in Judea and Samaria to that of Nazi Germany. The author, Yitzhak Leor, is a well-known Israeli Communist. (Two years earlier, Leor authored a poem that spoke of Jewish settlers "baking the blood of Palestinian youths into their Passover matzos.") *The Governor of Jericho* is a play about a brutal and stupid Jewish military governor and a poor, persecuted Arab terrorist who, along with a soldier who refuses to obey orders, are the two heroes of the play. The same playwright, Yosef Mondi, has written *The Gay Nights of Frankfurt*, about a German-Jewish brothel owner in Frankfurt, West Germany, and an Israeli army officer who has left Israel to live in Germany and who appears in the brothel engaging in a sex act. Sample line from the play: "You Jews are just as bad as the Nazis. You also murder Arabs. If you only could, you would do what the Nazis did." And: "Jews are not human beings at all, they do not belong to the human race. They are the crudest enemies on the face of the earth."

When the anti-Semitic play *Garbage, the City and Death*, by the German leftist gentile playwright, Rainer Fassbinder, was to be presented in Frankfurt, German Jews, Israeli Jews and world Jewry rose up in protest that an anti-Semitic play should be allowed to be shown. The play carried only a small part of the anti-Jewish lines and innuendoes that so many Israeli plays do. Little wonder that the religious parties in Haifa, in June 1986, demanded that the municipality cut off its funding of the theatre.

Invariably, the national masochists manage to intertwine their three main themes—love between an Arab and a Jew, the oppressed Palestinian and the oppressive Israeli army. Thus, plays such as *A Very Narrow Bridge*, *The Palestinian* and *To Share an Apartment* all attack the basic fundamentals of Judaism, Zionism and the State of Israel, especially the fundamental Jewish opposition to intermarriage. They join such films as *Ham-sin* by Danny Waxman, *A Silver Tray* by Yehuda N'eman, and *Pressure* by Michel Ohion. *To Share an Apartment*, a story about a Jewish woman (naturally) who shares an apartment with an Arab student, male (naturally), was hailed in the newspaper *Hadashot* as "an answer to Kahanism." That in itself should tell everything about the real meaning of the struggle between Kahane and his enemies. That should explain exactly what the enemies of Kahane really want.

All these plays poison the minds of tens of thousands of young people. All underline clearly what the real purpose of the opponents of Kahanism is. And as this spiritual and moral destruction takes place, does the Jew outside of Israel have the slightest knowledge of what is happening?

Among the worst of the abominations was the 1984 film *Beyond the Walls*, which was a Hollywood Oscar nominee in 1985 for the best foreign film of the year! This essentially undistinguished film was the winner of the "Israeli Oscar" last January, and the recipient of outlandish praise and exaggerated bombastism by all the decadent denizens of the world of art in Israel, the same camp that, in every country in the west, is in the forefront of the rot and moral suicide of the state. *Beyond the Walls* was directed by one Uri Barbash, an extreme left-wing pillar of Peace Now, who correctly grasped the principle behind the technique of destroying a society from within. A nation whose military prowess and technological skills are matched by a strong will to win and self-assurance as to the justice of their cause cannot be defeated. The only way to insure the collapse of that kind of nation and society is to erode its confidence from within, to implant within the people doubts concerning the justice and righteousness of their struggle, to inject within the body politic the viruses of guilt, moral confusion and self-hate. A people so infected will produce soldiers who lose the idealism and moral certainty that carry them to heights of heroism; soldiers who hesitate to use the force and strength that alone can assure their survival and who, thus, begin to fear to enter into certain situations and for whom the very name "Lebanon" strikes deep unease in their hearts; soldiers who, for the first time, refuse to obey orders to either serve in Lebanon or the "occupied territories" at all, or to participate in certain actions.

The Vietnamization of Israel—this is the program and plan of Suicide Now, and the blast that causes internal collapse will come from the barrel of the gun of the decadent and self-hating "artists" whose use of the media, of television and movie entertainment, provides the most effective brain-washing weapons of them all. Of all the guns in the hands of the enemies of the State of Israel, none is more powerful than that of the cultural cannon from within, the artillery of entertainment. And the finger on the trigger is a Jewish one.

Beyond the Walls is a film that sets about attacking the most powerful roadblock in the path of the leftist drive for Israeli collapse—namely, the normal, healthy and correct perception by

Israelis of the Arab as their enemy, and, more important, of the nature of the Arab as a cruel, brutal, murderous enemy. In particular, it is the Sephardi Jews—those who lived under Arabs and who are so acutely normal, who know the enemy well and who never again wish to "enjoy" Arab hospitality—who must, somehow, be neutralized and propagandized. This was the goal of Barbash and his film. It is a cheap film, pandering to the tastes of the masses by using a prison, with all its attendant violence, as the setting. Knowing that it is the natural tendency of people who are at the bottom of the social rung to resent authority of any kind, the leftist Barbash shrewdly used his film to center in on that resentment.

The film showed the prison with its two major populations, the Jews and the Arabs. Barbash's first task was to break down the negative picture of the Arabs while at the same time destroying the positive image of the Jew. Thus, the Arabs in the film are idealistic terrorists and the Jews ordinary criminals. The Arabs and their leader, the real star of the film, emerge as intelligent idealists, who are in prison only because of their higher cause, while the Jews are thugs, ignoramuses and hoodlums, jailed for selfish and ordinary crimes. The Arab terrorist leader was played by an Israeli Arab, shrewdly chosen by Barbash. He was light, blue-eyed (as typical an Arab as I am a Chinese), and thus physically and ultimately personally attractive to Israelis.

Having done this, Barbash moves on to the main goal of the film: To show that it is not the Jews and Arabs who should be fighting each other, but rather an alliance of the oppressed poor Jews (read Sephardic!) and the Arabs against the corrupt Jewish Establishment.

And so, the main theme of the film is the corrupt prison officialdom and how it mistreats Jews and Arabs alike, and the attempt by the wise and calm Arab terrorist leader to persuade the rather backward Jewish prison gang leader that Arabs and Jews are really brothers in arms against Jewish corruption. This film is a fifth column, a ticking time bomb, a gun aimed by Jews at the very heart of Israel.

Naturally, it was hailed in Israel by the colony of decadent artists, the ones who are among the pillars of Suicide Now. And, of course, the Philistine lemmings who are in eternal awe of "artists" fell in line and praised it to the skies, overlooking such lines as "What is the difference between a (Jewish) bus that is blown up (by terrorists) and a refugee camp bombed (by Israeli jets)?" And of course, it won prizes as the international leftist decadents who make up the international artists of the world leapt to nominate it as best foreign film of the year.

But most important, was the impact on the Israeli audiences who flocked to it (thanks in great measure to the rave reviews by the left-ists in the newspapers, radio and television). The overwhelming majority of the viewers were young people, Sephardic Jews, the very normal and healthy people that until now have stood as a massive wall against the efforts of the sick Barbashes to infect Israel with the virus of self-destruction. And those viruses have now been injected into the body politic of Israel.

It is not the first such film, it is not the first bullet or shell fired by the artillery of the enemy within. There have been many others, almost all centering on the theme of the "poor, oppressed Arab" (invariably finding solace in the arms of the Israeli Jewess). But this is the first that has succeeded in climbing the international ramparts. Its success will legitimize cultural treason and the rights of the enemy within to destroy us from there.

And then there is the great debate in Israel over the censoring of a Swedish film, *Gaza Ghetto*, an unabashed propaganda piece for the PLO, which shows an Arab mother whose son has participated in an anti-Israel demonstration and been killed, shouting to her children at the grave: "You will grow up and join the PLO and avenge his death!" The Israeli censor did what any normal country under the Arab gun would do. It banned the showing of the film in Israel. The outcry from the artists of decadence, Suicide Now, the cultural enemies from within, was immediate. "Censorship! Of what are we afraid?" Another shot in the war from within the Jewish state, from within the walls.

The question remains: What is it that drives artist types to hatred of state, people and self? What is it that drives them to an anarchy that attacks all that is normal and sane, that drives them to irrational hatred of all authority? What, in the case of Israel and Jewry, obsesses them, impels them to climb the barricades against Judaism and the Jewish State?

The answer, of course, lies in the very nature of that person who is an "artist." Almost by definition, the artist is an individualist, one who is driven by an overwhelming sense of self, one who is possessed by an ego that not only impels him to produce works of "greatness" and "beauty," but which grows in direct relationship to his success. A certain kind of person is moved to become a teacher or accountant or physician. A certain kind of person is driven to "art," whether it be painting or music or the entertainment world. The artist, in the broad-est terms, is a person with an all-consuming ego that finds himself needing the approval and adulation of the crowd which he secretly despises as being inferior to him in talent and in intelligence. And because of his ego, he cannot abide any tethering of his desires; he demands absolute freedom to do that which he wishes, in the name of his "art."

The state, by its very nature as an authoritative, coercive body that demands respect and obedience from the individual, is the natural enemy of the artist, and especially when, deep in his sub-consciousness, is the gnawing knowledge that the businessman and the politician and the military person are people of decisive action and decision in the real world, a thing that he shrinks from, for it is the very need to escape from reality that drives the artist into his own world. That is why the artist will heap calumny and contempt upon precisely those people who live in the real world, who must and do make the difficult decisions that the artist could never make. He hates them for their strength; he hates them for their authority; he hates them for being that which he would like to be but cannot achieve because of a weakness that is cloaked by a narcissism that destroys.

And of course, the ultimate enemy for the Jewish artist is a Judaism that demands, from each individual, the acceptance of the yoke of Heaven. Freedom? Judaism defines freedom in a way that no artist can accept: "For no man is free but he who occupies himself in the study of Torah" (Avot 6:2). The only freedom recognized by Judaism is that which is within the bounds, the framework of halacha. The Jewish ego must be harnessed by the yoke of Heaven. Art? Of course. But only within the limitations of goodness and halacha, and the beauty of Yefet can dwell only within the tents of Shem.

For the artist this is impermissible. It goes against that very soul that is consumed by self, by ego, by "I." That is why Judaism and the state are his sworn enemies. That is why authority of any kind cannot dwell within his camp. And that is why he is driven by self-destruction, to the desire to destroy all others along with himself. For the one who is obsessed by ego can never be satisfied, can never find happiness. His is the path of eternal damnation in this world, and since he does not believe in another one, his ultimate yearning is to put an end to his agony. In the meantime, we all suffer because of him.

And then there is Nadia. Another fascinating *must* for students of national abnormal psychology. Nadia was a 24-year-old Arab terrorist, captured inside Israel as she prepared to plant a bomb in Jerusalem that would have caused wholesale slaughter. She was sentenced to 12 years imprisonment and sent to the women's prison at Nvei Tirza. Since she was beautiful, cultured, wealthy, intelligent and talented, the Jewish mercy of fools won out and she was placed with regular Jewish criminals and not with other terrorists.

It is interesting to note an article that appeared in *Ma'ariv* (January 2, 1985) about a Jewish woman criminal who had been incarcerated in the same Nvei Tirza prison. Her name is given only as G., and the article states:

"G. is furious over the privileged position of the [women] terrorist prisoners, over the strikes they call if the food is unacceptable to them and over the fact that they are immediately asked if they would like something else. They utter hatred against the state and the army and sing Palestinian [terrorist] songs. The day of [the refugee camps in Beirut] Sabra and Shatila saw speeches and defamation against Israel, and the prison guard B. responded by saying: 'What can we do?' But on Independence day, when we blessed the state and sang '*Am Yisrael Hai* (The People of Israel Lives),' the warden silenced us so as not to cause provocations."

But back to Nadia. With uncanny instinct she went for the Jewish jugular—*guilt*. She taught music to the inmates, showed them how to dress and wear makeup (all the important Jewish things that Dizengoff instills in daughters of Israel). More important, she learned Hebrew quickly, composed Hebrew songs and sang Zionist favorites. During the Yom Kippur War she knitted woolen caps for the soldiers at the front and one theme was sounded by her, tirelessly: Peace, peace, peace, peace. The clever Arab terrorist knew her Jewish lemmings.

Everyone loved her. An Israeli intellectual visited the prison regularly. She asked him to mail letters for her (illegally). Of course he did. Who could argue with an Arab terrorist who spoke, wrote and sang of *peace*? Edna Pe'er, an Israel State Radio personality and interviewer, simply had to visit her and lionize her on a broadcast. With pathos and indigenous Arab sincerity, Nadia won Edna over. Needless to say, because of "poor health" and rich and influential Israeli lemmings, Nadia was pardoned after only three years. She left—a Zionist, woolen cap knitter and lover-of-peace, former terrorist.

In March, 1986, Edna Pe'er presented a second program on Nadia. It seems that the Israeli liberal radio lemming could not get enough of her terrorist friend who loved her and Israel so much (in prison she had told Edna Pe'er: "To be a Jew in this part of the world is to be a hero," leading one of her new-found Israeli friends to blurt out: "She's one of us! She's one of us!"). And so, Edna flew to Morocco to interview Nadia again.

Ashes. Weep for Edna and all the Israeli lemmings of Jewish persuasion. Let me quote the *Jerusalem Post* (March 21, 1986) report on the *second* Nadia program following poor Edna's return from Morocco:

"Nadia's whole performance during her imprisonment here, her enthusiasm for Zionism and Hebrew songs and her admiration for Israeli patriotism, was a sham.

"[Says Nadia] 'We got out messages to our brothers in the occupied areas through prison workers and in other ways. And those seemingly harmless unsealed letters I had sent abroad (through her Israeli intellectual), those, too, contained messages.'

"You Israelis are so sure you are right, and you so want people to believe and to understand you ...'" Bullseye for Nadia! Poor Edna. Poor Israel.

This erosion of the national will is manifested in more than plays and movies. It is seen in the *daily* doses of masochism and guilt and self-hate that are poured down the mouths of the Jews in Israel by the leftist-dominated radio and television. The news itself is incredibly slanted, and the Lebanese war saw such an insidious anti-war bias that the news media came to be known in nationalist circles as Radio and TV *Fatah*. Naturally, every demand for change and the banning of programs that can only be of invaluable service to the enemy (such as the long coverage given to a blatantly pro-PLO graduation ceremony at Shchem's An-Najah University) is immediately blasted as "censorship." (This from leftists who succeeded in banning a television program on intermarriage in Israel on the grounds that it was "racist.") Surely, one of the first things that any sane national party that achieves power must do is to throw the rascals out, remove the entire leftist-dominated state news media system—the producers, editors and commentators—and bring in Jews who are committed to Zionism, Judaism and a healthy proud approach to the State of Israel. Not people chosen for their political party affiliations but for their *ideological* thinking. It is a thing that must be done, and, please G-d, will be done. And let no leftist who barred Meir Kahane from appearing on state communications because of his views ever dare to complain when he is removed for the very same reason.

The sick, corrosive guilt of the intellectuals can be seen in myriad ways:

Thirty "artists," members of the Israeli Artists Union, left Jerusalem's Artist House on August 12, 1984, to travel to the Arab refugee camp, Jabaliya, in Gaza to protest the arrest of a PLO Arab artist Fatchi Rban for pro-PLO paintings. The Jewish artists carried signs reading "There is no art without freedom," and "An artist in prison—Kahane in the Knesset," and issued a statement on behalf of the PLO Arab which declared that "limitations on freedom of expression [sic] lead directly to fascism."

In March, 1986, a group called "Forum," made up of university people, held a seminar on Law and Citizen's Rights in the Territories at Tel Aviv University's "Seat of Law" hall. Naturally, pro-PLO Arabs from the territories were invited—after all were they not the featured victims of Israeli persecution?—and among them was one Mona Rashmawi, an attorney from Ramalla. During a break, the persecuted Mona pronounced that an Israeli flag standing in the hall was giving her a problem since the presence of both flag and Mona in the same room might be interpreted as her recognizing the "conquest." (Just what she meant by "the conquest" was not clear, though right-wing fascist types might point out that the flag was *in Tel Aviv*.) In any event, when it comes to Israeli intellectuals, whatever Arab Mona wants, Mona gets, and Professor Tina Reinhart rushed to move the offending Israeli flag to the other side of the room where it could not be seen by the persecuted Mona.

On January 9, 1985, some 2500 cheering Arabs sat inside An-Najah National University in the city of Shchem (Nablus), situated in Samaria. An-Najah is one of no less than seven universities in Judea, Samaria and Gaza, all of which were naturally created by the Israelis. (Jordan, needless to say, was far too astute to allow universities under its rule of the areas from 1949 to 1967.) If ever there was a formula for the creation of rebels and revolutionaries it is the creation of universities and the intellectuals they produce, no matter how half-baked. But the Jew—always merciful, democratic and intent on self-destruction—rushed to allow the Arabs to create the breeding grounds for PLO leadership.

Here is the Jewish Telegraphic Agency report (January 14, 1985) concerning the commencement exercises at An-Najah that day:

"Cheering Palestinians attended the fourth commencement exercises at the university which has often been the scene of violent clashes between Arab students and Israeli soldiers. They sang nationalist songs, chanted Palestinian slogans and listened to patriotic speeches, against the backdrop of a huge red-white-black Palestinian flag—an absolute no-no by the standards of the Israeli authorities. But the army kept away from the university; it did not intervene.

"As the 481 graduating students entered the hall to the strains of the Palestinian national song, 'My Country,' and raising 'V' signs (the PLO symbol), the crowd sheered with enthusiasm. Among the crowd were many of the national leaders, most of them deposed from their official positions—Bassam Shaka, who was removed as Mayor of Nablus, and Karim Khalaf, deposed mayor of Ramallah."

One *knows* that the Jordanians are torn between absolute astonishment and disbelief. Who but the incredible Jew would allow such an open display of Palestinian nationalism, which is guaranteed to create young student and intellectual leaders for the PLO? Who could not understand the immense pride that surged through the Arab breasts and the accompanying hatred for Israel as, against the backdrop of *their* flag, they sang their national song, "My Country"? And who could fail to grasp the Arab understanding that they were witnessing an Israeli retreat, yet another Israeli weakness and fear of America? For who was in attendance, too? The JTA report continues:

"Next to them (Shaka and Khalaf) sat a distinguished guest, Wat Clevarius, the American Consul General in East Jerusalem—quite openly an expression of American interest [sic] in the quality of life of the Palestinians under Israeli occupation."

"American interest"? Say rather American *pressure*, that forces even normal Israelis to step toward the brink of madness. This blatant interference by the United States in the most vital of Israeli interests is topped only by the humiliating insistence by Washington on *two* separate consulates in Jerusalem, one in the eastern (Arab) section and the other in the western (Jewish) area. This United States move is a stinging slap in Israel's face, a reminder that, for Washington, Jerusalem is *not* a Jewish city, but divided between East and West, Jewish and Arab. A people, a state, with the slightest element of pride would have long since barred foreign officials from entering the territories to agitate the Arabs, and would have ordered one of the U.S. consulates to close (whichever the Americans chose would not be important, since it is all one city—Jewish).

The Arab universities grow and grow (An-Najah has increased from several hundred when Israel set it up in 1977 to 3100 in 1986). They are hotbeds of radical anti-Israel thinking and activities. In the elections for the four main universities for Student Committees, the results were:

	Arafat Backers	Rejection Front- Leftist Terrorists	Moslem Brotherhood
Bir Zeit (Ramalla)	38%	36%	26%
An-Najah (Shchem)	50%	13%	37%
Hebron	50%	7%	43%
Bethlehem	44%	44%	12%

These are the monsters that Israel allows to be created under its own nose. These are the ones who will lead the terrorists and the

"Palestinians" in violent clashes and in revolution against Israel. How many Jews will be murdered because Israel allowed its enemies to create a leadership that would urge its people to attack Jews?

But to consider something even more insane—what about the far more serious danger of *Israeli* Arabs who are being educated daily in the higher universities of *Israel*? Each and every one of these students is part of the nucleus of the future revolutionary leadership of a "Palestinian" people inside Israel which will turn the country into a northern Ireland. Knesset member Muhamad Miari of the Progressive List is openly a supporter of the PLO and an opponent of a Zionist state. He is a graduate of Hebrew University. Mahmoud Muhareb, then chairman of the Arab Student Committee at Hebrew University and an Israeli citizen of Lydda, told *Ma'ariv* (January 20, 1978):

"We, the Arab students at the university, constitute an indivisible part of the Palestinian Arab nation, and we struggle in its service and in order to achieve its goals.

"As for me and my personal lot, I am first and foremost a Palestinian, a resident of Lydda. My Israeli citizenship was forced upon me. The law required me to carry an Israeli identity card and passport. As a Palestinian, I would prefer Palestinian ones. With the final solution common to the Arab of Palestine and Judea, Lydda will be within the sovereign boundaries of the democratic state. What will that state be called? Palestine, naturally....

"We do not recognize the right, which you call 'historic,' of the Jewish people in this land—this is our fundamental principle. In this land only the Palestinian Arab people have the historic right."

Mahmud was able to study at Hebrew University thanks to Jewish madmen. Including those Jews who so happily contribute to the school and all the others—Tel Aviv University, Ben Gurion University, Haifa University. At the latter, the Arab students published a paper called *Bian*, which said, among other things:

"We are an indivisible part of the Arab Palestine people and the PLO is our sole legal representative.... Zionism is a racist, colonialist movement."

For those who enjoy giving money to "Israel" to help the "Jewish State," take pride in knowing that of the 37 graduates majoring in chemistry in the spring of 1984, at Hebrew University, you helped no fewer than 17 Arabs to go to degrees and expertise. What will they do with it? What *could* an expert in chemistry do?

Prime Minister Peres in the Knesset boasted of the progress made by Israeli Arabs under their friendly and benevolent Jewish democrats. Whereas Israel in 1948 saw an Arab population that was abysmally illiterate, today, said Peres, there are some 4,000 Arabs studying in the universities of the Jewish State. Indeed, another such "accomplishment" for Israel and we are undone.

But, of course, it will continue, and the growing education of the Arab will not only give him the weapon of knowledge but will also create a qualitatively different Arab, totally unlike his pliant fathers. And so, when *Yediot Aharonot* (March 25, 1986) writes that since 1970 the number of Arab academicians has grown by five times and that the number of Arab high school graduates is now ten times that which it was fifteen years ago, one begins to understand the full extent of the bloody uprising that Israel will see in the near future.

Is there no one who feels that for an Arab to be privileged to receive higher education in the Jewish State he should *at least* be compelled, as a condition of admission, to state his allegiance to *and acceptance of Israel as the Jewish State?* Is that too much to ask before giving Jewish funds—so much of it raised from naive western Jews in the Exile—to Arabs who can use their education to work for Israel's destruction? Are there not tens of thousands of poor Israeli Jews—mostly Sephardic—who would dearly love to get the education and room and board that the Israeli Arabs, who hate Israel, are now receiving? Madness, Jewish madness.

And yet, even this aspect of lunacy cannot quite match another area of Israeli cuckooland. It would stand to reason that the purpose of Jewish schools in the Jewish State is to encourage love and faith and pride in Jewishness and Israel. Surely, that is not too far-fetched an assumption, even in these days of madness. And so it becomes difficult for even a jaded watcher of Jewish cuckooland to understand the decision by the liberal, progressive, all-tolerant Ministry of Education to introduce to Jewish high school students books and stories and Arab authors, all of course anti-Zionist and Pro-PLO, for the young Jew to see "the other side."

And so, the high schools of Israel have introduced an anthology of stories by Arab authors, called *A Place on the Face of the Earth.* The anthology was compiled by the infamous Van Leer Institute, a den of leftist and defeatist Jews, whose major achievement is to undermine Jewish confidence and certainty concerning the justice of the Jewish cause.

Here is one example of a story in the anthology read by Jewish students who are on the verge of entering the army in order to learn how to fight the Arab enemy. The story is called "The Land of the Sad Oranges," and was written by Asan Kanfani, born in Acre, Israel, from which he and other Arabs fled during the 1948 war that was launched by them to wipe out Israel. Kafani was active with the PLO in Lebanon and was killed by a car bomb there in 1972. In the story he describes the flight of his family from Acre to Lebanon in 1948. Consider the education of a Jewish high school student on the verge of his three-year military service. Consider how he will think about the Arabs he is being trained to fight:

"The women went down from the vehicles and walked over to a peasant sitting on the side of the road with a basket of oranges. My father put out his hand to get an orange. He looked at it silently and burst into tears like a baby. In Rosh Hanikra [near the Lebanese border] our car stopped.... In my father's eyes there shone the memory of all the orange trees that he left for the Jews, all those good and healthy trees that he bought, one by one. The tears flowed down his cheeks. When we reached Sidon that evening, we became refugees."

What possible impression can this leave on the young Israeli who already suffers from ignorance? An emptiness of soul, a vacuum of ideology. How can he possibly not feel a sense of injustice, guilt (more!)? Who will give him the real story? The Jewish story and truth? Who will teach him the reality of Arab attaks, murder and rape against Jews throughout the 1920s and '30s and '40s? The reality of Arab armies and mobs screaming for the throwing of the Jews into the sea as they rejected the very idea of a Jewish State in 1948? Who will tear apart the tissue of Arab lies to tell Jewish youth that the orange groves would have remained *along with their Arabs* had the Arabs not attacked the Jews? Who will tell the Jewish youth that it was a *Divine blessing* that the Arabs fled and have them consider what our fate would be today *had they not?* Madness, madness.

The artists, the intellectuals, the destroyers of the Jewish State. Those who so desperately need their own private couch; those who drive us to the national one.

Other glimpses from the couch:

The following is reprinted exactly as it appeared in *Yediot Aharonot,* June 16, 1986:

"The State of Israel is paying National Insurance benefits to families of terrorists from East Jerusalem who are serving long prison sentences in Israeli prisons. From an investigation of the East Jerusalem branch of the National Insurance Institute, it emerges that the Institute is paying benefits to some 20 families of security prisoners [terrorists] who have been sentenced to tens of years imprisonment for terrorists attacks."

Only G-d or Freud would understand.

And the following is reprinted exactly as it appeared in the newspaper *Ha'aretz* in 1984:

"Rauma Weizman [wife of Israeli dove Ezer Weizman] served as a defender of her husband Ezer in an argument that he had with Arab youths. It was in the Arab villages of Baka al Garbia in the Triangle. The couple were guests at a wedding of Arab acquaintances and an argument broke out during which the youths accused Weizman, saying that, in his eyes, Arabs have no names, that he does not call his Arab gardener by his given name but talks about him as "the Arab." Weizman called his wife to testify that this was not so. "Rauma," he asked her, "What do I call the gardener?" Rauma testified for her husband that he calls him by his first name, Muhammad."

What is one supposed to do after reading this? Laugh? Weep? The former Minister of Defense of Israel, the former chief of the Israeli Air Force, pathetically attempting to justify himself in the eyes of a group of young Arabs who look upon him with contempt for even discussing the issue with them! Rauma, Rauma, tell them that I really love Arabs. Tell them how much I respect my gardener. Show them what imbeciles we are.

In October, 1985, Labor Knesset member Aharon Harel, one of the most cooing of the Israeli doves, visited the Arab town of Tulkarm, near Netanya. Harel is known as one of the most violently anti-Kahane Knesset members because of Kahane's call for the removal of Arabs from Israel. How fascinating, therefore, for Harel to meet with the Arab mayor of Tulkarm who asked him from where he came. "Poland," was the reply of the little Jewish dove. "Then why do you not go back there, this is the land of the Palestinians," said the Arab mayor.

The stricken Harel, who hates Jews who speak of Arabs leaving the country, was able to "understand" the Arab who wants Jews out but "chastised" him by saying: "I am a dove and if I hear you say such things what will the hawks say?"

The hospitals and medical services of Israel are in deep crisis due to budgetary problems. Many hospitals are on the verge of closing down and all have made drastic cuts in their services. The following letter appeared on June 29, 1984, in the Tel Aviv paper, *Ha'ir*:

"Some time ago the military governor of Hebron appeared on television in an Arab broadcast to announce that a sizeable sum of money had been put into improving the Arab hospital in Hebron. And now another two million dollars had been set aside for a new wing. A similar project was completed in Gaza a few months ago. Despite this, we read about the financial problems of the Rothschild Hospital in Haifa which cannot run properly because of lack of funds.

"In the name of thousands of immigrants who came to Israel thinking they were settling in a Jewish state, I ask: When will we stop streaming our limited funds to the welfare of an Arab population free of income tax, military service and even medical tax, and begin to rehabilitate the Jewish citizens of Israel?"

Obviously, the demented letter-writer (who is clearly a racist, too) does not understand that unless the Arabs of the territories feel satisfied, they will all hate Jews and join the PLO. Indeed, this is exactly what the Minister of Defense told the Knesset in July 1986. "Let the Arabs sit quietly," is the policy. And, indeed they do.

They sit quietly and buy up Jewish land and Jewish houses and subsidize agriculture and industry to compete with the Jews and destroy them economically. But the main thing is to let the Arabs sit quietly lest they become anti-Israel.

On April 3, 1985, Chaim Herzog became the first President of Israel to visit the Arab town of Um-Al-Fahm. His visit was trumpeted as an answer to racism, to the effort of Knesset member Meir Kahane to visit there half a year earlier in order to dramatize the contradiction between Zionism and Arab aspirations. In his visit, Herzog declared: "I see in this visit a challenge to the evil spirit that carries on its wings the seeds of disaster, separation, and hate." The President, son of the late revered Chief Rabbi, had clearly proven why Kahane had referred to him by the Talmudic maxim, "vinegar, son of wine."

Um-al-Fahm, praised and flattered by Herzog as a model of coexistence and loyalty to Israel, had been chosen by Kahane with care. In the real world that Herzog rarely encounters outside his posh residence, the town has a reputation for enmity to Israel that would not shame any pro-PLO area.

Thus, the Associated Press carried the following dispatch in 1980: "Tel Aviv, Jan. 20: About 5,000 Arab soccer spectators shouting Khomeni!'and 'Down with Zionism!' stormed the field in Galilee where their team was playing a Jewish squad in a weekend game....

"'This is more than the usual sporting soccer riot,' said a police source. 'The Jewish players had to barricade themselves in their locker room for two hours while the Arabs tried to batter down the doors.'"

On September 4, 1980, the Arabs of Chaim Herzog's model Arab town rioted. The headline in *Ma'ariv* the following day read:

STONES THROWN AT POLICE IN MASS DEMONSTRATION AT
UM-AL-FAHAM

And on December 12, 1979, *Ma'ariv* carried a long story about the attacks by Arabs of Um-Al-Fahm and other villages in the Wadi Ara area on the lone Jewish settlement there, Mei Ami. Three fires, set by Arab arsonists, destroyed some 110 dunams of Jewish National Fund forests, and wholesale stealing of the settlement's agricultural equipment, led one of the settlers to say: "We have reached the end of our rope."

And an Arab attorney from Um-al-Fahm, Herzog's choice, told the newspaper:

"The Arab villages in the Triangle are sitting on a volcano. Feelings of discrimination grow daily and with them hate and frustration."

The truth is that Um-al-Fahm is a hotbed of Arab hatred of Zionism. It is a center of both the violently nationalist Sons of the Village Movement as well as Khomeni-type *fundamentalist* Moslem groups. Only the Arabs of Um-al-Fahm know how *much more* Meir Kahane understands them than does the Presidential Vinegar Son of Wine.

One can debate the merits or demerits of Peace Now endlessly and so it would appear that the best answer to the question, "Is Peace Now good for the Jews?" is to quote this unsolicited praise for the group by Ibrahim Tawil. Tawil is the former mayor of El-Bireh, the sister town of Ramallah just north of Jerusalem. Tawil, stridently pro-PLO, was deposed by Israel because of his membership in the PLO-front group, the National Guidance Committee. In an interview, and after blasting "Jewish control of Congress, the [U.S.] newspapers, the business world and the election system," as well as declaring that no Jews would be permitted to live in the Palestinian state he demands on the West Bank, Tawil declared:

"I hope that Peace Now will grow in size and stature, because its activities will hasten the rise of an independent Palestinian state." No greater exhibit could the opponents of Peace Now ever present. If Tawil praises Peace Now, let all normal Jews turn quickly in the other direction.

And the entire question of the slow Arab takeover of Israel, through money.

In September, 1986, a Turkish synagogue in Istanbul was attacked by Arab terrorists. The world was shocked. In June of 1986 another Turkish synagogue did not make headlines. In June of 1986 the Turkish synagogue building on Yefet Street in Jaffa Israel was sold. The buyers belonged to a group specializing in buying Jewish property in Jaffa, by offering more than the market value of the property and paying cold cash. And more. The group that is buying these homes is an open supporter of the PLO. This is what the Israeli newspaper *Hatzofe* wrote (June 27, 1986):

"Those who brought the synagogue for 'full value' did not hide the fact that they work within the framework of a group that is buying the buildings of Jews living in Jaffa. 'Jaffa was conquered with fire (by the Jews) and will be redeemed with money,' is the slogan of the group whose purpose is to remove the Jews from Jaffa. This is what one of the elders of the Christian community told a reporter from *Hatzofe*. The informant's name is in the paper's files. According to him, the group's method is to purchase the building of a Jew, even at high cost, and then let Arabs, mostly from Gaza, live there. The source of the funds is Libya and Saudi Arabia."

Since most people do not understand the full gravity of the situation, let it be understood that Jaffa was an all-Arab city until 1948 and was included in the original Arab state as envisaged by the United Nations Partition Plan of 1947. When the Arab rejected that and attacked the Jews in bordering Tel Aviv, members of the Irgun Zvai Leumi and Sternists routed the Arabs, who fled in panic. Jaffa was the largest Arab city in the country at the time (some 80,000 people), and they fled to Gaza. For years, clever Arabs who have come to be known as "moderates" have advocated "recognizing Israel" if she agrees to comply with ALL the U.N. Resolutions, including the "return" of the by now more than two million refugees who fled the Jewish State when their hopes to destroy it were thwarted. Obviously, such a thing would spell the end of the Jewish State, first by demography and then by pogroms, and Israel has rejected any such concept out of hand.

But the clever Arabs, by buying up Jewish houses in Jaffa and moving in precisely those Jaffa Arabs who fled to Gaza, are creating exactly that political fact which will be a precedent for the demand of the Arabs and the United Nations for a return of all the others. Insanity, sheer madness.

But there is more.

It is not only in Jaffa and other cities that the PLO and Arab states such as Jordan and Saudi Arabia are so cleverly buying up Jewish homes and turning the cities into *de facto* Arab ones. In a brilliant emulation of the original idea that was created by the Jews in the early days of Zionism to buy up Arab land, the Jewish National Fund, the Arabs have created a similar, huge reserve which could easily be called the Palestine National Fund. And, indeed, that is exactly what former Knesset member Ra'anan Na'im (Labor) said to the Israeli weekly *Yoman Hashavua* (October 29, 1982):

"It is very worrisome to learn that in various places in the Galilee, such as Upper Nazareth and Carmiel [set up deliberately as Jewish enclaves in the midst of Arab centers of population], the Arabs are acquiring land, property, homes and stores from Jewish residents. It is as if there is an Ishmaelite National Fund organization to acquire lands and Jewish property just as once the Jewish National Fund did....

"I suspect that we are speaking here of an organized acquisition of lands behind which stand wealthy Arab countries such as Kuwait, and even the PLO."

Let us understand what is happening here. The ownership of the land in the Land of Israel has always been understood as the foundation of the Jewish State. Indeed, within the by-laws of the Jewish National Fund it is clearly stated that public lands, i.e., those in the name of the Jewish National Fund, cannot be sold or leased to non-Jews. (This in turn, is a limited secular underlining of the Torah ruling that land cannot be sold to gentiles in the Holy Land.) The symbolism in the ownership of the land by Jews was always a clear one.

It is this that must be understood when reading the following item that appeared in *Ma'ariv* (January 6, 1984), under the heading, "The Arabs Are Buying the Lands of Israel":

"The farmer from Hadera (a city in the heartland of Jewish agriculture) apparently could not withstand the temptation. A. T., an Arab businessman, offered him the highest price for his 40 dunams of land. Kibbutz Gan Shmuel was also interested, but the price offered by A.T. was higher. The orchard was sold to an Arab.

"One of the Hadera farmers described the incident in these words: 'It is betrayal. There has never yet been such a thing as Jewish land sold to an Arab. If a veteran grower, from the first settlers of Hadera, can sell his orchard, there should be a thousand red lights in our minds. Without Jewish agriculture, the state is not a state.'"

It is not an isolated phenomenon. Nothing legal prevents Israeli Jews from selling their privately owned lands to Arabs, but such a thing was unheard of in the past, for many reasons: First, the national obligation to have Jewish ownership of the land in the Jewish State. Second, in the early years of Jewish pioneers, Arabs were eager to make profits by selling land to the Jews. Their children, educated in Israeli schools, are fierce nationalists who not only will not sell their land but, prodded by PLO and other Arab nationalist forces, see in the purchase of Jewish land not only a good private profit deal, but also an act of Arab nationalism. Third, and this speaks volumes for the insanity of Israel, the Arabs today have money, large amounts, that

Jews do not, in part because of the funds from the PLO and Arab states that come to them unhindered. But also because of the scandalous failure on the part of the Arab sector in Israel to pay anywhere remotely near its taxes and the absolute freedom of Arabs of the territories from Israeli taxes. Israeli Arabs cheat and laugh at the authorities who hesitate to move into Arab villages because of mass organized violence and also because of an Israeli government policy of overlooking Arab "peccadillos," following the mad concept of "let them sit quietly." They do, and gather up huge funds, to buy up Israel.

And so, in yet another article in *Ma'ariv* (February 15, 1985), under the heading "The Baron Rothschild Turns Over In His Grave," Aharon Dolev deals with the growing plague of Arab purchase of Jewish land in Kfar Tavor, where back in the late nineteenth century the wealthy Baron Edmund de Rothschild purchased and gave land to Jews returning to the Land. Says veteran resident of Kfar Tavor, 63-year-old Yehuda Cohen:

"Believe me, the Baron turns over in his grave. Not only the Baron. My grandfather and father. Ben Gurion and even Yigal Allon, who was born in Kfar Tavor....

"Did we receive the land in order to sell it to Arabs who want to destroy the State of Israel? We have already heard that the Arabs are buying Jewish land with Saudi money. The 'birds' in the Arab villages are chirping and even the Arabs who work in the village have told me that."

On February 7, 1985, *Ha'aretz* carried a front-page story quoting the head of the Kfar Tavor council, Micha Goldman. Goldman is a veteran Labor Party member, and the story begins as follows:

"For the first time, there appears to be a trend in the Galilee of Jews selling their lands to Arabs. Four residents of Kfar Tavor in the Eastern Galilee have received down payments for sale of their land to Arabs. Micha Goldman, head of the council, invited the sellers last Friday to meet with him in an effort to dissuade them." I cannot, at this point, in addition to emphasizing my total agreement with Goldman that this is a national tragedy, help pointing out the incredible insanity and hypocrisy in his words, the words of a man who condemns Kahane for "racism:"

"It is worrisome and serious and we must uproot the phenomenon of land sales immediately. I believe that we can coexist with the Arabs living in an Arab village and the Jews in a Jewish one. Each of us must keep his own nationality."

And fanatical anti-Kahane writer Gavriel Strassman writes in *Ma'ariv* (February 10, 1985):

"In addition to the violence of Arabs against Jews, they have now increased their acquisition of lands from Jews in the land of Israel. It is truly unbelievable. A dunam and another dunam, but this time it is not Israel but Ishmael who follows the time-tested pattern. The thought that Jews in Eretz Yisrael and especially in the Galilee, which already has more Arabs than Jews, should sell land to the Arabs is astonishing, and one simply cannot believe it. . . .

"Let there be no misunderstandings. I do not protest against these deals on the grounds of racism. I protest on the grounds of pure nationalism of which I am not ashamed."

I sit back and smile. With tears in my eyes for the confused hypocrites of Israel. When Kahane says these things, he is a racist. When Goldman and Shtrasman say them, they are nationalists. Perhaps Kahane is also a nationalist?

It remains for the self-hating but uninhibited Dan Ben Amotz to prick the bubble of hypocrisy:

"I don't understand something. If all our citizens are really equal before the law with no difference in religion, nationality, sex or race, as stated in the Declaration of Independence, and if this is really a democratic state, perhaps you can explain to me why a Jewish citizen cannot sell his private land to a citizen whose mother is, by chance, not Jewish" (*Hadashot*, February 15, 1985).

Of course, *my* answer is clear. In a Jewish State, in a Zionist Jewish State, Jews and non-Jews are *not* equal in national areas of life. But Ben Amotz the self-hater who disagrees with that, asks the anti-Kahane Zionist democrats a question that they, in their schizophrenic minds, cannot answer.

Any more than they could explain their objections to the Kach demand in the Jewish town of Kiryat Arba in Judea for Jewish labor only. When a furor arose and I asked in the Knesset how many Arabs worked *in the Knesset*, in any capacity (none), and stated that any Arab Knesset member, losing his seat, would not be hired as a waiter in the Knesset dining room, there was, of course, no response. How could there be? And when I asked why, in the 1930s, the Histradut fought violently against Jewish employers who hired Arabs instead of Jewish workers and why the Hebrew national poet Chaim Nachman Bialik came out against hiring Arabs and why former Finance Minister Pinchas Sapir, as a young Laborite activist, went to prison for protesting this in Kfar Saba, again, there was no reply. It is amazing how those who are so blessed with active mouths are so often stricken dumb.

Jews sell their lands to Arabs in the State of Israel and Jews are now selling land they just acquired in Judea and Samaria to Arabs also. In a story, "Jews Selling Land in Judea-Samaria to Arabs" (*Hadashot*, December 31, 1984), the subheading reads:

"A subsidiary of the Ya'eh-Yakir company seeking to sell 1500 dunams of land near Elkana [in Samaria] to Arabs from Judea-Samaria who brought money from Jordan."

It is an unbelievable story. The Jews of Israel, weighed down by insane and burdensome taxes and strangling bureaucracy, are losing money as their farmers and *moshavim* (agricultural villages) go bankrupt, while the Arabs of both Israel and the territories, free of such nuisances as taxes and regulations, grow rich, and buy up Jewish land. Arabs from the territories who, until the Jews came, were backward, poverty-stricken people who counted themselves fortunate if they owned two donkeys!

And so we read in *Ha'aretz* (November 22, 1984): "Representatives of an Arab land dealer, Mahmud Lafit, have been in contact recently with two veteran farmers from Zichron Ya'kov as well as land owners in Hadera and Binyamina with a proposal to purchase from them hundreds of dunams of private agricultural land. Lafit, according to his associates, is now in Jordan...."

The paper adds that a Jewish group which offered to buy the land could not meet the Arab's price, which was *four times higher* than the best Jewish one. Where does an Arab land dealer get that money?

"According to his associates, he is now in Jordan...." And the Jewish settlement of Ma'suah in the Jordan Valley, on the verge of bankruptcy, is offered a deal by an Arab from Jericho. I quote *Davar* (May 25, 1986):

"A few days ago a merchant from Jericho offered members of moshav Massuah to cover the $10 million dollar debt of the moshav [!] in return for the right to use their land and the water rights."

Mind boggling! Ten million dollars! How does an Arab from Jericho get that money? Of course, from Jordan, Saudi Arabia, the PLO, the Ishmaelite National Fund.... And we know about it, the government, the military administration in the territories—and *do nothing.*

The newspaper *Hadashot* (August 8, 1984) writes: "Some $400 million [!] has been transferred by the PLO to the territories (Judea, Samaria, Gaza) between the years 1979-83. This emerged from a document to the Joint PLO-Jordanian Committee published in the East Jerusalem paper *Almatak.*"

A national couch? Order instead a psychological storeroom for a Jewish people that has clearly lost its mind. This money, which comes in freely, subsidizes the Arabs, enabling them to buy Jewish land and houses, to undercut Jewish prices and drive Jews out of business as they cannot meet the Arab competition, to fan the flames of inflation and to destroy Israel economically.

An Israeli government allows the PLO and other Arab funds to subsidize the Arabs while it creates the condition where the Arabs of the territories are free of taxes, free of the need to get permits and free of all regulations that hamper the Jews. And so, in its special business section, *Ma'ariv* writes the following:

"The competition is difficult, destructive, in many cases hurting Israel industry. The source of the competition: Judea, Samaria, Gaza. 'Unfair competition' is what the industrialists in Israel call it and they refer to the fact that the factories on the other side of the 'Green Line' [in the territories] are not tied by Israeli law, do not have to meet Israeli standards, do not pay taxes, do not need permits and do not recognize the standards of the Ministry of Health.

"'The scope of our industry has dropped by 60%,' says Moti Chaimovitz of Kibbutz Zikim. 'The competition is not fair. They do not pay comprehensive pensions, do not pay urban taxes. They sell without receipts and do not pay the [approximately 15%] Value Added Tax at all. And who speaks about the army duty we have to serve each year...?'"

Yet another Jew says: "Their merchandise already comprises 30% of the market." The article gloomily states:

"The industrialists are stunned, the government looks away. The problem is complex, politically and economically. The only thing being done is hiding our head in the sand."

And Arab subsidies and insane Israeli policy lead to the slow death of Jewish agriculture.

"'Agricultural exports have dropped in half in the last three years, from $840 million to $480 million,' the head of the Farmers' Federation, Eliyahu Isaacson, said yesterday at a press conference in Tel Aviv." (*Ha'aretz*, Dec. 11, 1984).

And so as Jewish agricultural settlements close down and Jews flee them in the hope of eventually fleeing Israel, we read in *Davar* (March 21, 1986):

ECONOMIC GROWTH AND BUILDING SPREE IN THE GAZA STRIP

And *Yediot Aharonot* (May 4, 1986):

"Hundreds of citrus grove owners [Jewish] are threatening to sell their products to merchants from Gaza. The grove owners are attempting to get out from under the control of the Council for Citrus Marketing which controls the industry and they argue that the Gaza merchants offer them prices much higher than those of the Council."

Madness. The moshavim of the Negev, bankrupt, are forced now to break the law and rent their land to Arabs. Thus writes *Davar* (December 16, 1985):

"Some 40% [!] of the agricultural settlements in the Negev lease their lands, the agricultural products and the water rights to Arabs from the Gaza Strip, for 'good money,' mostly in foreign currency." And the Jews? Their madness knows no bounds. The Israeli Ministry of Foreign Affairs (September 4, 1983) issues the following chorus of joy to the press in a "briefing" to the gentiles:

"While the world focuses on daily events in Judea-Samaria, it has devoted little attention to the quiet drama unfolding in the region; a steadily growing economy resulting in increased prosperity for its inhabitants.

"While the big industrialized nations worry about high unemployment, the people of this region enjoy full employment. The per capita Gross National Product of the population of Judea-Samaria has increased by 8.8% per year since 1970. This success can be attributed in large measure to the 'green revolution,' a reformed economy based on agricultural development. The successful utilization of modern technologies is the direct and indirect result of contacts with Israel since 1967."

And the Jewish farmer drowns in the mud of debts and bankruptcy brought on by Arab competition that is maintained by Israeli development and aid to the Arabs and by the PLO funds that Israel allows to enter the territories to subsidize them.

Ma'ariv, in November 1985, carried an incredible story detailing Arab control of the agricultural market in Israel through Jordanian directives and Jordanian funds. The article reads:

"Five weeks ago, after the gang of murderers from the [Judean] village of Tzoref [who murdered a Jewish couple near Beit Shemesh] was captured, *Ma'ariv* writer Avinoam Bar Yosef went to the territories to retrace the steps of the five gang members. It appears that some of the members were employed by Jews in Beit Shemesh and Tel Aviv. The article disclosed that Cafe Stern in Tel Aviv belongs to a Jewish and Arab partner from Tzoref, a brother of the head of the gang. The discovery led to this expose:

"Thus, for example, it turned out that three merchants from the Gaza Strip were the deciding factor in the rise in the price of tomatoes a short while ago. State lands are leased to Arabs in violation of the law. They do with the produce what they wish and direct their activities according to the needs of Jordan, without any connection to Israeli agriculture. Respectable Israelis, among them former senior officers in the armed forces, are partners in these Arab dealings....

"In the Ministry of Agriculture, they confirm these facts. Hillel Adiri, the special advisor to the Minister of Agriculture, says: 'Most of the vegetable produce in the State of Israel is today in the hands of the Arabs from the territories. Most of the agricultural land in the south is in the hands of Arabs from Gaza. The Pituach Shalom area, for example, is a sad story. It was once a glorious export area but the economic crisis broke the people there. Arabs came with suitcases filled with dollars and Jordanian dinars. The Jews, on the verge of despair, could not withstand the temptation and sold them rights to the land.'"

Of course this is illegal. And of course the government does nothing. Of course these huge amounts of funds come from Jordan, Saudi and Kuwait, and the government does nothing. In October, 1984, *Ma'ariv* writes: "Saudi Arabia, with the aid of the United States, is transferring funds to the occupied territories [sic] to cover debts and to carry out development plans...."

Jordan, in blatant plans to ensure that the Arabs remain in the territories, subsidizes the building of houses, some magnificent ones. On December 2, 1984, *Hadashot* carried the following story:

"Whoever drives along the narrow road that goes down from the hills of Ramallah (in Samaria), sees blocks of new buildings peeping out from the olive trees. The first thought is—Jewish settlers. But approaching closer one sees that this is not so. Right and left, for kilometers, stand buildings empty of people...."

And why are these Arab buildings empty, and why were they built? An Arab explains:

"Anyone who has land gets a permit to build from the military government, then sends a request and receives 7,000 dinar (almost $20,000) from Jordan. Thus the land costs him nothing. The money comes in installments. When he lays the foundation, he photographs it and sends the photo to Jordan. He then gets the next installment. When he puts up the roof, he gets the next installment. Hussein is not so stupid."

Stupid? Would that Israel be that stupid.

The article continues:

"Why do the buildings stand empty? 'Most of the people have no money aside from the aid from Jordan....'

"Pinchas Wallerstein, [Jewish] head of the Benjamin Regional Council says that the idea of the housing lies in the desire to seize the lands west of Ramallah in order to prevent the setting up there of Jewish settlements."

And, of course, to insure that the Arab will stay in the Land of Israel. And the Israeli government? The newspaper concludes:

"In the civil administration [of the territories] no one is upset. The housing was built on private property and there is nothing we can do to prevent their going up...." Of course not. Israel cannot order the end to Jordanian money arriving in the territories. *Of course not.* And so, life is made easy for the Arabs, thanks to Arab states. Thanks to Jews. While young Jewish couples without funds are forced to live with their parents in crowded apartments, the *Jerusalem Post* (July 27, 1984) informs us: "The joint Jordanian-PLO coordination committee has decided to renew the allocation of housing loans to East Jerusalem...."

There is no better way to comprehend the extent of Arab control over the key agricultural segment of the Israeli economy, thanks to the madness of the Israeli government, than to study "the case of the expensive tomatoes."

In October 1985, the price of tomatoes in Israel suddenly leaped to 3,000 shekels a kilogram, an incredible rise in price. *Ma'ariv* explains:

"Economists rubbed their eyes in astonishment, journalists did not understand what was happening, people had to remove the tomatoes from the salad. The answer to the puzzle lay in great measure in the hands of three people—Salach a-Mata from Gaza, Nasser a-Sina from Gaza, and Salman Razaq al Attar of Rafiah [in the Gaza Strip]. These three are the "barons" of Israeli agriculture in the south of the country. The lands are registered, it is true, in the names of Jews, but control of the growth, the harvest, the transportation and the marketing is in the hands of these three and their families. In the last tomato crisis they proved, too, that the price is also, in great measure, set by them.

"The crisis began with a virus that attacked tomatoes in the Arava area, causing a shortage. All eyes now turned to Pitchat Shalom, which was once a center for export. Today the Jews there grow villas à la Dallas and the Arabs grow tomatoes. When the shortage came about, the Arab merchants proved their expertise in the game. The cheap tomatoes, of second- or third-grade quality, they sold in the Gaza and Rafah market. The top-grade ones reached the Tel Aviv marketplace with frustrating slowness and with startling prices. The Jews who had sold the produce before the crisis held their heads. But it was too late. In Rafiah and Gaza new wealth was born."

Fear of world opinion and a mad Jewish policy of thinking that a happy Arab is a quiet and good Arab has given birth to a policy that allows Arab money to come into the country and subsidize competition that destroys Jews. The same policy leads to a condition under which Arabs who do not pay taxes or acquire permits can easily undercut competition. Is it any wonder that more and more stalls in the Jewish marketplaces are sold or leased to Arabs who can sell their produce well below the prices of their harried Jewish competitors?

And still, the madness goes on. Indeed, it increases.

Defense Minister Yitzhak Rabin rises in the Knesset, announces his support for the establishment of a Palestinian bank in the city of Shechem. Now, it is clear that the bank will be under the thumb of our enemies and will serve as an important conduit for huge amounts of Arab funds arriving from Jordan, Saudi Arabia and all over the world for the purposes of establishing an economic infrastructure for the new Palestinian state. It is also evident that much of the money that comes in will go to subsidize Arabs who wreck the Israeli economy by charging severely lower prices than Jews for contracting work, for produce, for production. Not only will Jewish business people be wiped out but the money will also go to purchase Jewish apartments and houses in Jewish cities at twice the going price in order to tempt the Jews to sell. Jaffa and Acre and Lydda and Ramle and Upper Nazareth will become Arab cities during the course of the purchase of the Jewish State.

The Palestine Bank of Shechem will be the underpinnings of the Arab National Fund, the modern-day reply to the little blue-white box Jews knew in their childhood. But in this case, it will not be nickels and dimes but billions of dollars that will go to destroy the Jewish State, collected cleverly and with sophistication. Rabin's Arab bank will be the greatest weapon in the establishing of the Arab West Bank state on the west bank. It will be the financial heart of the new Palestinian state; you can bank on that.

No matter. Rabin and all the other Rabins of the Jewish world are convinced that it is imperative to buy the Arab's heart in order that, through economic advantage, he will forget his desire for a state of his own, his anger at what he calls the Jewish "occupation" of his land, his national self-esteem. The mind of the Jewish liberals and leftists who believe that one can buy the Arab's national pride through giving him indoor toilets, television sets and banks. The liberal, the liberal. He never changes. You can bank on that.

And on and on it goes. As economic depression threatens to wreck the Israeli economy, a band of American Jews with Israeli and U.S. government blessing decides to join with American Arabs to help buy it even sooner. In the finest tradition of Jewish masochism, guilt and love-thine-enemy, American Jewish liberals have joined in the indoor brigade to uplift the poor suffering Arabs, and are raising millions of dollars to invest in Judea and Samaria in order to enrich the lives of our Arab friends there.

The names of the Jewish capitalist members of JAM (Jewish Association of Masochists) who are preparing to build the factories for Arabs that they do not build for Jews, and which will compete with Israeli Jews and put them out of business, include some of the famous and wealthy: Howard Squadron, former head of the American Jewish Congress and chairman of the President's Conference; Philip Klutznick, former head of the World Jewish Congress; Lester Crown of Chicago, general director of General Dynamics; wealthy Syrian Jewish financier Steve Shalom (whose saintly, philanthropic late father would turn over in his grave); Henry Kaufman, the Wall Street economist; real estate magnate Lawrence Tisch; Alfred Moses of the Anti-Defamation League and Jewish aide to Jimmy Carter; Arnold Foster, former head of the ADL; Edith and Henry Everetz, active in the UJA; and many others. This group of Jews is driven by a double demon. Not only are they believers in the contemptuous theory of "buy that Arab," but they are driven by liberal guilt and self-hate and obsessive need to "compensate" for perceived injustices to the oppressed "Palestinian." They are a sick lot, but they will plunge blindly on in their effort to improve the economy of the Arabs who hate and dream of destroying Israel, even as the poor Sephardi Jews of the development towns and the poverty-stricken urban neighborhoods sink deeper and deeper into the morass of economic collapse.

They are the patricians of Jewish masochism but they are joined by the pathetic faceless young Jewish liberals and leftists who babble in inexplicable guilt, in a manner that delights but confounds the Arabs who would kill them tomorrow if they could. They are represented by the student at the University of Rochester who, in response to my statement that "it is better to be a winner than a loser," cried out angrily: "That is a fascist statement!" One can see them in the person of the Israeli female student at UCLA who is famed for her love of Arabs, and who protested against attacks on the "freedom fighters of the PLO."

The Bank of Shechem is only one more example of Jewish masochistic insanity and contempt for Arabs. It is only one more link in a chain that wraps itself around the necks of the Jewish guilty, the chain of *selbsthas* (self-hate). It is a thing of sickness, but of *permanent* sickness. As long as the disturbed Jewish liberal and self-hater exists, there will be a bank in Shechem to create the financial infrastructure for a "Palestine" that will attempt to destroy Israel. As long as Arabs exist to attempt to kill Jews, the Jewish liberals will be there to attempt to buy them, to apologize to them. You can bank on that.

And the Arabs, seeing the kind of lemming of the Mosaic persuasion with whom they can deal, go further. Jewish trepidation and timidity have always bred Arab contempt and gall. And so, despite the fact that in order to build a house or even add to an already built one, citizens of Israel must ask for permits which are as difficult to obtain from the bureaucrats as the proverbial splitting of the Red Sea, Arabs have no problem. They simply do not ask.

And so in the Galilee, more than 8,000 buildings in the Arab sector were built illegally over the years. Eight thousand. Court orders were issued to knock them down. Enter Ezer Weizman, husband of Rauma, friend of Muhammad the gardener. Patron of the Arabs. Shocked, not by the 8,000 examples of Arab contempt for the law, but by the news that the court had ordered that the illegal structures be knocked down, the Israeli sheik of Araby hastened to intercede with Prime Minister Shimon Peres. The Prime Minister and Weizman thereupon moved to interfere with a court process, with judicial orders, and told the police not to implement the directives of the courts, not to knock down any illegal Arab buildings until a committee that would be set up could "study" the matter. And thus, on February 7, 1986, Minister of Police, Chaim Bar Lev, told the press:

"I have issued an order to the police not to assist in the demolition of buildings in the Arab sector. The order went out after agreement with the Prime Minister and the ministers involved."

Oh, to be an Arab and not a Jewish soldier named Ephraim Cohen Tzemach or his new wife, Orly! They are not Arabs; they do not live in an Arab village in the Galilee. They are only Jews in the slum area of Ezra, in Tel Aviv. Ephraim lived for years in a three-room apartment with his parents and his brothers and sisters. Hoping to marry, the soldier decided to build a second story over the small house of his parents. For one and a half years, every day after work, Ephraim would come home and spend every waking hour building with his own hands the one story for himself and his new wife. It was finally built. Ephraim married Orly. Four days later, while Ephraim was at work, the police arrived, with Border Police to put down any resistance and five Arab workers from the municipality of Tel Aviv, and destroyed the entire second story!

When Peres and Weizman defied the courts and arbitrarily ordered that illegally built Arab homes not be knocked down, Justice Minister

Moshe Nissim said: "Ministers have contempt for the law." Worse, they have contempt for the Jewish State. And themselves as Jews.

And of course only G-d and Freud can understand the complex terror of Jews in stating what they truly believe and fear about Arabs. Consider this fascinating piece of abnormal psychology in the Knesset in November, 1985, concerning the sale of land by Jews to Arabs. The motion was raised by Likud Knesset member Benny Shalita and responding was Minister of Agriculture, Aryeh Nachamkin:

NACHAMKIN: We have to gather every shekel and establish a public fund to buy every dunam of land up for sale.

SHALITA: But outside foreign forces offer much more.

At this point Abdal Darwasha, an Arab labor party member of Knesset, interrupted:

DARWASHA: Mr. Minister, are the Arabs of Israel a foreign factor?

NACHAMKIN: I didn't say that.

DARWASHA: Shalita did.

SHALITA: I didn't say that.

DARWASHA: You did.

SHALITA: Did you hear the word "Arab" on my lips?

DARWASHA: But you meant it.

SHALITA: I never said "Arab."

DARWASHA: I read your thoughts.

Now, of course, Shalita meant Arabs and Nachamkin was calling for a Jewish fund to buy up the land for sale before Arabs did, and the whole debate was over Arabs buying land from Jews. But neither the cabinet minister nor the Knesset member dared to say the word "Arab," which was the key to the whole problem. Only G-d or Freud...

PART IV

JUDAISM VERSUS WESTERN DEMOCRACY

"For My thoughts are not your thoughts, neither are your ways My ways, saith the L-rd. For as the heavens are higher than the earth, so are My ways higher than your ways ..." (*Isaiah* 55)

Chapter 10

Jews and Gentiles

Terror awakens in the Jew at the terrible thought—and subconscious realization—that liberal democracy is not only incompatible with Zionism, but with the very bone of his bones, flesh of his flesh, the *very Judaism* that is his religion and tradition, his basic Certificate of Identity.

But before we can even consider the relationship between Judaism and liberal democracy, it is imperative to define what we mean by "Judaism." Indeed, most of the problems that arise in the entire debate over "Kahanism" originate in the lack of defined terms, a situation which is mostly a deliberate effort on the part of Jewish leaders too terrified to debate clearly and concretely and who thus resort not only to personal smears but to definitive fraud.

Judaism. In order to decide what it *is*, we must first firmly and clearly define *what it is not, what it cannot be*. If we wish to speak about "Judaism," it cannot be the intellectual creation of man, the product of the intellectual meanderings of the people. That is surely philosophy, and, indeed, given the subject matter of G-d, it may even be the philosophy of *religion*, but religion it is *not*; *Judaism* it is not.

Religion, and in this case Judaism, can only be defined as the product of Divine Revelation or it has no meaning in any debate against "Kahanism." If Judaism is merely the product and result of the intellectual thought processes of men, no matter how clever or incisive, it is but sham and fraud to wheel it out in the battle against "Kahanism" and triumphantly shout: "You see; Judaism differs with Kahane!"

If "Judaism" is merely the ideas of other people, human and finite, what relevance does it have to absolute truth and the defeat of "Kahanism" in the marketplace of ideas? If a Jewish thinker differs with Kahane, who is to say that he or his is any greater in mind or theory than Kahane or "Kahanism"? The only intellectually honest use of the weapon of "Judaism" against "Kahanism" is when the one wielding that weapon of Judaism believes that it rests upon Divine, hence omniscient, law. *That* automatically excludes the Reform and Conservative religious movements and their spokespersons who do not recognize Torah and Talmud, Written and Oral Jewish Law, as being Divine, as being the literal word of G-d and His direct laws. Let us, therefore, simply ignore the deceit and hypocrisy of Jewish leaders—religious or lay—who, themselves, do not believe Judaism to be Divine but who hypocritically wave its flag against Kahane. Of such did the Jewish King Alexander Yannai speak when he advised: "Fear neither the Pharisees nor the Sadduccees, fear rather the hypocrites...."

Reform and Conservative leaders simply have no moral right to participate in this debate on *religious* grounds. They are not relevant to the question of Kahanism and Judaism, since their "Judaism" is nothing more than a potpourri of human, finite, personal choices and thoughts. When Reform Rabbi Cohen who does not recognize the Divinity of Judaism speaks, he is not speaking about Judaism. He is expressing "Cohenism" and what makes his personal "Cohenism" more Jewish than "Kahanism"? And when Reform chief Alexander Schindler emotes on "Judaism" he is really speaking about "Schindlerism" and it behooves him to admit it rather than intellectually defraud Jews. Far better an honest Schindler than a dishonest swindler. The "rabbi" who does not accept the Divine authority of the Bible via-a-vis the Sabbath or kosher food or ritual purity reaches the height of arrogant *chutzpaism* (gall), when he then quotes an "ethical" verse in the same Bible whose other verses he rejected a dozen times over when he "disagreed" with it.

The truth is that Reform and Conservative rabbis are paragons of ignorance whose greatest blessing is the fact that their congregations are Jews who know even less than they. The Jewish congregational sheep, so empty of any basic Jewish knowledge, look upon the rabbinical donkeys who lead them and see "scholars." Heaven help us! The reality is "rabbis" who know less than orthodox yeshiva students in high school. "Rabbis" who are truly abysmally ignorant of basic Judaism, who could not open a tractate of the Talmud to any page and calmly and surely understand what is says. Their ignorance combines with a stupefying arrogance that flaunts their lack of knowledge before the congregation in the sure knowledge that the mesmerized ignoramuses will not understand the charade being played out before them.

It is these ignoramuses in the form of rabbis who have the *chutzpah* to talk about "Judaism." Aside from their refusal to accept Judaism as the Divine, literal word of G-d, they have not more than the barest idea of what Judaism really says. And if they did, they would reject it! How dare these shallow empty vessels twist, pervert and corrupt Judaism, especially in those areas in which the very lives of millions of Jews is at stake!

And if this is true for rabbinical fraud how much more so for the Jewish *lay* leaders in their irrelevance to "Judaism." The vessels of ignorance of B'nai B'rith or the American Jewish Congress (or Committee) or Hadassah would not know a Jewish value or concept if they tripped over one. If we wish to *honestly* debate the relationship between Judaism and "Kahanism," between Judaism and liberal democracy, it can only be on the basis of knowledge and scholarship, a thing that eliminates the overwhelming majority of Jewish leaders. And it can only be based on the honesty of a Judaism given at Sinai, as Divine, absolute truth. Anything else not only has no relevance to whether Kahanism is "Jewish" or not, it merely opens the even more terrifying can of worms—the question: Why be Jewish *at all*, when one can be a moral human being?

And so, for the sake of the Jewish people, it is time to speak about the ignorance, the perversion, the corruption, the counterfeiting of Judaism. It is more than time to bring down what Judaism really says about Jews and non-Jews, about the status of both in the world, about the concept of Israel as a special chosen people and the place of a non-Jew within the Jewish State, about the contradictions between basic Judaism and basic western democracy and liberalism. It is time that the average Jew knew who leads him, what incredibly shallow and ignorant people they are; what the truth of Judaism really is and how far from that truth are the comfortable pulpiteers and feudal barons who run and run down the Jewish communities of the world. So that never again will they dare to raise the flag of "Judaism" in the service of their perverted schizophrenic Hellenism and gentilized concepts, it is time to instill terror into their hearts.

Jewish terror grows, is magnified beyond endurance, at the realization of the profound, immense, unbridgeable differences between the Judaism to which the Jew pays lip service and the liberal western values before which he prostrates himself and to which he is so keenly committed.

He will do anything—this schizophrenic, pathetic creature from an over-two-millennia Exile—to deny it. He will climb the highest mountain, ford the deepest river, burrow into the deepest of depths, to escape the awful truth and realization that his heritage, his Judaism, his umbilical cord on the one hand, and his real beliefs in western values, his unbiblical cord on the other, are, in the words of the Psalmist, "as the heaven is high above the earth ... as far as the east is from the west." The thought is so agonizing, the implications so horrifying, that he must shut it from his ears or shut up those whose dinning of it given him no peace. But, of course, it avails him nothing: "Whither shall I go from Thy Spirit or whither shall I flee from Thy Presence? If I ascend up into heaven, Thou are there; if I make my bed in hell, behold, Thou art there."

How numerous and how profound are the differences between the Torah of the Jew and the civilization of the gentile! Let me count the ways.

The liberal west speaks of the rule of democracy, of the authority of the majority, while Judaism speaks of the Divine truth that is immutable and not subject to the ballot box, or to majority error.

The liberal west speaks of the absolute equality of all peoples while Judaism speaks of spiritual *status*, of the chosenness of the Jew from and above all other people, of the special and exclusive relationship between G-d and Israel.

The liberal west speaks of subjective truth, of no one being able to claim or to know what absolute truth is, while Judaism speaks of objective, eternal truth that is *known*, having been given by G-d at Sinai.

The liberal west speaks of freedom and the right of all people to live their lives as they see fit as long as they do not harm others, while Judaism declares that there is no such thing as "victimless crime," since the sinner becomes himself a victim and the very act of not following G-d's law will bring down punishment and harm to all.

The liberal west speaks of tolerance and the obligation to respect all views regardless of their rightness or wrongness, while Judaism demands that the Jew choose truth and the path of right and not tolerate evil in his midst. And so the homosexual, the prostitute, the abortionist, the addict are not permitted the tolerance of living their own lives as they see fit, for Judaism is not a certificate of license, but of obligation.

The liberal west speaks of the purpose of life in the attainment of joy, happiness and man's desires and fulfillment as he sees it, while Judaism sets down for man what his fulfillment is and what his goal in life should be.

The liberal west categorically negates certain concepts—i.e., vengeance, hate and violence—almost *a priori,* while Judaism speaks of "a time to love and a time to hate, a time for war and a time for peace," with the need and commandment to love the good and hate evil, to seek peace but to go to war against the wicked, with vengeance, at the proper time, *an obligation,* in order to show that there is a Judge and there is justice in the world.

The liberal west speaks of the most important thing being life itself and thus moves easily into a concept of better anything than dead, while Judaism speaks of the quality of life, with the yardstick being the doing of G-d's will in life and the commandment being to give up one's life if necessary in order to obey certain of G-d's laws.

The liberal west speaks of the pragmatic and practical, with reality being that which we can see and touch and feel, while Judaism rests on a foundation of faith and belief in a G-d who is Omnipotent and who is the G-d of history.

But above all, Judaism differs from liberal *and non-liberal* western values in that the foundation upon which it rests is that of *"the yoke of Heaven,"* the acceptance of G-d's law and values and concepts as truth, without testing them in the fires of one's own knowledge, choice, desires and acceptance. One does not weigh and mull over Jewish values as presented in Torah authority. One does not test them to see if they are acceptable to the taste, sweet to the palate. One does not test them by his own standards to see if he believes them to be just or decent or merciful or good. It is the Almighty who created the world and the word, who created finite and stumbling man, who created justice and decency and mercy and good. That which He created is just and decent and merciful and good, and we accept it because of that. It is this yoke of Heaven, the setting aside of our will before His because He is truth and His Torah is truth, that is the fundamental of Judaism.

Of course the Jew must study and analyze and grapple with Torah and its concepts. And is there another religion in the world that places so much emphasis and obligation to study as does Judaism? But that study is not to twist and concert Judaism's concepts so as to confirm our own. It is an attempt to analyze and understand them; and whether we succeed or do not, we obey, nevertheless. We bend our neck, we bow the head, we soften the heart and accept the yoke of Heaven. That and not our "rationality" and our "approval" is what guides us and obligates us.

And though there be concepts that we, because we were so sadly raised in foreign and gentile environment with foreign and gentile concepts and values, find difficult to accept and understand and carry out, we nevertheless climb the Jewish mountain in the certainty that G-d, the Omniscient, has given us the truth that we must follow. That is the difference between Judaism and the western idea that elevates Man, rational man, to the throne of the universe; that gives man the ultimate right to determine justice and goodness and values. That is the ultimate contradiction between Judaism and western culture and nothing can ever bridge that gap. The Jew must choose.

And there is more. Let us magnify Jewish terror.

Liberal democracy and Judaism

The differences between liberal democracy, as modern man knows and defines it, and Judaism are profound. Democracy is based on the notion of the will of "the people." The people are supreme and the majority of the people have a right to express their will and make the state act in accordance with that will.

And liberal democracy defines "the people" who have these rights. Who are they? Who are the "people" who have the absolute right to demand all the rights granted by the state? Liberal democracy is crystal clear on this point. The "people" are those individuals—*all* those individuals—who are citizens of the state, whether through birth or through sufficient time of residence within the particular, geographical area of the state. All of those people have an absolute right to be citizens of the state and to absolutely enjoy those equal political, economic, social and all other privileges that exist in human development and within that state. Democracy is color blind and religion blind and national-origin blind, and it is only the geographical area of the state which determines citizenship and equal rights and enjoyment of state privileges.

And the right of this defined "people" to express their will and have the majority of that will accepted as rule of state, derives from liberal democracy's premise that man cannot know the truth, that, indeed, there is no "truth" as such. Liberal democracy is a sociologist's Garden of Eden, a kind of Paradise Found, of Margaret Meadism. Having discovered that there exists a Pacific island with natives who eat their mothers-in-law, the liberal democrat postulates that there is surely no objective prohibition to eat mothers-in-law, that the failure to eat mothers-in-law is rather a specific cultural aberration of the west, and this holds true for all taboos and prohibitions. Truth, says liberal democracy, is in the mind of the believer and no one has the right to declare that he possesses it and therefore demand the right to impose it on a majority that disagrees or denies it as being truth. Democracy declares that "truth," being a matter of subjectivity, the only "fair" and equitable system of government is majority rule and majority decision as to what it desires—be that "truth" or not.

And if this is so, democracy also implies "liberty," and here, again, the differences between Judaism and western liberal democracy are awesome.

Liberty means the right of a person to affirm his own "essence," to "realize himself" in the manner that he sees fit. So long as he does not harm his fellow, nothing should be barred to him, no act disallowed by the state, no outside morality imposed on him to bar him from reaching his personal happiness or unhappiness. No one can tell him what is good for him, what is right for him. His is the right to reach great heights or fall to great depths; it is his affairs. It is his liberty.

This is liberal democracy, and breathes a western Jew with soul so dead who does not subscribe to it? And can we find a Jewish leader who will not swear and pontificate that this *is Judaism*? But of course, it is not, and it is time that we forced ourselves to know it and admit it.

Judaism's definition of the state, of citizenship, of national rights is based on the specific unique definition of the Jewish people. It is based on the Jewish people's role and on their purpose in this world. And it is based on the connection of the Jewish people to their Land, the Land of Israel. And both people and land have existence and meaning only inasmuch as they adhere *to Judaism*. It is from *Judaism* that the Jewish people derives its reason for being. It is only Judaism that prevents "Jewishness" from descending into the nonsense of "nationalism" and the racism of irrational "Jewish pride." It is Judaism alone that gives the Jews the moral right and obligation to wave his separate identity and shout: I am a Jew!

For Judaism, the Jewish people is not merely one more people of all the many who inhabit the earth. For Judaism, the Jew is a chosen and special and holy people, and if not, there is not the slightest reason to be a Jew.

Of course, Judaism lays down the love of G-d for all human beings who are not wicked and states that all men are created in the image of G-d. And, of course, Judaism enjoins the Jew to respect and deal decently and properly with the non-Jew. And, of course, the Jew is enjoined not to harm, and, indeed, to help the worthy non-Jew. But that has nothing to do with the *legal status* and difference between Jew and non-Jew, a thing that is poles apart from the western democratic outlook on political equality.

Let us therefore consider what Judaism really says about the relationship of Jew and non-Jew, about their dual status in the world and about the status of Jew and non-Jew in the Jewish State. Let us see what Judaism really says, no matter how terribly painful that may be for those who are the products of an admixture of Judaism and western civilization with all the contradictions between the two. Let the truth cut through the mountain and let it never be forgotten that the pain of truth makes it not one whit less truthful for it. One can, indeed, as so many do, flee from it, but neither does flight change its status as verity.

The beginning of Jewish wisdom in this matter begins with the basic Jewish axiom that the Almighty chose the Jewish people to be His special, holy nation, armed with His Divine Law, the Torah, given at Sinai before the eyes of all the people. This election of Israel created something very different from that found in any other "religion" or "faith." Judaism became more than a religion. It became a totality of life with laws that, through study and practice, bound the Jew in every aspect of his life, personal status, government, state—his totality of existence.

"And the L-rd spoke unto you out of the midst of the fire; you heard the voice of the words but saw no picture, only the voice. And He declared unto you His covenant which He commanded you to perform..." (Deuteronomy 4).

"This day the L-rd thy G-d commandeth thee to do these statutes and ordinances; thou shall therefore observe and do them with all thy heart and with all thy soul. Thou hast avouched the L-rd this day to be thy G-d and that thou wouldst walk in His ways and keep His statutes and His commandments and His ordinances and hearken unto His voice; and the L-rd hath avouched thee this day to be His own treasure as He hath promised thee and that thou shouldst keep all His commandments. And to make thee high above all nations He hath made, in praise and in name and in glory, and that thou mayest be a holy people unto the L-rd thy G-d as He hath spoken" (Deuteronomy 26).

"To love the L-rd thy G-d and to hearken to His voice and to cleave unto Him, for that is thy life and the length of thy days" (Deuteronomy 30).

A covenant at Sinai that created a Jew committed to a *total* life of holiness!

But Judaism was created for more than the *individual*. It transcended the individual Jew and made him part of a Jewish religio-nation, that obligated all Jews together, that made each responsible for the conduct of all other Jews and culpable for the sins of fellow-Jews:

"There is not a single *mitzvah* (commandment) written in the Torah concerning which there were not covenanted 48 treaties of 603,550" (The Talmud, *Sota* 37b), and the Talmudic commentator, Rashi, explains:

"The 48 treaties were for each and every one of the 603,550 Israelites who were in the desert, since each one became a guarantor for all of his brethren" (Ibid.).

Judaism is a *people-oriented* belief, an idea that is common to all Jews and that not only binds them together as Jews but imposes upon them the obligation to create a national society that is unique, special, *holy—Jewish!* It enjoins on the Jew a people and society that is separate and separated, that is set apart from the others because only in this way can it be free of all the un-Jewish and unholy influences of the other nations.

"Now therefore, it ye will hearken unto My voice indeed, and keep My covenant, then ye shall be Mine own treasure from among all peoples, for all the earth is Mine. And ye shall be unto Me a kingdom of priests and a holy nation" (Exodus 19).

And the rabbis of the Talmud comment:

"Holy—hallowed and sanctified, separated from the nations of the world and their abominations" (*Mchilta, Yitro*).

The concept of a holy nation is inevitably coupled by Judaism with the concept of a separate nation for the clear reason that the mixture of holy and profane dilutes, destroys the purity and totality of holiness. And that is exactly the reason for the Biblical injunction:

"Lo, it is a people that shall dwell alone and shall not be reckoned among the nations" (Numbers 23).

And that is exactly the comment of the rabbis on the verse (Leviticus 20):

"And ye shall be holy unto Me, for I the L-rd am holy, and have set you apart from the peoples, that ye shall be Mine." "If you are separated from them, then you are Mine; if not—then you belong to Nebuchadnezzar [King of Babylon] and his comrades" (*Sifra*).

No, not hatred of the other nations but an understanding and deep assurance of belief that the Jews are indeed the blessed recipients of Divine truth; that that truth is a thing to be studied and acted upon and lived every moment of the Jew's life; and he and his children and theirs must live in a society of Divine holiness that is unique and untouched or influenced by the profanity and commonness of the other nations. Not hatred for others, but deep pride and thanksgiving that we are the chosen.

And this concept of chosenness, holiness and separation is an integral part of the Jewish ritual. When called up to read in the Torah scroll, the Jew recites the blessing, "Who has chosen us from all the peoples..." When he performs the Sabbath night ritual on the exit of the Sabbath, a ritual which itself is called *havdala* (separation), he raises his cup and blesses G-d who divides "the sacred from the profane, light from darkness, Israel from the nations." When he recites the holiday prayer he stands and murmurs, "You have chosen us from all the peoples, loved us and desired us, raised us from all the tongues and hallowed us with Your commandments."

No, not a hatred of other nations but a refusal to bow to the nonsensical leveling of a fraudulent democratization of values. Not all values are equal. There is truth and there if falsehood, and blessed is the one who has truth. And not all peoples are equal, and blessed is that people who has been chosen and given truth. And the rabbis, after declaring that all humans were made in G-d's image, continue: "Beloved are the Jews who are called the children of G-d. A *special* love was granted unto them..." (*Avot* 3). And again: "The Holy One Blessed Be He created the seventy nations but of them all found pleasure only in Israel..." (*Tanchuma*, Bamidbar 10).

The era of false democracy in which there is nothing better than anything else and in which everything and everybody is brought to a common denominator, invariably among the lowest, is not that of Judaism. G-d is truth and G-d chose a special people and gave them that truth. If any of the nations wish to share that, they are welcome to join the Jewish people. But until they do there is a *difference*, there is the difference of the *havdala* intonation: "He who separates Israel and the nations...."

The injunction upon the people of Israel to separate themselves from the nations of the world in order to create a Torah society in an effort to, as well as possible, escape the influences of the nations, makes Judaism *a land-centered faith*, a concept that follows inexorably from its people-centeredness. For if the Almighty wishes the Jews to live as a collective people and so to create a special, holy, unique nation, it is obvious that this can only be done if they live in a single, distinctive land of their own, isolated—yes, isolated, not integrated—from gentile and foreign influences which can and must corrupt the pure totality and distinctiveness of G-d's society.

And so Moses tells the Jews: "Behold, I have taught you statutes and judgments ... that you should do *in the midst of the land* whither you go to possess it" (Deuteronomy 4). And again: "And the L-rd commanded me at that time to teach you statutes and judgments that you might do them *in the land* whither you go over to possess it" (Ibid.).

And thus do the commentators speak:

"For the Holy One Blessed Be He, told Moses *two* things: That he should go down to save the people from Egypt—and this would have been possible in the land of Goshen [Egypt] itself or close to it. But he promised *another* thing: To take them out of that land [Egypt] totally and to the place of the Canaanites" (*Ramban*, Exodus 3:9).

And: "For G-d knew that they [Israel] could not fulfill the *mitzvot* [commandments] properly if they would be in countries ruling over them" (*Ibn Ezra*, Deuteronomy, 4:10).

And: "And since in our servitude we were unable to acquire the completeness directed by Him, G-d did wondrously to take us out and to bring us into the land where we could acquire that completeness" (*Sforno*, Deuteronomy 6:21).

The concept is clear. G-d, wishing to create a society and life of Torah totality, knew that, with the Jews living as a minority in a foreign country, not only would it be impossible to create the *national* laws and forms of a Jewish society, but even the individual would be influenced by the majority culture and thus warp the *completeness* of the Torah teachings, never able to *properly* observe Torah. And that, of course, is the meaning of the astounding rabbinical *midrashic* statement:

"Even after you are in Exile, be distinguished with *mitzvot*; place *tefillin* [phylacteries], make *mezuzot* [on your doorposts] so that they will not be foreign to you when you return."

The question leaps at us: Is *that* then the reason for Jews to observe the commandments? So that they should not be "foreign" when we return? Why are we not commanded to do the commandments simply because all the commandments that are not tied to the land are the obligation of the Jew anywhere? And the answer is clear: The commandments were given *only* for the Land of Israel, for there *only* could they be done properly and completely, the only way that G-d could have wished it. Only there could the Jew build a Torah society uncorrupted by gentile concepts. And the sole reason to observe them in the Exile is indeed the need not to forget them *when we do return to Eretz Israel.*

And so, knowing that G-d wished the Jew to create a unique, total, pure and complete Jewish life, society and state, who can honestly believe that He then sanctioned the democratic right of a non-Jew, who is totally alien and outside the Jewish society and who is free of its religious obligation, to have the slightest say in its workings?

Eretz Israel means "the Land of Israel." Meaning the land of the people called Israel. Precisely as Moab was the land of the people of Moab and Edom that of the Edomites. The concept, the logical concept of a land, is that it serves as the home and the receptacle for a people to lead their own unique and distinctive lifestyle. It is not the geographical area that defines the person, it is the person who controls the land. No non-Edomite was ever a citizen of Edom just as no non-Philistine was a citizen of Philistia or had any say in its national concerns or characters. So, too, with Israel—the Jewish people. The Land of Israel belongs to the people of Israel. It is they who control it, define it. It is their vessel, their territory in which to create the society of Israel, the Torah society of G-d. Only Israel, only the Jew, has a proprietary interest in it.

And thus, Judaism lays down legal, *halachic*, conditions for the privilege of a non-Jew being allowed to live in the Land of Israel, the Chosen Land of G-d, given to His Chosen People, Israel, to create a Chosen Torah society.

And this is, of course, the heart of the matter. It is not merely that the land belongs to the Jewish people. It is the land that belongs to *G-d* and which He gave to the Jewish people for a specific reason and under a specific condition. It is the land that was indeed taken from other people—the Canaanite nations—because it is G-d who made the world for a specific purpose—goodness and holiness—who holds title to the entire universe, to all the land within it, and it is His to do with as He sees fit. And the rabbis, in asking why the Torah—a book of law—begins with a story, the story of the Creation, reply that should the nations point to the Jews entering the land and taking it from the seven Canaanite nations, Israel rejoins:

"The world and all that is in it belongs to The Holy One Blessed Be He. When He so chose, He gave it unto you and when He so chose, He took it from you and gave it to us, and this is the meaning of the verse (Psalms 111): The strength of

His deeds did He recount unto His people in order to give unto them the inheritance of the nations'" (*Bereshit Rabah* 1:2).

It is the Almighty who created all—the world, the lands, the peoples in them—for a purpose. And it is He who took the Holy Land from others for the same purpose and gave it to the Chosen People, for that purpose:

"And He gave them the lands of nations and they inherited the labor of peoples that they might observe His statutes and keep His laws" (Psalms 105).

To observe His statutes and to keep His laws. And that is why non-Jew who wishes to live there can do so only under certain conditions, the most important being that he has nothing to say concerning the state, its character, its workings.

This is so for all non-Jews. Any grant to them of citizenship that implies ownership and a right to shape the destiny and character of the state destroys the uniqueness and entire purpose of giving the land to Israel. It invites spiritual assimilation and eventually demands for political autonomy.

How much more so for the non-Jewish residents of the land who lived there *before* the L-rd gave it to the Jews. Those residents refuse to recognize such a fact. They believe the land to be theirs and dream of the day when they will regain it. To allow them to remain as proprietors, or even freely living with restrictions, is to ensure not only the general spiritual assimilation that is threatened by any large number of non-Jews, but also the threat of revanchist political and military attack.

And that is the clear concept given by the great Biblical commentator, Abarbanel, in explaining why the Children of Israel were forbidden to agree to a covenant of peace with the Canaanite nations which would give both equality and rights in the land.

Abarbanel brings down the verses in Exodus (34:11-12):

"Observe thou that which I command thee this day; behold I drive out before thee the Amorite and the Canaanite and the Hittite and the Peruzite and the Hivite and the Jebusite. Take heed to thyself lest thou make a covenant with the inhabitants of the land that you come upon, lest it be a snare in your midst."

And here is what the great Biblical commentator says:

"For having taken their land from them there is no doubt that they would always seek the harm of Israel. And that is why the verse says 'the land that you come upon,' i.e., since you, Israel, came upon the land to take it from its inhabitants and they are 'robbed' of it, how will they observe a covenant of love? It will rather be just the opposite, for they will be a 'snare in your midst' and when there will be a war, they will join your enemies and fight you."

What sheer clarity and logic and normalcy! What understanding of the normal workings of people's minds and national feelings! And what a difference between the great Torah scholar and the tiny Hellenists whose cowardice and fear of facing truth lead them down such pathways of contempt for the Arabs. Of course the admonition prohibiting a treaty of friendship and equality with the Canaanite nations is exactly the same for the Arabs of Israel, and for precisely the same reason. In both cases we deal with people who lived in the land before Israel returned. Of course, they do not accept the truth of Divine ownership of the land by the G-d of Israel, hence Israel's right to take the land with sovereignty and ownership. Do we expect them to? Of course the ultimate, only reason that they surrender and live quietly is fear and their understanding that they are too weak at present to change the situation. But of course they never accept that situation as permanent and of course they dream of the day when they will return their "stolen land" unto themselves. And so, apart from the reason that *any* non-Jews, even those from a people who never lived in the land, cannot be granted national and citizenship rights in a Jewish state, there is a far greater reason in the case of the Canaanites and the Arabs and any non-Jewish people who once lived in Israel and who see it as their land, stolen by the Jews.

(And, indeed that is why so many of the Torah commentators deny the right of the Canaanites to live in the land at all, under any circumstances, because it is impossible that they would not plot revanchist plots.)

There is no essential difference between the feelings of the Arabs and those of the Canaanite nations concerning the land they believe to be theirs. And while we may accept the view of those commentators who would grant the Arabs the limited rights of all other gentiles in the land, it behooves us to watch them far more carefully than we would people who never lived there. So basic and important is this concept that, as the Jews prepared to cross the Jordan into the Land of Israel, as the waters rose to enormous heights and the Children of Israel rapidly crossed to the other side, as they were in the middle of the now-dry riverbed, suddenly Joshua told them to stop, gather together. And he spoke to them. What was so vital that could not wait until they had crossed safely to the other side? What had to be said *now*, in the middle of the Jordan, as the waters piled higher and higher?

"While still in the Jordan, Joshua said to them: 'Know why you are crossing the Jordan! In order that you drive out the inhabitants of the Land from before you as it is written' (Numbers 33:52). And you shall drive out all the inhabitants of the land from before you. If you do this—it shall be good. If not—the waters shall come and inundate me and you" (Talmud, *Sota* 34a). Nothing was more urgent than this message, for allowing the gentile nations who inhabited the Land of Israel to remain there freely was to invite physical and spiritual threats; military or political efforts on the part of bitter, angry, revanchist people to regain the land; spiritual and cultural assimilation; and disintegration of the uniqueness of the special society that the Jew was commanded to build.

And so, the Talmud tells us: "Joshua sent three messages to the inhabitants [of Canaan]. He who wishes to evacuate—let him evacuate; who wishes to make peace—let him make peace; to make war—let him make war" (*Vayikra Rabah* 17).

The choices are given. Either leave, or prepare for war—or make peace. The choice of "making peace" is explained by the rabbis as involving three things. To begin with, the non-Jew must agree to adopt the seven basic Noahide laws, which include prohibitions against idolatry, blasphemy, immorality, bloodshed, robbery and eating flesh cut from a living animal, and a positive action—adherence to social laws. Once he has done this, he has the status of a *ger toshav* (resident stranger) who is allowed to live in Eretz Israel (Talmud, *Avoda Zara* 64b), *if he also accepts the conditions of tribute and servitude.*

Biblical commentator Rabbi David Kimchi (*Radak*) explains Joshua 9:7: "If they uproot idolatry and accept the seven Noahide laws, they must also pay tribute and serve Israel and be subjects under them, as it is written (Deuteronomy 20:11): 'They will be tribute and shall serve you.' "

And Maimonides (*Hilchot Mlachim* 6:11) declares: "If they make peace and accept the seven Noahide laws we do not kill them, for they are tributary. If they agreed to pay tribute but not accept servitude or accepted servitude but not tribute we do not acquiesce until they have accepted both. And servitude means that they shall be humble and low and not raise their head in Israel. Rather they shall be subjects under us and not be appointed to any position over Jews ever."

Far better than foolish humans did the Almighty understand the dangers inherent in allowing a people that believed the land belonged to it to be given free and unfettered residence, let alone ownership, proprietorship, citizenship. What more natural thing than to ask to regain what it believed to be rightly its own land? And this over and above the need to create a *unique* and distinctly separate Torah culture that will shape the Jewish people into a holy nation. That "uniqueness" can be guaranteed only by the non-Jew's having no sovereignty, ownership, citizenship or say in the state that could allow him to shape its destiny and character. And so, concerning any non-Jew, Maimonides says: "'Thou shalt not place over thyself a stranger who is not of your brethren'" (Deuteronomy 17:15). Not only a king, but the prohibition is for any authority in Israel. Not an officer in the armed forces... not even a public official in charge of the distribution of water to the fields. And there is no need to mention that a judge or chieftain shall only be from the midst of the people of Israel.... "Any authority that you appoint shall only be from the midst of thy people" (*Hilchot Melachim* 1:4).

The purpose is clear. The non-Jew has no share in the Land of Israel. He has no ownership, citizenship, or destiny in it. The non-Jew who wishes to live in Israel must accept basic human obligations. Then he may live in Israel as a *resident stranger*, but never as a citizen with any proprietary interest or with any political say, never as one who can hold any public office that will give him dominion over a Jew or a share in the authority of the country. Accepting these conditions, he admits that the land is not his, and therefore he may live in Israel quietly, separately observing his own private life, with all religious, economic, social and cultural rights. Refusing this, he cannot remain. Those are the conditions for the gentile who wishes to remain in the Land of the People of Israel, of *the Jewish* people. A stranger who is allowed to reside as a resident but never with citizenship, never with anything to say about the country.

Then, by all means, he must not be ill-treated or oppressed. *Then*, by all means, we should treat him properly, kindly, heal his sick and support all his needs. *Then*, we must treat him with the same kindness we would show any decent human being who is not Jewish if we lived in the Exile outside of Israel.

Then he is entitled to personal rights, economic and cultural and social rights within Torah law. But *national rights*, the right to say anything about the structure, the character, of the state—never!

And certainly nothing of even this to one who does *not* accept the Jewish sovereignty over the land, the tribute and servitude that *goes along with it*. And a thousand times never to a gentile, the Arab, who is the *enemy*, who claims the country is really his and who declares his right to retake the country through war or through population

growth and democracy! And concerning those who do not accept the
permanency and legality of Jewish sovereignty, the Torah clearly
commanded: "And you shall drive out all the inhabitants of the land
from before you.... But if you will not drive out the inhabitants of
the land from before you, then it shall come to pass that those which
you let remain of them, shall be thorns in your eyes and thistles in
your sides and shall torment you in the land wherein you dwell. And
it shall be that I will do to you as I thought to do to them" (Numbers
33:53-56).

The Biblical commentators are explicit: "And you shall drive out
the inhabitants and then you shall inherit it, you will be able to exist
in it. And if you do not, you will not be able to exist in it"
(*Rashi*—Rabbi Shlomo Yitzchaki).

"When you shall eliminate the inhabitants of the land, then you
shall be privileged to inherit the land and pass it down to your children. But if you do not eliminate them, even though you will conquer
the land you will not be privileged to hand it down to your children"
(*Sforno*—Rabbi Ovadiah ben Yaakov).

"... The verse speaks of others aside from the seven Canaanite
nations .... Not only will they hold that part of the land that you did
not possess, but even concerning that part which you did possess and
settle in—they will distress you and say: Rise and get out ..." (*Ohr
Hachayim*—Rabbi Chaim ben Atar).

That is Judaism, and if it be painful to the western secularized Jew
because of its all-too-obvious contradiction of western political
democracy, so be it. And if the westernized, secularized Jew will have
to *choose*, to make an agonizing, painful choice—then so be that, too.
But at long last, let honesty ring. For Jewish honesty is infinitely more
preferable to the dishonesty of Schindlerism or the ignorance of
Peresism. Far better to look at Judaism truthfully, though that will
mean realizing that we are seeing "Kahanism."

Some 2500 years ago, Elijah stood on Mount Carmel and spoke to
the Jews. Their problem at the time too was deformed Judaism. They
had created a comfortable form of Judaism mixed with Baal worship
and felt quite at home in this progressive admixture. Their temples
were a bit of this and that, their Judaism and Zionism an ideological
coexistence of paganism and monotheism, and they certainly felt
themselves good Israelites. And yet, Elijah rose and boomed out at
them:

"How long halt ye between two opinions? If the L-rd be G-d, follow Him; but if Baal, follow him."

Because Judaism cannot abide the admixture of Torah and fraud, there is no Jewish coexistence between honesty and falsehood. And that is why it is so necessary that we rid ourselves of the irrelevancies and evasions and fraud of terrified Jews, from Reform and atheist to Moderdox (modern orthodox), who avoid the clear rulings of Jewish law and conceptual values because of their inability to deal with the immutable conflict between them and western, non-Jewish values.

That is why they bring high-sounding irrelevancies, moral and ethical concepts that no one argues with, that no one disagrees with, that are all magnificent and glorious—and irrelevant to what we are talking about. Hear them, the frightened sellers of Jewish red herrings:

"The highest value of all is peace. Rabbi Yochanan of the Torah would even greet a gentile in the marketplace with '*shalom* (peace).'"

The greatest value is peace? Of course, and what relevance does that have to anything that I say? Of course, the Torah calls for peace between Jews and gentiles and of course Rabbi Yochanan greeted a gentile with "shalom" and—so what? The Jew greets the gentile with peace, and he deals with him with respect and honor and decency in all his private and personal relations with him—but not as a *citizen* of the Jewish state. Not as one who has any *national* say in the Jewish state. And certainly not even "shalom" to an *enemy!*

"All men are made in the image of G-d." Agreed, embraced wholeheartedly. And what relevancy is that to all of the above? All men are made in the image of G-d, and when they are decent we owe them the basic decency and respect we would owe to any Jew. But again, this is limited to the private and personal sphere. The national sphere—state and people and citizenship and equal political rights in a Jewish state—are not the province of non-Jews. One is obligated to run miles to help a decent gentile in his personal problems but not an inch in the sphere of national equality.

And, of course *none* of this has anything at all to do with the evil men who were indeed created in the image of G-d and then proceeded to destroy it and corrupt it and turn themselves into worse than beasts. None of this concept of "made in the image of G-d" has the slightest relevance to truly evil people, as far as what our attitude toward them should be. Were not the Nazis—*Hitler himself*—made in the image of G-d? Of course. And Stalin? And Genghis Khan? And the Amalekites for whom the Torah decrees extermination? Was not the Moslem Mufti of Jerusalem who led massacres of hundreds of Jewish men, women and children in the Land of Israel in the 1920s and 1930s made in the image of G-d? And Arafat and George Habash? Of course they were. The question is: *What did they do with that image? To it?* How did they—through their evil—defile and corrupt it? And how much love and mercy do we owe to these who would destroy us if they could? The theological fishmongers continue with their red herrings:

"But the Bible tells us to love the stranger. The Bible declares that there shall be one law for you and the stranger."

Again, even if it were true that the Hebrew word in the Bible—*ger*—which is wrongly translated "stranger," meant the *non-Jewish* foreigner, of course it would mean that one should not oppress or persecute that non-Jew who is allowed to live in Israel as a *ger toshav*, resident stranger. That one must help him and feed him and heal him and treat him with decency and mercy and respect. It does *not* mean that he must be given the right to be equal politically, a citizen, one who has a say in the character and running of the state.

But more than that, the rabbis make it clear that the general use of the word *ger* in the Bible refers to what they term a *ger tzedek, a gentile who has converted and become a Jew.* The warning is not to offend him or treat him in any way differently from the one who was *born* Jewish. And this is what is expressly stated in the *Chinuch* (Commandment 63):

"'And you shall not oppress or persecute a *ger...*' (Exodus 22). We are prevented from oppressing a *ger* even with words. *And this is one of the seven nations who converted and entered our faith.*"

And the rabbis (*Torat Kohanim,* Leviticus 19), on the verse, "And if a *ger* shall live in your land you shall not oppress him; as an *ezrach* (citizen) of you shall he be" (*Ibid.*).   "'As an *ezrach*': just as an *'ezrach'* is one who accepted all of the Torah, *so is a ger, one who accepted all the Torah.*"

And when the Bible uses the term *ger* in the context of the "stranger" and the Jews who were in Egypt, as in the verse, "And you shall love the *ger* for you were *gerim* in the land of Egypt" (Deuteronomy 10), the greatest of the Aramaic Biblical translators, Onkelos, who was himself a *ger*, a convert to Judaism, carefully and painstakingly uses *two different words* to translate *ger* and *gerim*, and thus to differentiate between the meaning of the two in the verse. Concerning, "And you shall love the *ger*," Onkelos says, "And you shall love the *Giora* [meaning convert to Judaism]. But in translating "for you were *gerim*," he writes: "for you were *dayarim* [meaning 'residents'] in the Land of Egypt."

Of course the use of the word *ger* by the Torah refers to the stranger who converted to Judaism and who is now a full Jew. The Torah understood the danger of discrimination by "natural-born" Jews against the "new" Jew who, but yesterday, was a gentile. That is why the emphasis on the need to treat the *ger—converted Jew—*as yourself. And that is, of course, the reason for the injunction: "One law shall there be for you and the *ger* who dwells in your midst" (Exodus 12).

Is it logical to suppose that this "one law" which refers to the commandment to eat of the Paschal lamb is incumbent on that non-Jewish resident when the Talmud *forbids* the non-Jew to eat from it?

No, the injunction to "love the *ger"* refers to the stranger, but it is an injunction to love the *ger tzedek*, the gentile who converted and is now Jewish. In that respect the love is one that demands *equality*. As for the non-Jew, indeed we must treat kindly and decently and with love all gentiles who have accepted the minimal laws of civilization, the seven Noahide laws. But they are not Jews and are not part of the Jewish people that, alone, has not the right but the *obligation* to live in the Land of Israel and create there their unique and special Jewish State. This is the very warp and woof of Judaism, the very fundamental of Jewish fundamentals: the separation of the Jew from the non-Jew in order to create the complete and total Jewish society.

And, of course, Judaism never leaves its fundamentals within the realm of the ethereal and philosophical. Judaism is first a creed of concepts and then a meticulous path of ritual that symbolizes those concepts. The ritual of Judaism, the commandment, is the outer expression and manifestation of the inner concept. And, clearly, Judaism took great pains to impress upon its followers the vital importance of separation through precise and exact laws, laws and rules that are not only in opposition to "progressive thinking" but, in this era of "Kahanism," have become the objects of an hysterical, irrational orgy of defamation and condemnation.

The clearest and most painful example of the agonizing contradiction between liberal-democratic-western thinking and Judaism, the one that has led to the most violent and hideous hate and wildly irrational defamation is surely the clear and ringing Jewish ban on intermarriage and sexual relations between Jews and non-Jews, a thing that has become the centerpiece of the hysterical attack by the Hellenist Jews on "Kahanism."

From the know-nothing, religion-hating left, whose Shulamit Aloni cried, "Kahane is a Nazi," to balding Likud Knesset member Michael Eitan who drew up a table of Kahane laws and Nazi Nuremberg laws to show the "similarities," this subject has brought down the most emotional and irrational attacks. But of course, sound and fury and heat and hysteria have not the slightest relevance to or effect upon the reality of a situation, and if it is indeed true, as leftist Aloni and rightist Eytan say, that Kahane is a Nazi for calling for a ban on intermarriage and sexual relations between Jews and non-Jews, let it be known that so then were their grandparents—*and those of every other Jew.*

It is not Kahanism that the neo-Hellenists attack when they hysterically condemn his war on intermarriage, but Judaism, and, though it is excruciating painful, let the truth be known. Intermarriage is the Waterloo, the Valley of Death, for the desperately confused Jewish Hellenist and defamer. And Judaism's clear and unmistakable total opposition to it, more than any other thing, marks the secular Jewish Hellenist as standing outside the pale of that Judaism which, to his horror, is the "Kahanism" of his grandparents as far back as Sinai. And never was there a mightier Tower of Jewish babbling than this Hellenistic edifice complex.

Breathes there a Jewish leader with soul so dead who does not pay homage and obeisance to Judaism and its great books? Is there an Israeli Prime Minister, Knesset member, Reform rabbi, Federation head, Jewish Congress (American, Canadian, *World!*) president who does not respectfully rise in respect and salutation to the Book of Books, the Holy Bible? Search if you will, as for leaven on the eve of Passover, and you will never find a Jewish humanist, liberal leader who does not shower us with praise of the Bible and its Judaism of "ethics, morality and brotherly love."

And so, let me suggest a game. It is called: "What If?"

It is really a rather simple game. One simply opens the ethical and humanistic Bible and chooses a passage or event. Then, he selects a modern-day Jewish leader or leaders, and asks the sublime question: What if? What if they had lived at the time? What would their reaction have been? Such a simple game. And with such momentous implications. Let us begin. What if...?

What if Shimon Peres, the Israeli Knesset, the World Jewish Congress, the Reform Rabbinate, B'nai B'rith and the Jewish Federations had been in the desert when Moses, fresh from Sinai, declared: "Neither shalt thou make marriages with them (the Canaanites); thy daughter thou shalt not give unto his son nor his daughter shalt thou take unto thy son" (Deuteronomy 7).

Can one even begin to imagine the vitriolic condemnation on the part of all the above-mentioned "progressives" against this racist, Kahanist decree?

And then, what if they had been in the desert when Pinchas (Phineas) rose out of the congregation: "And behold, one of the children of Israel came and brought unto his brethren a Midianite woman in the sight of Moses..." (Numbers 25).

The man is Zimri, prince of the tribe of Shimon, leader of Israel, respected, honored, famous. The woman is a gentile, well-born, daughter of a king of Midian. He has relations with her—not only a victimless crime, but he may, in fact, love her. What is the reaction of Pinchas?

"And when Pinchas saw it, he rose up from among the congregation and took a javelin in his hand; and he went after the man of Israel into the tent and thrust both of them through, the man of Israel and the woman through her belly..."

The game becomes more exciting. What if? What if all the above and Alexander Schindler and Shulamit Aloni and Balfour Brickner and Edgar Bronfman had been there; what would they have said? What would the rabbi of the Stephen Wise Free Synagogue and the head of the World Jewish Congress—humanists and liberals, par excellence—have done? What arises in the hearts and minds of the ethical Jews when Pinchas kills a Jew and a paramour merely because they wish to have adult enjoyment that does no hurt to anyone? What kind of Declaration does Balfour deliver at this gross violation of human rights and base violation of basic tolerance? And what does Edgar—married to the same kind of *shiksa* (well born) whom Pinchas thrust through—think as he contemplates the Bible that sits in every temple, Orthodox, Conservative, Reform, Reconstructionist or Gay? And which describes all this and G-d's *rewarding* of Pinchas for his act. "Behold, I give unto him My covenant of peace." Reward? Where are the anti-racist, anti-Pinchas demonstrations? And how do the progressives continue to raise high that Torah scroll?

What if?

What if they transported them centuries later to Jerusalem, where, as the Second Temple is being built, Ezra, leader of the Jews, is suddenly told shocking news: Jews are intermarrying! What would Alexander Schindler and Knesset Speaker Hillel have said to the following paragons of Jewish morality:

"For they (the Jews) have taken to their daughters.... So that the holy seed have mingled themselves with the people of the lands ... (Ezra 9).

Holy seed? What kind of racist philosophy is this? Does it not smack of ... ? And then, in response to this intermarriage, Nehemiah acts: "In those days I saw Jews that had married wives of Ashdod, Ammon and Moab.... And I quarrelled with them and cursed them and smote certain of them and plucked off their hair..." (Nehemiah 13). Why surely the entire Knesset and Conference of Presidents of Major American Jewish Organizations would have risen up in fury and created some league Against Racism and Coercion and demanded an immediate anti-racist law had they been there.

The truth is that had they been there, these Jewish leaders of the school of neo-Hellenism and gentilization would have never accepted the Torah, would have never embraced the Judaism of Sinai and of their ancestors. For all that they find abhorrent today in the emphatic war on intermarriage and relations between Jews and gentiles that they call "Kahanism" is really Judaism, pure and simple.

Maimonides, whom Jewish leaders, either through ignorance or hypocrisy, so praise today unto the heavens as the progressive codifier, did indeed codify such Jewish laws as:

"A Jew who had relations with a gentile through marriage is whipped according to Torah law. But he who has relations with a gentile immorally [not through marriage] is whipped by rabbinical decree lest he come to marry her.... And this leads to cleaving to the gentiles from whom the Almighty separated us, and thus to turn away from G-d and to betray Him" (Maimonides, Laws of Forbidden Relations, 12).

It could not have been put more clearly or pithily. Intermarriage and sexual relations between Jews and non-Jews lead to the breaking down of the separation that G-d commanded, a separation that alone keeps the Jew as a distinct and unique entity, building a life of beauty and holiness and—above all—handing down the torch to his child who in turn will pass it on to his. No, not hatred nor "dislike" of the non-Jew, but a deep belief that G-d gave the Jewish people His Truth and nothing could be more stupid or criminal than losing that truth by losing our distinctiveness and separateness.

That is why the rabbis so painstakingly created "fences" that would as much as possible assure the strengthening of this separation:

"The rabbis forbade the eating of bread baked by the nations because of intermarriage ... for if he eats their bread he will come to eat with them" (Code of Jewish Law, *Yorah Deah* 114). And:

"It was decreed not to drink their wine because of their daughters [i.e., it would lead to intermarriage with their daughters]" (Talmud, *Avoda Zara* 36b).

No, no, no—not hatred and not contempt, because the very same gentile, truly desiring to be Jewish, can convert and thus become as Jewish as the greatest of the rabbis.

But having made that clear, the converse is just as clear. For the Jew, *vis à vis* the gentile, there remains a gulf, a division, a separation, an apartness that yawns in its immensity. Two worlds, two separate beings. Yes "Kahanism" is Judaism, and all the hate and curses and defamations and stones and frantic efforts to silence that truth are both unavailing and irrelevant.

The Almighty never intended that this world be an easy one for the Jew—only a holy and spiritual one. And so, he must choose. He must choose because Judaism and Zionism on the one hand, and western, liberal culture on the other. They are different. The one represents spiritual life and the other death, the one truth and the other falsehood and delusion, the one blessing and the other curse.

"See I have set before thee this day life and good and death and evil ... therefore choose life!" Therefore choose Judaism so that you and your children and your children's children shall live upon the land which the L-rd swore unto our fathers to give them as the days of the heavens above the earth....

But the Hellenists of Israel and the Exile cannot. The gentilized Jewish leaders cannot choose. They know, all too well, that Judaism, the faith unto which they were born, is in fundamental conflict with the westernized values to which they have always cleaved and which have become flesh of their flesh. They are victims, trapped in their own personal ideology which stands in contradiction to their Judaism, and they cannot bear being forced to choose.

And yet, not even *that* is the worst of their agonies. There is an even more terrible horror, emerging directly from the contradictions of their lives and ideologies and which is the worst of all. It is a terror that shakes the very reason for the existence of Israel as a Jewish state and that of the Jews as a separate people.

Even if there were no Arab physical threat to the existence of Israel, the far greater question, the far greater threat, exists in the *struggle among Jews over what kind of state will Israel be*. Will it be a *Jewish* State or a sickly, carbon copy of the non-Jewish ones with all their foreign cultures—a gentilized Hebrew-speaking entity? And if it is to be *that*, the terrible question arises: Is this what we waited for, dreamed of, hoped for, over two millennia, for nearly 2,000 years? For a pallid copy of the United States or Britain or Canada or Australia or France or Germany or the west in which we could live in far greater comfort and safety? If this is the product and not a state of Jewish identity and specific Jewish character and Jewish specialness, do we really need it? That is the terrible question that shakes the thinking Jewish Hellenist who has no answer to it. And his agony grows in proportion to the reality of Israel as a state indeed most un-Jewish, in truth most alien to all that Judaism and the Jewish soul ever yearned for.

Chapter 11

Jews and Jews

Some time ago, an opinion poll was given to Arabs and Jews by Sociology Professor Ephraim Ya'ar of Tel Aviv University. Ya'ar gave his respondents a list of 14 factors that may or may not influence the course of peace between Israel and the Arab states, and asked them to rank the list in importance, from one to 14. The Arabs placed "the will of God" first, the Jews placed it last.

One need not be "Orthodox" to understand that we are beholding the unfolding of tragedy in Israel. For nearly 2,000 years a Jewish people, pious and cleaving to G-d through deep faith in Judaism, prayed to return from the depths of the Exile to the heights of their own state. It is doubtful if any of them could have dreamed that when that miracle of return would happen and the Jewish state would be in place, the Jewish citizens who were privileged to see the incredible miracle of the return from twenty centuries of Exile would rank, in the list of factors that move history, their G-d dead last.

And *one* need not be a "fanatic" to understand the spiritual holocaust taking place in the Jewish State when one reads in the newspaper (*Yediot Aharonot*, January 5, 1983) the following:

"About a quarter of the public that calls itself secular, or about 15 percent of the adult population of Israel, is prepared to have themselves or someone in their family marry a Christian. Most of those who are ready for marriage ties with a Christian are not prepared for similar ties with a religious Jew. These figures emerge from an opinion poll taken by the research institute Dahaf under the direction of Dr. Mina Tzemach."

Nor need one be a "Kahanist" to be shaken by the following news item from the *Jerusalem Post* (February 25, 1986), written by one of its resident Hellenists, Benny Morris:

"Tomorrow evening Israel television is scheduled to screen a program against Jewish-Gentile intermarriage. Citizens Rights Movement MK Shulamit Aloni, the Knesset's leading and veteran crusader against racism and other civil rights abuses, has appealed to the

Broadcasting Authority to halt the broadcast and if the authority refuses, intends to ask the High Court of Justice for an order to prevent it.

"In the program a young Jewish woman relates how she slept with a man called Yoram. But then she found out that 'Yoram's' real name was Ahmed. 'I then felt polluted, defiled,' the young woman says.

"Aloni regards the program, prepared by the *Yad Le'Ahim* Orthodox anti-missionary organization (which is financed in part by the Education and Religious Affairs Ministries), as 'a sign of the times.' It's like the Nuremberg Laws, in which Aryan Germany tried to 'protect' its women from having sexual intercourse with Jews. That's how these things start.

"Aloni fears that the country is on a downward slide into racism, even 'fascism.' She stops short of saying it's inevitable. Maybe she doesn't want to depress me....

"Recently, she adds, the country's Orthodox establishment has begun to 'use the terminology of Nuremberg' openly, preaching against marriages between Jewesses and Arabs and against meetings between Jewish and Arab schoolchildren."

The broadcast was, indeed, cancelled on the grounds of "racism" and one can only shake his head in disbelief that in the Jewish State, a program against intermarriage can be banned because of "racism." One can only rend his garments when a Knesset member compares such a program to "The Nuremberg Laws" and one begins to understand the real meaning of the comparisons of Kahanism to Nuremberg.

And one can only grit the teeth in anger at the obvious sympathy of the writer for the views of Aloni, and then add the following footnote.

The week that Israel banned a television broadcast against intermarriage its board of censorship decided to allow the presentation of the play *Oh Calcutta*, in all its nudity. It was in response to tens of telegrams from American playwrights, authors, actors and other such liberals (including Arthur Miller and Edward Albee), who wrote: "The difference between the democratic governments in the United States and Israel and the authoritarian ones is that the democratic regime has principles within the area of freedom of expression and creativity." They added that "from many aspects Israel is a ray of light unto the free nations and it would be better that it not turn into a nation that limits freedom of art."

And so it did not. It allowed nudity and degradation in the name of freedom of art and expression. And it banned a television program against intermarriage. In the name of ... ?

And one need not be a reactionary to look at the State of Israel, dream of centuries, land of Judaism and Jewishness, and to shudder at the following from the newspaper *Al Hamishmar* (January 14, 1986), under the heading, "A Family Picture With a Christmas Tree." It deals with a family in the leftist Kibbutz, Yad Mordechai:

"On Christmas Eve, a holiday atmosphere filled the home of the Rothstein family in Yad Mordechai, also. True, there was no snow and no full-fledged Christmas tree, but there was a tender little sapling in a vase and in the shadow of its decorated branches lay wrapped gifts from overseas and on the tablecloth with its red and green ornaments were pork chops and rice dipped in sweet cream. Some of that had been placed in a dish and placed outside for Santa Claus.

"What can one say except that Alice and Gadi Rothstein and their children, Pia and Danny, spent a very pleasant Christmas. Once again, the credit [sic] goes to Alice who came to Yad Mordechai as a volunteer and married Gadi (in church and in the kibbutz) in 1967.

"Q: Do you intend to convert?

"A: Why should I convert? Would you change your faith if you lived in a different country? The fact that I am not Jewish never bothered me, not even outside the kibbutz; neither in terms of society nor in my occupation as a teacher.

"Q: And the children?

"A: They learned from us not to make any problem out of it and because of that there is no problem.

"Q: And Christmas is one of your more pleasant holidays?

"A: Yes. With a holiday meal and the Christmas tree in the vase.... By the way, on Chanukah we dance around the Christmas tree and sing Chanukah songs. It works out beautifully."

Perhaps more sickening than the babbling words of the Christian member of the kibbutz is the clear sympathy for the entire abomination on the part of the newspaper. This, too, is the culmination of the longed-for Return to Zion.

And one need be nothing but a decent and heartfelt Jew to be appalled at the result of the "best in secular Israeli education," Amal. At the time of the interview she was 25. A graduate of the prestigious High School of the Hebrew University in Jerusalem, graveyard of Judaism, Zionism, and—heaven help us—of the Jewish state. A classic example of the "new Israeli," she comes from a prominent Israeli family. Her grandfather is Baruch Ben Yehuda, first Director of the Ministry of Education, before that principal of the classic Herzliah high school in Tel Aviv, and member of the equally classic kibbutz,

Degania Aleph. And, of course, winner of the prestigious "Israel Prize" for his contributions to Israeli education.

Her mother is Netiva, and she is the prototype of the Exodus girl. A member of the Palmach shock troops in the 1948 War of Independence, she served in several assaults in the Negev. She then studied at Hebrew University (language and philosophy) and then in London (art) which she concluded at the Bezalel School of Art in Jerusalem. A sculptress, an author, an intellectual; in short, the perfect Israeli product. And mother of Amal.

And Amal. What does the product of a laborite, socialist grandfather who was Director of the Ministry of Education and a mother who was a fighter in the Palmach and sabra extraordinaire think about Israel and the Jewish people?

Her answers appeared in an interview in *Ma'ariv* (January 26, 1979):

"I do not see any Divine right (of Jews) to the land because I am not religious. I do not see any national right to the land just because of our suffering. My right is simply because I and my mother were born here.... And because of this I feel a much greater obligation to the Arabs who paid a price in order that there be a Jewish state.... We have a right to a Jewish state because of the facts that were created here over three generations."

It is difficult if not impossible to be stunned by the lack of anything Jewish and, more, the sheer fascism of the views of this creature from outside of Jewish space. Rejecting religion and nationalism, the only "right" to Israel her tortured and empty mind can come up with is that "there have been created facts." In short, aggression, illegality, brutality, occupation, robbery, become legitimized by "the creation of facts over three generations."

One shudders to see Amal, the product of the Israeli secular education for which her grandfather won the Israel Prize, in a debate with an Arab as he loudly proclaims *his* national and religious right to the land stolen by the Zionists and vows that he will never accept the dictum that "time creates facts," and that this allows a stolen land to become that of the thief.

And one reads the following article (*Ma'ariv*, January 28, 1983) about an American Jewish family in Minneapolis who sent their daughter to study in the Jewish homeland, the Jewish State, at Tel Aviv University. Read. Read and weep, loudly:

"'What didn't we do in order that our daughter should be a good Jew?' ask the parents, for whom the events of the past few weeks have left deep furrows in the foreheads." And the story goes on to detail a good, Jewish family, who attended the local Conservative temple, were very Zionist and invested time and deep thought in making sure that their daughter, Liza Leah, would stay Jewish and, of course, marry a good Jewish boy.

"'It is not easy to raise a Jewish child in a foreign country,' sighs the mother. 'In Israel, Jewishness is a natural thing but here one has to emphasize it, love it, fight for it.' They allowed their daughter a free hand in regard to boys but were insistent that she dare not go out with those that were not 'ours.'

"'As long as no gentile entered our house I did not worry. I had faith in my daughter and in the Jewish education [sic] (after-hours Hebrew school) that we invested in her. I said to myself that it was impossible that she not marry a Jew....'

"How great was their happiness when their daughter told them of her decision to attend Tel Aviv University.... There was no doubt that in Israel she would find her Jewish dream prince and, if in the wake of her love for her Israeli husband she would decide to settle in the land of our forefathers, that would also be acceptable....

"And then, one wintry, snowy evening, the phone rang and the operator asked if they were willing to accept a collect call from Zurich, Switzerland. They were surprised since they had no acquaintance or relative there, but when the operator mentioned the name of the caller they hurriedly agreed to accept the call. Even before they had a chance to ask their daughter what she was doing in Zurich instead of Tel Aviv, she shouted into the phone:

"'His name is Taga [an Arab). I met him in the student lounge. We got married this morning in a civil ceremony.'

"Two months passed since then. The happy couple, as part of their honeymoon, flew to Minneapolis to meet the parents. The latter, in a desperate effort to swallow the bitter pill, sought to find a slim chance of his converting and the rabbi agreed to a lightning conversion.

"The groom refused. No, thanks. 'My religion is as dear to my heart as yours is to you.'

"And the daughter quickly drops the subject, saying: 'Oh stop being so Jewish. Isn't Taga a doll?'

"And both thanked the parents from the bottom of their hearts for sending their daughter to Israel. If she had not come to Tel Aviv, the meeting would have never taken place."

How good it is to have a Jewish State where Jews can meet Jews. And how good it is to have a democratic Jewish state where at Tel Aviv University Arabs can meet Jewesses freely and marry them.

And what do the Jews of centuries who went to the stake and died as martyrs to cleave unto their Jewishness, until there would once again rise up a Jewish state, say to the following article that appeared in the publication *Olam HaIsha* (*Women's World*), August, 1985?

"Some 3500 mixed marriages, the man an Arab and the woman a Jewess, live today in Israel [the actual figure is, of course, higher]... The figures show that the highest amount of mixed marriages are to be found in the large Arab villages of Israel, such as Taibe and Um al Fahm. Says Ra'a'nan Cohen, head of the Arab department of the Labor Party: 'Mixed marriages have become a practical problem since Kahane was elected to the Knesset. Before this, hardly anyone dealt with it, despite the fact that it is not a new phenomenon.'" And the article goes on to mention Jewish Nehama and her Moslem husband, Yusef. Nehama is from an Iraqi Jewish family and she lives in her husband's Arab village of Taibe. The magazine says: "Their four children are registered in their identity cards as Jews but in the village they are recognized as Arabs. Yusef says that he will not send his children into the army. 'They have nothing to do there.'"

Indeed they do not, if they are Arabs. The tragedy is that thousands of Jewish children, products of mixed marriages, walk the ground of the Jewish state, identifying themselves as Arabs, cut off from their army, state and people. This, too, is the realization of the dream of 2,000 years.

And in the Jewish State, the following item appeared in the *Jerusalem Post* (June 21, 1984) under the heading, "Rabbi Sentenced for Disturbing Missionaries":

"Tiberias (*Itim*)—The head of the Yad Rambam Yeshiva here, Rabbi Idan Makhlouf, was sentenced yesterday to three months in jail and another three months suspended for disturbing a missionary gathering and threatening the participants. The offence was committed four years ago."

The Jewish State. In which missionaries are free to snatch Jewish souls and a rabbi is sentenced to jail for fighting them. The Jewish State. Where a Knesset bill aimed at outlawing missionary activity is ruled illegal because it is "racist"! The Jewish State of Chelm. But it is not funny.

Israel, where the irony of ironies finds young Jews lost and bereft of all Jewish identity except that given them by the Arabs who hate them for being the Jews that they, young secular Israelis, do not even want to be!

The kibbutz. O gem of socialist Zionism, the apex of the secular humanist leftist Jew who, in disgust, threw away the reactionary Judaism and racist Judaism of his forefathers to create a proud, new, secular society that would produce a proud, new, secular Zionist socialist. Mishmar Ha'emek is one of the proud Marxist kibbutzim of Israel. A member of Hashomer Hatzair's kibbutz network, it holds within its boundaries a major educational institution, Shomriah, that caters to the children of other kibbutzim, too, Hazoreah, Givat Oz, Megido. Its purpose is to produce the proud Zionists and Jews who will give Israel its future leaders and, indeed, generation.

On December 1, 1985, the newspaper *Ha'aretz*, reported on the latest edition of the kibbutz institution's school newspaper. The heading of one of the pages reads, "Herzl and Zionut" (a mixture of the words "Zionism" and the slang sexual word for intercourse). Below it is a picture of Herzl, father of Zionism, with his beard ending in the form of the male sexual organ. Under the picture appear the words: "Herzl, as a youth, was almost ignorant of his Jewishness (despite the fact that he masturbated intensively as every other youth and certainly realized the cut in his organ)." Yet another drawing in the magazine shows a couple making love and under it the words:

"The book, *The Jewish State* [by Herzl], is the Hebrew translation of *Kama Sutra* [the Indian book of sex]. With its initial appearance it was clear to many that many of its positions [a double entendre] were incapable of being carried out."

Needless to say the kibbutzim were outraged and according to the newspaper *Al Hamishmar* (December 2, 1985), "in the wake of the publicity the kibbutzim met to discuss and clarify the events."

There was of course little to clarify. The empty children of empty Zionism who had been emptied of Jewishness were repaying their educators with the fruits of their work. The kibbutzim were the classic examples of Divine measure for measure, of the absurdity of hoping to empty Israelis of Judaism and a special meaning for the concept of a Jewish people and expect them to idolize Zionism, now merely another empty, stupid form of nationalism which may, in addition, also be a form of aggressive imperialism and colonialism. And so, what wonder that when the Chief of Staff of the Israeli army, Moshe Levi (himself a member of a Marxist Hashomer Hatzair kibbutz), visited the summer camp of Kibbutz Sdei Nahemiah, the proud young sabras, the new Hebrews of our time, and paragons of manners and respect, began clapping in unison as he kept speaking, a reminder for him to finish. And later, four of the young Hebrews went up to the stage and urinated in front of everyone.

And so, at a symposium on the question of emigration from Israel, Shmuel Lahis, former director of the Jewish Agency and now head of a group to prevent emigration, tells the educators that "there exists a large amount of emigration among youth of the kibbutz movement and especially Hashomer Hatzair" (among the most viciously anti-religious and anti-nationalist of the movements in Israel). This says Lahis, "because their educators did not give them the message of belonging to the land, and they grew, too, without a national identity." And so a poll in January, 1986, revealed that fully 25 percent of high school students of Hashomer Hatzair kibbutzim refuse to condemn emigration from Israel and six percent of all the kibbutz members between the ages of 25-45 have left the country.

In response to the breakdown of Jewish, Zionist and basic values in the Kibbutz, leftist Assistant Minister of Agriculture, Avraham Katz Oz, contributed this comforting thought:

"The youth of kibbutzim, as the general kibbutz population, are a part of the entire state and have been influenced by the general atmosphere that has been created in the country" (*Ha'aretz*, November 15, 1985).

Small comfort. No comfort. For, indeed, the atmosphere within the Jewish State is that of anarchy when it comes to any kind of values. Ruth Meged, a secularist par excellence, wrote a classic sociological document of primary importance in *Yediot Aharonot* (October 9, 1980). It should be required reading for all the opponents of Kahanism, Jewish "Khomenism" (!) and "dark ages" Judaism. It should be required reading for all the secularists who have produced a new Jew in Israel, liberal, free, progressive. The article is titled "A Disco Bat Mitzvah."

"Pretty Danny, king of the class, said that in his house there is a stereo system with six speakers and he deliberately pushed Gai into our stereo system, putting out of commission the 'Papa' group. Tzutzikit, aged 12, said that it was impossible to dance when the boys were making noise and that they should douse the lights already. A gay caballero announced that someone who does not have a color television is worth nothing.

"It all began at eight o'clock on Friday night, at the Bat Mitzvah party for our older daughter. We agreed that we had to celebrate it and that it would be nice to invite the members of the class. What is the problem? You arrange for a cake, pita with humus, a little singing and group games. But my daughter notified us that without a stereo and a bunch of disco records there is no party because the dances are the hit of the evening. She then told us that parties are only held on the Sabbath eve, Friday night, because during the week it is impossible to stay late.

"'It also has to be dark because we don't dance in the light and the parents can't be home and there must be a lot of food because after the dancing people are very hungry.'

"Eight o'clock, the house is ready. Salads, fruit, decorations, gaiety, really pretty, and then the pogrom begins:

"The food disappears within minutes. Three little men take over the stereo and raise the basso to its loudest. The lights are out—almost total darkness. The house shakes as with an earthquake and every effort to ask them to lower the sound is met with, 'We can't hear the beat.' There is an atmosphere of boredom, unfunny jokes, and confused giggling.

"The final damage of the successful party: A broken record; a scratch on the television screen; filth everywhere—paper and food on the floor, on the upholstery and the furniture, ripped and punctured decorations and balloons. The principal of the school tried to comfort me by telling us that last year there were parties that ended with broken furniture....

"And they are only twelve years old. G-d, where have we gone wrong?"

It would take volumes to tell the Hellenist, because the simple truth is a thing she is not willing to accept....

Nor would Yeshayahu Tadmor, secular Zionist who writes in *Yediot Aharonot* (February 25, 1986) under the heading: "Not for This Child Did We Hope":

"A few days ago I participated in a discussion that took place with two classes in our local school. We wanted to see the students' positions on Zionism and how they saw the Zionist future....

"The results of their positions as expressed by them through statements and votes were as follows: 'In 15 years, about a quarter or perhaps a third of the children would probably live outside of Israel; there would undoubtedly be another war between us and the Arabs and in the coming war we will win, but there is no certainty of that; we might lose; in 15 years,' said many of the students, 'Israel will exist but that is not 100 percent certain.'" Participating in the discussion was the director of the Haifa region of the Ministry of Education. He told me that he found similar expressions in many other schools which he visits. "The picture that was revealed was horrifying. I knew about it Out did not realize it was so serious.... The expressions were honest and authentic and their message shouted: Confusion, fear, insecurity and lack of faith in the Zionist future." Of course, Given the pragmatic realities of Israel and the Middle East, given the removal of faith in G-d and of Judaism from the lives of these youngsters, what is the surprise? And given the fact that the Hellenists and anarchists of Jewish values are permitted to destroy Jewish values and confidence, should we expect anything different?

Among the artistic and "educational" institutions that undermine values and confidence of Israelis is Bet Lessin and its director Yaakov Agmon. The following appeared in the Histadrut paper, *Davar* (April 2, 1986):

"High school principals have decided to protect their students from the play *Deserted*, at the Beit Lessin Theater, because it is likely to injure the morals of youngsters about to be drafted into the army.

"The principal of the ORT school, *Yad Singelovsky*, Chaim Giron, stated his objection as follows: 'Its influence on the youth in the country is likely to be terrible. A picture is presented of war that is dreary and frightening. Militarism is forced on us by the Arabs, wars are an existing fact and there is no need to frighten youth that stands before military service. It creates demoralization. There are in this play effects that are hair-raising.'"

Indeed, they are. And the play, which shows an Israeli and Arab soldier speaking of peace together, wipes away the reality of the Arab states' wishing to destroy Israel and presents instead a deliberately false picture of peoples who could live in peace if it were not for their governments. The horrors that war brings on the ordinary people are only because of those governments, including the Israeli one. The self-haters who comprise the artistic and theatrical elements of Israel have embarked on an unholy crusade and their victims will be young sabras who do not know to begin with why they are Jewish and why they need Zionism and a Jewish State, if they must go to war for them.

Behind the surface that the tourists see, far from the sight of the American Jewish Congress climbers of Masada and the weepers and filmers at the Western Wall; out of mind of the happy neo-Zionists of Hadassah and the Long Island temple tour (with rabbi along for a free ride to tell them what he knows about Israel, one of the great fiction efforts of our time), is the reality of an Israel struggling for its soul, in a battle between Jews and Jews to decide what kind of a state it shall be. A Jewish State—home of a Divine, chosen, special people, cloaked in holiness and wrapped in the mantle of difference? A people proud and confident, radiating the joy of being G-d's special people, blessed with the Divine truth at Sinai that raised it above the common and profane, and divided from the nations who know not holiness and sanctity?

Or will it be the shabby imitation of cheap cultures that sully the greatness of Man; the disgusting limitations of all that is animal and degrading of the soul, leaving the youth of Israel as nothing more than

Hebrew-speaking gentiles without the slightest logical reason to remain Jewish, and certainly not in the pressure cooker and potential danger that is Israel? Will Israel be the dream of centuries or the nightmare of modern times? This is the meaning of the struggle today between the Jews of Jewishness and those of profane Hellenism and gentilization. The Jews against the Hellenists, far more than the Jews against the Arabs, is the real struggle. And the Hellenists with their destructive anarchy of worthless values have already created a spiritual holocaust within the Holy Land.

A nation rejects its special distinctive holiness for the common, the universally profane. The Sabbath mourns in humiliation, its Garment of Sanctification removed for the nakedness of desecration. Jewish mouths created to take in food sanctified by G-d and to give out words of purity and sanctity, instead hungrily swallow the "white steak" of the pig and the impurity of the shrimp even as they give forth profanity and filth. The dessert they gorge themselves on is the cultural diet of pornography, violence and license subtly and less subtly fed them by the cultural barons of communications. The Jew who, but yesterday, watched his father sway in prayer, today rolls to rock and shakes with the agitation of a need for drugs. Perversion and self-indulgence—the worship of self, of the great "I"—becomes the religion of a state infested by Hellenism.

"Go through the city ... and set a mark upon the foreheads of the men that sigh and cry for all the abominations done in the midst thereof (Ezekiel 9).

The external face of the nation becomes indistinguishable from that of any other people as the Hellenists—disturbed artists, intellectuals and writers, the barons of television and radio and theatre, epitomizing all that is arrogance and ego, placing their own needs, desires, and illnesses over that of the sacred yoke of Heaven—destroy a people and state from within. A people that was Chosen by G-d rejects with contempt its Divine blessing.

"And Esau said ... Why do I need this birthright?... So Esau despised his birthright" (Genesis 25).

How hath Jacob become an Esau! Woe unto that which is gone.

The external face is but the outer manifestation of the internal values. And the values of Judaism struggle to the death with the secular, gentilized, foreign, corrupt ones of the Hellenists. If there are those who deplore the huge rise in foreign imports, let them know that more despicable than the foreign automobiles and luxury items are the foreign ideas, values, concepts. If we fear the importing of drugs from the outside, let us know that the worst of the opiates are the gentilized ideas that the intellectuals of Hellenism, the artists of gentilization, dance about as some Calf of Dross, shouting: "These are your gods, O Hellenes of Israel!"

This is the real struggle—the war of ideas, of values, of civilization. Will it be the victory of Judaism with its specific, separate, distinct views of holiness and purity, or the triumph of the Hebrew-speaking gentiles whose self-hate, a twisted product of cancerous ego, leads them to reject and stomp upon Judaism of discipline and embrace instead the malignancy of gentilization with its license, total self-indulgence, and self-destruction?

"The wicked walk on every side when vileness is exalted among the sons of man" (Psalm 12).

The war is being fought over the soul and destiny of the people and state. And the destroyers from within do their job well, eating away at the morality and values of a people once chosen for purity and who today throw off the greatness of the yoke of Heaven—which alone guarantees true freedom—for the rotting incense of foreign altars and strange temples of the "I."

"Who have said: With our tongue we will prevail; our lives are with us; who is lord over us?" (Psalms 12).

The Hellenists rampage through the Temple of the L-rd, scattering its sanctity, destroying its nation of priests. A people rejects its chosenness and specialness, its sanctity and elevation, its separation from the impurities of the nations, their profanations and abominations. It pants after the gentile; it seeks to be as all the nations.

"'For My people have committed two evils; they have forsaken Me, the fountain of living waters, and hewed them out cisterns—broken cisterns—that can hold no water" (Jeremiah 2).

The Jews against the Hellenists. The real struggle.

The dream of materialism fills the streets of Israel and the acrid smell of yearning for pleasure assails the nostrils. In the parlor, on the bus, in the cafe, the talk is of money and what it can buy. The gentile world of magical sensualism and gratification of desires fills the bowels with painful need and the holiness of Israel is exchanged for the dream of pagan America.

The curse of drugs—as some locust plague borne by the western winds—rages through society and the young Jew is destroyed, daily, by his search for pleasure and escape from the reality of life and the values and challenges of Judaism and holiness. The Labor party chairperson of the Knesset's Labor and Welfare Committee, Ora Namir, babbles that "there is no school in Israel in which there are not drugs," failing in her obtuseness to add that she and her ideological colleagues who destroyed Judaism and the Jewish child are directly responsible. And failing—deliberately—to add that the religious schools of Israel are noticeably free of the poison. And in the alleyways of Tel Aviv and Haifa young Jews die in an agony of heroin—the children of Jews who once lived on the high of Judaism.

And the reality is an alarming growth in emigration, *yerida*, as the Zionist dream falls beneath the American one. Los Angeles and New York and Toronto and London and Amsterdam and Hamburg become Blue-and-White as hundreds of thousands leave the Jewish State for the Exile that Herzl sought to end. Their places remain empty for there is hardly any *aliya*, immigration, to Israel from the fleshpots of the west. Even those who must flee prefer some other land. The Zionist dream falls victim to the bankrupt education and values of a state that is not Jewish but a Hebrew-speaking Portugal seeking to be a caricature of America.

"The more they were increased, the more they sinned against Me; I will change their glory into shame.... And they shall eat and not have enough, they shall commit harlotry and not increase" (Hosea 4).

For the cows of Dizengoff there can never be enough of the silks and dresses and gold and silver and good life of the gentile west, of the nakedness of gentile culture, of the throwing off of holiness and modesty.

"Because the daughters of Zion are haughty and walk with stretched-forth necks and wanton eyes, walking and mincing as they go ... therefore the L-rd will smite with a scab the crown of the head of the daughters of Zion and the L-rd will lay bare their secret parts" (Isaiah 3).

The Jews against the Hellenists. The real struggle.

The reality becomes a land whose music rocks to gentile beat and rolls to the depths of ugly violence. Values that raised the Jew to but a little lower than the angels are exchanged for those so base that he plunges lower than the beast. Judaism loses all meaning and Jewishness follows it into the junk heap of antiquity as Zionism becomes a word of mockery and cynicism. It is a land that raises its eyes unto the gentile films and televised pornography and cheers its pagan heroes even as it worships at the feet of uncircumcized basketball players. Sinai is cast away for Times Square and the purity of the Chosen people is exchanged for the material vomit of Los Angeles. The modesty of holiness is contemptuously abandoned and the nation wallows in the nakedness of gentile culture.

The breakdown of holiness and sanctity; the fall from the mountain of discipline and heavenly yoke. The transformation of a people of

G-d, yearning for the heavens, to a herd of men and women seeking the pleasures and aspirations of the beasts. Worse than the Jews for Christianity or Jews for Gurus or Jews for Marx are the Jews for Nothing ... absolutely nothing of any value. The Jews of emptiness and vanities and shallowness and grossness and ugliness and bestiality. And all this in the Holy Land. And all this on the part of the sons and daughters of Jews who clung to greatness in the Exile. The Jews of Israel who have been destroyed by the Hellenists and the empty vessels of gentilization. They exist in a vacuum that is valueless, and live for transitory pleasure, regressing to the paganism from which their father Abraham climbed to the One G-d.

A gross and grotesque creature named Nina Hagen, a punk singer as depressing and as shallow as possible, comes to Israel (from East Germany, yet) and thousands of empty sacrificial lambs leap and scream in a mass exhibition of sickness. And a home-made product of depressing degradation, Shalom Hanoch, brings 30,000 Jewish youngsters, for whom the heart must weep even as the eye blinks in sad disgust, into Hayarkon Park in Tel Aviv to sink deeper yet into the mud of animalism. *Ha'aretz* (October 3, 1985) describes the Hebrew tragedy:

"Hanoch sings, 'I don't know how to tell you how much I love,' and the crowd grows excited. There is a smell of hashish in the air. Hanoch sings 'Morena, Morena' and the smell of hashish grows stronger. The crowd sings with him, screams. He sings 'The Messiah Has Not Come,' and the crowd is on its feet singing and dancing with him: 'The public is idiotic so the public pays ...'" This is Israeli culture. For this they threw away Judaism. We are all in an insane asylum.

One opens the newspaper to the entertainment section. Every single sick aspect of the gentilized society of the Hellenized west is reflected there. A nation of priests, a holy people, is in the gutter. The sex movies, the ones that are symbolized by the permanent huge sign over the Tel Aviv Central bus station with a couple making explicit love and the words "sex" on it. The word is not even given its Hebrew name. The English word is transliterated in Hebrew letters. Night clubs advertise sex acts on stage as ads announce the glorious movies of Sylvester Stallone. A full page ad in the daily yellow rag, *Hadashot*, that enters tens of thousands of homes in Israel, carries a full-page ad from the chain of "Sex Style Stores," the largest and most reputable chain. Honest. Reputable.

Its four stores proudly sell high quality video cassettes and 8 mm. films on "unusual subjects." It also offers "fat and daring booklets on anal, oral and animal sex," as well as all manner of sex equipment for

the pervert of the Hebrew persuasion. And all of this in the holy
tongue, the language of the rabbis, of Moses, of Sinai. A State of
Israel, state of valueless anarchy. A ridiculous joke of a "poet" named
David Avidan is found to be sufficiently important to be interviewed
concerning a poll taken concerning whether Israeli women are satisfied with their sex life. *Ha'aretz*, which incredibly would care to be
known as *The New York Times* of Israel, finds both poll and poet sufficiently important to be made the subject of their page two "Conversation of the Day." The little worm comes up with a deathless statement that is headlined by the somewhat less than *Israel Times*: "With
me, women lose their embarrassment soon enough." Once Jews wrote
poetry such as the Psalms. Under the secularists the poetry is as cheap
as the shallow and empty Hellenists who write it.

"Thou hast built thy lofty place at every head of the way and hast
made thy beauty an abomination and hast opened thy feet to everyone
that passed by and multiplied thy harlotries" (Ezekiel 16).

And this is what the children are fed. These become their values.
And so half of the students have had sex by the time they enter high
school and the discos become the centerpieces of their empty lives and
they become pregnant at 15 and have abortions in a land in which
some 30,000 Jewish babies are murdered yearly by irresponsible
women who murder after careless sex. Thirty thousand a year, more
than a million since the Jewish State came into being. And how many
soldiers would they have produced and how many Jews to fill Judea
and Samaria and the Galilee? The poor sabras, the ones who are being
destroyed daily, the ones who are given the poison of an empty life
so that suddenly an epidemic of teenage suicides shocks Israel, and
all ask: Why?

The values of Judaism are replaced by those of Dizengoff Street in
Tel Aviv. The results can be seen in the crime, murder, robbery, rape
and increasing brutalization of society. It can be seen in the prisons
of Ramle and Beersheba and Shata where, sadly, mostly the children
of the religious Sephardic immigrants of Arab lands sit. It can be seen
in the Jewish prostitutes whose clients and pimps are so often Arabs.
It can be seen in the growing number of Jewish girls who date and
sleep with and marry Arabs. Who easily bed the foreign laborers and
foreign soldiers. The incredible pollution of the sacred Jewish seed
that preserved its purity in the Exile only to become abominated in
the Holy land.

"Shall not the land tremble for this and everyone mourn that
dwelleth therein?" (Amos 8).

"For they have taken of their daughters for themselves and for their sons; so that the holy seed have mingled themselves with the peoples of the lands" (Ezra 9).

"... and she doted on her lovers, on the Assyrians, warriors clothed with blue ... handsome young men all of them riding upon horses. And she bestowed her harlotries upon them ... and they poured out their lust upon her" (Ezekiel 23).

This is the reality of secular Zionism; these are its victims. Children of Zion who suddenly find Jesus in Tel Aviv and pagan Indian idols in Jerusalem, whose sick soul of ignorance seeks refuge in cults and strange gods of stranger lands far beyond the seas.

The lonely, lost, searching Israeli youngsters. See them in Tzachi, Tzachi is a graduate of the prestigious Gymnasia high school in Jerusalem, a student of theater at Hebrew University. "I always searched for truth," he tells the newspaper *Ha'aretz* (April 15, 1986). At the age of 27 he left his home, left Israel and travelled to America. In Florida he met a young Christian girl who introduced him to the New Testament. The lost son of Abraham, grandson of Jews murdered by the Christian mobs, suddenly found "truth"—Jesus. Tzachi returned home to Israel. He is a Messianic Jew. The ignoramus who never studied Judaism remains an ignoramus, ignorant of his faith and its teachings. But he has found Jesus.

And in the streets of Israel, the same simplistic cartoons of Jews for Jesus that appeal to the lost American Jewish youngster find their way—this time in Hebrew—into the hands of the lost Jewish youngsters in Israel, who read the following:

"Jesus of Nazareth indeed came and was crucified for us. He was tortured for our sins and in his wounds we will all be healed. How sad that the Messiah came and the people did not recognize him. But Jesus will not disappoint us; he will come again as king and judge.

"Today, know the Messiah."

And a coupon and an address and another lost Jewish soul in the hands of the missionaries.

The lonely, lost, searching Israelis, robbed by their parents and their leaders of their most precious gift: identity, reason for being, knowledge of what life is about and where they are supposed to go. And the vultures, the spiritual bloodsuckers, the missionary soul snatchers, smell the blood of the Jewish sacrificial lamb, smell his fearful search for answers, identity. As a swarm of locusts they descend on the Holy Land to "save" Jewish souls, knowing that the insanity of liberal democratic western Hellenism will allow them to do what they wish, with no interference from the Jewish government. And they are correct.

The Mormons, a missionary cult whose spiritual foundation is the attempt to convert one and all to their faith, see Israel as a goldmine for their conversation efforts. Their "center" in Jerusalem, which has been built despite vigorous protests by religious Jews, went up in great measure due to active support for their "democratic rights" on the part of leftists and liberals whose hatred of Judaism does not stop even at the knowledge that the missionaries will have a field day in their conversion of the weak-minded, empty-headed Israeli youngster and equally lost western Jewish tourist and student. The Mormon "pledge" not to proselytize is waved high by the hypocrites of liberalism who know that a Mormon who does not attempt to convert is like an Orthodox Jew who does not attempt to observe the Sabbath. The Mormon Center on Mount Scopus next to the university is red meat for a lion, tragedy for Jews, yet another symbol of the bankruptcy of a state that places foreign gentile values—democratic freedom of speech—over the Jewish ones.

They are everywhere, the missionaries. In Tiberias they openly proselytize among the young tourists. On Jerusalem's Narkis Street, the Baptist Church, under its minister Lindsey, laughs at Jews who rush to donate funds for their burned church, even as they openly lie about their refusal to convert Jews. In Nahariya, the Hebrew Christians, under Tzipi Hason, baptize Jews in the nearby Mediterranean. Moshe Cohen, 24, a young Jew baptized by Tzipi, now lives in the Emanuel Church in Jaffa.

And the cleverest of all the missionaries is the so-called Christian Embassy" in Jerusalem, run by a cunning Dutchman named Jan William van der Hoevan, former warder of the Garden Tomb. It is this "Embassy" that directs the operations and tours of countless Christians who come to Israel and express their total support for the Jewish state, a thing that emerges directly from their belief that the Jewish state presages the coming of the Messiah and the conversion of the Jewish people. Meanwhile, they use their reputation as lovers of Zion to quietly and methodically convert Jews while the Israeli government refuses to stop them. Every single absorption center and *ulpan* has them. Jewish public funds help the missionaries to snatch Jewish souls.

And as they sense not only the red meat of the lost Israeli Jew, but also the unexpected support from Jewish leftists and liberals, the missionaries grow bolder. In an article in the *Jerusalem Post* (October 20, 1984), the bold change is spelled out:

"Israel's Christian missionaries, or, as they prefer to be called, Evangelicals, who bear witness to the Jews about Jesus, are coming out of the closet and openly stating their intentions for the first time.

"The forthright declaration of missionary intent comes in the form of the *Mishkan, A Theological Journal on Jewish Evangelism*, recently published in Jerusalem by the United Christian Council in Israel. In the words of its editor, Rev. Ole Kvarme, it is a 'clear statement that we do want to witness and to promote evangelism among Jews.'

"Kvarme heads the Caspari Institute, a Christian study center in Jerusalem's French Hill, and the financial support for the publication of the journal comes from, among others, the American Board of Missions to the Jews, and Jews for Jesus."

Every conceivable type of missionary group has come to Israel, a happy hunting ground for Christian sects of all stripes, as well as Eastern sects that stagger the imagination. Thus, the Witnesses with all their weirdness have opened a center in the heart of Tel Aviv and tens of Jews join and participate weekly in their prayers and beliefs.

They knock on doors and reach everywhere. In Lydda, where thousands of Georgian Jews live after leaving the Soviet Union, Shalom Tzikashvilli, 62, sits as a mourner. His daughter, Roseta, has joined the Witnesses and he says softly: "This is a humiliation for our family; for me my daughter has died." The Witnesses offer money, a thing which is not allowed by the tepid Israeli law that "limits" missionaries. But few know that not one missionary has been tried under the law and that the Justice Minister at the time of its passage, Shmuel Tamir, immediately vowed that he would never prosecute anyone under it.

And so, confident, the Witnesses stand outside schools with their literature and their inducements. Eliyahu Leviashvilli, whose son, Avraham, was accosted by the Witnesses outside of his school, says: "Who heard about missionaries in the Soviet Union? Here, in our own land, land of the Jews, I have to fear such a thing?"

A telling question. No answer is forthcoming from those who stand at the helm of the Jewish ship of state and run it unto the rocks. And in the streets of Jerusalem one can find such posters as the one that reads:

KRIYA YOGA MEETING
of
INTERNATIONAL BABAJI YOGA SANGAM
at East-West Center
on 46 Bezalel Street, Jerusalem
Yogi S.A.A. Ramaiah speaks on
Tamil Kriya Yoga Siddhantha

Yes, the cults of the east have found homes in Israel with all their sheer paganism and idol worship. At least several thousand Israeli

Jewish youngsters have joined cult groups during the past decade, according to government estimates. A recently formed organization called Concerned Parents Against Cults, however, says the number is now "over 10,000." In a country the size of Israel, either figure is alarming.

The problem became so severe that the Education Minister ordered the formation of a special ministerial committee to investigate what it called "Eastern sects" operating in the Holy Land,

According to *Yad L'Achim*, an anti-missionary organization, the cults "have found Israel is an excellent target ... [they] operate with more freedom [here] than they can in their countries of origin.... They prey on the lonely, the hard-pressed, and the "Wandering Jews" who, although at home, are still searching for their roots."

Nearly every major U.S.-based cult has a branch in Israel.

The Guru Maharaji's "Divine Light Mission" is among the largest. With almost unlimited wealth at its disposal—devotees surrender most or all of their possessions to the cult—the movement has established two communes in Ramat Gan, purchased two factory buildings in south Tel Aviv, and set up groups in Jerusalem and Haifa.

Over 500 Israelis are active members of the Guru Maharaji cult. They believe that the Guru—an obese 19-year-old Indian youth—is a god; they pray before photographs of him in their Ramat Gan temple.

Their center is officially called a Yoga Academy, but the Guru's fanatical followers are unabashedly engaged in idol worship; a devotional letter written to the Guru by one of these young Israelis, and displayed on a commune wall, reads: "Guru, You are the King of the Kings, Master of the World, giver of Life, Love, Light, and Purity. Give me the perfect devotion to You and Infinite Love that will never end. Let me be at your feet forever."

A bewildering variety of other so-called "Yoga" or "Meditation" groups dot the Israeli scene as well, including the notorious Hare Krishna group.

A visit to the East-West Center on Bezalel Street reveals that its bookstore in fact showcases a veritable Who's Who of Eastern and other cults: literature from Hare Krishna, Guru Maharaji, Scientology and nearly every bizarre "meditation" or "yoga" cult under the sun is all that is for sale. The spiritual shopper is offered a wide variety of idols to worship.

And thus writes *Yediot Aharonot* (February 6, 1986); "A group of young Israelis, mostly from elite units of the IDF, that believe in the teachings of the Guru Rina Shein who died two years ago in India, have established a commune in Spain. They continue to believe in the guru and practice a sensual way of life as she ordered in her will.

"The leader of the group is an Israeli who was a former teacher of drawing and close friend of the guru. His followers continue to worship the Indian guru, Bhagwan Shree Rajneesh, who was active in the western U.S. and taught free sex and varied sex, and gathered thousands of followers." What a sadness, what a tragedy.

"Thy sons and thy daughters shall be given unto another people and thine eyes shall look and fail with longing for them all the day; and there shall be naught in the power of thy hand" (Deuteronomy 28).

The Jews against the Hellenists. The real struggle.

Worst of all is the inexorable breakdown of the fundamental bottom-line of Judaism—spiritual and national self-preservation. As an immutable law of society, the mad Israeli dash to weaken, befog and eventually do away with exclusive precise, exact and separate Jewish identity that—alone—preserved the Jewish people, brings the most inevitable and ultimate of disasters: A Jewish people who, seeing nothing special about being Jewish, leaps into the waters of intermarriage and dreams.

The kibbutzim, like some nightmarish Abu Ben Adam, lead all the rest of the spiritually destroyed Jews. The *Jerusalem Post* (April 20, 1986), writes:

"The marriages of non-Jewish volunteers with members of the kibbutzim they work in have been increasing over the past five years and are creating a 'serious' problem for the identity of their children, many of whom are not considered Jewish because their mothers have not converted. These conclusions, from a study of the subject, made by Haifa University's kibbutz research institute, were published in Friday's issue of the Kibbutz Artzi (Hashomer Hatzair) weekly, *Hashavua.*

"In a survey of 137 kibbutzim the institute found 739 mixed couples with a total of 1200 children.

"'... But most important, as the phenomenon grows, so does the danger of its jeopardizing the Jewish character of the kibbutz,' the writer of the article, A. Ginat, notes."

One must pause to admire the gall of the leftist kibbutz writer. A movement that destroyed Judaism among its members and which rails against the "racist" opposition to mixing Jewish and Arab students, suddenly bemoans "the Jewish character" of the kibbutz. Why, the very term smacks of the rankest of racism. Who can plumb the dark depths of the agonized secularist Hellenist soul? The confusion, the schizophrenia, are awesome.

The pitiful leftist writer continues: "Four hundred children of the mixed couples in the Kibbutz Artzi settlements are receiving a bi-national education [read Jewish and Christian]. The Christmas tree has become a common sight and is no longer considered strange. Gradually quantity turns into quality and this will determine the national character of kibbutz society. In one of the Artzi kibbutzim, 13% [!] of the members are non-Jewish."

But of course, it is much more than the kibbutzim. All over the Country young Israelis see not the slightest reason not to marry a gentile, and so they do: Arabs, U.N. soldiers from Finland, Sweden, France, Holland; Portugese laborers in the Negev; any gentile tourist in Israel or just any gentile met while the Israeli is a tourist. Consider the spiritual emptiness and holocaust erupting in Israel:

• More than 4,000 Jewish women are married to Arabs, with many living in Arab villages, having converted to Islam.

• Thousands of Jewish women live with and regularly have relations with Arabs, including large numbers of married women.

• Hundreds of Jewish children live in Arab villages (their mothers are Jewish and their fathers Arab, making them halachically Jewish). They are raised as Arabs, speak Arabic and hate Israel.

• Almost all the prostitutes in the cities of Israel are Jews and the majority of pimps are Arabs.

• Arab pimps wait at the Tel Aviv Central Bus Station near stops that are terminals for young Jewish girls from *moshavim* and poor development towns, and there offer them "help" and "financial assistance." The next step is drugs, drug dependency and prostitution. Some Arab pimps "rent" out Jewish prostitutes for the weekend or week to wealthy Arabs from the territories.

• Arabs have lists of schools and institutions for young girls, mostly poor Sephardic girls from development towns and *moshavim*. They wait outside patiently and repeat the pattern of the Central Bus Station.

• The beaches and shores of Israel are frenetic hunting grounds for Arabs whose own women are securely locked into their villages and homes. Armed with money, the Arabs—often posing as Jews—seek and easily find Jewish girls.

The bankrupt schools of Israel, which make so many Jews proud as they turn out Jewish doctors and lawyers and pilots, fail of course to do what they were most meant to, to put out good and proud Jews (who will *then* be good doctors and lawyers and pilots). Little wonder that we read this happy and positive article in the *Jerusalem Post* which will undoubtedly do much to condition other young Israelis not to even think of intermarriage or love with gentiles:

"Love songs and romantic music are the strongest protest one can make today, says folk-rock singer Don McLean, who has arrived in Israel to promote his four concerts here scheduled for this month....

"Love is also the main reason for McLean's frequent visits to Israel. Two years ago, a group of teenagers came backstage to see him after his performance. Among them was a shy, slim girl, who hung apart from the others. An intense romance began, with McLean calling Orly Tzarfati, of Kiron, every day after she returned from school and inviting her to stay on his farm in upstate New York when she finished high school.

"About six months ago, McLean came to be with Tzarfati on her last day before she was recruited to the Israel Defense Forces. She had insisted on serving her full term before considering marriage to the non-Jewish singer.

"'Of course, I came for Orly,' McLean said last week in his Tel Aviv Hilton suite. She spent every moment off from the army with him, while he spent as much time as he could sun-bathing on Tel Aviv's beach, between interviews about his approaching four concerts here."

Again, the worst of the abomination is the sympathetic, positive, encouraging tone of the article. Indeed, the very fact that it was printed is guaranteed to encourage other lost, empty Israelis to seek love with the gentile. The State is in the hands of an Establishment, from the political to the news media, which is so gentilized and so foreign to Jewish values that it sacrifices its children to the Molech of Hellenism daily.

And so multi-millionaire Meshulam Riklis, an Israeli citizen who left for America to make a fortune, leaving behind his army duties (a small crime that was overlooked in lieu of his large contributions to Israel), came to visit the motherland in May 1985. Meshulam came with three things: A check for $2.5 million for the Tel Aviv Museum and Foundation, a wife and an infant daughter. The wife, Catholic actress Pia Zadora and the infant, *shiksa* Katie. To say that the Israelis of Hellenistic persuasion fell over themselves in flattering and fawning over Riklis would be to fail to describe the picture adequately. The man who deserted his country and openly flaunted his gentile wife and child was the subject of effusive compliments by such as Tel Aviv's mayor Shlomo ("Chich") Lahat and cabinet minister Ezer Weizman. And thus wrote the *Jerusalem Post* (May 31, 1985):

"Chich's effusive thanks ('he showed his greatness by his business recovery') and Ezer Weizman's tribute to his childhood pal ('His father courted my mother in Damascus') were at times drowned by the wailing of the Riklis grandchildren, brought in from New York with their parents and (the first) Mrs. Yehudit Riklis. All eyes were riveted on the second Mrs. Riklis, 24-year-old rock singer Pia Zadora, who brought their four-month-old baby girl, Katie. Mother and daughter wore matching white outfits.

"The rock singer confirmed that since she met him when she was 17, her career changed. Declaring that 'it would not be honest to convert to Judaism,' Zadora said her daughter will be reared as 'a good Catholic. But she'll go to synagogue on Saturday and church on Sunday.' Her doting hubby commented: 'Why not? I've got enough Jewish children and grandchildren.'"

What does the Talmud say? "Money will purify bastards." But the real point is that these are the values of the state in the hands of its secular Hellenists. Money and power far outweigh the Jewish values that their forefathers clung to and were convinced would be those of the new-born state, too. And the message is sent loudly and clearly to the youth: You too can be wealthy and married to a beautiful gentile and honored by famous people if you leave Israel and make it in the golden land of Uncle Sam. The destruction of Judaism, or Jewishness and of Zionism by the leaders of Israel. But the real danger is, of course, Kahanism.

The cancer of intermarriage and assimilation rages through the country. It is not only Arabs. It is soldiers of the United Nations and Portuguese laborers working on the Negev airfields and volunteers who come to work in the kibbutzim. Consider:

The Amar family in Nahariya was composed of a two pretty daughters and a youthful, divorced mother. Then one of the daughters met a Finnish member of UNIFIL (United Nations Forces in Lebanon), and "fell in love." Not many weeks later, the second daughter met a *bon vivant* French member of UNIFIL and love won again. One day, the Frenchman brought a friend of his, also a U.N. soldier, along to the home and soon the friend had won the mother. Three "happy" Jewesses, married to U.N. gentiles, one living in Finland and two in France.

Thus, another phase of the frightening growth of intermarriage and assimilation in the State that lost its Jewish way. There have been at least a hundred weddings between Jewesses and U.N. gentiles, the vast majority of them *not* involving conversion to Judaism, the Israeli girls not seeing much need for it. Many other hundreds live with U.N. soldiers, without a marriage contract, and many other hundreds satisfy the U.N. needs as prostitutes or occasional dates. In the words of a U.N. Scandinavian soldier: "After two difficult weeks in Lebanon, you seek a little warmth, quiet and love. In a word, you want a girl." Since the Arabs in Lebanon would kill any Arab girl who would dare have sex with a stranger, it remains for liberal Israel to show the way to hospitality and *hachnasat orchim* (the taking in of guests).

There are some 6,000 U.N. personnel today in Lebanon with another 1,500 or so serving as observers in the Golan. Most of the civilians and many of the officers have rented apartments in Israel—in Jerusalem, Safed, Tiberias and Nahariya. The regular soldiers get a long weekend off (Thursday to Sunday) every two weeks. That is when they all hunt for Jewish girls. The hunt is not difficult since the prey is more than willing.

There are several meeting places that have become permanent rendezvous over the years. The information about the Jewish girls, places and prices for favors is passed on from unit to unit and the "fame" of Israeli Jewesses has spread so that even U.N. people stationed in Cyprus prefer to spend their vacations in Tel Aviv where the sex and girls are "easier."

The disgrace and *hillul Hashem* (desecration of the Name) that is the result of modern Zionism's Jewish bankruptcy is nowhere seen more clearly than in an interview in the newspaper *Ha'aretz* (April 30, 1981) with two colored soldiers from Barbados. Eddie and Steve live with a third male in a rented apartment in Nahariya. They told the reporter from *Ha'aretz*:

"In our country girls are not as free as in Israel. Precisely this is what we like. At first we were astounded. We were not used to a girl chasing a boy or a girl willing to go to bed with a man that she only met two or three hours earlier. We were not familiar with that kind of lifestyle. But we got used to it. The fact is that we continue to serve in the region [the two renewed their contract with the U.N.]. We get good money and have the good life—what can be bad!"

Such is the state of disgrace to Jewishness and Judaism in the State of Israel. What kinds of girls are so eager to bed and hopefully wed U.N. gentiles? For the most part they are young Sephardic girls from poor families. They see in the U.N. soldiers an opportunity to leave their house and even country and begin a new life in what they visualize as an exciting foreign land. Others simply hope to temporarily escape boredom by having a fling with a foreigner. Both are classic examples of the product of the modern secular Zionist movement that created a bankrupt state in terms of Jewish values. The divestment of Judaism from Zionism led, of course, to the divestment, in turn, of nationalism, and what is left is a crass materialism and an "Israeliness" which has no different coloring than "Swedishness" or "Barbadianess."

Denise Ben-Haim is a young girl from Kiryat Haim near Haifa. She met her U.N. lover, a colored soldier, in the "Club 120" in Haifa. They soon began to live together in a rented apartment in Nahariya. For three years Denise and the U.N. civilian worker shared the apartment, he paying for all expenses. She readily admits that she wanted to marry her lover and did not care about her parents' objections to her living with a non-Jew or the glances she would get from some people in the streets.

"The main thing is that he was good to me. I wanted very much to marry him. I am not a child. I am already 29. He was sweet to me and spoiled me. I was treated like a queen. We had a common language that I never found in my home. My father is sick and my mother suffered in her life. The problem was that he did not want to get married. He said he wanted to wait till he was 30. (He was 26 at the time.) I couldn't wait. We separated. I admit that I am very sad."

Yes, but not half as sad as Jews who weep over the destruction of Jewish values in the state destroyed by secular Hellenism.

There are, of course, those Israeli women who do regret it. Not for reasons of sudden Jewish consciousness, but rather for personal disappointment. There are at least 40 Israeli women who married U.N. gentiles eagerly and have since been divorced. Not a few have children. It turns out that the exotic and blissful weekend rendezvous is very different from the ordinary, unexciting wedding years.

Ma'ariv (July 7, 1986) writes: "Tens of Israeli women who travelled to Finland over the past few years in the wake of Finnish soldiers of UNIFIL, have been left stranded there. Some were deserted before the promised marriage and others after finding out Finnish society is not overjoyed at absorbing the foreigners into its midst." The wandering Jew. The wandering Jewess. Losing the anchor of Judaism, they drifted out into the terrible sea of tragedy. Will this convince other Israeli Jewish women to remain true to their people and land? Hardly.

The source of the evil is the curse of secular materialism that has captured the minds and very souls of the Israelis. Says one girl: "After all, how much can a secretary earn? Or a clerk? These days it is hard to get along on a regular salary. The girls are happy to be able to pick up a few liras extra. No one ever connects it to prostitution." But of course, that is what it is. And more. It is the reality of the gentilized Israel that was once supposed to be a Jewish State.

But, clearly, it is the assimilation with the Arabs that is the worst of the tragedy and the most dangerous. Again, it is, sadly, the Sephardic women, who never knew what assimilation and intermarriage meant when they were in the Exile, who are the greatest victims of the criminal Hellenism of Israel that deliberately destroyed their Judaism and, eventually, themselves as Jews. Etty Davidov is the classic case of the weeping for generations of the State of Israel:

The Davidov family is a pious, observant one, the father a learned man. They live in Jaffa, a city that, thanks to the insanity of the government, is rapidly becoming an Arab city again (as it was until 1948). Thousands of Arabs mix with Jews and they look for Jewish women. It is not difficult to find them. The Arabs do not serve in the army, hence make money while Jews of that age are away for three years. They work for less and do not pay taxes and the money in their pocket is more than sufficient to entice a young Jewish girl of 16. Etty Davidov was 16 when she ran away with Yichya Harub, 21, an Arab who lived near her. For three years she had dated him, telling her parents that he was a Jew named Yoram. The parents, like so many other Sephardic Jews who had come to Israel, were too often lost in the new country, not understanding the pitfalls and dangers of the land they had eagerly come to, thinking it was a Jewish State. Certainly, that is why they made the incredible mistake of allowing a daughter from a religious home to study at the Tichon Chadash, the leftist-oriented, secular high school for the progressive Hellenists of Tel Aviv.

For three years Etty dated an Arab, as did a whole group of her Jewish girl friends. On New Year's Eve 1986, she and two other friends went out with three Arabs. They stayed out all night. The next day she ran away with her lover and was gone for nearly a month. When the police found her she told her parents: "I love him and will not return to the house." For this her parents left Morocco.

The destruction of the Jew. Jewish holiness and morality. The defiling of the Jew after twenty centuries of sanctity. The weekly Beersheba magazine *Sheva* carries a story about two teenage girls who regularly work as prostitutes for Arabs in Gaza, Jaffa and Beersheba. *Yediot Aharonot* (January 8, 1986) tells of the 12-year-old girl from Ashdod who served as a prostitute for Arabs from Gaza. The Jewish woman who was praised throughout the ages as the woman of virtue comes home to the Holy Land to become the lady of the night. Shall we not weep for the spiritual holocaust of Israel?

Or shall we shake our heads in disbelief at the insanity of a Jewish state that long ago lost its way?

In 1980, a Jewish woman, 23, appeared before the Moslem court in Nazareth, declared that she loved her Muslim boyfriend and wished to convert to Islam in order to marry him. The Moslem court converted her and they were married. Two children were quickly born to them and then their relations soured. The husband beat her, a common occurrence, as the Jewish woman found out too late, and she fled with her year-old daughter to a home for battered women. At the same time she announced that she wished to return to Judaism and asked for custody of both children as well as child support from the husband.

The State of Israel, the Jewish State, in defiance of Jewish law which does not recognize the right of a Jew to change his religion—once a Jew always so—*does* recognize conversion from Judaism and ruled that the religious court of the "conversion" has jurisdiction. The Moslem court held that a "Moslem" (the Jewish woman who converted to Islam) who leaves the faith (of Islam) testifies that she is not reliable and thus it is impossible to give that person his or her child. And so, in the Jewish state, the Jewish children of the Jewish mother were taken from her and given to the Moslem father to raise as Moslems (December 31, 1984).

The Moslem courts will also thumb their nose at the Ministry of the Interior. Thus, in the case of a young woman, daughter of a Moslem from Nazareth and an American Jewish mother, the Ministry of the Interior registered her as Jewish under Jewish law that sees the child following the mother's religion. The Moslem *kadi* (minister) of Nazareth, however, ruled that the woman was Moslem (under Moslem law that follows the father) and the *kadi* angrily ordered the Ministry of the Interior to change the recording since the woman was under Moslem jurisdiction and the Koran ruling. The Koran ruling did, indeed, decide the case of a Jewish woman in the Jewish State.

And as the Arabs grow in numbers and spread throughout the cities of Israel, the curse will become a veritable plague. This is a letter sent by a group of Jewish residents of the northern, mixed city of Acre (which had just 1,000 Arabs remaining in it in 1949):

"We are a group of *baalei tshuva* (returners to religion) who live in Acre.... The city of Acre has some 45,000 residents of whom 18,000 are gentiles [Arabs]. It is a city whose major problem is the large and daily growth of non-Jews in alarming numbers since they have large amounts of money available to them which they use to purchase every apartment and building that empties—even in the luxury sections of the city. They penetrate with no problem and especially since the flow into the city comes from all the Arab villages in the area.

"The situation is so serious and painful that one neighborhood [Kiryat Wolfson], which until two or three years ago was populated by Jews, is today almost 50 percent non-Jewish. This [Jewish] population is made up of families with many children that live door to door with the Arabs and are subject to continual influence since their children play together and they are good friends.

"Therefore, on the Sabbath, instead of going to synagogue, they prefer to go to the beach or the football game with their gentile friends and, of course, want to study with them in the same school, which will surely not be a religious one....

"Elementary and high schools are mixed and Jewish boys and girls study in the same class with Arabs with whom they spend most of their time in school and in the afternoon in the neighborhood clubs, as well as hiking together. Is this the way of Jewish girls?

"Even worse is the flight of young Jews from Acre, and, especially, the best ones. When you go out on a *tefillin* campaign you do not know if you are dealing with a Jew or gentile since every third person who passes is an Arab....

"The most serious thing is the problem of assimilation in the city and by this we refer to intermarriage. Every day we hear of intermarriage of Jews and gentiles. Not long ago, a Jewish girl wanted to marry an Arab but for various reasons they did not allow her and refused to convert him. She therefore married him in a Moslem ceremony and they now live together with her holding a Moslem identity card ...

"If the situation does not improve soon, the flight, especially of the good youth, will grow and even we—of good will—will not be able to continue and will be forced to leave.... For an ordered life according to Torah and *halacha* is very difficult in this city, and the raising of a family with children alongside the gentiles and their children is simply not possible...."

And in the face of this spiritual holocaust that will surely become much much worse as the young gentilized sabras, sans Judaism of any kind, grow up, the Minister of Education of Israel, Yitzhak Navon, obsessively (and I do not use this lightly in regard to the man or his program) plans, directs, pushes a program of *mifgashim* (meetings) between Jewish and Arab children whose purpose is to break down even further the barriers, and direct Jewish and Arab children into social contact that will bring the tragedy of America and western Europe to the Jewish state.

What would the reaction of the Jewish community of Los Angeles be to news that their Federation had planned and was implementing programs to integrate Jews and non-Jews in schools and in various aspects of their social life? What would the reaction be to learn that the Jewish leadership was planning programs and allocating funds for the following:

The setting up of purposeful mixed Jewish-gentile summer camps in order that young Jews get to learn and mix with non- Jews in order to break down barriers?

School programs in the Jews schools to visit non-Jewish com munities, live with non-Jewish families for three to four days and, later, invite non-Jewish youth to visit and live with the Jewish families?

A program to begin to integrate Jewish schools by mixing non-Jewish children in the classes.

In the wake of a disastrous cancer of intermarriage and assimi lation that sees young Jews breaking off from the Jewish people by the hundreds of thousands, can one imagine what the outcry would be if such a program were announced and funded by the Federation and UJA in Los Angeles or Boston or Kansas City? Surely it would top the record for outrageous explosion on the Jewish Richter scale.

But it is happening. Not in Los Angeles or Boston or Kansas City. The abomination of planned assimilation and breaking down of Jewish barriers to spiritual destruction is taking place at this moment in the State of Israel, a state that never was a *Jewish* State, but at least presumed to be a State of Jews. The Ministry of Education, with Jewish funds (some through the auspices of the UJA) has embarked on a mass, mad mission of the spiritual destruction of Jewish youth.

The truth is that it was not Navon who began the insane march toward spiritual genocide in Israel. He has merely escalated it into a mad race.

I have before me a directive from the Ministry of Education from June 1, 1982. Under paragraph 342, headed "Meetings of Jewish-Arab students," we read:

"a) The Ministry of Education and Culture encourages meetings of Jewish and Arab students, the purpose of which is to aid in mutual recognition and lessening of unfamiliarity. The Ministry sees in them an important part of social education for all ages, especially teenagers.

"b) It is important that there not be only a single meeting, but a number of reciprocal ones and joint activities in order to insure the attainment of the goals."

The Ministry of Education has even appointed a "coordinator of meetings," whose office is in the Department of Arab Education and Culture, Paran Street, Ramat Eshkol, Jerusalem. From this office comes the tragedy, the Hellenism, the assimilation, the gentilization, the destruction of Jewish children as they are passed through the fires of the Molech.

And I have before me a booklet, printed by the Ministry of Education in Israel, and dated Tishrei, 5741 (when the presumably religious Zvulon Hammer of the NRP-Mizrachi party was minister). It is titled "We and Our Neighbors" and is described on the cover as "A handbook for the teacher and class discussion and activities on the subject." The subject is, of course, the best way to break down the exclusiveness, the difference and separation of the Jew. The best way to destroy the Jewish child is not through the chimneys of Auschwitz but through the fires of the Molech. And this sickness of secular Zionism that is incredibly abetted by the practitioners of Jewish ritual who hide their Hellenism beneath their *yarmulkes*, is summed up at the end of the first article (p. 12): "We must build social relations between the peoples in Israel, tighten personal contacts, smash barriers and puncture intolerant views." And, indeed, the booklet presents various concrete ways to do just that and destroy the medieval "intolerance" that lies in the very existence of a separate Jewish people.

Thus, the principal of the Bachar school in Even Yehuda and the Arab principal of the Bir-al-Sikka school in the village of Yamma describe joint excursions and visits of Jewish and Arab students to each others' home. In the words of the Jewish principal: "The seeds of friendship between the students from both sides began to sprout." Indeed. And there is no telling what kind of noxious needs we will yet harvest.

In Jerusalem, children from the predominantly Sephardic and traditional families of Talpiot were taken on a joint exclusion with the Arabs of Beit Tzefafa. The "intellectual" describing the experience (which she, of course, delighted in) admits that some parents feared that "it could be dangerous; it could lead to romances between the children," a thing that only leads me to nominate those parents to take over the school.... The results are described ecstatically by the article: "In a class discussion (after the trip), the children registered their surprise at the discovery that 'the Arabs are just like us,' and all wanted more meetings."

And in an article on the "summer camp at Herzliya Beach" we are told of a joint "religious" ceremony in which a Jewish youngster describes the rituals of Sabbath (which he will never practice) and an Arab youth tells about the fast of Ramadan, which he does and will.

And when the author of the article, Zion Haham, describes the visit by the Jewish children of Herzliya to the Arab villages of Taibe and Baka, he writes: "Each Arab child took a Jewish child and ran with him to his home to present him to his parents. The hospitality was total and touched the heart." And so, the Ministry of Education finances and sponsors all these abominations that will lead, not to "peace," but to Jewish women marrying Arabs. Jewish women sleeping with Arabs. Jewish prostitutes working for Arabs. And, of course, a total breakdown in everything that is meaningful in Jewishness and Judaism. The ultimate irony: that the confused babbling secular Zionists will never be able to explain to their children why they should be Zionists or Jews, rather than "human beings." Why it is necessary to have a Jewish State rather than a "democratic secular Palestine" in which there is no difference between Arabs and Jews. More, what will the young Israeli soldier, taught to fight the Arab enemy, say after he has met Ahmed and Mustafa and, in his shallow naiveté, thought to himself: They are good Arabs; why am I learning to fight them?

I spent an hour in the Negev town of Sderot last month, attempting to make the principal Jewish. His school had just sent some 20 Sephardic children, all from traditional homes, to spend four days in the Arab village of Taibe. Now, a reciprocal visit was being planned. The principal, a decent sort of a Hellenist, a product of secular Zionist gentilization, simply could not comprehend a thing I said. We seemed from two different worlds, and, indeed, we are. And this is the real struggle in Israel today. The battle between the Jews and the Hellenists, the struggle over the Jewish souls of our children.

The worst of it is the mocking hostility of the gentilized Hebrew. In the almost totally Sephardic town of Beit Sh'an in the Jordan Valley, where all the families were once religious, the secular schools began a program of meetings between Arab and Jewish students. The Sephardic Chief Rabbi Eliyahu Cohen, pleaded with the principal of the ORT school to put a stop to them. "Parents told me that children ate Arab food in their villages," he said, "and I was horrified. There is a halachic [legal] ruling of the Chief Rabbis of Israel forbidding the parents to send their children to schools that hold such meetings." The principal told the chief rabbi that this was a directive from the Ministry of Education within the context of "education to democracy."

Rabbi Cohen, to his eternal credit, took it upon himself to wage a personal war against the meetings. He called tens of parents and told them that if they did not put a stop to the meetings "there will be mixed couples, Rachel and Mustafa." He forbade sending children to the secular schools. Proof that he was doing something successful came from the Director General of the Ministry of Education, Eliezar Shmueli, a man who has been in the forefront of the battle to topple the barriers between Jews and Arabs that, alone, have saved Jews from assimilation and intermarriage. He bitterly attacked the rabbi, saying: "There is no precedent for the rabbi's politics that polarize secular and religious!" The newspaper *Hadashot*, one of the bitterest enemies of religion in Israel, carried a mocking headline that read:

HEAVEN FORBID! JEWISH CHILDREN IN AN ARAB VILLAGE ...

I want to put an end to such things as the joint project between Kiryat Ata's Jewish youth and the Arabs of Rama village, a project sponsored by the Ministry of Education with funds given to the Reform abomination known as Interns for Peace. I want to eliminate funds for the joint Jewish-Arab "camping experience" at Meir Shfeya village, sponsored by the Reform movement with Ministry of Education funds. And I want, never again, to read another news release such as the one below:

"Jerusalem, July 27: Some 9,000 students from the Arab sector are presently participating in summer camps organized by the Youth Department of the Ministry of Education and Culture... There also are summer camps in which Jewish and Arab students spend time together."

And never, never do I want to read an article such as the one that appeared in the newspaper *Yediot Aharonot* under the heading: "Erez Sat next to Samir and Irit Next to Hasan."

The article describes a joint class of kindergarten children, Jewish and Arab, and after a lyrical description of the Messianic era, it concludes with the following reaction of two Jewish educators:

"They melted at the sight of the dancing children. 'Why, it is impossible to tell who is Jewish and who is not,' they said."

And, indeed, that is the purpose of the entire program. A program created by Hellenists wracked with doubts, complexes, guilt and self-hate, in order to eliminate the source of their guilt: The existence of a separate Jewish people.

And, surely, this is why, even as they insist on breaking down the uniqueness of Judaism and the Jewish people by opening wide the doors to assimilation and intermarriage, for the first time in Israel's history the Ministry of Education bars from the schools rabbis who lecture on Judaism and the need to return to it. The following appeared in *Yediot Aharonot* (June 2, 1986):

"For the first time in the history of the Israeli education system, the Ministry of Education is working actively against the Return to Judaism movement. The Director General, Eliezer Shmueli, has drafted a direct order according to which it is forbidden to speak about returning to Judaism, either in courses of Judaism or within any other framework.

"The decision was taken by the Ministry after lengthy discussions in the Knesset Committee on Education, following many complaints from parents and teachers against rabbis urging a return to Judaism in secular schools....

"From now on, rabbis will have to be careful in what they say. Should they attempt to urge a return to Judaism in secular schools they will be forced to leave the school."

What can one possibly say to the madness? The Ministry of Education looks about, sees a youth devoid of all Jewishness, of all values. It sees a lost youth that has no identity and that wanders blindly and aimlessly, threatening the very existence of the State. And its solution? The banning of a call to return to Judaism in the schools. Of course the reason is obvious. The Hellenists of Israel, naked and bankrupt of any answer to their children who ask why they should be Zionists, why be *Jewish*, know that the only ones that have the answer are their bitter enemies, the religious. Far better in their eyes that the State itself go under than that it become religious and Jewish in the way of their forefathers.

And that is why the mayor of Givatayim, the very same one who cried out, concerning the Kach people, "Kill them while they are still small," and a man who comes as close to being a Jewish anti-Semite as is imaginable, barred the pasting of posters on city billboards by a religious group that holds regular sessions in Givatayim for young Jews seeking their roots. Despite the fact that every group has the right, on paying, to have its posters pasted up, the religious group was told that "there is no room." Hardly a bunch of fools, the religious Jews sent a young woman with posters advertising a yoga group to the municipality. Naturally, the posters were accepted and pasted up. When the head of the religious council protested to Mayor Yitzhak Yaron, the gentilized mayor of Givatayim, wrote a letter that said, in part:

"These lecturers are nothing but missionaries [sic] who wish to confuse boys and girls and topple them into the net of 'returning to Judaism'.... We will do our best to capture the insect, the poisoner of the wells, and drive him beyond our borders." The language is almost incredible. The man is sick, sick with hate; and, of course, it begins with a self-hate so massive that he is totally capable of any act that will destroy those whom he hates.

In the Knesset, when I raised a proposal to cut off funding to all Ministry of Education projects for mixing Jews and Arabs, I turned to the Minister of Education, the Sephardic turned Hellenist, and said: "You, a member of an Iraqi Jewish community that for 2500 years nurtured the flame of Judaism—how can you take part in the destruction of Judaism? If your grandfather were here, what would he say to you?"

Instead of thinking and contemplating, he turned white. Instead of turning his scarlet sins into deeds, he turned pale, in guilt and anger and hate. He moved, in one sentence, without bothering to answer any of my allegations and proofs, to remove the proposal from the agenda. Navon, of whom King Solomon, the truly wise, said: "As a dog returneth to his vomit, a fool returneth to his folly."

I came across an item from the Jewish Telegraphic Agency which stated:

"An overwhelming majority of parents ... indicated that a central reason for sending their children to Jewish Community Center-sponsored camps across the United States and Canada is to 'strengthen their Jewish identity.'"

The official reason given by the Hellenists at the Israeli Ministry of Education for mixed camps in Israel is the fight against "racism and for democracy." I suggest to the American Jewish parents who seek Jewish camps for their children and Jewish identity to ponder their racism and anti-democratic tendencies.

On February 5, 1985, the President of the Council of Jewish Federations, Shoshana Cardin, declared: "Jewish identity and continuity is a world wide concern now." And former CJF president, Morton Mandel, wailed: "Jews are not maintaining affiliation and identification."

What are we to make of this racist and anti-democratic nonsense!

We have come full circle. The Jews of the Exile are fighting to stay Jewish, even as the State of Israel's Hellenists struggle to become like all the other nations. We are not a normal people. The Jew of Israel wish to *kechol hagoyim* (as all the nations). Those in the Exile struggle to remain *bechol hagoyim* (in the midst of all the nations).

Again. In ancient times the peoples of Canaan would pass their children through fire to appease the god Molech:

"And they built the high places of Baal in the valley of Benhimmon, in order to sacrifice their sons and daughters unto the Molech...."

The question, as we see the purposeful destruction of young Jewish children in Israel, is:

Who can save us from ourselves? And who can save our children from us, we who would pass them between the twin fires of Molech:

those of the Auschwitzes of the Exile and those of the Ministry of Education of the state of gentilized Hebrews?

Yes, we reap the sterile seeds of secular Zionism, a dream of Jewish gentiles who sought to cut away Judaism from Jewish nationalism and who thus guaranteed the death of the latter. Secular Zionism is bankrupt; see its epitaph on the streets of Dizengoff, in Hebrew Christians, in Jewish women with Arab men, in the Jews fleeing the Jewish State for the golden one of California. On the day that Judaism was separated from Zionism, the latter became one more form of vapid, empty, meaningless, ugly, secular nationalism. It died the day it was born. See the reality.

Chapter 12

Father's Grapes and Children's Teeth

At the bottom of it all festers the ultimate question that painfully crushes the ultimate layer of Jewish soul tissue, that becomes the ultimate of Jewish nightmares buried just beneath Jewish consciousness. It is the ever-clanging bell that pounds the Jewish head and creates an army of pounding frightened Jewish hearts.

It is the questions of questions that, if left unanswered, does away with any reason for Zionism, for a Jewish State, *for a Jewish people.* And it is the question for which the secular Jew of Hellenism indeed has no answer, and, therefore, his child—more honest by far than he—indeed sees no need for Zionism, or for a Jewish State, or *for a Jewish people.* Is it surprising that the poor Jewish leader, intellectual, neo-rabbi, crumbles before our very eyes, lashes out in animal fury at those who raise it, even as he and the Jewish state and the Jewish community themselves writhe in agony of soul?

Such a simple question that in its non-complexity it creates so many Jewish complexes. The hauntingly simple question that has led to the spiritual disappearance of more young Jews than ever perished in Hitler's death camps. The siren song-question that beckons to young Jews and Israelis, swallowing them up in the misty, befogged grave of assimilation and national destruction. The Jewish Question of our times which in its awesomely brutal honesty attacks the very intellectual and logical underpinnings of Zionism, Israel, Judaism, the Jewish people.

The One question that displaces and replaces the classic four at the Passover Seder table. The One question that becomes a perpetual mini-Seder every night and day of the Jewish year. How few young Jews still ask the original four questions and how many *do* ask the one: *Why be Jewish at all?*

Secular fathers of the nation, let me ask you the one question: Why must this Jewish people be different from all others? Why must this Jewish people *be*? Why must this *particular* Jew insist on remaining a member of a tribalistic, particularistic, separate, isolationist people rather than a universalist human being with no barriers to intermarriage and assimilation? Why in all other people is there no bar to marrying a pretty, intelligent, decent young woman, leavened or unleavened, Jewish or non-Jewish, and in this family the insistence on only unleavened—Jewish? Why in all other families is there an effort to break down primitive, atavistic trends to isolation and particularism, with a call for dipping into all cultures and religions and nationalities, while in this family we dip only once—into narrow Jewishness? Why must we, in Israel, live in a continuous state of war because of our insistence on living in a perpetual state of *"Jewishness"*? Why must we be "Zionists" and insist on a Zionist, Jewish State when it is this that leads to a never-ending war with Arabs? Why can we not have a democratic secular Israel-Palestine? Why do all democratic nations eat all kinds of greens while we insist on eating only bitter herbs of Zionist-Jewishness? In short, tell me, O fathers of the nation: Why be Jewish?

Poor child. Confused, lost, bewildered. Poor fathers. Confused, lost, bewildered. Poor Jews. Confused, lost, bewildered. For here is the ultimate racism: A stubborn, irrational insistence on being "Jewish," without the slightest logical, morally ethical reason to be so. A Jewishness and a Jewish State built on nothing more logical than a peculiar special status built on an obsession with being "different." Truly the ultimate in racism.

The secular Jew of both Israel and the Exile is not Jewish for any logical, non-tribalistic reason. He could not in a millennium explain rationally why he persists in being a JEW, thus different from the rest of the world. The secular Jew in both Israel and the Exile is Jewish for only one of two most irrational, emotional reasons, a syndrome I have called *"cholent* and *goyim."*

Cholent is the traditional Jewish Sabbath food, meat and beans that cook all night and morning on the fire (since one is not allowed to light a fire on the Sabbath itself). I use it to symbolize the "nostalgia" or "stomach culture" of the Jew for that Orthodox family (parent or grandparent) and the customs, way of life and traditions that he remembers fondly and emotionally, even after having jettisoned them. He, the Jew of the present, clings to a Jewishness that is based on his fond memories of *others* observing real Jewishness. He builds his links on the Passover Seder he remembers, the Sabbath candles he remembers, the Jewish prayers and lessons he once learned as a child. Judaism? Hardly. Call it rather the *nostalgia* of Judaism—"cholent."

On the other hand his "Jewishness" arises so often, not because of anything positive that he learned in Judaism, if he ever, indeed, learned anything about Judaism. His Jewishness is so often imprinted upon him by the *goyim*, the gentiles who do not allow him to forget he is a Jew no matter how he might like to. Indeed, anti-Semitism has always been the greatest guarantor of "Jewishness," forcing the Jew to acknowledge who he is, whether he really wished to or not.

Cholent and *goyim*; both went into the making of Zionism. The fathers of political Zionism, who threw away authentic Judaism, remained Jewish only because of the dual influence of *cholent* and *goyim*. On the one hand was the reality of brutal anti-Semitism in East and Central Europe. The Czar was the greatest proof in the minds of the Jews of 1880 and 1980 that there must be a Jewish State and that the Jew would never be accepted as anything but that. And *cholent*. No matter how he tried, no matter how much he professed his opposition and enmity to religion, the early Zionist could never really escape the bondage of *cholent*, nostalgia. It was Judaism, the *cheder*, the little Jewish school in which he studied as a child in the Russian or Polish shtetl-village that made him Jewish and Zionist. It was his religious father and mother and grandparents and memories of the home and holidays that really created the secular Zionist. He could never escape them, no matter how he tried. Political Zionism arose—with all its secularism and dropping of Judaism—only because of *cholent* and *goyim*.

But these two intensely emotional factors could never be roots of permanence. If this is the entire reason for Zionism and a Jewish State, then only those who ever felt them could continue to be impressed by them. One certainly cannot pass on an emotion to one who has never felt it. And thus the secular Zionist founding generations whose "Jewishness" and "Zionism" were built only on these emotional reasons could never hope to pass them on to their children or grandchildren who never lived or felt them. And that is indeed why secular Zionism began to die the moment it was born. The reason for its success lay in the very temporary, specific circumstances of the era of its creation. The moment it succeeded in creating a Jewish State and thus, automatically, grandchildren who never knew the *goyim* of the Czar or anti-Semitism of any kind and who—raised in the irreligious, utterly non-Jewish homes of their parents who had neither *cholent* nor candles nor any Jewish nostalgia—it could never hope to continue to pass on a flame that was never fire but merely a pot that had once sat on the flame of Judaism. Once having been removed, it grew colder with every passing hour. The young sabra of Israel, knowing neither *goyim* nor *cholent*, is left with not the slightest emotional reason to be a Jew. And having been ripped by his parents from Judaism, he has not the slightest *logical* reason to be one. And when all this apathetic and indifferent attitude towards Judaism and Jewishness is compounded by the reality of a state that offers only a constant threat of war, annual army service, heavy taxes, and depression of soul, is it any wonder that the young Jewish Israeli—rootless and spiritless, as gentile as any gentile—dreams of living elsewhere? That he is as un-Jewish as one could possibly be, that he turns his back on all the valueless values of the founding fathers of Zionism and the "Jewish" State? For when one considers it, it is precisely the founding fathers of modern Zionism who created this monster.

Modern or political secular Zionism arose, not only in order to bring the Jews out of the physical dangers of the Exile, but, in the hands of so many of its ideologists, to create a new and totally different Jew, a Jew who would no longer be tied to the laws and rules and regulations of religion.

For nearly two millennia, the Jewish people were clearly identified as a religio-nation. When one spoke of a Jew one automatically thought of Judaism. A gentile who wished to "become Jewish" certainly did not do the same as anyone wishing to become English or French or German. One who sought to join the Jewish people had to join the Jewish *religion*. That was what Judaism was—a religio-nation. And for nearly 2,000 years, Jews were not only followers of religion, but were *religious* observers of Jewish laws and of Jewish concepts. The Jew walked with his G-d, bowed his head beneath the yoke of his G-d, saw his personal destiny and that of the entire Jewish people as linked to G-d. There was no such concept as "secular" in the mind of the Jew. There was no such thing as a "nationalism" that stood by itself. If the Jews were a nation, a people, that was only because of Torah, of Judaism.

And all that changed with the rise of modern political Zionism.

Political Zionism arose to make the Jew "normal," like the other people of the earth. It arose to create a "new" Jew, a new Jewish people instead of the one that the secular Zionists so deeply despised (and, in the end, this self-hatred of the secular Zionist would carry over into the state he created). The first of the truly influential modern secular Zionists, Leo Pinsker, wrote of making the Jews a nation "like all the other nations, a people with a common language, common customs and common land." That was the main thing, and because of it, Pinsker was prepared to suggest that Jews *not* think about going back to their Holy Land.

"If we would have a secure home, so that we may give up our endless life of wandering and rehabilitate our nation in our own eyes and in the eyes of the world, we must, above all, not dream of restoring ancient Judea. We must not attach ourselves to the place where our political life was once violently interrupted and destroyed. The goal of our present endeavors must not be the 'Holy Land' but a land of our own ... from which no foreign master can expel us."

And the father of political Zionism, Theodore Herzl—his Zionism hardly arose out of any positive Jewish feelings, but rather through the shock of a Dreyfus trial in which he saw civilized, liberal France rage with anti-Jewish passions. The great irony is that the father of modern Zionism was turned into an active Jew not by the Jew, but by the Jew-hater, not through Judaism but through the gentile. The *goyim* syndrome. Little wonder that his dream of a state as outlined in his last book, *Altneuland* (*Old-New Land*), reflected all the liberal views of his Vienna transmitted to a State of Jews, but surely there was nothing in it that suggested a *Jewish* State. In the gentilized Jew that was Herzl, the entire concept of a Jewish nation based on Judaism, that nation that existed from time immemorial and was the idea that alone kept Herzl's ancestors Jewish so that he could suddenly begin to dabble in it, went out the window. In his description of his idylic Old-New Land, he wrote: "Matters of faith were once and for all excluded from public influence. Whether anyone sought religious devotion in the synagogue, in the church, in the mosque, in the art museum or in a philharmonic concert, did not concern society. That was his private affair."

Not even Hebrew would be the official language of the "Jewish" State. In his major work, *The Jewish State*, Herzl wrote: "We cannot converse with one another in Hebrew. Who amongst us has a sufficient acquaintance with Hebrew to ask for a railroad ticket in that language? Such a thing cannot be done. But the difficulty is very easily circumvented. Every man can preserve the language in which his thoughts are most comfortable. Switzerland affords conclusive proof of the possibility of a federation of tongues."

This was the founder of political Zionism. A man who rejected the Hebrew faith, the Hebrew language, who was even prepared to accept Uganda (!) as a Jewish State and whose dream of that "Jewish" State turned out to be a gentilized, liberal kind of wiener schnitzel of the blue Jordan-Danube. Here, at the very outset of the new Zionism was the declaration of war on Judaism and upon a Jewish people that was a religio-nation, rooted in Sinai.

Gershon Shocken, editor of the Israeli paper *Ha'aretz*, and a secular Zionist whose obsession with fighting Judaism is pathological, delivered a paper in 1984 to a seminar on the subject of "Judaism's attitude toward the foreigner." He put most clearly the reality of modern secular Zionism and what its adherents seek today in the State of Israel:

"Zionism in Eastern Europe was, perhaps first and foremost, a rebellion against the Jewish religion. They wanted to uproot it so that there would be no trace of it in the new Jewish society they wished to create....

"If we wish to create and develop our state as a modern one... we must create a situation in which the religious circles tend to their affairs in their homes, their synagogues and *yeshivot* (religious schools), but will not influence the life of the state and society beyond those boundaries."

Shocken's claim that Zionism arose as a rebellion against Judaism is not an exaggeration. It is seen in its utmost clarity in the writings of the early Zionist thinkers and poets.

Thus, one of the most famous modern Hebrew poets, Saul Tchernichowsky, celebrated paganism and the pagan Hebrews who, in his eyes, were virile and magnificent, in contrast to the pallid Jewish scholars of Eastern Europe. To the ancient Canaanite gods of the Hebrews, Tchernichowsky paid homage through poems such as "Before the Statue of Apollo," and thus did this Jew, son of Monotheism, speak to the Greek god:

I bow before thee, life's strength and beauty,
Bow before youth which like a whirlwind
Frights and chases away those withered, dried-up people
Who have tried to take my god's life
And who fetter with their [tefillin] prayer straps
E-l Sha-dai, the lord of the deserts,
Who led Canaan's daring conquerors.

And Micha Joseph Berdichevski, who glorified Nietzsche and his ecstatic affirmation of primitive nature, who borrowed the German's concept of "transvaluation of all values." Berdichevski declared war on Judaism and on the "Jews" which it produced: "We have come to a time of two worlds in conflict: To be or not to be! To be the last Jews or the first Hebrews.

"It is not reforms but transvaluations that we need—fundamental transvaluations in the whole course of our life, in our thoughts, in our very souls. Jewish scholarship and religion are not the basic values—every man may be as much or as little devoted to them as he wishes. But the people of Israel come before them. Israel precedes the Torah.

"We are the last Jews—or the first of a new nation."

Jews throughout the world were shocked in the spring of 1986 when a synagogue in Tel Aviv was burned and a religious school attacked, the vandals tearing up hundreds of religious books. The cries of shock were unanimous in centering around the theme: How can this be? How have we reached such a level of self-hate and hatred of our own religion?

As usual, Jews forget. In a long letter (May 6, 1903) to Theodore Herzl, Chaim Weizmann, one of the *gurus* of modern Zionism, President of the World Zionist Organization and first President of the State of Israel, wrote: "Children are in open revolt against their parents. The elders are confined within tradition and Orthodox inflexibility. The young make their first step a search for freedom from everything Jewish. In one small town near Pinsk, youngsters tore the Torah scroll to shreds. This speaks volumes."

He then added his own warning against any effort to attract religious Jews into the modern Zionist camp: "This will lead straight to catastrophe. If there is anything in Judaism that has become intolerable and incomprehensible to the best of Jewish youth, it is the pressure to equate its essence with the religious formalism of the Orthodox." Jewish youth, he added, could be saved through Zionism and a return to Jewish culture, "but the latter should no longer be confused with Jewish religious worship."

Political Zionism, that which created the State of Israel, was dominated by ideologists and politicians who wished to separate Judaism from state, and create an entire new concept of Jew. Religion, tradition, G-d, were no longer the relevant aspects of Jewish people. The new Jew, the Hebrew, would be freed of all religious restraints and would be "normal," like all the others.

And so, Nachman Syrkin, ideological father of "moderate" Socialist

Zionism, from whose teachings came men like Ben Gurion and Katzenelson, and the present Labor Party of Israel, stated in "A Manifesto of Jewish Youth":

"Zionist Socialism sees, in the applied Jewish religion, which is not a religion but a tragedy, the major impediment confronting the Jewish nation on the road to culture, science, freedom."

And Jacob Klatzkin, head of the Jewish National Fund and editor of the organ of the World Zionist Organization, *Die Welt*, declared: "Zionism began a new era, not only for the purpose of making an end to the Diaspora but also in order to establish a new definition of Jewish identity—a secular definition. . . .

"To be a Jew means the acceptance of neither a religious nor an ethical creed. . . . In short, to be part of the nation, one need not believe in the Jewish religion or the Jewish spiritual outlook." And:

"The 'spiritual' criterion is a grave danger not only to our national renaissance, but even more, to our renaissance as individuals. It binds our spirit with the chains of tradition and subordinates our life to specific doctrines, to a heritage and values of an ancient outlook. We are constrained by antiquated values and, in the name of national unity and cohesiveness, our personalities are crippled, for we are denied freedom of thought" (from the essay "Boundaries").

And the war on Judaism, so rooted in self-hate, was put most nakedly by the proletarian writer, Joseph Chaim Brenner, who wrote:

"[Previous generations] lived not on the Sanctification of the Name but on various schemes aimed at fulfilling for their own benefit the commercial functions demanded of them by the general populace; they lived to safeguard their money and increase the interest rates.

"Yes, indeed, we have survived, we live. True, but what is our life worth? We have no inheritance. Each generation gives nothing of its own to its successor. And whatever was transmitted—the rabbinical literature—was better never handed down to us.

"[E]ven our faith and our religious concepts were, for the most part, taken over, borrowed, and influenced in every way—and vulgarly so—by others, angels, demons, hocus-pocus and sorcery in the Talmud" (from *Self-Criticism*).

The self-hate that emerged from the hearts and minds of the secular Zionists was mindboggling. The Jew of the Exile was reviled, spat upon, abominated as a coward, parasite, weak, vulgar, socially flawed, non-productive, all the attributes that the Nazis would later use to describe the *Jude*. What was really happening was that the secular Zionist was giving vent to his feelings not about the Jew of the Exile but about Judaism itself. And his was a product of an awesome self-hate, a self-hate that would exist as long as Judaism did, a self-hate that ultimately lead to the tragedy of a State of Israel today, driven by hate and by a desire on the part of the secular self-haters for a civil war that will put an end to the Judaism that has become for them a thorn in their eyes and thistles in their sides.

At best, the new Zionists who rejected Judaism and G-d as a factor in Jewish national life, tolerated Judaism. Even Ahad Ha'am, the cultural Zionist leader who differed with Herzl and the other political Zionists who saw Zionism as a purely political issue, hardly thought to insist on the Jewish people cleaving to religion. His was "cultural Zionism," and the Jewish State was a means to cultural survival, a thing he defined most vaguely as the "ethical teachings of the prophets of old." Little did these foolish men whose Zionism was born only because they came from traditional home, whose ancestors had survived as Jews only because of religion and whose Jewish impulse derived only from the Jewish tradition that they rejected, realize that their children and grandchildren, totally removed from Judaism, would eventually turn their backs on *Zionism*.

Secular Zionism was Jewish gentilization. Like all the other gentile nationalist movements it perceived secularism as the progressive enlightened option of the day. In this respect there was no ultimate difference between Right or Left, so that even the non-leftist nationalist Zev Jabotinsky could write to his son (who later became an atheist, condemned Judaism in the first Knesset to which he was elected and called for a "Canaanite" nation of Hebrews instead of Jews in the country) and say; "I, myself, see no holiness in the Jewish ritual." And while he treated religion with far greater respect than the left, Jabotinsky made it clear that the kind of people and state he envisioned were simply not based on Judaism.

Even the leading *American* Zionist, Louis Brandeis, was a non-believer who conceived of Zionism as an ideal that would replace Judaism. Jewish nationalism was to Brandeis "an attractive substitute for the Jewish religion."

And so, there was an active attempt on the part of the New Zionists, particularly the socialists, to eradicate Judaism and replace it with their new ideology, often—less than honestly—taking religious themes and perverting them for their own.

Thus, Ber Borochov, radical socialist-Zionist, took the "wicked son" of the Passover Haggadah and praised him for rejecting the freedom from Egypt given by G-d. The "wicked ones" in our generation, he argued, are attaining freedom through their own efforts, and a kibbutz *Haggadah* declared, "We, the generation of free men, will celebrate our holiday without the spirit of enslavement to tradition." And one of the most popular Chanukah songs of modern day Zionism took the traditional phrase of the prayer book, "Who can retell the glories of G-d," and changed it to, "Who can retell the glories of Israel."

It was, of course, only a step from that to the kibbutz *Haggadah* that proclaimed: "Hear O Israel, Israel is our destiny, Israel is one." And the ultimate was reached in the change of the prayer for the dead, the *kaddish*, when the socialists of the kibbutzim stood at the grave and instead of the classical words, "May His Name be glorified and sanctified," could now be heard, "May the working man be glorified and sanctified."

In an article in the newspaper *Ha'aretz* (June 20, 1986), Natan Dunevitz recalls the most famous of Zionist high schools in Tel Aviv, Herzliya, "where teachers used to humiliate any student who wore a skullcap during a lesson in Bible by saying, 'Is your head cold?'" And in the very Declaration of Independence of Israel lies a phrase that reflects the refusal of the leaders of political Zionism to allow G-d to intrude on the Creation of the Jewish State. The leaders of the Zionist-Socialist parties adamantly refused to have G-d's name expressly mentioned in the Declaration, and so it was decided that an ambiguous phrase, *Tzur Yisrael* (Rock of Israel), be written, one which could mean all things to all men, women, socialist and rabbis.

Secular Zionism thus came into being as Jewish "nationalism." The religio-nation of Sinai was exchanged for the "national liberation movement of the Jewish people." G-d was irrelevant. Judaism was, at best, unimportant. And from that moment, the basic, built-in contradiction that today rips apart the State of Israel and the whole basis of modern Zionism was created.

The Israeli Minister of Absorption and Immigration, Yaakov Tzur, is a son of a kibbutz, a leftist progressive humanist whose hatred of racism is so clear-cut that when Kahane speaks in the Knesset he walks out (an action no Knesset member who is Arab or member of the Israeli Communist Party has ever yet merited). And then this progressive humanist, whose commitment to democracy and the equality of all people "made in the image of G-d" (a Being the minister may not even believe in), rises in the Knesset and makes the following deathless paean to universal values of democracy and equality:

"Today we are fighting over the will of the Jewish people to continue to be Jewish. This is the whole truth. Never was there an easier period in Jewish history *not* to be Jewish. More than 70 percent intermarry in France.... This is part of the struggle for the survival of the Jewish people."

What in the world is the minister, son of the left and the kibbutz, hater of racism and discrimination, child of democracy and equality of human beings, talking about? Warnings against intermarriage? Why, the very opposition to intermarriage is a contradiction of the progressive outlook upon all people as being equal? What greater discrimination could there be than that which attempts to prevent Jews from marrying someone merely on the grounds of being different—a gentile? "Survival of the Jewish people?" Breathes there a progressive with soul so dead who never to himself would cry out: "Reactionary! Racist! The struggle of our age is over the integration of *all* peoples and the ending of nationalistic and tribalistic barriers that divide them!"

Of course the minister is the classic babbling, confused schizophrenic, thus the perfect candidate to sit in the Israeli cabinet of split-souls.

They are all of them, naked, bankrupt, "groping in the day as a blind man at night." They cannot answer the one neo-Seder question: "Father, tell me—why be Jewish?"

And so, because they cannot answer the question of the child, they lose him. Only Judaism gives any remotely rational reason and logical excuse to be Jewish, *specifically* Jewish, distinctly and separately Jewish; and because the secularized, Hellenized, gentilized Israeli father does not believe in Judaism, he remains bereft of answers and loses his child.

Delicious. Divine irony puts into play the Iron Law of the New Jew. Those who cast off Judaism and determined that their children would be free of religion—and who, instead, worshipped at the new temple of Jewish nationalism, Zionism—watch in impotent frustration as their children now turn their backs on both Judaism *and* Zionism.

The "fathers of the nation" destroyed their own children as they smashed the temple of Moses and the altar of the rabbis, replacing them with the paganism of socialism and Marx and universalist assimilation of ideas and the culture of foreigners and gentiles. The kibbutz produced a Hebrew-speaking Hellenist who trampled Sinai in the dust even as he worshipped at the Pantheon of the *goy*. The original settler, fresh from Eastern Europe, retained a semblance of "Jewishness" because of his father who remembered the *shtetl*. The exquisiteness of Divine punishment is that *his* child sees not the slightest difference between Jew and non-Jew, not the slightest reason not to marry the Swedish or German gentile volunteer who works on the kibbutz. *His* child sees not the slightest guilt in leaving both kibbutz and country to live with gentile spouse in Europe or America. *His* child, of a secular Zionist father who rejected Judaism, exquisitely repays him by yawning in the face of Zionism.

Indeed, consider the case—the incredible case of Mordechai Bar-On, leftist Knesset member and one of the stalwarts of Peace Now.

Mordechai Bar-On was chief Education Officer for the entire Israel Defense Forces before being appointed head of the Youth and Pioneer Department of the Jewish Agency. Consider. Here is a person who was entrusted with the vitally important job of taking the overwhelming majority of Israeli youth, who serve in the army during the formative final years of the teens, and instilling in them values. Presumably these are the Jewish and Zionist values that are so vital in creating a proud Jewish youth who understands the supreme reason for being Jewish, the clear need to be different from the gentile, which alone would given him reason to insist on remaining in a country that offers heavy taxes, regular army reserve duty and constant threat of war.

In light of all this and in light of the fact that he was in charge of the Jewish Agency's Youth Department, which gives culture and education to all youth groups in the world, it is of some interest to note that Mordechai Bar-On's daughter, Tal, is married to an Arab from Nazareth, a member of the Communist Party, an open supporter of the PLO. Now, one certainly cannot always blame parents for all their children. No, it is not the fact of the intermarriage alone that brands Bar-On. It is rather his views concerning it.

Bar-On, former chief Education Officer for the Army of Israel and guider of Jewish youth for the Jewish Agency, says:

"I personally always looked upon intermarriage as a very harmful phenomenon for the Jewish people. But on the other hand, each person has to have priorities in his family circle and cannot dictate the path of happiness for another person. If two young people, after careful and serious thought, choose their own path, who am I and my wife to stand in their way? Just the opposite. My wife and I see our support of them as a higher value....

"I would describe the education that my daughters received as 'humanist.' I would add that when you meet a young Arab intellectual who speaks fluent Hebrew and who has absorbed much of our culture and is also a sensitive young man, there has already been laid the infrastructure for dialogue with him. The fact is that there does not exist between me and my son-in-law any substantive tension on 'spiritual and cultural matters.'"

Or to quote Tal, the daughter, concerning her father's attitude to her Arab husband, named Dahar:

"*Avi 'met' al Dahar* ... [My father 'dies' (Hebrew slang for 'is wild over') Dahar ...]"

This is the Educator. The educator of Jewish children. The one who declares: "I am a person with secular values. I do not believe in G-d's intervention in what occurs on earth."

Bar-On is a terribly confused man, a man whose nationalism is an illogical, hence truly racist, concept. He will stand up before Jewish youth and speak of the importance of being Jewish, and not have the slightest logical support for that outlandish, reactionary statement. He will say that intermarriage hurts the Jews and then point out the right and even "higher value" of people choosing their own personal way to happiness, even if that is intermarriage. He will calmly mix himself a drink of light and darkness, truth and falsehood, Jewishness and humanism, and down it with drunken abandon, not realizing that he is wallowing in the street of Jewish spiritual destruction. He is a sad and spiritually disturbed person who never understood truth and thus co-mingles it with falsehood, who reunites light and darkness. Until infinity he could never teach a young Jew why it is important to be Jewish, because he himself does not begin to understand. And his liberalism that cries out against racism psychologically draws its intensity from the fact that there is no greater racism than his version of the Importance of Being Jewish While Embracing the Humanism That Destroys It.

It is of passing interest to note the (sympathetic) comment by one James P. Rice, a Federation of Jewish Philanthropies functionary, concerning Bar-On. It is taken from his book, *We Are One, But I Am Many*, and reprinted in *Moment* magazine (July 1977). After telling of meeting Bar-On at a Jewish dinner (but of course), Rice writes:

"Bar-On tops me with the story of his first trip to Sde Boker to see (David) Ben Gurion [first Israeli Prime Minister]. Paula [Ben Gurion's wife] greeted him: 'You don't look Jewish.' 'I can't help it if I had a German Catholic mother!' he replied truthfully. 'It's all right,' Paula says, 'my son married a *shiksa*.'"

Rice, the American Jewish functionary who helps destroy his community, then says, concerning his Israeli counterpart: "My admiration for Bar-On increases as he talks and he'll certainly have my help in Chicago!"

One wonders whether Rice gave Bar-On his "help" when in 1984 the Israeli leftist and educator of soldiers arrived in America as part of a tour sponsored by the violently anti-Zionist American Friends Service Committee (AFSC) and the American Peace Now brand known as New Jewish Agenda (the "New" apparently applied to the name since it is most difficult to find anything that was ever *originally* Jewish about it). Along with Bar-On came a PLO "moderate," former mayor of the Judean town of Halhoul, Mohammed Milham. The moderation of Mr. Milham must surely be seen as one of the great political sleight-of-hands of all time. In a speech before the AFSC in 1979, "moderate" Mahammed issued the following moderate demands: The return of all the "occupied" land of 1969 including Jerusalem, as well as the "right" of the Arabs who fled in 1948 to return to Jaffa, Haifa, Acre, Ramle, etc. That same year the moderate told the leftist Congress of World Peace in Switzerland that "a conquest like that of Israel has not been suffered by the European peoples even under the Nazis." That year, moderate Milham and yet another bearer of peace, Hebron Mayor Fahd Kawasmeh, brazenly agitated and incited Arabs to riot. In an interview with an Arab paper Milham boasted that he was a member of the PLO National Guidance Committee formed "to recruit the masses to act against the Israeli authorities."

Then, in March, 1980, at a rally in Hebron, Milham said: "This rally will produce many forces and many deeds. The *jihad* [holy war] must go on." Five weeks later, six Jews were shot down in cold blood and murdered in Hebron. Milham and Kawasmeh were expelled from the country and the former threatened to "pursue the Israelis all over the world," saying that in Israel there were "no doves, no hawks, only pigs."

Nothing, however, bothered the Educator of the Israeli army. Bar-On travelled with Milham throughout the United States (was even given a hearing by the Jewish Establishment in San Francisco; try that with Meir Kahane), and when questioned about Milham's use of the word *jihad*, thus spake the Israeli army Educator: "There is a war-speak and a peace-speak...." He added that his "good friend Milham was known throughout Israel as one of the group of the most moderate leaders of the Palestinians on the West Bank." One can hardly wait to see the extremists.

Bar-On as a leader of Peace Now and the suicide left once again proves that the left is far more than a political group that speaks merely of boundaries and land. He and his camp represent all that is non-Jewish and Hellenistic in Jewish life.

The Educator. Now one can understand why the sabra has fallen from being Jewish to the depths of a Hebrew-speaking gentile. Now we can understand the death of Zionism in Israel, the emigration from the country, the loss of moral values. With an Educator such as Bar-On, what can we expect from the "educated"?

Nothing. And it is indeed the most "educated," the sons and daughters of the kibbutzim—the heart of Leftistland, the sons and daughters of the upper class and comfortable bourgeoisie, the enlightened and the progressive—who most reject anything Jewish and who, indeed, cast off all restraints. The use of drugs among young "progressive" Jews is staggering and the sexual anarchy and license is massive; and more than half of the children of the kibbutz leave it (a higher percentage than that of any other sector), continuing on to leave the country. Indeed, the pitifully small number of immigrants notwithstanding, the overwhelming majority of these is religious, while the exact converse is true for those leaving the country. The arrivals come with *yarmulkes* on their heads, those who leave are overwhelmingly bare of Jewish head-covering or head.

The monster-child of the secular Zionist realizes that nationalism is, at best, a stupid thing. With all respect to Swedes and Finns, if you see one you indeed see the other. And the same with all the flags and parliaments and prime ministers and anthems. What absurdity, what sterile lack of any meaning at best! But worse, what a *danger*! How many wars have been fought and how many people died because of the artificial differences between peoples!

And when this reality is not only a theoretical one but a very real one for the young Israeli; when he knows that the war with the Arabs is over the "Jewishness" of the state, over a Zionism that insists on particularism and separateness with no logical, progressive, democratic reason; when he knows that this is why he must go into the army at 18 for three years and for 30 to 40 days every year after that he will be on reserve duty; and when he knows that he must live in constant tension and expectation of the possibility of war; and when he knows that his is a poor country with crushing taxes and a bankrupt economy; and when he meets a pretty (or not so pretty) gentile volunteer on his kibbutz or a gentile tourist on the beach at Tel Aviv, or on a trip to Holland or Chicago; and when his cousin, who has moved to Los Angeles and done quite well for himself, then writes him a sarcastic letter that reads, in part: "Imbecile, what are you doing there? Come here and I'll arrange for you to get a 'green card' (work permit); you'll marry an American and stay here and make money and be free of army service and all the madness there"—*why should he stay?* The young sabra, victim, sacrificial lamb of a secular educational system that never says a word to him about being a good Jew.

The young Israeli who brays, "I am an Israeli, not a Jew." The one who has cast off the anchor of Judaism and who now drifts helplessly at sea, seeking to escape the ship of Zionism and its flying fools called Zionists.

And because so many *cannot* escape and are doomed to remain in what they fear is a potential death camp, why is it a surprise to so many that they grasp delusions as straws and madly march for a peace that is sheer insanity, while calling for concessions to enemies who will massacre them tomorrow as they did their fathers yesterday? What wonder is there that as blind lemmings they demand that their state commit suicide? A people that has cut itself from its past has no future. A people with no faith in G-d must, in the end, have no faith in itself. It will doubt everything about itself, including its rightful claim to its own land. It will roam and moan in the streets, losing that sweetest and most precious of weapons—certainty of self-confidence. A state once so happy and confident; it had begotten children shaken to the core by doubt and fear. This is the reality; this is the natural consequence of the state that lost its faith.

The Jew against the Hellenist. The real struggle. The struggle of those who truly believe that there is a G-d in Israel against those who openly deny it, in alliance with the lip movers and payers of lip service.

This is the reality of the secular Zionism that cut out its own heart—Judaism—and lost its head, its direction, its youth. The State of Israel reaps the sterile weeds of secular nationalism, secular Zionism, a dream of gentilized Jews who sought to cut away Judaism and build a proud new nationalism, and who, immutably, guaranteed the death of the latter. Look! Have the courage to see the reality of the Jewish State that has turned into a Hebrew-speaking caricature of the gentilized West. Look at the reality of the change of the dream of Zion as a land of holy, special, chosen people to what it is today.

What can we give these sad, lost sabras when they hear only the worst of anti-Semitism and self-hate from their own intellectuals and artists? Consider the following fascinating example of the New Hebrew:

In December, 1985, the newest wing of the Israel Museum was dedicated and the whole complement of Israel's artistic anarchists came for the cocktails, including sculptor Yigal Tomarkin. Unfortunately, cocktails were not the only thing on the agenda. It was Tomarkin's bad luck that the holiday of Chanukah fell on that evening and Israeli President Herzog rose to light the traditional candles. Not only did

Tomarkin flee as from the plague, but he then wrote the following protest:

"A museum is the opposite of a synagogue. It is the symbol of culture and progress. If the power of the Maccabees would today be as great as it was then, the museum would be a wreck of destroyed art. Chanukah is the holiday of backwardness and reaction, not that of the artist and intellectual."

What shall we feed these sad young Jews, victims of spiritual malnutrition? And what do you offer young Israeli Jews who have no logical reason to be Jewish and every material, rational one *not* to be, when the wandering Jews of the George Steiner stripe tell them that nationalism is the tragedy of mankind that may destroy the world because of nonsense such as flags and sovereignty?

Shall we tell them that only Israel as a Jewish homeland will save them from another Auschwitz when they do not believe that gentiles hate Jews enough to bring on another Holocaust, and, more, reject the inevitability of anti-Semitism as a tenet of their faith? When they believe that the Arabs pose a greater danger to survival of Jews in Israel than does anybody else to Jews in the United States, Canada, Australia or Western Europe?

Or perhaps we will satisfy them by babbling about the importance of Jewish "culture" and thus resurrecting the "cultural Zionism" of Ahad Ha'am? Consider the convincing arguments of secularists today telling young sabras of the "specialness" of the Jewish "national spirit" and "national ethic" when every young secular Israeli *knows* that Jews have no monopoly on either spirit or ethic. The existence of a Jewish "culture" does not give the young sabra the slightest reason not to marry an ethical shiksa or move to ethical Boston. Shall we then persuade the young Israeli Jew of the greatness of being Jewish through the writings of that secular mystic, A.D. Gordon, who wrote:

"The Jewish soul, its very nature, is entwined with the Land of Israel. The nations do not understand this spirit. This bright and enlightened spirit is unknown to them."

Poor A.D. Gordon, were he to rise from the grave and speak these words to the sabras of Israel he would find that they, along with "the nations of the world," have not the slightest idea what he is talking about. The *Jewish* soul? The *Jewish* spirit? Does an enlightened progressive, non-racist, democratic humanist Jew believe in a special *Jewish* soul and spirit? Poor A.D. Gordon, who rejected pure Judaism for sheer nonsense.

But even worse, in this insane era of mindless, flailing defamation when the cry "racism" is so mindlessly bandied about, consider one of the great philosophers of Jewish nationalism. Consider, for example, the guru of the confused and perplexed, Martin Buber—and never was there a better candidate for a god for the confused and perplexed. Buber, who should be best remembered for his protest against the hanging of Adolf Eichmann (on "ethical" grounds), is the master of befogging, inexplicable meaningless writings, all-things-and-nothing-to-all-men. His writings which are so confusing to any normal person automatically make him a candidate for deep philosophical perplexer to the circle of the guides.

Buber, that sad, tortured soul, so desperately in need of his own spiritual help, blindly trumpets his solutions to the blind.

The Jew, according to Buber, must integrate the individual in the "blood" continuum of the people, blood signifying "the creative mystery uniting the generation...."

One can imagine what a massive impact this will have on the young Israeli Jew. What pride, what noblesse oblige. What balderdash... if not blatant racism.

"In the way that a man measures, thus shall he be measured.' The words of the rabbis proclaiming the immutable law of measure for measure. The secular Zionist fathers have eaten the sour grapes of secularism and their children's teeth are set on edge as *they* reject Zionism and *everything* "Jewish."

And who can blame them, in any way. Not only did the "fathers of the nation," the founders and thinkers of Zionism, lay the infrastructure for their spiritual and ideological destruction, but the Hellenists of *today*, in their psychotic and psychopathic drive for self-destruction, lead the way to the annihilation of Jewish youth and Jewish State both.

How can we possibly be serious about pleading with the young Israeli Jew to retain his Jewishness and not marry the decent, good, pretty, intelligent gentile when the editor of *Ha'aretz*, Gershon Shocken, writes a long article in his *blatt* (August 29, 1985), entitled "Ezra's Curse"?

The title refers, of course, to the struggle of Ezra and his compatriot Nehemiah, the Jewish leaders of the Jewish community that returned to Israel from Babylon and rebuilt the Holy Temple, against intermarriage. Both Ezra and Nehemiah were horrified at the spiritual destruction of the Jewish people when just as today a large section of the leadership, particularly the priesthood, was guilty of intermarriage. Unlike today, however, the main leadership and the power were in Ezra's hands. Without hesitation he gathered all the returning Jews and covenanted with them not only not to intermarry but to remove

the gentiles whom they had already married from their midst, saying
that whoever would not gather and swear, "all his substance should
be forfeited and himself separated from the congregation."

There is not the slightest doubt that this step by Ezra was among
the greatest blessings for the Jewish people in their history, and not
for nothing does the Talmud praise Ezra as having been worthy of
giving the Jews the Torah at Sinai. But that which the Jewish Jew
understands to be a blessing must, in the eyes of the Hellenist, be a
curse, and Shocken, one of the bitterest foes of Judaism extant,
launches a vicious attack on the entire Jewish ban on intermarriage,
writing:

"For a sovereign people obligated to arrive at coexistence with people of another origin and to create normal relations with neighbors
across its borders, this prohibition that symbolizes the estrangement
between Jews and other groups, has turned into a curse. If it continues,
it will contribute to eternalizing the tension in the land and Israel's
isolation in the region. We must free ourselves of Ezra's curse."

Here is the gauntlet thrown down to Judaism by the self-haters, by
the Hellenists. Nowhere could there be a clearer challenge to Judaism
and a more open declaration of war. But most of all, Shocken the fool
is greater even than Shocken the enemy of Judaism and the Jewish
people. For every secular young Israeli Jew who reads his words will
carry the message to its logical conclusion. If separation isolates the
Jew and if his isolation is a curse, why have a *Jewish* State with all
its particularism and difference, since clearly *that*, so much more than
individual Jewish tribalism, is what bothers the Arabs? If Judaism's
individual ban on intermarriage is a curse, what shall we say, asks the
young Israeli Jew, to Zionism's *national* decision to create a Jewish
State only? If Ezra's is a curse, what shall we say about Herzl?

The young Israeli Jew is no fool. Of course he will agree with
Shocken and then carry it the one logical step further that Shocken,
the ideological coward, cannot. Why be Jewish in a "national" sense
at all? Why not agree with Arafat to the democratic, secular Palestine
or Israel (the name is totally irrelevant) in which it will not matter
whether the majority is Jewish or Arab or Chinese? And most to the
point—*why be Jewish at all?* Following in the blind, mad footsteps of
the secular founding fathers, Shocken lights the way to the destruction
of the Zionism he supposedly follows. Of course, in his heart of
hearts, torn and agonized by the clear difference between the faith he
was so unfortunately born into and the gentilized values he so much
believes in, that is exactly what Shocken wants.

The destruction of the young Israeli Jew continues on many fronts.

Following Shocken's article, a letter appeared in *Ha'aretz* in support of it, from "the point of view of health [sic]." The writer was a member of Kibbutz Ayelet Hashachar, the well known guest house to which unwary simple, naive Jewish tourists go and spend money. How few know that the kibbutzim which they visit and around which is spread the aura of proud new Jewishness are among the great enemies of the Jewish people and against everything in which the simple Jew believes. The writer, one Chaim Catzori, writes:

"The religious ban on intermarriage in Israel will weaken the nation in the long run from a physical and genetic point of view. We must look upon every Israeli citizen who fulfills his national obligations, whether he be Jew or Arab, as a candidate for intermarriage—for the sake of the immunization of the nation."

Of course, the Jewish people, over the thousands of years of "Ezra's curse," has been thoroughly weakened. Its list of scholars and intellectuals and scientists and artists and Nobel prize winners clearly proves the kibbutznik's thesis. Its armed forces are clear evidence that the leftist is correct and that we must hasten to ban the ban. This pitiful tripe is Exhibit One in the trial of Israeli Hellenism. It is hatred of Judaism *par excellence*. The young Israeli secularist watches and learns. He has watched for years. He watched in the wake of the magnificent Six Day War. At that time Golda Meir, speaking out against assimilation (she was one of those who of course believed Jews should be a separate people but could not articulate why to the new Hebrew she was raising), and told a group of visiting rabbis:

"Anyone who intermarries joins the six million [killed in the Holocaust]."

Immediately, the political party Moked, the forerunner of the present *Ratz* party of Shulamit Aloni and Yossi Sarid, placed a large ad reading:

"Is that true? Is Jewish identity determined today by ties of birth alone? Would Saul Tchernichovsky [the pagan Jewish poet who intermarried] be considered dead to Hebrew culture?

"Remember! A nation is not a tribe and society is not a community. A state is not a ghetto."

Of course this attack on the basic identity of the Jewish people is not lost on the young Jew who will always be braver and more logical than timid elders. What is being sown is the death of any logical reason for a Jewish State or for being "Jewish" at all. For the young Israeli Jew will carry the logic of Moked to its conclusion. He will reason:

"A human is not a tribe or a nation or a state. He is part of a world community of humans that sees no difference between peoples and rejects flags and all other national symbols of 'difference,' including Zionism and its separation of Jews from other people."

The war against Judaism is one that, if successful, would destroy Zionism and the Jewish people. It is impossible that the Hellenists do not understand it. The conclusion is that they do, but that this is precisely what they want and have not the courage to come out and say it.

Their attacks on Kahane and Kahanism are attacks on *Judaism*, and when they say that Kahane is a racist, what they really mean is that Judaism is racist, *per se*. That opposition to intermarriage is racism. That our grandparents and those who died at the stake for a separate Jewish people were, indeed, more than fools. They were racists.

That is why the campaign continues unabated:

The weekly Jerusalem paper *Kol Ha'ir*, one of the more openly anti-Jewish papers in the land, publishes a long article by Yoram Binur. The article, sadly translated and reprinted in a number of uncomprehending Jewish weeklies in the United States, has one point: The author has dressed up as an Arab and openly gone out with a Jewish girl through Jerusalem seeking to rent an apartment, to gain entrance to a private social club, to have the right to intermingle with a Jewish woman and live with her. The tragic result is that the bigoted, prejudiced Jews refuse to allow him to. This is what *Kol Ha'ir* and the Hellenism it represents wish to change. They wish to put an end to the ban on Jewish-Arab relations because it is "racist." But their real target *is Judaism*, because that to them is the ultimate source of racism.

And the confused, babbling Hellenist Yoram Peri writes in Histradut's paper *Davar* (October 15, 1985):

"Assimilation is a basic problem for the Jew of the Exile.... In Israel it is no problem at all [sic]. Our basic problem is relations between Jews and Arabs. And it is more than worth it to 'pay' a small price of intermarriage in order to prevent our turning into a racist, anti-democratic society."

This is the voice of Hellenism. This is the meaning of the forces that are ranged against Kahane. Their real target is Judaism, their real goal the end of the Jewish people as a separate, distinct, chosen one. Democracy and humanism are their values and, as I have said so many times, they run counter to and stand in contradiction to the basic principles of Judaism—Zionism and a Jewish people.

And so every aspect of the Jews as a holy and sanctified people is attacked, as the young Israeli Jew watches—and learns. The religious parties have introduced a bill forbidding the sale of pork in Jewish communities. The Hellenists rally to the defense of the pig. The Hellenist and the pig stand on the barricades in defense of freedom of abomination. And, of course, to attack that Judaism that made the Jewish people separate and disciplined, and raised them high above the animal desires and passions, by limiting their freedom to eat any and all things.

The *Jerusalem Post* allowed one Joseph Franklin to write a long article attacking the attack on pork. Attacking Judaism:

"Pork is not being defended on its merits as a tasty meat; rather, the battle is against the relegation of secular thought and practice to subject status. The traditions of secular humanism, nominally supported by a major segment of Israel's populace, are in fact fighting a battle against marginalization in an environment of Middle Eastern extremism.

"Though Kibbutz Misra's pigpens and Kranzdorf's butcher shop in Jerusalem may seem queer sites for philosophic engagement, political conflict inevitably tends to revolve around symbols. No better symbol than the pig is available to Israel's invigorated religious forces in their present challenge to secular culture."

And Michael Handelsaltz, "cultural" writer for *Ha'aretz*, not content with the censorship board's allowing the abomination *Oh Calcutta* to appear in Israel, writes (March 5, 1986):

"The fact, that a majority of the [censorship] Council ruled that adults are capable of deciding if they wish to see nudity, is merely 'happiness for the naked.' For there was no majority to rule that adults are capable of deciding what they wish to think. A tie vote prevented the acceptance of an appeal in the case of the play *Ephraim Returns to the Army*." [The anti-war play that, as always, made the Israeli army look like a brutal, Nazi-like conquering force, which is, of course, perfect for Israel's youth when Israel is at war with Arabs who wish to destroy her.] "As long as this shameful and foolish [censorship] law exists, we must continue to struggle against it in every way."

It is clear that while Israel faces a war of survival against the Arabs, by far the greater struggle is between Jew and Jew over the character of the state and its Jews who live there. And it is a conflict that is hardly a new one. It is rather the latest phase in an ongoing conflict, thousands of years old. Perhaps its most famous phase is commemorated, rather ignorantly, as the holiday of Chanukah. The bitter battle some 2500 years ago was between those Jews who sought to create a truly Jewish culture and society as opposed to those who sought to be Greeks in form and idea. The latter came to be known as the Hellenists and the real battle of the Maccabees was against them, against the perversion and corruption of the Jewish people into a hideous, Hebrew caricature of foreign, gentilized culture.

That is precisely what the struggle is today in the Jewish State that has become the State of the Jewish and which sinks into something far less than even that.

Shall this state be the home of a Divine, chosen, higher people, cloaked in holiness and wrapped in the mantle of difference? Shall it be a separate, distinctive nation, divided from the abominations of the others, isolated from foreign cultures that sully the purity, that plunge the special people from the heights of the sacred to the depths of the profane? Shall it be the chosen freedom of G-d?

Or will it choose to be as all the mediocre and worse? Will it decide on a dream, turn sanctity into commonness, fall from the greatness to the ordinary? "Thus saith the L-rd: learn not the way of the nations" (Jeremiah 10).

The choice, the decision, will determine the very lives of the people of Israel. Redemption or tragedy depends on the reply. And the decision is made daily as the new Hellenists extend their deadly hand of mediocrity and profanation.

And they are joined, these gentilized Hebrews of Israel, with the Jewish Establishment denizens of the Exile, the leaders who Federate the Jewish Community, who Unitedly Appeal to it, who preside over the temples and, of course, serve as its rabbis, *sans* Sinai or sometimes even G-d.

How intellectually stimulating an encounter between a Jewish child and a Reform-Conservative rabbi! What an exciting thing it would be to record a meeting between the Jewish child and his Jewish leaders, ignoramuses, at a mini-Seder at which he asks the One Question:

"Fathers, O Jewish leaders, tell me why in the name of peace and brotherhood I should insist on being Jewish and not a human being?"

What a spectacle it would be to gather all the simple sons of Abraham, Isaac and Jacob to a huge stadium and there, facing the Barons of Jewishness, the Counts of the Jewish Establishment, the Lords of Jewish Leadership, the directors of the Federations and Councils and UJAs and Reform-Conservative Rabbis, all who pay such obsessive and obsequious service to democracy and equality and brotherhood and the universality and brotherhood of all men, even as they insist that their youngsters take pride in being "Jewish," support Israel, the Jewish state with its special status for Jews, fight intermarriage and assimilation, and support the United *Jewish* Appeal, their local *Jewish* temple and *Jewish* Center.

What an exciting event would be this confrontation, this New Seder, with its New Passover Agenda whose centerpiece would be a whole host of New Jewish Questions! Consider the agony of soul for the Jewish Barons of Ignorance and Rabbis of Hypocrisy as the Jewish child asks the fathers of the community:

"If all human beings are equal and if we are all spiritually alike and (if we must bring in G-d) are made in His image, and if "one world" of human brotherhood is the ideal, why do you Jewish leaders insist on our being 'Jewish' and creating a barrier, a 'difference' between 'Jews' and non-Jews? Would it not be better to be 'human beings' with no barriers between us? Why should I not marry a nice, ethical, pretty (or handsome), intelligent gentile without this absurd farce of 'conversion'? Why not just be ethical without reference to Jews or non-Jews, for what in the world are *'Jewish'* ethics, and are you telling me that non-Jews cannot be ethical?

"The essential difference between Orthodoxy and Reform-Conservatism is that Orthodoxy believes that the Torah, *as is*, was actually, literally given by G-d to the Jewish people at the literal Revelation at Sinai. Whether we agree or not, it must be admitted that if that *is* so, it is certainly the compelling reason to be a Jew, (and, of course, to observe all the Divine Laws of that Torah), and thus different from other people.

"But if, as you Reform-Conservative leaders claim, this is not so, and the Torah was not given literally by G-d but only 'Divinely revealed' then as honest Jews we *must* ask ourselves:

"What in the world does 'Divinely revealed' mean? If G-d did *not* actually appear at Sinai to give the Torah, how does our rabbi know that it was 'Divinely revealed'? Perhaps Christianity then was also 'Divinely revealed.' And Islam and Buddhism. Perhaps Marxism or Adam Smith. Perhaps what I or my gentile intellectual friend perceive. How does our rabbi know that *only* Judaism was 'Divinely revealed,' and if others were too, why do Jewish leaders insist on a racist, separatist division of Jews and gentiles?

"Fathers of the community, could you please put down the ham sandwich for a moment and tell me: If Torah, if Judaism, is *not* the direct precise word of G-d, why bother to observe any of it as "Judaism'? Why does the temple rabbi insist on my observing certain laws and not others? Who is to tell me which laws are 'in the spirit of the times' and which are not? Why have any formalized ritual? Why be a 'Reform' or 'Conservative' Jew, adhering to rules that other people decide for you? Why go to a temple to pray in a fixed form and book that someone in New York City or Cincinnati wrote? Why not be me and do my thing? Perhaps I too am 'Divinely revealed.'

"Why must I want to go to Israel to visit and to work and to volunteer when there is greater poverty and need for me in Ethiopia or in Peru? What is this racist, narrow, obsession with being Jewish when we are all G-d's children? Why should I go on a walk for the United Jewish Appeal when I could walk for the United *Human* Appeal?

"I am really mind-boggled by you, Fathers of the community. You do not observe Sabbath, you do not eat kosher, you do not believe that Judaism is G-d's literal word. More and more of you are married to non-Jews, and yet you insist on being 'Jewish' and, worse, on *my* being so? Why?

"And the worst are my non-Orthodox *rabbis!*

"According to Reform's Lenn Report (1972) no less than 14 percent of their rabbis admit to being atheists or agnostics. What kind of *religious* movement can spawn such 'rabbis'? Is it not better to have an honest atheist with no ties to a temple than this kind of confusion? Furthermore, another 14 percent admitted to a 'non-traditionalist' belief in G-d, similar to that of one of Reform's leading rabbis, Roland Gittelson, who stated: 'I don't believe in miracles; I don't believe that G-d is a person or discrete being.... I believe that G-d is a Force, an Intelligence.' [*Reform Judaism*, Winter 1983] Now, *truthfully*, do you know what this means? Is it intellectually honest? Is it not more logical and honest to say as the Orthodox do that G-d controls all destiny, performs miracles and is the G-d of history? Or just honestly admit that He does not really exist as someone you can pray to, and stop going to Temple?

"But what truly gets me angry is the fraud and racism of these rabbis. Despite the fact that Reform denies that G-d appeared at Sinai and literally revealed Himself and the Torah, at their convention in Jerusalem [June 30, 1983] they declared: 'We believe that G-d has ordained a religious purpose for the people of Israel which distinguishes it from the nations of the earth.' As liberal humanists, *are you not* appalled at this rank racism and parochialism? If G-d did not appear and tell us, how do we know that we were 'chosen'? If the Torah is not Divine, absolute truth, how do we hallow books that have 'barbaric' and 'archaic' portions in them? If ethics are our yardstick, are there not gentile works that are ethical and beautiful? Is it not an emotional cowardice on the part of Reform-Conservative leaders and parents that prevents them from breaking with narrowness and becoming simply human beings?"

What a magnificent confrontation *that* would be!

The secular Zionist Frankensteins created the child-monster Jews who oppose Judaism. What they never foresaw was the unleashing of the monsters in a war against Zionism and Jewish nationalism. That will come too, Israel. Fathers and children. Jews against Judaism. And, inevitably, against Zionism. And, finally, against the very concept of a Jewish people.

PART V

UNCOMFORTABLE QUESTIONS FOR COMFORTABLE JEWS

Chapter 13

No Guilt!

G-d made Man normal, healthy, complete. He created lungs within him so that he might breathe. And so, Man breathes oxygen, the breath of life. That is normal. Jews tend to breathe guilt. That is not.

The AIDS of the Jewish people of our times is guilt. Needless, destructive, corrosive guilt. A guilt that leads to incredible self-hate. A self-hate that leads to self-destruction. It is a guilt and a self-hate and a desire to destroy themselves that stems directly from the existence of the Jew as a minority persecuted and oppressed and degraded and terrified for 2,000 years of Exile. It is this agonizingly long Exile that has made so great a proportion of the Jewish people psychologically abnormal.

A people cannot be normal without a state of its own any more than a child can be truly normal without a loving family and home that he can call his own. It is in the nature of the nation, as created by G-d, that normalcy and natural healthy growth be within the context of the sovereignty, self-rule and proprietorship of its own land.

To be a minority is to be the immutable victim of the fears, complexes, insecurities and guilt that are unshakable and permanent parts of the essence of minority status. It is impossible to escape this; it comes along with the "lease."

One who is a minority for even a relatively short period lives in constant wariness of what he says and does, in constant fear of the reaction to his words and actions on the part of the majority. Concern with "What will 'they' say and what will 'they' do" becomes a permanent part of the minority member's psyche. And how much more so for Jews whose Exile was such a long and brutal and scattered one, in which Jews *everywhere* were defamed and attacked and made pariahs. What begins to happen to a member of the minority is the inevitable growth within him of the victim complex, which becomes self-contempt for his own weakness and unconscious jealousy and admiration for the prowess and strength of the oppressor. Worse, as nation after nation and attacker after attacker continue to defame and condemn the Jew, he begins to ask himself: Is it possible that they are all wrong and I, alone, am right? In a word the centuries of defamation and slander cause the Jew to believe the attacks and lies of his enemies. And with that inner belief comes terrible guilt, agonizing guilt. And the worst of self-hate.

No man can live believing that he is as bad and obnoxious and terrible as his enemies say he is. No man can live, normally, despising himself. From his terrible secret belief that perhaps his enemies are indeed correct and that perhaps his basic faith and very being are indeed rooted in evil, comes forth the kind of self-hate that is awesome to behold, so compelling, so agonizing, so awful for these afflicted by it that they yearn to destroy the roots of that which causes the "evil"—the Judaism and Jewishness that bring them such pain. And, of course, in their tortured souls they seek their own personal final solution, self-destruction as a people.

The rise of the era of Enlightenment and Emancipation, the fall of the ghetto and the opening of the doors of freedom and integration to the Jew have not only sharpened his perception of guilt and self-hate but opened for him, too, the way to put an end to it, to his Jewishness and Judaism that so destroy his troubled soul.

And so, what we have seen in our days is the fruition of the guilt-ridden, self-hating Jew, the creation of the lemming of the Mosaic persuasion.

The lemming is a small animal, about the size of a rat. The lemming is a strange animal with a very strange custom. Every few years, lemmings gather together and march to the sea. The lemming and all the other lemmings march shoulder to shoulder and when they reach the sea they do a very strange thing: they jump in and drown. The lemming is a very strange animal and few can understand it. But the Hebrew lemming, the lemming of the Mosaic persuasion, is the strangest of them all. Psychologists and sociologists and anthropologists and biologists and students of irrational behavior from far and wide gather to study the march of the Hebrew lemming.

The Hebrew lemming of guilt is the rodent who is haunted by the thought that he is not only an oppressor and aggressor in the "occupied lands of 1967," but also a thief and robber of a people he calls "Palestinians," and really has no right to any of the land that was once "Palestine." The Hebrew lemming of Suicide Now is haunted by the thought that his family had no right to come from Russia or Poland or Galicia or England or Canada or Argentina or the United States to create a "Jewish State" on lands that were owned by others.

But since the lemming lacks the courage to honestly follow up his convictions and stand up before the "Palestinian" and say, "I am a thief and I hereby return my kibbutz to you," he must, instead, fight all the harder for the poor "Palestinian" in Judea, Samaria, Gaza, Lebanon. His weakness and inability to give up his house in Kibbutz Mishmar Ha'emek or the artist colony of Ein Hod or the tennis courts of Ramat Hasharon or villa in Savyon drive the Hebrew lemming into even greater depression of guilt and self-hate. His need to prostrate himself before the poor Arab becomes an all-consuming, obsessive one.

And, of course, the guilt goes much further. The Hebrew lemming, who is a small animal, about the size of a rat, deeply despises with a psychopathic passion everything that smacks of Judaism and the curse of fate that made him Jewish. In his little heart the lemming knows that Judaism's values are at odds with everything that he wishes his life to consist of. The separateness and exclusivity of Judaism vis-à-vis other peoples is anathema to his universalistic desire to intermarry, assimilate, amalgamate with all the goyim and thus find love and escape in their midst. The concept of chosenness repels him, for he seeks anything that will enable him to eliminate the barriers between Jews and others. The holiness that decrees discipline and sanctity and abstinence and personal limitations is diametrically opposed to his materialistic need for total freedom, anarchy, limitless right to license. He sees in Judaism racism, primitiveness, parochialism, concepts that he abhors because he seeks to be a universal rodent. And faced with this Judaism, he is faced, too, with the fact that he is a Jew. This is the horror that he cannot abide. From guilt emerges self-hate, black and ugly self-hate.

This lemming cannot survive self-hate. No one can survive with that terrible malignancy growing within him. The Hebrew lemming must escape, and his escape is through the sea. The Sea of Suicide.

Suicide Now. Let the state that he feels to be a robber state go under. Let the people and faith that he sees as reactionary and racist and abominable cease to exist. "Let my soul perish with the Philistines." The cry of the Hebrew lemmings of Suicide Now.

The tragic story of the Hebrew lemmings. But, if it must be, it would be sufficient if they leaped into the sea themselves. The real tragedy is that while ordinary lemmings take the plunge themselves, the Hebrew ones seek to take all of us with them.

And that cannot be. That is why the lemmings of Israel must be fought. Because they have become more than an interesting zoological phenomenon. They threaten the existence of normal, healthy, true Jews.

The great danger and most powerful weapon of the Hebrew- speaking gentiles and lemmings of Israel is their ability to so instill guilt and doubt in us, so that we close our mouths and minds and fear to say what we know to be true.

The small circle of leftists and guilt-ridden liberals, intellectuals and frustrated artistic types possesses a weapon of overwhelming power, and it is this that enables them to march toward victory. Their control of the news media affords them the opportunity, daily, to influence, indoctrinate, pervert, corrupt an entire generation that is their captive audience. They decree the gentilized foreign culture that becomes the passion of the masses. They decree the ideas and perverted gentilized values that are heard and propagated over the waves. An entire generation of youth is in their hands. And they are aided by the frustrated, spiritually sick, lost artists who join them in a parody of perverted "peace and love." They din this message of perversion into our ears every day, every hour, every minute.

Guilt, guilt, guilt. The poison of spiritual corrosion, the destruction of self-confidence and belief in oneself and one's people and faith. The end of certainty and normalcy. Guilt that leads to self-hate, to national self-destruction. Guilt. The weapon of the Hellenist, of the gentilized and sick Jew of the lemming persuasion. Guilt.

I feel no guilt. Not the slightest. I feel no guilt about the fact that I am a Jew. I feel no guilt about the fact that I believe *and know* that the Jew is a Chosen person who stood at Sinai and was selected to be G-d's elected. I feel no guilt over the fact that I believe *and know* that the Land of Israel is the exclusive home of the Jewish people, and that no other people has the slightest right to it. I feel no guilt over my knowledge that Arabs are thieves who entered my land when the Jewish people was forcibly exiled from it, and I feel no guilt over the fact that I am prepared to use every possible means to insure that they will never again murder Jews and threaten the existence of my state. I feel no guilt over the fact that I prefer winning wars to losing pogroms, that I choose living over dying. It is infinitely more satisfying to win. *I feel no guilt over feeling no guilt.*

Having lost, been losers for so many centuries, too many Jews have difficulty dealing with winning. I have no such problem. It is infinitely more satisfying to be a winner than a loser. It is exceedingly more pleasant to live than die; there is little of any positive value in Holocausts or pogroms. And I totally prefer a powerful and proud Jewish State that is hated by the entire world than an Auschwitz that is loved by one and all.

And I feel no guilt about making sure that the faces of Shchem, the largest Arab city in Samaria-Judea, will never be seen again in the Land of Israel.

The faces. The faces of Shchem. The faces of Arabs, freed for the moment of Israeli army restraint, glowing, shimmering with hate as they marched, ran, raced through the streets of Shchem. What a pity that all the Jewish liberals and humanists, Hellenists and Moderdox together, all the ones who prattle about "Jewish values" and Arab-Jewish coexistence and democracy and brotherhood and the horror of Arab expulsion could not have seen the faces.

It was a miraculously clear day in Shchem, so clear that even the most obtuse Jew could have seen tomorrow, could have understood what that tomorrow holds for the Jew if those faces would suddenly appear, free to race through the streets of Jerusalem, Tel Aviv, Gush Etzion or Bnei Brak. The faces of naked Arab hate and wild abandon as the Israeli army left the city to them for the day.

It was the day of the funeral of the puppet mayor of Shchem, Al-Matzri, praised and eulogized by the head of the shallow and base kingdom, Shimon Peres, as a "moderate Palestinian." His "Palestinianship" is, of course, as fraudulent as his "moderation," and the name Al-Matzri (Egyptian) is more testimony than 1,000 speeches to the origin of so many Arabs who arrived in the Land of Israel over the last century from Egypt, Iraq, Syria and other Arab countries, and who, voila, became "Palestinians." And he was a moderate as much as any Arab moderate, meaning that the difference between that and the extremist is that the latter says what he means—"Slaughter the Zionist!"—while the moderate thinks it, but has cunningly learned the pragmatic lesson that if you behave quietly and praise Jews they will throw money at you. Or the Sinai. Or Palestine.

There are no Arab "moderates" or "extremists." There are stupid Arabs who cannot hide their true feelings and so babble them for all to hear and see. And there are clever ones who mean the same, but do not say it. They bide their time.

And, so, the "moderate" was assassinated by an "extremist," meaning that one PLO wing who feared to lose power to another "Palestinian" wing killed Al-Matzri, thus continuing the magnificent vindication of the Biblical description of Ishmael: "And he will be a wild man, his hand against everyone and everyone against him." And the crowds, tens of thousands of them, roared into the streets, snatching his body and holding it aloft as the Israeli army was given orders to leave the towns to the Arabs for the day. They did, and we were given just a taste of the stinging honey of Arab autonomy, of what they will do when given self-rule, and worse—the independence and power to sweep our city of Shchem into Jewish cities, towns and neighborhoods.

The hysteria, the mass shouting of "Arafat, Arafat!" The curses and slogans against Zionism and the Zionist State. The chant, "Yes to revolution, until final victory!" The PLO flags, the pictures of Arafat. But most of all, for all the humanists and Hellenists, the "good" Jews and moralists, most of all—the faces.

The faces of naked hatred. The faces shining in anticipation of tearing Jews apart even as their Zionist State is trodden beneath the boots of marching Arabs. Their faces sang, and in an unremarkable way they sang their own version of "Hatikva (The Hope)": "The hope is not yet lost, to return to Palestine, to destroy the Jews." We saw the faces of hate and let the sick "humanists," who are so moral and merciful at the expense of Jews, who, G-d forbid, will pay the ultimate price because of liberal regurgitation of suicidal and gentilized phrases, know that not only did we see tomorrow by *yesterday*. For these were the same faces that marched and ran through Eretz Yisrael in the 1920s shouting "*Itbach al Yehud* (Slaughter the Jew)!" And they did. By the hundreds. Men, women, children. Slaughter and rape and mutilization. "And he shall be a wild man...."

And the Israeli army allowed them to spit in the face of Zionism and the Jewish state and swear its destruction and gain more confidence in themselves and more certainty that the Zionist entity—thanks to the Hellenists and humanists and Moderdox—grows weaker, more unsure, more hesitant. And it is that image that guarantees the most terrible of tragedies for Israel. I am only comforted by the thought that if, G-d forbid, tragedy strikes, we will be the beneficiaries of the most ecumenical of eulogies, from Brickner to Schulweis to Bernstein (no, dear friends, not a double play combination for Kansas City).

The faces of Shchem. The faces of "Palestinian" Arabs who are as

"Palestinian" as I am Tasmanian, whose Palestinian legitimacy is seen in the name they use for Shchem—Nablus. Nablus? The *Arab* name for Shchem? But surely you jest, oh New Agenda, oh Brickner, oh Balfour and your daily bleeding declaration for the suffering Palestinians! Nablus, an *Arab* name?

The name is Shchem. It is in the Bible. It and the entire country were ripped from us by the invading Romans who changed the name to Napulus (as in Naples or Napoli). G-d having afflicted Arabs with some difficulty in pronouncing a "p," Napulus became "Nabulus" and Italy's loss was Ishmael's gain.

Nablus is *not* Shchem. Shchem is *Shchem*, not Nablus. And Eretz Yisrael is Eretz Yisrael, and there is not and never was and, I promise you, please G-d, there will never be a "Palestine," in Eretz Yisrael. The faces of Arab hate and murder that glowered at us from Shchem are able to do so only because we are cursed with unclean birds of Peres, and leftist Hellenists, terminally ill with self-hate, and the little men of little faith whose empty heads are topped all-too often with yarmulkes that proclaim the glory of ritual even as their wearers deny the existence of G-d.

No, with G-d's help, I promise you that the faces of Shchem will never be seen in Tel Aviv or Beersheba or Haifa. Indeed, dear Jewish humanist, I promise you that they will not be seen in Shchem. *And I say this without the slightest feeling of guilt.*

I am stricken with a strange condition. It is called normalcy.

Over the years, I have gotten used to living. I enjoy it. I certainly prefer it to the alternative. And I intend, with G-d's help, to continue that condition despite Arabs in Shchem or Jewish leaders in their gilded ghettos or kosherless kibbutzim. Someday, we will continue to see tens of thousands of Arabs, racing and raving and ranting through the streets, shouting their hatred for Jews and Israel. But they will be in Baghdad or Teheran or Pakistan or Disneyland. But one thing is certain: Never, never again in Shchem.

I feel no guilt in making exceedingly certain that the Arabs, who massacred Jews mercilessly when they had the power, will never again have the opportunity. I feel no guilt in making certain that the Arabs will not destroy my state through either bullets or babies. And because I feel no guilt, that is why the guilt-ridden lemmings of the Mosaic faith hate me so. No matter.

And that is why I feel not the slightest guilt about implementing my proposal, which is so Zionist, Jewish and sane, to insure that Israel will always remain a sovereign, independent Jewish state.

I do not hate Arabs. I love Jews. And because of that I will do everything to insure that they survive. When we achieve power, with the help of G-d, we will offer the Arabs of Israel, who so understandably hate the Jewish State and so dream of its demise, the following options:

1) Within a certain limited number, to be set by security considerations, all Arabs who are prepared to accept the State of Israel as the exclusive state of the Jewish people and of no one else, will be allowed to remain the land with the status of "resident stranger," as per Jewish laws. They will be granted personal rights but no national ones. They will have general economic, social, cultural and religious freedom but will not be citizens of the Jewish State and will have nothing to say in its future in any way. Accepting this status, they are welcome to remain and are entitled to all the respect and decency that Judaism demands we grant to all humans who are resident strangers in our land and who bow to its laws and concepts.

2) Those Arabs who are not prepared to accept this will be offered the opportunity to leave voluntarily and peacefully with set compensation for their property (more than they ever dreamed of offering the 800,000 Sephardic Jews who fled Arab lands beginning in 1948). Those who are not prepared to leave willingly will be forcibly removed from the land.

Is this cruel? Hardly. What would be cruel would be to succumb to the sickness of non-Jewish guilt and allow the Arabs to remain to destroy us politically and, later, physically. Those who preach Jewish-Arab coexistence would do well to first raise the banner of Arab coexistence in Lebanon, for example. It is indeed a comforting sight to see Shiite Moslems, Suni Moslems, Druze and Christians coexisting so magnificently together; it offers magnificent possibilities for Arabs and Jews in Israel.

Will the Arabs of Israel fight? Hardly. When the Poles and Czechs after World War II licked their wounds bitterly and recalled the fifth column that was the huge German minority in their countries, they expelled no less than 12 million of the ethnic Germans, many of whom had lived for centuries in Poland and Czechoslovakia. Did the Germans fight? No. It is not very wise to fight soldiers and few are so foolhardy. The Arabs of Israel, when faced with a government of Meir Kahane and his soldiers, will not fight. Whatever else they may be, they are not fools. Indeed, on the day they turn on their radios and hear that the new Prime Minister is Kahane, the movement out of the country will have already begun.

Where will the Arabs go? Those who leave willingly can travel to any of the 22 Arab states that the "Arab nation" has been blessed with or to any other state that will have them. Those who do not leave willingly will be sent across the border to Lebanon or Jordan.

Will those states take them? Surely no one will ask them. We are dealing with the survival of Israel. This is not a game that we play. Lebanon is not a country; it is a series of feudal baronies and Israel controls as much of it as it wishes to. Southern Lebanon will take the Arabs that Israel sends it. As far as Jordan is concerned, the very last person in the world to talk about legitimate national and sovereign rights is any ruler of Jordan, a state that was conceived in duplicity and born in illegality. That area that is now called Jordan (sic), the east bank of the Jordan River, originally was home for 2½ of the tribes of Israel and was given by the League of Nations in trust to Great Britain as a mandate, to hold until a Jewish state would be established on both sides of the Jordan. Perfidious Albion, faced with a problem of Arab puppets, illegally and by fiat suddenly cut off that east bank of the Jordan, fully 80 percent of the League of Nations mandatory territory, and gave it to their puppet named Abdullah, grandfather of the little monarch Hussein, who fancies himself king of an independent state. Let him sit quietly and be gratified that Israel does not do to him what he tried and would love again to do to it.

If necessary, the Israeli army will seize the bridges across the Jordan for two days, send over the Arabs who would wipe out Israel, and then return the bridges to the little king. Every one of the Arabs he would get would consider himself a "Palestinian" and thus would join the 75 percent of the population of "Jordan" who also consider themselves Palestinians. We are speaking of Jewish survival, and normal Jews who feel no guilt about the urge to do just that, *survive*, do not ask illegal kingdoms whether they have permission to do so.

Will the Arab states not call for a *jihad*? The Arab states tend to call for *jihad*s every so often. They did so in 1948 and in 1967. With most disappointing results. Few Moslems cared to die for "Palestine." Israel survived. Israel survives. No, no Arab state wants to die for Palestine. Certainly, if they believed that they could destroy Israel, the Arab states would have gone to war long before Kahane, since it is not Meir Kahane who upsets them. It is the existence of the Jewish state, *per se*. The reason why Syria is not at full-fledged war with Israel, and the reason that Jordan and Iraq and all the others, including our new friend Egypt, is that these states know that if they attacked Israel, they would be badly beaten. And an Israel under Meir Kahane, they know, would be capable of and prepared to use any and every weapon in its arsenal, and the Arabs know what those weapons are. Any mad Arab attempt to go to war, they know, would go into the records as the six-hour war. No, not one Arab state wants to die for Palestine.

Will not the world react vigorously and angrily? The world? Yes, Ghana and Burma and Mozambique will vigorously and angrily condemn Israel and call for sanctions in the United Nations. The protests will be deafening. African states that just renewed their ties after breaking them with the non-Kahane Israel in the Jewish State's "war of aggression" in 1973, will break them again. The Third and Fourth and Twelfth Worlds will make terrible noises and the non-aligned and unaligned and what-have-you will send messages of solidarity to Arafat and he will appear with a hawk on his shoulder in a speech to the United Nations General Assembly. I feel the chills of fear run down my spine.

I recall when Menachem Begin bombed the Iraqi nuclear reactor near Baghdad. The protests were truly frightening. One had difficulty sleeping for a month. The condemnations, the demonstrations, the threats had all Israel terrified.... And then they passed. And there is no reactor. And that is the way of the world.

But what if America cuts off aid? Poor little Jew, who has turned worry into an art form. Who in the world says that America will cut off aid? What kind of ghetto mentality is it that persists in believing that America or any other country supports any nation merely out of considerations of morality and ethics? Since when do nations weigh their foreign policy on the scales of "goodness"? Consider all the moral and decent states that the United States has supported. Franco's Spain and Salazar's Portugal and the colonels of Greece and South Korea and Taiwan and Tito's Yugoslavia and a host of "democratic" Latin American states. What incredible balderdash is this insipid Jewish fear of American instant morality! The United States does not support Israel out of some kind of love affair between the American President and the Israeli Prime Minister. Nor because Israel is the "only democracy in the Middle East." The United States supports Israel as it does any other state—*out of a perception of self-interest*. And on the day that the perception changes, on the day that America ever feels that support for Israel is against its self-interest, it will change its policy, even if the most dovish of the doves is the Prime Minister.

The United States policy in the Middle East is rooted in the search for strong, loyal anti-communist allies. America can choose between Israel and Oman. Washington knows that an Israel under Meir Kahane would be the strongest, most powerfully anti-communist state in the region. Of course America will condemn Israel. It did so in the war in Lebanon. But it is a *pro forma* kind of action, deliberately toothless.

Israel will survive. What is important in any case is to make it clear that never will fear of American actions prevent Israel from taking all possible steps to guarantee its survival.

But above all, in answer to all the fears and trepidations of timid and frightened Jews of little faith:

What is wrong with you? Whatever happened to the people of perfect and classic faith? Did it ever occur to you that the G-d of Israel is mightier than Ronald Reagan or any other American President? Why is it that you do not understand that when the Jew does G-d's will, that He protects him and saves him from his enemies? Whatever happened to the people of the book, the people of faith in the G-d of Israel?

The pity is that we have long since stopped opening the book, hence have long since stopped having faith. Well, open it again and study it and practice it and believe in it. We are the chosen people and if we do His will, why, *He must* do ours!

The State of Israel is G-d's hand, the greatest miracle for the Jewish people in well over 2500 years. It is the beginning of the redemption, and we sit, small, tiny, dwarfs, rather than the giants of the earth that we can be. Washington? The United States? The "World"?

"The king's heart is in the hand of the L-rd, as the rivers of waters; He turneth it whithersoever He will.... When a man's ways please the L-rd He maketh even his enemies to be at peace with him." The words of the Bible. Know them. They are your words, Jew. The words of the wisest of men, Solomon. They are commended to his people. There is no doubt of it. With G-d's help the Arabs of Israel will go to live in their own lands and, while this will not bring peace, there will be existence and Jews will not be murdered each week and fear will not stalk the buses and markets and streets and highways of the Jewish state. And Arab babies will not threaten the very existence of the Jewish State.

Jew! Get up from the national coach; throw away the sick, corrosive guilt. Be strong and proud *and comfortable with Jewishness and Jewish survival!*

"The praises of G-d in their throat and a two-edged sword in their hand..."

Faith and a powerful Jewish arm. Is that not the Jewish way? Of course it is. And so, no guilt, no apologies. Only pride and strength and Jewish belief and survival.

Chapter 14

A Jewish State

A Jewish State, and the State of Jews that exists today in Israel, stand in stupendous opposition to each other in terms of the very character of the state, its values, its laws and its institutions. Judaism, if it is Divine and G-d's word, simply cannot and does not countenance the secular, liberal democratic state that the west postulates and that the gentilized Jewish leaders of Israel and the Exile swear by.

Can one begin to imagine that Judaism or any rational belief can accept with equanimity and approval the kind of secular state that the west produces today? Can anyone begin to believe that G-d or Judaism can look with acceptance on the kind of state that Israel is today? What possible social redemption is there in a state and society and people for whom pleasure, total freedom, materialism and the race for hedonism are at the center of their lives? What conceivable greatness is there in a state that is wracked with drugs and drink and sex and violence and hate and boredom and flight from responsibility and flight from the state itself? What kind of state is it whose basic tenet is a democracy and liberty guaranteed to allow Man to do evil and destroy himself? This is a positive value? For this we dreamed and hoped? This is the culmination of a chosen people? This makes us proud of Israel, the Jewish State within the Holy Land? This is what makes it important and vital to be a Jew and die for it, if need be?

It is far more than a question of the Arabs and non-Jews of Israel. The ultimate question is: what kind of a country shall it be for the Jews who live there? And the answer to that is to know why G-d made the world and what the role in it is of man in general and of the Jew in particular.

The Jewish people and their vessel, the Jewish state, in which they are to create the Torah society of the Almighty, were created by Him in order to bring to fruition His purpose for the world itself. A world that would accept Him as the Divine Creator and Omniscient King, that would accept His sovereignty and heavenly yoke, do His will and sing His praises. And this is surely what will be in the end of days:

"And many nations shall go and say: Come, let us go up to the mountain of the L-rd, to the house of the G-d of Jacob, and He will teach us His ways and we will walk in His paths, for out of Zion shall come forth the law and the word of G-d from Jerusalem" (Isaiah 2).

The Almighty made the world for "good," an *objective "good"* that He created and knows and defines, an objective "good" that he insists the world shall follow. Judaism rejects emphatically a world of freedom that is license to a world that insists upon the right to do what it wishes, a world that defines its own path. Man is not free to do that which he wishes; he is free to do that which he must. "Good." He is free in the sense that he can refuse to do that, but let him know that there is Divine punishment for that refusal. Man is not a creature of accident. He did not suddenly appear. He was created by G-d, with purpose and for purpose. His obligation is to cleave unto that purpose. And that purpose is the "good" that the Almighty created and gave man as his challenge on earth, in life.

For G-d created man as the most unique, single, specific, special creature of all. Alone of all His Creation, Man has choice, freedom of will. The ability to do good and to do evil. No angel or celestial creature can ever claim glory or reward for doing good, since he cannot do aught but that. And no beast of the field can ever be punished for his "evil" actions since he cannot ever do "good." Both heavenly creature and beast of the field are locked into an existence that precludes choice. Only Man has the power, the Divine power to choose, to be great, if he but choose to go that way. Or to be small, tiny, irrelevant, should he choose to go that way. And herein lies his true greatness. The ability to choose good, though it be terribly difficult. The ability to reject that which is evil, though it be so wonderfully tempting and sweet. That is the greatness of Man, that is his uniqueness, that is why he was created. To choose good, to do good, to appreciate the magnificence of good, and to sing the praises of the One who is the totality of Good. G-d.

Man alone was given the opportunity to climb the higher mountain or Creation. His is the challenge to take the ego that is such an integral and deliberate part of him, to take the "I" that is the source of all that is selfish and egotistical and coveting and self-centered and sanctify it through limiting it, through self-discipline and self-sacrifice, through denial of that which he could freely take if he were unfettered.

That is the essence of the "good" that G-d gave and obligated Man to accept. And he defined it specifically in the form of seven basic laws for all humankind:

1) Prohibition against idolatry
2) Prohibition against blasphemy
3) Prohibition against murder
4) Prohibition against immorality
5) Prohibition against robbery
6) Commandment to set up laws and courts for the proper, just working of society
7) Prohibition against the eating of a mutilated animal

These seven basic laws take wild, primitive man, the one who is totally free, the one born in supreme, sublime anarchy, the idol of Rousseau, the one who, if he were to follow his natural bent would be worse by far than the beast of the field as he added cruelty to his evil actions, and raises him up by the greatness of free will. To bend the knee and bow the head and accept the Divine yoke as one does "good" unto humanity in the way that the Almighty commanded, and then appreciate and hold Him in awe and love Him in a totality of body and soul. That is the purpose of Man.

Humanity is called, in Judaism, the "sons of Noah," for it was the flood that destroyed all the rest of the descendants of the first man, Adam. And that flood came as awesome punishment to teach man that which is among the greatest of all lessons:

There is no purpose for the world except that it do "good," except that it follow G-d's will. Totally in opposition to those who see the end of life as the worst of all possible nightmares. For Judaism there is not the slightest meaning to having a world except that it follow "good." The worst of all nightmares for the Jew is a world that rejects G-d and His Will, for the doing of good is more important by far than life itself. Life, the world, has no purpose at all, no value, if one swerves from the purpose for which it was created, and that is why the Almighty destroyed a world with a flood and swept away the creations of His own Hand. To engrave on our hearts the lesson that more important than life is living that life in the proper way. The doing of good, keeping from evil, is an eternal challenge in the world. There is a perpetual battle between good and evil and, in that sense, between G-d and the people who defy Him and commit evil. And thus did the rabbis proclaim it: "As long as the wicked rule in the world, the Almighty, so to speak, does not sit on His throne. And when does He sit on His throne? As it says: 'And the redeemers shall go up to Mount Zion to judge the mountain of Esau, and the kingdom shall be that of the L-rd'" (Obadiah 1) (*Yalkut Shimoni*, Psalms 47).

How totally different this concept of the world from that of the secular, gentilized Jew, rooted in that materialism and self-centeredness that is the precise opposite of Divine will and law!

And that is why Judaism, in such total contrast to the liberal and permissive west, cleaves to the concepts of punishment for evil, as over and over again the Bible cries out: "And thou shalt eradicate evil from thy midst," and the rabbis explain: "And thou shall eradicate *the doers of evil* from Israel (*Sifrei*, R'ey 86).

"All Israel shall hear and fear and shall not continue to do such wickedness among you."

The world is not a game, a plaything. G-d made a world for good, and when there is evil within it, *that* destroys and pollutes and defies G-d's creation. There is no place in this world for evil. There is no coexistence with it. Good and evil must be made separate, and, indeed, the very first act of the Almighty was separation—the separation of light and darkness since, in the words of the commentator Rashi: "G-d saw that it was not good that the two serve together." Unlike liberal Man who so wants and needs a befogging, clouding, confusion of values so that he may be permitted a maximum of freedom, of personal anarchy, Judaism clearly defines good and evil and then goes much further: it forbids and punishes for the committing of that evil.

"For My thoughts are not your thoughts, neither are your ways My ways, saith the L-rd" (Isaiah 55).

And because of this, G-d chose, out of all the peoples on earth, a single one that would be His chosen one. A nation that would be an example of the magnificence of Divine life as practiced in totality by man. A life that is pure and holy, free from the abominations of ego and materialism and "I." The Jewish people was chosen to accept and observe and bring into fruition the laws of G-d, so as to show how magnificent and wonderful human life can be when Man, in every phase of that life, in the totality of life, bends the knee and cleaves to G-d and the yoke of heaven. The Jewish people was chosen to be a light unto the nations by practicing fully and exactly the laws of the Almighty, as individuals and as a nation within a specific, isolated state of their own—within the Land of Israel.

What magnificent glory, but what awesome obligation, too! For along with the greatness and the privilege came a life far more difficult and demanding than that of any other of the sons of Noah. To be pure and holy and elevated is wonderful, but difficult and exacting. Judaism is not the plaything, the fraud, of Reform and Conservatism. It is not a "religion" created by Garment Center man to fit the client. G-d is not made in the image of man. G-d exists as the Creator, as the One who rules history and who is not a Santa Claus figure, perpetually smiling and doling out gifts to little children. We are not little children but adults who are expected to live certain way-the good way-and if not, to be punished for our refusal. There is sin and punishment just as there is goodness and reward. It may be unnerving to most Jews, unsettling and uncomfortable. It may, indeed, be frightening and unacceptable. No matter. It is true, and Jewish destiny on both a personal and a national level is based on that scale of reward and punishment.

"If you walk in my statutes and keep my commandments and do them ... you shall dwell in safety in your land and I will *give* peace in the land."

The G-d of Israel, in His deep love for His people and the world, gives them an opportunity for a wonderful life, for a life that makes them great and elevated and holy, *a life that is good for them.* "And thou shalt do that which is right and good in the sight of the L-rd *that it may be good for thee ...*" (Deuteronomy 6).

But it is more than an opportunity for magnificence. It is a demand, an obligation. It is an ultimatum, and there is no escaping it. "The Almighty wished to purify and benefit Israel, therefore He gave them Torah and many commandments." What a magnificent gift, indeed! On the one hand the degrading, bestial, animalistic life of wallowing in the mud of cheap materialism and ego and selfishness and violence and pettiness, the utter waste of a life that passes all too quickly, the kind of society that we see daily in the west, and on the other, the life of greatness and holiness, of spiritual elevation, of reality and permanent, of Torah life. A magnificent gift that the Jew must accept, is not permitted to reject.

"And if you shall despise my statutes and if your soul abhor my judgments so that you will not do all My commandments so as to violate My covenant... I will set My face against you and you shall be slain before your enemies.

"And if you shall not listen to the voice of the L-rd, thy G-d, to observe and to do all His commandments and statutes that I command you this day, then shall all these curses come upon you."

The people of Israel, given a Torah, given a land in which they were ordered to create a Torah society, were given the choice of observing or not, the choice of life or death:

"See, I have set before you this day, life and good, death and evil... therefore choose life, that both thou and thy seed may live."

There is no escape from it. It does not matter that one agrees or not, finds it "acceptable" or not. The Almighty has chosen us, and our destiny is fixed and clear. That is why a Jewish government in a Jewish State is established and precisely fixed by *halacha,* by Jewish law, and commanded to see to it that the Jewish nation within the Jewish state will, indeed, obey the will of G-d. *For our own sake!*

"Judges and officers shalt thou make thee in all thy gates which the L-rd, your G-d, giveth thee throughout thy tribes and they shall judge the people with just judgment" (Deuteronomy 16).

And the commentary *The Chinuch* explains: "We are commanded to appoint judges and officers to compel the people to observe the laws of the Torah and to return those who stray from the path of truth unto it by force and they shall command what is proper to do and prevent that which is abominable."

The Jewish concept of government differs totally from that of the liberal west. The liberal, gentilized society, lacking any concept of objective truth and, indeed, not wishing to have any such concept, desiring the anarchy and totality of freedom to sink to the depths in the mire as they please, is institutionally and ideologically opposed to government coercion in the area of personal life. But Judaism knows that it is *precisely* the area of personal life of the individual that shapes his character and soul and that will lead to evil or good. And G-d sees in immorality and self-indulgence and materialism, in anarchy, all the things that are evil and obscene and destructive of man and the world. That is why there is Jewish government: To teach man the path of "good," and to insure that the individual and society follow that path of "good."

Of course we want "freedom." What child does not want the totality of freedom to do exactly as he wishes, when he wishes, regardless of responsibility or lack thereof? And when in human history was there any wider era and area of adult children indulging themselves in their pleasures and freedoms under a society that they have created to justify and legitimize that "freedom"?

But the freedom of the west runs counter to the basic Jewish concept of freedom as enunciated by the rabbis: "And the tablets were the work of G-d ... engraved on the tablets" (Exodus 32); the rabbis take the word, "engraved" (in Hebrew *"charut"*) and the word "freedom" (in Hebrew *"cherut"*) and declare the sublime and magnificent basic *law of society,* the law that divides man from the animal and, eventually, Israel from the nations and material philosophy: "Read not *'charut'* but rather *'cherut'* . For no man can be free except one occupied by the study of the Law" (*Avot* 6).

Of course, and what *lack* of freedom is there in an individual and state addicted to materialism which have long since lost any ability to escape the narcotics of pleasure and hedonism! Both the individual and state in the material west have long since lost the power and freedom to break the shackles of the need, the yearning, the bondage of pleasure, drugs, sex, "I"!

Western man and western state are prisoners of their own egos and material selves. The great "I," the utter concentration on self, turns them into captives of the animal lust and power within themselves. They are prisoners of what they call "freedom," sentenced to life imprisonment in the camps of license and anarchy.

For Judaism, true freedom, authentic freedom, can only be when man is free to break the power of his "I," of his material ego over his free will. Only within the obedience to laws that place the soul over the flesh, the commitment of the will to be holy and sanctified over the lust to be an animal, can man truly be free. Judaism and the Jewish State create the true freedom of that unique Creation called man, through a society of Divine laws of sanctity that raise the Jew to the Heavens of holiness and that grant him freedom from animalism.

The state that the West has created under its perverted "freedom" is a state and society that have institutionalized slavery of the soul within their citizens. The western state has legalized imprisonment of the soul and murder of sanctity. Do you think that this kind of state is what G-d wanted and desired for the Jew? A state in which all the ugliness and obscenity of animal hedonism and bestial selfishness can be given free rein in order to enslave and then destroy the special Divine image that was given to man? A state in which drugs and pornography and abortion and perverted sex and immorality are licensed and enthroned as kings and queens on the two-legged stool-throne called "democracy?" A state in which the worst of man can seduce a child within him? A state in which the child is exposed to the worst and the most ugly and dangerous, all in the name of a perverted and twisted "freedom" that is in reality the very opposite of the term? A state in which all the nausea and vomit of greed and lust for pleasure are declared legal by a society which is drowning in the great Sea of Boredom and lack of direction?

Do you believe that that is the kind of state the Almighty chose for the Jews? And do you believe that that is the kind of state we could ever offer him or allow to go unchecked, a foreign, imported cancer eating away at the bodies and souls of our children? What conceivable positive and substantive values does such a society-state possess over and above the cool refreshing and life-giving ones of the true freedom of Judaism to be man the unique and holy, and to climb the spiritual mountains of greatness and sanctity?

I will never accept the "right" of man and state to be ugly and selfish and addicted to evil and animalism. I will never accept a state that insanely sanctifies the concept of "freedom" of pornography and unbridled, illicit and perverted sex; and murderous abortions; and artistic national suicide; and drugs that ravage the soul and kill the spirit of Heaven within the unique child called man. Never. That is not freedom. That is slavery. That is bondage. That is tyranny most foul. And the Almighty who took the Jew out of the physical bondage of Egypt never meant to then take him up to his own land to build a state of slavery of the soul and spirit. The state that freely allows values that create the Jewish child lying dead of an overdose of "pleasurable" drugs in a urine-ridden doorway near Tel Aviv's Central Bus Station is not the Jewish state of G-d—or Kahane.

The Almighty never meant such a state for His people and never will allow it. He is not some plastic god invented by clever Jewish entrepreneurs to fill a need of people to feel something "spiritual" as long as it does not interfere too much with their material pleasures. He is not an artificial Cabbage Patch doll created for our pleasure and desire, a perpetually laughing Santa Claus come down from the Heavenly North Pole to perpetually dispense gifts and the counterfeit "love" that modern theologians, in cowardly prostration before the mob, have created to cover every possible sin and abomination. The G-d of Israel postulates and decrees truth and greatness and true freedom. He does not ask, He *demands* that the Jew choose that truth and greatness and freedom. And He warns and guarantees awesome punishment for the Jew who, given the freedom of choice, rejects Good and chooses Evil.

This is the essence. G-d is truth, G-d has given us truth and G-d demands from us that we follow and observe and live by that truth and the perfect goodness within it. There is no "choice." There is no concept of "live and let live." That is the most un-Jewish of all concepts! The Divine reward and punishment that must be is not one that is granted to the individual Jew, in this world. His personal blessings will be granted in the world to come. Here, all Jews are one. All Jews—as the one, chosen people of G-d—are judged together. They stand together; they fall together. One's sins are visited upon all; we are all brothers and sisters; we are all surety and guarantors for each and every Jew.

How did the rabbis put it? "It is similar to a group of people in a boat. One suddenly took a tool and began to knock a hole in the boat. Said the others to him: What are you doing? He answered: What concern is it of yours; am I not knocking the hole under my side? They replied: But the water will rise and sink the entire boat" (Vayikra Raba 4).

There are no individual seats or sides in the Jewish boat. The sinners, the choosers of evil, knock holes in the boat and we all go under. There is no freedom of choice for the Jewish individual. He has no luxury of demanding live and let live! All of us live together and all of us fall together.

Jewish history is replete with exactly that punishment, the national punishment of Jews who, by their refusal to be chosen and special, do away with any reason for a world, for creation, and thus bring the world itself to the brink of destruction. I will never lend my hand to a "freedom" and democracy that are the freedom and democratic right to destruction of the individual Jew, his state and the world. For that too, I feel no guilt. Not the slightest.

We must be honest; above all, we must be honest. We must be honest, no matter how painful it is and no matter how it shakes our personal illusions and lives. If we are not interested in Judaism, if it is not the ruler of our lives, that is one thing; but, in that case, let no one raise it as a weapon in the battle against Kahane. But neither can one use a fraudulent Judaism as an intellectual weapon unless one is intellectually dishonest. Judaism is either authentic Judaism or it is not, and if one chooses Reform or Conservatism or any of the "wings" that fly on the words of human beings, no matter how "wise," then understand that this is not Judaism but the personal views of people who set their own view and their own beliefs as their G-d and their "Judaism"; know that it is fraud. Judaism is Divine and it is G-d's literal word or it is worthless. It *is* Divine! It *is* G-d's word! And He gave us not only laws concerning our personal lives but those that establish and control and direct the way a Jewish State and Jewish government must be.

And the basic truth, no matter how bitter for Jews raised and influenced by the non-Jewish cultures of the West, is that Judaism does not postulate a state based on democracy in western form. Consider:

If it is true that Judaism is a Divine Law given the Jew at Sinai by the Almighty, is it really logical to assume that the state which is sanctioned by Judaism should sanction, too, a system of government under which every four years or so the people shall decide whether to observe the law of G-d? Would any religious code sanction such a political system? Obviously not, and clearly Judaism is not western democracy, as we know it. The Talmud clearly states the Jewish concept of government.

During the days of the First Holy Temple, as King Hezekiah

reigned in Judea, the mighty Assyrian empire ruled the Middle East. Its armies poured over the area, conquering nations and states, never defeated. The northern Jewish kingdom of Israel fell to the mighty Assyrians, and they ravaged the southern kingdom of Judea, conquering every city and town except the capital, Jerusalem. The powerful army, led by Sanacherib, laid siege to the city and delivered an ultimatum to the Jews standing behind the city's walls: Surrender and live, be taken to another land where you will live lives of quiet comfort, or fight—and be exterminated.

Within the city a bitter debate broke out, with King Hezekiah placing his faith in the Almighty, calling for resistance and refusal to surrender. A second camp, however, led by the scholar and scribe Shevna, called for surrender and peace. And thus, says the Talmud (Sanhedrin 26a):

"Shevna spoke before 130,000 people and Hezekiah before 110,000. Hezekiah (seeing that the majority was with Shevna) was fearful and said: Can it be, G-d forbid, that the Almighty wishes to go after the majority and since the majority wishes to surrender, we, too, should agree to surrender? The prophet [Isaiah] then came and said: 'Say you not a confederation to all that the people shall call a confederation' (Isaiah 8). It is a confederation of the wicked and *a confederacy of the wicked is not counted.*"

The votes and the majority of those who do not follow G-d's law and will are not "counted," are not considered in making a national Jewish decision. Of course, there is a concept of democracy within Judaism. But that is within a context of Jewish law, when the majority does not go against Judaism. Certainly the Sanhedrin ruled on the basis of the majority decision of its members and certainly the vote for people who are committed to Judaism and Jewish policies is based on the principle of democracy. But democracy can never be used to vote against Torah and Jewish concepts and values and laws. Democracy must bow before the truth of Judaism. That is logical and that is obvious if one is speaking about Jewish values on a Judaism based on Divine law. And that is logical and obvious to any Jew who is honest and open.

Democracy is indeed the only political system for people and societies that are not privy to absolute truth. Then, with no other choice, one must accept democracy lest the state fall into anarchy or secular dictatorship. But if Judaism is Divine truth and if the Jewish State is to be based on Divine truth, it is simply the height of absurdity and madness to speak of a democratic vote by the people to abide by that law or not. Democracy is not Judaism, no one has the right to defy G-d's law. But, alas, there is a tragic "but."

The pity is—the tragedy is—that most Jews do not believe that Judaism is Divine and therefore do not accept it as the foundation of the state. And so, because of that—but only because any attempt to establish a true Torah state would lead to a bitter civil war among Jews—I would not be prepared to establish a state that would bar elections involving parties that do not accept Torah law as authority. But know that punishment will be forthcoming against a people that refuses to create the kind of society that G-d demands. Tragedy. But we cannot ever create the conditions that will lead to certain civil war among Jews.

But let two things be clearly known. One, western democracy is not Judaism and not the form of government that Judaism postulates. Jewish leaders, particularly the rabbinical officials who say otherwise, are frauds who pervert Judaism and who twist and corrupt Torah law.

Secondly, should I through the democratic system gain power, it is totally acceptable for me, within that democratic system, to pass laws that would make people conform to Judaism. If a democratic election gives mandate to a particular person and party which pledges to accept that democratic process and allow the nation the choice of change or not in the next election, let no demagogue dare to shout that Torah laws passed by that democracy are "undemocratic."

Every law that is passed by any state and under any form of government, be it the purest of democracies, limits freedom, is a contradiction of "freedom." For the original state came into being on the heels of a people that was totally free. The state arose with a mandate to restrict that absolute freedom for what is accepted by almost all as the necessary greater good. All authority, every state *per se*, restricts the absolute right of free people to do as they please, but that is the very nature of state and government. We sacrifice absolute freedom for benefits that are more important to us, i.e., safety and protection from hoodlums or the enemy, as well as social and economic benefits.

Numerous are the laws passed by democratic governments, laws that we oppose, find absurd, obnoxious or worse. That is not relevant to the democratic concept. Laws are not necessarily expected to be appreciated or accepted by all the citizens of a democracy. Indeed, many of the laws may be bitterly contested. As long as the majority has decided upon them and as long as the political process allows for some future change in them, the minority is expected to respect the law and the process. And there is no difference between a law that limits the right of a citizen in his economic life and that which limits his social and "personal" existence. All laws limit "personal" existence, but if done for what the majority conceives to be the good of society, the state has a right to demand that they be obeyed.

Judaism does not accept western democracy, but if, for the sake of avoiding civil war, religious Jews do agree to it, they will not be lesser citizens for it. "Religious" laws are no worse in the eyes of the democratic process than economic or political ones. All laws limit man's freedom but the difference is that the so-called religious ones will help to save the state from tragic Divine anger and punishment.

The Jewish State that we will attempt to establish within the forced necessary democratic framework will attempt to save the Jewish people from the immutable Divine decree of reward and punishment. It will attempt to convince Jews to establish a truly Jewish State that will do away with the ugly present form, a cheap imitation of the western gentile state, a tragic copy of the worst of foreign culture. It will be an *authentic* Jewish State, with *authentic* Jewish values, with *authentic* Jewish ethics and morality. And we need no critical braying from the liberal moral prostitutes and the ethical perverts of the left.

Certainly, those who deliberately murder Jews and who deliberately destroyed the souls of hundreds of thousands of others should be the last to pontificate to others about "Jewish morality and ethics." I need no moral lesson from them. Nor any lesson in "Judaism" from those who so violently hate and oppose it. We know what Judaism says about morality and ethics and we know exactly within what context they are. And unlike the ignoramuses and the deliberate perverters of Judaism, we take nothing out of context of the *totality of Torah*. Those who accept the totality of Torah as the precise Divine word of G-d accept *all* of it, and know what justice is and is not. They know the precise place in this world for kindness and for mercy and for hardness and revenge. They know the importance of peace and the time for war, when to be merciful and when to be cruel, and know the Biblical words: "For everything there is a season and a time to every purpose under the heaven."

Of course, the rabbis tell us: "Who is honored, he who honors human beings." And, of course, the rabbis said: "Thus did the Almighty say unto Israel: My children, what do I ask of you? To love each other and respect each other." And of course Maimonides writes: "It is a commandment to love each and every one of Israel as himself."

And of course we are told: "Greet every man with peace, shalom." And of course we are told that "the property of your comrade should be as dear to you as your own." And of course the rabbis tell us: "Be similar to Him: Just as He is merciful and gracious and merciful, so be you gracious and merciful." And of course we are told: "Follow in the attributes of the Almighty: Just as He clothed the naked, so you clothe the naked; just as He visited the sick, so you visit the sick; just as He buried the dead, so you bury the dead." And of course it says that "*Tzedaka* (the giving of money to the needy) is as great as all the other commandments combined." And of course the rabbis tell us that "Torah begins with the doing of kindness and ends with the doing of kindness" and that "anyone who denies the doing of kindness is likened to one who denies the Almighty." And of course the rabbis tell us: "Let your home be open wide and let the poor be members of your household." And of course we are told that "the Almighty did not find a greater vessel to hold blessings for Israel, than that of peace." Of course, these are essentials of Judaism.

But none of those who never regularly give ten percent of their income to charity need give us ethical lessons, and none of those who never voluntarily went to prison and suffered for fellow Jews need apply for the job of official chastiser. Let the hypocritical chastisers of the liberal Left look at the state they have created and behold all the wonderful values of ethics and morality and holiness they have created within it....

Of course our authentic Jewish State will be one of immense justice and kindness and goodness and all the spiritual values the leftists and material secularists so hypocritically quote when they so hate and despise Judaism in its totality. But that is exactly the kind of Jewish State that is the only authentic one: *A state of Jewish totality.* What kind of state will it be? Here is a partial program:

With the help of G-d, we will establish that state whose first and primary concern and action will be to build a proud and loyal and believing Jewish youth, a youth to whom we will restore their spiritual identity card.

We will establish a program of education aimed at creating Jewish identity, proud and maximum and certain. All the public schools of Israel will receive a thorough overhaul of their curriculum with a large percentage of the studies given over to Jewish content, to Judaism. Never again will youngsters say, "I am an Israeli, not a Jew." Never again will they wander about, lost and indifferent to their identity. Judaism will be taught by professional teachers who know and believe in the subject. Jewish pride will be the first order of business. A Jewish youngster will know that being Jewish is, indeed, special, and he will know the reason for that special status—Judaism, Torah from Sinai. He will wake each morning with the age-old Jewish prayer: "*Ashrenu*; happy are we, how good is our portion, and how sweet is our lot and how beautiful our inheritance!" He will attend the burial of Jewish guilt and be present at the birth of the old Jew of certainty, of pride, of strength—of himself. He will know that he lives in Eretz Yisrael, the Land of Israel, the exclusive home of the Jewish people and of no others. He will learn the *tefillin* of the hand and heart and head, which give the Jew wisdom and mercy and, also, strength of arm.

All the public schools of Israel, those which today so destroy Jewish children through their paucity of Judaism (and even the Bible that is taught, is taught as Jewish "culture," à la Shakespeare in the United States and with as much value), will teach Judaism. There will be no "secular" schools to educationally castrate Jewish children. And those parents who do not desire this are free to create their own private schools where they can supervise the death of their children. But even in such a school there will be a minimal amount of hours of Judaism, as important in the eyes of the Jewish State as are mathematics or art. The schools of Israel, the Jewish State, will, indeed, first create good Jews who may then be good doctors or pilots.

And the Jewish State will be precisely that, the state of the Jewish people, with responsibility for all the Jewish people, not only those who happen to be Israeli citizens or who live in the country. Israel was created by the Jewish people to be the trustee of the Jewish people, their protector and defender. There are no boundaries when it comes to Jewish pain and oppression. There are no Soviet Jews or Syrian Jews or American Jews. There are only Jews who live *in* the Soviet Union or *in* Syria or *in* America. There is one Jewish people, indivisible, that the Jewish State, which has the power and expertise and professionalism, is obligated to defend in every way, across and within any border. When the State of Israel demands support, monetarily and politically, from Jews all over the world—and properly so—it is because Israel is the Jewish State. But that is a two-way street. The Jews outside of Israel have a right to demand and expect help and support from that Jewish State.

We will create a special anti-terror and Jewish defense unit that will deal with attacks on and threats to Jews outside of Israel. Let neo-Nazis know that they cannot, with impunity, threaten or attack Jews in a country outside of Israel and be free from fear of Israeli retaliation. Let those who murder Jews in Turkey or Italy or France know that they, who live in Italy or Turkey or France, will die there. There will be no sanctuary for murder *of Jews*, Israelis or not.

And when arrangements are made to exchange prisoners, never

again will Syrian soldiers be exchanged only for Israeli soldiers. There will be an exchange of Syrians *for Jews*, including the Jews of Syria.

At the same time, the Jewish state must overcome its fear of the reaction of the Jewish Establishment in the Exile and—for the sake of Jewish survival there—cry out:

The commandment to live in the Land of Israel brings with it the threat of mass tragedy for those Jews who refuse to leave the Exile. The Jewish State is the sanctification of G-d, and to remain in the Exile, the personification of desecration, at a time when it is possible to return home, is to consciously choose to reinforce the desecration. The Almighty will never allow it, and the Exile is being ended whether the Jew agrees to it or not. The signs are already plentiful as Jew-hatred and world political conditions combine to shake the ground under the feet of the Jew in continent after continent. The Exile will end, either in glory, through mass, voluntary Jewish emigration to Israel, or through terrible tragedy, G-d forbid. There cannot be coexistence between sanctification and desecration, and so, the Exile is doomed.

The Jews of the Exile, including those of the United States, face a horrible growth of Jew-hatred that will be triggered by economic and social upheaval in the world. At the same time, they face a possible nuclear confrontation that will wipe out large areas of the Exile but never that of a Jewish State that the rabbis of the Talmud guarantee can never become a third exile. Before it is too late, they must leave the graveyard and return to Israel. It is the obligation of Zionist leaders in the Exile to take the lead in emigrating to Israel.

And there is more.

The Jew is forbidden to give up any part of the Land of Israel which has been liberated. The land belongs to the G-d of Israel, and the Jew, given it by G-d, has no right to give away any part of it. All the areas liberated in 1967 will be annexed and made part of the State of Israel. Jewish settlement in every part of the land, including cities that today are sadly *Judenrein*, will be unlimited.

This will be part of a policy, that, once and for all, puts to an end the insane delusion of "peace through concessions."

The Arabs do not want peace. It is illusion and delusion to believe that the Middle Eastern problem is a dispute over the "occupied lands of 1967," or the creation of a "Palestine" that would exist next to Israel. Those who understand the Arabs and are free of contempt for them know that the essence of the problem is the Arab belief that the Jews have stolen the entire land from them. Arabs went to war with Israel in 1967 and 1956 when the "occupied lands" of today were in their hands. Arabs turned down the United Nations 1947 partition plan and went to war then, too. Arabs murdered Jews in the 1930s and 1920s when there was no Jewish state and no "Zionist occupation force."

There are no Arab moderates (witness the Jordanian "moderate" who in 1967, in possession of the lands of Judea and Samaria and East Jerusalem, went to war). The Arabs differ in tactics, not goals. Foolish Jews who call for concessions have already cost us dearly and we will pay terribly for those concessions that were made on the assumption that Arab "moderates" would seek peace with Israel and be its allies. Similarly, it is mad delusion to insist that Arab terrorists do not represent the "Palestinians." Of course they do, because the "Palestinians" as a whole, are committed to the destruction of an Israel they see as a robber state.

The true issue is the refusal of the Arabs to recognize a Jewish State of any size or shape for any permanent length of time. It is not an Arab-Israel issue but an Arab-Jewish one, and it is more than a political dispute: It is a religious war. We should not be surprised that Christians and Moslems who kill each other join against the Jews, or that a Pope meets with Moslem terrorists. The very existence of the Jewish State is proof of the truth of Judaism, a thing that neither Islam nor Christianity can accept. Peace is not possible under the above circumstances, but Jews need not weep or wail. Zionism, from the first, was not created primarily for peace but for a Jewish State. Hopefully, it was believed, this could be accompanied by peace. But with or without peace, the primary goal was and is a Jewish State.

And Jewish self-respect and honor must be resurrected with an end to the humiliating obscenity of carefree political relations with the *Amalek* of our times, Germany. Was there a greater abomination than that of Israel establishing relations with Germany less than a decade after Auschwitz? And for money reparations, of course! Today, there is not the slightest feeling of guilt on the part of Israelis who happily travel on business or vacation to Munich and Frankfurt and Hamburg; many of whom—40,000 Jews (!)—*live* there. There is no guilt on the part of a state that regularly sends youth on cultural and sports excursions to walk on the land stained with Jewish blood. There is no guilt felt when Jewish and Israeli leaders, even the "nationalist" ones of Likud, travel to Germany and eat and drink with the Germans at state dinners, or when a high-ranking German official arrives in Israel and the Israeli army band plays the German national anthem, *Deutschland Uber Alles* as the new Hebrews stand at attention with respect.

The Germans *owe* us reparations. The money does not absolve them of one sin, of one crime, of one murder. But they owe reparations for property and we owe them nothing. Political and cultural ties will be cut with the Germans and they will be expected to fulfill, to the letter, their obligations to the Jewish people.

And because the Jewish child is shaped by his environment and because a Jewish state would be an abomination in any other form, *the public character*, of the state will be Jewish. There will be no stores or restaurants that publicly sell non-kosher food, or which wave leavened bread, *chametz*, about on Passover. Book stalls and newspapers kiosks will no longer titillate and destroy Jewish minds and souls with pornography, and movies and theatres will no longer be free to stand on the soapbox of "freedom of expression and art" to demolish the purity and sanctity of the Jewish soul. And no one will be allowed to murder unborn children, and abortion will be regulated by Jews law, permitted only in case of danger to the mother. And missionaries will be allowed to proselytize in China but not in the Jewish State, and Mormon Centers and other such places of soul snatching will be closed down and nationalized. People of other faiths who are not idolaters will be given total freedom to pray and worship and observe as they see fit, but never, ever to proselytize.

And an end will be put to the awful threat of the splitting of Jews into two different peoples, one unable to marry with the other. The definition of who is a Jew will be clear, uniform, as it was before the deniers of Divine *halacha* rose to defraud it. A Jew will be defined only as one born to a Jewish mother or converted according to authentic *halacha*.

And normal and acceptable decency in dress will be demanded and the foreign tourists who flock to Israel and its Eilats will be greeted at the airports with polite welcomes to the Holy Land and with instructions on how they are expected to behave and dress and conduct themselves in our Holy land. And intermarriage and sexual relations between Jews and gentiles will be forbidden by law; respect for the gentile will be demanded but that will not include sharing his or her bed.

The Talmud tells us that G-d would not give the Children of Israel the Torah until they put up a pledge, a guarantee. That pledge and that guarantee was their children. We have no intention of losing our pledge, our children. Our sacred oath and obligation to them is to shape them and produce yet another Jewish generation, yet another link in the golden chain of Judaism, a generation that is holy and decent and proud and free of all the ugliness of western license and anarchy that is packaged as "freedom."

And there will be a five-day work week in Israel with work ending at 2 p.m. on Friday, the eve of the Sabbath, and leisure extending until Monday morning. And from Saturday night on, Jews will be free to do what they please in terms of sports and vacations and leisure, *but the Sabbath day shall be holy.* No one will check to see what the Jew does in the privacy of his home but the public character of the Sabbath will be respected and demanded.

The Temple Mount, holiest site in all of Judaism, will be freed of the Moslem outrage and contempt for Judaism and its holy places. The Moslems will be taken down from there along with their mosques, which will be carefully removed to any other site where the Moslems can then worship in peace.

And finally. The Jewish people, with their financial genius, have made countless nations wealthy and prosperous. All the more reason to stand in astonishment as the Jews, finally achieving their dream of their own state, have plied its economy as shoemakers, instead of financial wizards. The country is riddled with economic inefficiency; it is in shambles. What can possibly be the cause of this incredible phenomenon?

The answer is clear. Israel is a country which refuses to allow people to breathe economically. It is a place of economic strait-jacket and strangulation. In the United States, a person who seeks to open a store finds a vacant location and opens a store. Not so in Israel. There, the act of opening a store is an adventure. Licenses must be obtained and innumerable and frustrating visits made to a dozen governmental offices and bureaucrats. And then taxes. All manner of taxes, invented by a genius or a demon. The heavy hand of the bureaucrat and government forces people to be thieves or go out of business.

Foreign investors, Jews, good ones, good Zionists, want very much to invest in Israel rather than Taiwan or South Korea. But coming to Israel and meeting with the governmental bureaucrats, they go through the seven circles of Jewish hell. In the end they leave, in anger and frustration, and do indeed build their factory in Taiwan or South Korea.

What is the matter with the Israelis? Do they not understand that Israel needs investment and business? Do they not know that business gives jobs to Jews, and factories produce and export goods and bring in badly needed foreign hard currency? Do they not see Israelis who leave the country in disgust and then, going to America or Canada or Europe, work with an energy and effort no one dreamed they possessed? What is the problem? Do they not know that Israel cannot continue to remain as some *shtetl* beggar, with its hand out to America or Germany or the UJA or Israel Bonds? That Israel must learn to stand on its own feet and work and produce and export?

Of course they do. But they also know that political power comes out of the barrel of economic power and the government bureaucracy deliberately adopts its agonizing policy of choking and throttling and frustrating the individual so that finally the spirit of independence within him is crushed and he bows to the fact that he needs the government and must play its game. And that is why the Israeli power Establishment really does not want western Aliyah. For western Jews, raised in democracy and independence, in freedom-minded countries, have been taught to look upon government as serving *them*, whereas that attitude is anathema to totalitarian types. The socialists who founded Israel prefer the East European Jews and those from Arab lands who accept government's fiat much more pliably. They want western Jewish money but no western Jews.

If we want Israel to grow and economically expand and prosper, there is an immediate need to dismantle the socialist bureaucratic system that strangles the individual Jew and prevents him from striking out on his own economic path. Only free enterprise that brings in foreign investment and that encourages domestic capitalism and incentive will allow Israel to escape its present position as a beggar basket-case. And only the dismantling of the socialist bureaucracy and ingrained vested interests of the political Establishment will bring in Jewish funds to build factories and give jobs, will allow the "black money" to come out of Swiss bank accounts and from under the tiles, will stop the flow of money and people from Israel. *Cut* the taxes, do not raise them. Allow people to gamble with their money in business, in the hope of making a profit. No need for arbitrary permits and licenses. Let the people breathe! This will be the economic underpinning of the Jewish State.

Of course, this will dismantle the political power of the Establishment. Of course it will be bitterly fought. No matter, the Jewish State transcends political parties and bosses.

And another economic need. Jews must once again learn to work with their hands and be prepared to do so, for wages that are fair and capable of allowing them to support their families. Every soldier, regardless of his background, who is drafted into the army for his three-year service, will—in his second year—be taught a manual trade. *Every single one.* Then, in the third year, except for intervals of army training, he will be sent home—but still be in the army. And as part of that military service, he will have to report each morning to the labor exchange (employment bureau) and work in his field.

Why should Arabs build our houses and do our manual work? Who did these things before the Six Day War? A normal state must have normal people *who work*. Not every Jew can be a Ph.D....

A Jewish State. Strong in body and powerful in soul. With mighty right arm and mighty faith in G-d. That is what, please G-d, will be.

PART VI

OUTRAGE OF TYRANNY

Chapter 15

Israel

And so, that is the *other* side. Kahane's side. Finally. Finally, the opportunity to hear and read Kahane, not *about* him from frightened and hate-filled enemies. And having read it, consider: Is it really "racism"? Is it really an echo of "fascism"? Of Nazis? Of *Hitler? After having heard and read so much about the evils of "Kahanism" from those who so hate Kahane, is what they say really true?*

Is what Kahane says so abominable that the government of Israel, in defending the right of schools to ban him from appearing before students, was justified in 1983 in comparing his statements and program on the Arab issue to Hitler's *Mein Kampf* and the Nuremberg Laws? Is there ever any justification for any Jew to even dare to compare another Jew to Hitler, of cursed memory? Is there not something immensely sick in the hearts and minds of people who can so cheapen the Holocaust by removing it from its exclusive place in historical infamy and equating it with what a Jew proposes in order to save his people from precisely the repetition of such horrors? Is there not something unbelievably obscene about such a thing, and does it not speak volumes for the kind of people who do it and about their inner twisted motivations?

Can Kahane, who recognizes the absolute right of any Arab, through proper Jewish conversion, to become as good a Jew as anyone so born; who agrees to the right of any non-Jew, including an Arab, who accepts a status of "resident stranger" to remain in the land with full personal rights; who never remotely calls for the deliberate, premeditated killing of Arabs—can he be conceivably compared to the monster of Germany, except by cynical, frightened men who seek to silence his agonizing questions that destroy both their reasons for being and their political and economic power? What kind of twisted mind can possibly compare the German Jews to the Arabs of Israel? Did the German Jew sit quietly and seethe with anger and hate and declare that Germany was a country stolen from the Jews and that when they—the Jews—would achieve power or population or opportunity of any kind, they would reclaim it and call it Israel? Did German Jews stone German soldiers and plant bombs in German market places and murder Germans on the basis of nationalist hate? Did German Jews dream of eliminating the German state? Or did German Jews wish nothing more than to be the best Germans who ever lived, who accepted and loved Germany in a way that was pathetically abnormal in their groveling desire to be accepted and loved?

And does the Arab of Israel love and accept the Jewish State and want nothing more than to be a loyal less-than-first-class citizen of a country that is labeled "Jewish"; that has a Law of Return that applies to Jews and not to him; that has laws that forbid the leasing of national land to him; whose holidays and anthem and heroes and entire atmosphere *are Jewish*? And does the Arab of Israel never plant bombs, or murder Jews, or call for "Palestine" in place of Israel, or see himself as a "Palestinian," or recognize the PLO as the legitimate representative of the "Palestine people," or never demonstrate for autonomy in the Galilee, or never shout "Jews out"?

What kind of tortured, guilt-ridden soul is it that rises up to compare Nazism with a Kahane who sees the Arab threat and who cries out against the very real danger of an Arab who sincerely and totally rejects Zionism and the Jewish State even as he dreams of a "Palestine" in its place? What disturbed Jewish leader can equate Kahane, who calls for giving the Arab enemies an opportunity to peacefully leave with compensation for their property, *with Nazis and Hitler—accursed* enemies of Jews and mankind—who took loyal Jewish citizens and, on the basis of their origin alone, deliberately and murderously exterminated them?

Is there anything in what Kahane says that can remotely excuse the outrageous refusal of Knesset Speaker Hillel to table three of his proposed laws with the statement, "I will not lend my signature to the contempt of the Knesset through *Nuremberg* laws," when Kahane deliberately copied two of them, word for word, from the great Jewish law codifier, Maimonides, and the other from the bylaws of the Jewish National Fund? What does that say for both the intelligence and character of Kahane's opponent? What does that say about the real belief of Kahane's enemies that it is the Bible and the Talmud and Maimonides who are "Nazis" and equatable to "Nuremberg laws"? (And, indeed, in the debate on the anti-racist bill in the Knesset on August 5, 1986, leftist Knesset member Matityahu Peled did not hesitate to compare the Bible to *Mein Kampf* because it prohibits intermarriage, and the same Speaker Hillel sat quietly and did not demand a retraction.) And what does one make of the Black Comedy of Hillel declaring 1985 as the Year of Maimonides; along with UNESCO?

And what possible excuse exists for the Prime Minister of Israel, Shimon Peres, to dare stand in the Knesset and read a Jew out of the Jewish people, declaring: "A Jew who preaches racism is, in my eyes, not a Jew" (February 3, 1986). Can one even begin to imagine the outcry—led by Peres—if a religious Jew would ever exclaim: "A Jew who preaches Marxism is in my eyes, not a Jew?" Can one even begin to measure the heights of indignation—led by Peres—if a religious Jew would ever exclaim: "A Jew who preaches violation of the Sabbath is, in my eyes, not a Jew?" The truth is that no religious Jew would ever read a Jew out of the Jewish people, since *halacha* Jewish law,proclaims that "a Jew, though he sins, remains a Jew." But the fanaticism of those who are so quick to decry fanaticism will out. Beneath the demagogic cloak of tolerance and liberalism and democracy lies the reality of sheer vindictiveness and hate that can erupt into violence and worse against those they fear and see as a danger to them. It is hardly strange, therefore, that the same Peres who, in response to the religious demand that the definition of conversion to Judaism be based upon traditional Jewish law, so cleverly cloaked his political opposition to the bill with the stirring cry that he would never split the Jewish people by denying the Jewishness of any Jew, was suddenly capable of doing just that when it came to Kahane. The hypocrisy is indeed a garment that cloaks an immensely dangerous person, immensely dangerous *persons*.

And, indeed, what an outrage is this deliberate, deceitful twisting and misuse of the term "racism." A word that has a definite, precise meaning is cynically manipulated by an entire army of leftists and liberals and intellectuals to deliberately destroy a person who instills the deepest of ideological fears in them. They know that "racism" means hatred or discrimination based upon opposition to a person's *race*—i.e., racial background, skin color. They know that Meir Kahane and the Judaism he represents could not care a fig for a person's skin color or racial or, indeed, ethnic or national origin. They know that Kahane cannot—as Judaism cannot—ever differentiate between white Jew or black or yellow; cannot ever distinguish between Jew of the East or West, Africa or Europe. They know that Kahane is bound by Judaism that is color blind and ethnic blind and racial blind. They know that any human being—any *Arab*—who seeks to become Jewish and converts according to Torah law will be accepted by Kahane as a Jew at least as good as Shimon Peres. They know that the difference between Jew and non-Jew has nothing to do with race or color, or national or ethnic origin, but only with the ideological religious belief of the person. White Swedish gentiles are not the same as Jews, but Black Jewish converts are. The hideous and obscene charge of racism on the part of the Israeli and other Jewish Establishments are coldly calculated and cynical attempts to defame, smear and destroy a man they fear more than anyone else, a man who threatens their very ideological sanity. Obscene is too mild a word for them.

And what conceivable sickness can so possess the soul of a Jew that he can write about the trial of Nazi war criminal John Demjanjuk, accused of the cold-blooded murder of thousands of Jews during the Holocaust, and say: "The [court] dock is no longer holy, it has ceased to be pure as long as there walks in our midst an admitted [sic] racist. As long as the Knesset delays its drafting of a law against racism, our dock cannot serve as an arena to judge a racist who marched with racism to its logical and frightening end. As a nation that demands justice and that has suffered more than any other from racism we are liable to lose something of our moral right to judge in the trial of John Demjanjuk" (Sami Michael, *Hadashot*, (February 27, 1985).)

How utterly, utterly obscene! How sickening to compare a single sentence of Kahane, a Jew, to the acts and murders of a Nazi and then to question, even remotely, our moral right to try him! What a confused mind and what a diseased soul!

And what rational, sane person cannot but shrink in horror from the kind of mind and soul that is emerging in Israel when he reads the following item that appeared in the newspaper *Ma'ariv* (October 10, 1985)? Because it is so significant, I bring it down in full:

"Two ultra-Orthodox [Jews] surprise a young secular woman in her home and announce that she has been charged with the crime of murder. According to secret information that has reached them, she has had an abortion performed on herself, and their leader, Rabbi Ra'ana [sic], gave his authority to kill her: 'We will take a blood test. It if turns out that you are pregnant, we will apologize and leave. But if you are not pregnant we will carry out the sentence,' they tell her. The young woman cries out in terror that she is not pregnant, and the two carry out the murder.

"Does it sound frightening and imaginative? Perhaps, but Etti and Shlomi Sandak see in it a possible scenario if Kahanism conquers us. In the war against Kahane and fascism we see a vital thing, say the couple, who studied film at David Greenberg's School for Film, and they determined to produce a film that would serve the struggle against Kahanism. Coming to their aid was Yamin Suissa who helped them to get funds from former Knesset member Yaakov Gil, from the Center for Peace, the Center for Community Centers and The Jerusalem Fund.

"The people at the Jerusalem Fund approved the script and said that if the final result is satisfactory they will have the film shown in the schools, said Shlomi."

The item is more than frightening. It is an open call for war, not only against Kahane, but against "ultra-Orthodox" Jewry (read: religious Jews). It is a compendium of sheer hate and vicious ignorance. The two religious Jews are pictured in the crudest of manners, indeed, in a way that would have done justice to the very Nazis the two Hellenist Jews pontificate against. The concept that religious "zealots" will kill Jews because of abortions performed is not only the grossest of ignorance (Judaism does prohibit abortion but there is *no* death penalty for a Jew who performs it), but it is a deliberate opening of the door to killing religious Jews "before they kill us...." The fact that the Center for Community Centers, a group that gets its funding from government sources, and the Jerusalem Fund, the private fund of Teddy Kollek (now under investigation for all kinds of irregularities), gave money to this thinly veiled "hate Judaism" film is so outrageous that it cries out for investigation. And the fact that it will be shown in the public schools of Israel to indoctrinate young children with hatred of Judaism and religious Jews is nothing short of criminal.

Here we have the key to the war against "Kahanes." A war that is really only the tip of the iceberg in the unholy war against Judaism.

It is part of a campaign of pathological hatred of Judaism which sees *Hadashot* carry a full-page picture caricature of a Dracula type wrapped in prayer shawl and rising up to cast a shadow over Israel, with the sardonic words "Light unto the nations," as its caption (January 3, 1986). Or the poster being sold by *Twentieth Century*, a "progressive" boutique store in Tel Aviv. It shows a naked young baby tied up in phylacteries, with his penis exposed, and the poster is labeled: "The Festival of Freedom." Or the magazine *Know How to Respond*, whose cartoon was reprinted in the Histadrut's *Dvar Hashavua* weekend supplement. It shows a religious Jew inside a building calling to a youngster: "Child! Come spend a sweet Sabbath with a family that has values." The windows of the house are labeled: Destruction, quarrels, discrimination, hoodlumism, violence, killing, robbery, corruption, obscene actions. Or the article in *Ha'aretz* under the heading: "The Religious Are Endangering the State." Or the vicious attacks on the Return to Judaism movement and the fact that thousands of secular Israelis, empty of all values in the bankrupt secular state of Israel, have returned to religion. The fact that no force or coercion was ever used on any of them is immaterial to the naked Hellenists who understand all too well that *they* have nothing to give or sell to their children. That their youth is lost to Judaism, to Zionism, to anything that has higher spiritual value. They know that their children's bankruptcy is admission of their own, and so the leftists and liberals and secularists lash out in the kind of hate and murderous rage that is all too common among the humanitarian and ethical moralists of the world.

The bottom line in the struggle against Kahane is that it is the ultimate war *on Judaism*. The Hellenists and gentilized Hebrews understand all too well that Kahanism *is* Judaism, that Kahane speaks the authentic Jewish truth that others are too fearful to utter. *And the ultimate awful reality is that the Hellenists and leftists of Israel want a civil war against Kahane and against the Judaism he represents.*

You think not? It is hard to blame the ordinary Jew for being shocked and for refusing to want to believe such a thing. But it is all too true, and it is, ironically, the cold logic and sheer clarity of the contradiction between a Jewish State and a western democratic one, between Judaism and western liberal values, that drives Jewish leaders up the ladder of fulminating defamation and desperation. The clearer the contradiction, the more obvious the correctness of the solutions of "Kahanism," the more chilling becomes the intellectual and emotional terror, and the need to lash out, defame, silence Kahane. To go to war if necessary. It is more than mere dishonesty on the part of the political leaders of Israel, its intellectuals, its writers, its news media. It is more than the mere dishonesty of the community leaders, the rabbis, the intellectuals of the Exile. It is a supremely ugly kind of hate caused by the truly awesome awareness of a dichotomy of soul suddenly thrust upon them by Kahane. Suddenly they are forced to recognize that a lifetime of fraudulent efforts to wed Zionism and Judaism to western democracy and secularism is an abysmal failure. They stand before their flock and their pretensions, stripped naked of philosophy, barren of ideology, forced to choose, finally, between honesty and fraud. The terrible moment of truth is suddenly thrust upon them and they must select one or the other, for no longer can they deceive others or themselves. Zionism or western democracy. Judaism or western values. A *Jewish State* with Jewish values and character, or one in which all, Jew and Arab, are politically equal and free to be the majority that chooses a non-Jewish one. A state based upon Jewish values and that conforms to them, or one modeled on liberal anarchy. A life of honest, authentic *Judaism* or the knowledge that otherwise there is no non-racist reason to be a Jew. Never was there a more agonizing, tortuous moment of truth for the Hellenists and other deceivers of Jews, creators of castles in Israel.

Little wonder that they flee as from the plague any intellectual confrontation with Kahane. They may attempt to cover their terror of any such debate or forum with patently absurd excuses such as "We do not wish to dignify him" (the conceit of the dwarfs of Mosaic persuasion is laughable), but those who call for dialogue with Arabs or with Black militants and other enemies of the Jewish people on the grounds that one must speak with his enemy look more than foolish when they refuse to debate a Jew, a rabbi and a Knesset member. Those who welcome a Jesse Jackson or "moderate" PLO thug into their temple have a great deal of explaining to do about their adamant, stonewalling refusal to hold dialogue with a Jew.

No, the real reason for their unanimous, hysterical refusal to debate Kahane is their paralyzing knowledge that he will destroy them intellectually. That he will force them to stand barren of all logical argument before congregations and constituents and followers. That suddenly, it will be apparent to Jews that this is *not* the Kahane they were told about by Jewish leaders. That he makes a great deal of sense. *That they agree with him.* That the defamations and smears against him were worse than false. They were premeditated efforts at character assassination in order to save Establishment sanity and power.

For the westernized Jewish leaders, indeed for the general westernized Jew of Hellenism, the one who yearns for a "heritage" that is an admixture of "Judaism" and Thomas Jefferson, there can be nothing worse than realizing that the two are incompatible, that all of his precious western values are often opposite to the Jewish faith into which he was born, *and that he must choose between them.* He faces the stark reality of a Judaism that opposes many of his most basic western beliefs. He hates Judaism but was born into it.

And the gentilized Hebrew in Israel as well as his Hellenistic counterpart in the Exile suddenly understands that Zionism—even of the most secular and, indeed, atheistic kind—is the antithesis of a western democracy that demands total, equal political rights for all citizens of the state and the right to citizenship based on total nondiscrimination.

His world of Hellenism totters and all the delusions he has been fed by his teachers now emerge to haunt him. And so, he now hates Zionism, too, but it is the basis of his country.

Everything is against the bankrupt, secular Jew—including time. Here is a Jew who has few (if any) children, his lifestyle and that of his wife precluding such obstacles to the partaking of the good life as progeny. He has no children, but the religious Jew does. The enemy not only grows bolder. Worse. He just grows.

And here is a Jew whose few children who do emerge into the air of this world are empty of all the values of Jewishness and Zionism that, alone, can insure their wishing to remain in the country and their sacrificing for it. The Hellenist has brought forth children who are empty of Judaism because he wanted that. But he is also the father of children who look upon the Zionism he sees as sacred with all the enthusiasm of a deep yawn. They have no interest in a Zionism that for them is a sterile, empty vessel. Zionism as the "national liberation movement of the Jewish people" may have sounded valiant for the father in Europe or for the handful of American Zionist youngsters in Manhattan or London, but for the son and daughter of the Israeli Frankenstein, it is at best hollow and, worse, the cause of problems with the Arabs.

The child of the Hellenist has no identity. He quite literally does not know who he is. To proclaim himself an "Israeli" is to state his *identification*, but never his identity. Identification is a transitory, passing thing, superficial and of no great import. It is a driver's license or a social security card or a passport, exchangeable at will. *Identity* is a part of the person, existing before he was ever born. The nation and the religion are identities and the person is born into them. They become part of his entirety even as he emerges into the air of the world for the first time. Identification has no past, hence not necessarily a future. It carries with it no great ideology or *challenges* or pride. Identity has a past that began long before the young new child entered into it. And because it has a past, it also gives him his guide to the future, direction, purpose, connection to glory. But one who has no past, who rejects it, also casts aside the lamp to link up his future. He is doomed to wander in the dark, to grope, or be lost.

The young secular Israeli has a hundred identifications—his permanent identification card, his army card, his tax card, his bank card. But not one identity card. He does not accept religion. He waves his hand away at Zionism. He does not know what being Jewish is and cares less. If not for the Arab danger, the very word "Jewish" would seldom trespass into his head. His values are gentile values, his dreams gentile dreams; he would leave Israel tomorrow if he had a) the money, b) the permanent visa or, better still, c) the gentile girlfriend.

The secular parent sees it all. The bankruptcy of his own life and that of his child. He knows that he has no future. But worse, he sees "the others." The religious. The ones whose identity card is proudly marked on their phylacteries and prayer shawls and prayer books and Sabbaths and holidays and lifestyles and Jewish beliefs and Jewish values and Jewish certainties and Jewish willingness to sacrifice for their Jewishness and large families. Theirs is the future. Theirs is tomorrow and the secular Jew knows it. The state and what it will be will be theirs to determine. They will shape its destiny and they will determine its character, and it is a destiny and character that the secular Jew abhors, despises.

There is only one way the desperate, bankrupt Hellenist Jew of secularism can defeat the future he sees as so terrible. He must rise up and with his own hands and with his own strength, prevent it from happening. He must have civil war.

The secularist haters of Judaism want a civil war because they need a civil war. Because if they allow time and democracy and peaceful change to take place they are lost. The irony is that they are more willing to allow the Arabs to take the future than the religious Jews. The sickness is that they hate the religious Jew more than they hate the Arab. And, again, now clear ring the words of the rabbis through the ages: "Greater is the hatred of an ignoramus for a scholar than the hatred of the non-Jew for the Jew." Indeed. And greater than that of the secular Jew for the Arab.

That is the reality of the camp of the secular haters. When their own interests are threatened, gone are the values they flaunt before our eyes, *ad infinitum*. Gone are democracy and tolerance and law and order and ethics and love of Jews. Suddenly there are no means that are not justified by the end of destroying the Jews of Jewishness, the Jewish values they so abhor.

And the preparations have already begun—in the most obvious way. What, after all, is the way to prepare for a civil war if not to begin to claim that the other side is already preparing for it? Every violent hater and aggressor has always waved high the flag of supposed threat of aggression on the part of their intended victim and the psychopathic haters of Judaism are no different. They are laying the propaganda groundwork for the violent assault on Kahane and religious and nationalist elements. The news media is filled with dire warnings about the kind of fascist, totalitarian dictatorship Kahane will establish if he is allowed to take power. The airwaves and newsprint, daily, trumpet the dangers of "Khomenism," of the "fanatical" ultra-Orthodox, of the equally fanatic "Ultra-nationalism" of *Gush Emunim*. How cleverly cynical and cynically clever are people who control the news media that control the minds of people! Everything is "ultra"; everything is "fascist"; everything is "dangerous"!

A letter appeared in *Ha'aretz* (October 8, 1985) under the heading "To Answer Kahane with Strength": "It is not too late to go into the streets and deal with the hoodlums of the Right in the one language they understand: strength. Otherwise we will find ourselves in a short while under their rule and then we will be unable to even send letters to the editor."

The infrastructure of the civil war is laid in a daily flood of brainwashing. Shulamit Har-Even, a progressive, enlightened humanist and democrat of massive hypocritical proportions, writes in *Yediot Aharonot* (February 13, 1986) concerning the physically violent demonstration against the Kach convention:

"We will never be helpless against fanaticism, against racism.... Yesterday in Jerusalem, thousands of demonstrators who daily are foolish supporters of tolerance and democracy, because of the failure of the Knesset, were left with no choice but to cry categorically: Kahane—out!"*

Or the letter from the leftist, veteran kibbutz member Dov Yirmiah:

"Must blood be spilled in order that there be put to an end the weekly granting of licenses for incitement rallies by Kahane throughout the country?" (*Ha'aretz*, December 30, 1985).

The "democratic" lesson is clear. Kahane is to blame if blood is shed by "democrats" determined to prevent him from speaking. And that blood is a legitimate weapon and price to pay in the struggle against "racism."

And the "blood" theme is emphasized again, this time in the wake of the desecration of synagogues by secularists. Avraham Fried, head of the Committee Against Religious Violence (sic), tells *Ha'aretz* (June 18, 1986):

"I have no doubt this will continue. In my opinion, there will be someone killed in this struggle."

And religious-hater Knesset member Yossi Sarid writes an article in *Ha'aretz*, titled "The Revolt of the Secularists,.." and calls for barring religious areas within secular towns and villages:

"We have no choice except to keep separate boundaries: The entire land is before you—lords of religious coercion—separate yourselves from us."

And the ongoing pathology of hate in the intellectual's Bible,

Ha'aretz: "The religious are threatening the State," "The religious are conquering the State," *ad nauseam*. An atmosphere of hate and fear is deliberately created by both the yellow sheet mass circulation rags and the more sophisticated rags that cater to the devotees of English phrases in their columns. It is clear that the deliberate spread of this hate and fear on the part of all the news media led directly to the attacks on synagogues. It is clear that it is a careful propaganda brainwashing campaign meant to prepare the public to "understand" and accept a civil war against the "Khomenites" of Judaism.

And the haters of the left intend to sweep away the settlers and settlements of Gush Emunim, too, and Yosi Melman did not hesitate to write an article in May, 1985, in *Davar*, under the heading: "On the Verge of Civil War." The operative sentence was: "He who fears a confrontation with the foundations of the Right, the nationalist and the religious, will find himself in a year or two in an even more inferior position. He who fears the threat of civil war may find that in the near future a civil war will pursue him." The call is blatant. They *want* a civil war.

And the irony of the leftist recruitment of yarmulke-wearing Prof. Yeshayahu Leibowitz, the confused professor in his eighties, who prays to G-d and votes for an anti-religious party, a mad professor who delights the leftists by a speech in February, 1986, as he wonders why some people "refrain from admitting that there might be causes within a single nation that can set people at war with one another."

Civil war. And the leftists applaud wildly.

And there is real fear of the leftist net of psychological terror, a terror that includes threats on the part of angry, twisted people who hide behind the masquerade of ethics and morality. Thus, the weekly *Kol Ha'ir* (June 20, 1986) carries a story under the headline: "Professors of the Right Afraid to Come Out of the Closet." The story tells of a number of conservative and nationalist professors at Hebrew University who wrote to Foreign Minister Shamir, explaining that a statement made by radical leftist physicist Professor Daniel Amit (known on the campus as "Red Danny"), that professors would boycott the graduating ceremony of the school because of Shamir's presence did not represent their views.

The article continues: "All those who contacted [Shamir] refused to identify themselves, explaining that they feared that their academic advancement would be blocked by the leftists who, according to them, control the key positions at the university."

This is the face of the real haters, the real fascists of Israel. This is a look at the dark soul of people who are so prepared to kill other

Jews in the knowledge of their own bankruptcy and because of the most agonizing of jealousies, the coveting of a life of certainty and truth and satisfaction and true joy. Only by understanding the dark other side, the ugly soul that lies within the "progressive" masquerade, can one explain the out-and-out lies and fabrications concerning Kahane on the part of intellectuals and artists and political leaders, deliberate lies from people for whom nothing—no means—is forbidden to be used against the man who so threatens their ideological sanity.

What else can explain the outrageous lie by author-intellectual Amos Elon, one of the lions of Israeli and American Jewish comfortable society, writing in *The New Yorker* (yet another paragon of intellectual arrogance), and saying: "His [Kahane's] platform is openly racist. Arab men caught sleeping with Jewish girls should be 'castrated.'" News media in the west are all too guilty of twisting and slanting news, but rarely is there the *total, complete* lie served up unblinkingly to the public. Elon knows that Meir Kahane never made such a statement. Elon knows that in Judaism one is forbidden to castrate not only humans but even animals. Elon is a deliberate liar, but Elon represents an entire class of deliberate liars whose flawed characters see nothing wrong in deceit when used against their enemies.

And so that is why they were capable of the following. On the morning of January 3, 1986, members of the leftist kibbutz Dalia woke up and went down to the dining room for breakfast. They were stunned and angered to find the windows and the walls of the kibbutz smeared with slogans that read, "Kahane to power," "Kibbutznikim are traitors," and others in that vein. Posters had been torn from the bulletin board and one wall of the dining room was also covered with slogans.

Outrageous? Of course. But more than one can possibly realize, at this point. The real outrage is that the kibbutz leadership planned and approved the action which was done by four of the kibbutz members. "We did it," they said with a smile [!], "in order to arouse our members to the fight against racism" (*Hadashot*, January 5, 1986). Or, in the words of the kibbutz secretary, Nahum Sivan: "They wanted to awaken the members from their lethargy and to paint a possible scenario as if Kahane's hoodlums had painted up the dining room" (*Al Hamishmar*, January 6, 1986).

It really is difficult to comprehend the obnoxious and outrageous mind of the fascist left, the haters of Kahane, the ethical immoralists. But know it, for it is there, and capable of doing much worse. Aharon Papo, a Tel Aviv attorney and former member of the board of the leftist-dominated Israel Television Authority, put it best in an article in *Hadashot*, December 9, 1984:

"One does not have to agree with the views and statements of Rabbi Meir Kahane in order to rise up against the public lynch that is being organized against him by leftist Knesset members with the massive aid of an artillery of news media that stand at their service at any time. One need only be an honest man with a feeling of justice and fairness, in order to reject totally this smear campaign. Mordechai Virshubski, Yossi Sarid and Ron Cohen [leftist Knesset members] vie with each other in foul mouthed attacks on the man. In *Ha'aretz* (December 6, 1984), its Knesset correspondent reports on a rich collection that these pious saints cast upon Kahane within one minute alone:

"'Gangster,' 'creature,' 'abomination,' 'disease,' etc. Not a single explanation, not a single serious argument—only a flood of curses in the language of the marketplace, in the gutter language of the communists and their 'liberal' allies, in a technique whose purpose is to delegitimize, to instill fear, to permit bloodshed. This is the political technique of the left: To shower upon a rival a huge amount of defamation and contempt without reason, until the public is so brainwashed that all people think that they are dealing with Satan himself."

That is the reality, and the great danger is that so many have heard *about* Kahane, have read *about* Kahane, and so few have heard *Kahane*, have read *Kahane*. Instead, millions of Jews, like other people living in the modern totalitarian age of mass news media, are pathetic victims of the deadly, defamatory news, concepts and images that a handful of men and women decide upon. But in the case of Meir Kahane, it is more than the news media. Within Israel the totality of the political, intellectual, educational, government and general establishment join the news media in an assault on Kahane and on "Kahanism" that is truly breathtaking in its sheer psychopathic hatred. It becomes a compendium of defamation, smears and sheer lies, from which one can almost smell the reek of bile, a steady, non-stop obsession that drives out of sight and mind almost all else.

True falsehood always recognizes and trembles with hate and fear before real truth. True falsehood always recognizes its real enemy, the one that threatens its very existence. And that is why the real falsehood within the Jewish entity, both in Israel and without, recognizes within Kahane and "Kahanism" the real Judaism they cannot ever allow to conquer, the real Judaism they hate, abhor, fear. That is why they hate Kahane and that is why with every step of his advance to victory, they will grow more and more desperate, stopping at nothing, not even murder, to prevent the victory of real Judaism.

It began the very night of the election. As soon as a stunned Israel—conditioned by the news media to deem such a feat impossible since everyone "knew" that Kahane had only a handful of backers, all Americans or Russians, and almost all teenagers—heard that Kahane and his Kach Movement had won a seat, radio and television devoted more time to this than to the question of whether the Likud or Maarach (Alignment) would head the government. Professional anti-religious and anti-nationalist Shulamit Aloni literally stammered in her angry hatred and could not bring herself to mention the name "Kahane." So much for the liberal defender of the rights of "conquered and oppressed" Arabs, homosexuals and missionaries. Luba Eliav, aging, veteran intellectual and leftist, failed to qualify for the Knesset. But it was not that that bothered him as much as the success of Kahane. "That murderous psychopath is in the Knesset and I am not," he babbled. Defamation has always been the desperate weapon of people incapable of debating and challenging—intellectually—the ideas they fear.

Editorials, television programs, radio debates—all a veritable Niagara of hysteria over the election of Kahane. And all this, of course, despite the election of two members of the new pro-PLO party, the Progressive List, blatantly anti-Zionist, committed to support for Arafat. All this despite the fact that four Communist Party members were elected.

And it never stopped. The hatred, the fear, the obsession. How do they hate Kahane! Let us count the ways. The ways that add up to pathological soul-consuming *jihad* (holy war) on the part of people who converse, drink coffee, and socialize with enemies of the Jewish people and state. Ways that would fascinate and serve as a lodestone for a student of abnormal psychology.

Prime Minister Shimon Peres describes "Kahanism" as a "Sword of Damocles" hanging over a Jewish and democratic Israel. He denounces Kahane's views as the greatest danger to democratic Israel and vows and that "we will fight against this incitement and defend the values of Israel."

Minister of Police Haim Bar Lev asks Attorney General Yitzhak Zamir if there are any legal ways to prevent legal rallies by Kahane. There apparently being none, the police refuse permits in various cities anyway and only appeals to the court cause them to retreat. Instead, they now allow rallies but not in the areas asked for and without loudspeakers! Or they seek to ban rallies because they might lead to violence (i.e., because *others* will commit violence against Kahane, he should not be allowed to hold the rally).

The police also deliberately hold up approval of permits requested weeks in advance until the actual day of the rally, thus barring the hanging of posters announcing the rally until that day itself. The police allow counter rallies requested in less than the legal time required and also permit them to rally right in front of the Kach rallies with loudspeakers, eggs and rocks.

The Ministry of Education issues instructions banning Kahane from speaking in schools despite the fact that anti-Zionist Arabs and leftists of all kinds have free access to them.

The schools themselves have been given compulsory material to be taught to all children on the dangers of Kahane and Kahanism, material produced by the Van Leer Institute, a dangerous agency dominated by leftists opposed to Kahane, to religion, to the Israeli "occupation" and to the settlements of Jewish settlers. Kahane is not allowed a single opportunity to speak and rebut the attacks and defamations.

The army, supposed to be totally non-political and above stands on political matters, is brought into the fray with a vengeance. Its education department (so reminiscent of the Politrucks of yet another army) has produced literature against Kahane for the soldiers' benefit (Knesset member Ehud Olmert protested that one section had been lifted *in toto* from Commun ist Party literature). And in response to a protest by one of the soldiers, who like so many others was forced to sit and listen to lecture after lecture by leftists against Kahane, Colonel Shulamit Ligum, public relations officer for the manpower division of the Israel Defense Forces, wrote:

"We agree with the institutions of the state and with the vast majority of society that thinks that Kahane's messages are racist and they hurt us first because they carry within them the destruction of Israeli society and threaten the existence of the State of Israel." This is the army of Israel and this is the attempt to indoctrinate the Jewish soldier.

President Chaim Herzog is eminently suited to be the chief of state of the Israel of today. His actions, too, defy logical explana tion. Following the custom of 36 years under which the president, after national elections, meets with representatives of all political parties to discuss formation of a new government, Herzog met with the Communists and the PLO-backing Progressive List, all paragons of Zionism and democracy. Then, he broke tradition and refused to meet with Knesset member Meir Kahane, the "racist."

Within a year, Herzog, who had come to be obsessed with Kahane—he brought him into every discussion on every possible issue

—announced that he would be the first President of Israel to honor the Communist Party's convention with his presence. The Israeli Communist Party is not only one of the most slavishly loyal of the Red parties, but for years it has been the vehicle through which the Arabs express their anti-Zionism. Nothing bothered Herzog. Declaring loftily that he was "President of all the people," he attended a convention that heard a message of greeting from Yasir Arafat. To cheers from the delegates, the message was read:

"Dear Comrades,

"I am delighted, in the name of the PLO, to turn to comrades in battle and in common fate, at the time of your 20th convention, with appreciation and respect. I emphasize, at the same time, that the PLO, the sole, legitimate representative of the Palestine people, is proud of your glorious struggle whose purpose is to defend the immutable national rights of the Palestine people and to stand against the Colonialist-Zionist aggression against our people and tradition."

Yasir and Chaim. Both greeting and welcoming the Communist Party which recognized the PLO as the sole representative of the Palestine people. Of course, one can understand Yasir. But who can possibly fathom the depths of vinegar?

And having, "As President of all the people," attended the Communist Party convention, Mr. Herzog then inexplicably turned down an invitation to attend the Kach convention of Meir Kahane. Apparently "all the people" are somewhat less than that. Mr. Herzog remains an aristocrat, special. Like fine wine—or vinegar.

• The army radio *Galei Tzahal* (which broadcasts to all Israelis), set aside an entire day in October, 1985, to harangue against Kahane and Kahanism. It does not shrink from using as its major warning against Kahane that he wishes to establish a Torah state. The outrage of the army of Israel diving into political questions is compounded by the outrage of its attack on a Torah state in the Jewish one.

• State television and radio announce that they will not allow Kahane to appear on programs or talk shows or be interviewed. They refuse to attend any of his press conferences. They do not cover events organized by Kahane. Jordan's Hebrew television news becomes the major way to follow Kahane in Israel. Newspapers refuse to allow Kahane to write articles in response to attacks on him.

• The Knesset, led by Speaker Shlomo Hillel, conspires to crush and eliminate Kahane in a way that would do credit to the best of totalitarian governments. On the first attempt to present a motion of no-confidence in the government, the Knesset secretariat rules that Kahane will not be allowed to present such motions. The reason? In the Knesset by-laws it says that "one Knesset member" shall not be allowed to do so and Kahane, whose party has only one seat, is "one Knesset member." The blackness of the comedy is apparent to all. The by-law was created to prevent a single member of a party that has *many* seats in the Knesset from independently raising such a motion. Clearly, if the entire party *has only one seat*, it does not apply. No matter; Hillel, the Knesset Dwarf, rules imperiously. Only an appeal to the High Court finally forces Hillel to allow Kahane to present that most basic of all parliamentary motions, that of no confidence in the government.

In ridiculous, childlike emulation of the Arabs of the UN, the Knesset members walk out when Kahane speaks. The same righteous indignation never seems to overcome them when PLO-supporting Arabs or Communists address them.

Despite the fact that the Knesset grants immunity of many kinds to its members, including the right to travel freely throughout the country without being prevented by the police, the Parliament of Israel decides to take that right away from Kahane.

In an unbelievable move, the Knesset allows the Speaker to refuse to table a bill that would ban missionaries (not churches) on the grounds that the bill is racist!

The Israeli government and the United States conspire to attempt to revoke Kahane's United States citizenship, in one of the most outrageous legal steps taken by the State Department since the anti-Communist days of the 1950s. Kahane, born in the United States, is a dual citizen as are some *six million* other Americans who also hold the citizenship of other countries. Suddenly, the State Department informs Kahane that he has lost his citizenship by taking on his Knesset seat! This, despite the fact that Golda Meir, Moshe Arens and Marsha Friedman were all United States citizens and also members of the Knesset. Mrs. Meir never gave up her U.S. citizenship nor was she ever asked to despite the fact that she was Prime Minister of Israel. Moshe Arens served for years in the Knesset and was Chairman of the Knesset Foreign Affairs Committee. He was never asked to give up his citizenship voluntarily and never lost it. (Twenty years later, when he became the Israeli Ambassador to the United States, he gave it up, voluntarily.)

As of this writing, a United States citizen, a Brooklyn dentist, serves as U.N. Ambassador from Grenada. The United States State Department ruled that he did not lose his citizenship because he had not shown any "intent" to give it up. Kahane went further. Before taking his oath, he sent both a letter and a telegram to the State Department saying specifically that he had no intent of giving up the U.S. citizenship. No matter. The Israeli government, desperate to prevent Kahane from going to the United States to speak and raise funds, moves heaven and earth to have Washington do its dirty work for it.

Similar Jewish action succeeded in barring Kahane from both Canada and Great Britain. In both cases, pressure by Jewish groups on their respective governments persuaded them to prevent Kahane from entering their countries and speaking. In the case of Canada it was the joint efforts of the Canadian Jewish Congress and B'nai B'rith, and in the case of Great Britain it was the prestigious Board of Deputies. It is of more than passing interest to quote the Kadima Movement of the Canadian Council of Reform Zionists, which passed a resolution as its convention that expressed "to the Right Honourable Joseph Clark, the Minister of External Affairs, our support of the Government's refusal to grant a visa to Rabbi Meir Kahane to enter Canada." (The same conclave resolved to ask the Israeli government not to make any ideological commitment to retain Judea and Samaria.)

And the very proper and respectable and democratic and tolerant *Jewish Chronicle* of Great Britain. In response to a letter from a reader asking why, in view of the paper's almost hysterical obsession with Kahane, the latter is not allowed the right to reply, the following letter was sent by the editor of the prestigious paper. His name is Geoffrey D. Paul. I quote it in its entirety:

"Sir:

"Not only is Kahane a neo-Nazi but so are all those who, like him, employ exactly the same kind of lies, half truths and hate propaganda against the Arabs of Israel as Hitler and Goebbels used against the Jews.

"It would be better for both of us if you read your selected New York newspaper and stopped reading ours."

Indeed. Far better than anything I could ever do, this letter exposes the truly sick, hating mind of the Jewish Establishment.

Little wonder that they seek to bar me from their country. They could never hope to debate me on the issues. Their frothing at the mouth as some wild animal is their surest sign of intellectual bankruptcy, a thing that is a hallmark, too, of the American Jewish leadership.

Chapter 16

The United States

Outside of Israel, within the fiefdoms of the United States Jewish Establishment, the dictatorship of the Liberal Jewish Totalitarians went to work in the organized steamroller fashion it has honed to perfection. And because the American Jew is even more naive and even more an ideological captive than the Israeli; because he is such a slave to the mass media, to his B'nai B'rith leader and to his temple rabbi, it is important that he fully understand the awesome propaganda campaign of "hate Kahane" that has been aimed at him. It is important for him to see what a victim and what a captive he is in the hands of the puppeteers, the Jewish feudal barons who dominate the community. Above all, it is necessary that he understand the poison and the lies—the deliberate lies—that emanate from the men and women who take his money, who control his money, who speak in his name, who direct his Jewish fate. It is important that he know them for what they are and consider, too, that if they lie and deceive Jews on this issue, what do they do on other major and controversial ones? For they really are small people, and so ignorant and frightened, too. They really have no business being Jewish leaders, for they really do not know what they are supposed to do.

On July 1, 1986, I wrote to the newly chosen head of the United Jewish Appeal, Mr. Martin F. Stein of Milwaukee, congratulating him on his new position and suggesting that it would be important that we meet so that he might have the opportunity of hearing another view of issues that hold within them the future of Israel and the Jewish people, issues that UJA checks would not be able to resolve. Mr. Stein's reply was as follows:

"Dear Rabbi Kahane,
"Thank you for your letter dated July 1, 1986, in which you requested to meet with me during your visit to the United States in August. Unfortunately, I regret that I will be unable to meet with you *due to substantial differences in our viewpoints.*"

For years, the Palestine Liberation Organization, the governments of Syria, Saudi Arabia, Iraq and such, have adamantly refused to meet with Israeli government officials, Zionists, because of substantial differences in their viewpoints. For years, Jews have piously condemned such an attitude. And yet, Martin Stein, Jewish leader, refuses to meet with a Knesset member. Is it possible that an Arab has infiltrated the very highest levels of the United Jewish Appeal? Surely, no liberal, open-minded Jew refuses to meet with people merely because of "substantial differences" in views, for that is exactly the reason for meeting with people—so as to narrow those differences. And is that not what every liberal, dove-like Jew insists that Israel do with its Arabs enemies? No liberal Jewish leader would ever refuse to meet with Jesse Jackson merely because of a "difference" in view. Indeed, one might wager that not a few of the progressive Jewish leaders would welcome a request by Louis Farrakhan to meet and "dialogue." Yet not with Meir Kahane.

The Stein refusal to meet with me is hardly unrepresentative. No U.S. Jewish leader will meet with me to discuss the issues. No Jewish leader can discuss the issues. Every main Jewish organization refuses to permit its members to listen to Meir Kahane. Almost every single temple rabbi adamantly bars his doors to Meir Kahane, refusing his congregations the right to hear him, despite the fact that the pulpit is open to Arabs and to not a few Black anti-Semites. That the attitude of hate is contagious and has infected the ordinary Jew is clear from the following.

Harold Schulweis is a wealthy, well-known Conservative rabbi in the affluent San Fernando Valley of southern California. He is a man who has been in the forefront of the invective, lies and defamation concerning Meir Kahane. At the same time, in his liberalism, he has opened his pulpit to many a person whose commitment to Judaism, let alone Zionism, is doubtful, to say the least. He has refused, adamantly, to do the same for Meir Kahane. Instead, his poisonous invective against Kahane—always refusing to deal with the issues that he raises—has infected his congregants in a manner that is almost inconceivable.

In early 1986, Schulweis's congregants received form cards with the question: "Do you agree that Rabbi Kahane has the right to be heard in your synagogue or in a debate with Rabbi Schulweis?"

Normal expectation might be a negative reply on more or less rational, logical grounds. Instead here are some samples of replies received:

"Gas chambers for Hitler Kahane. Kahane is a disgrace to the human race. Another Hitler."

"Kahane is not a rabbi."

"Rabbi Kahane is a racist, maniac, no different than KKK or Nazi."

"We don't want a bigot in our temple! How dare you send out a card like this to the temple members."

"Did Hitler learn from the Bible or did Rabbi Kahane learn from Hitler."

"Kahane should be banned from speaking anywhere. He is a *shanda* [disgrace] for the Jewish people."

"You are all a bunch of nuts! Give it up you jerks. No one is interested in Kahane or his ideas. Go crawl in a hole and shut up."

There is more, but the lesson is clear. Thanks to the feudal dictators who control the American Jewish community, a viciously distorted image is created and the puppets move in tune to the directed message. If we are warned of "hate" in the Jewish community, here it is. If there is bigotry and threat of totalitarianism it comes from precisely those who impute it to Kahane. It is an incredibly frightening example of the manipulation of an entire community.

Yet another example of the utter irrationality and psychotic hatred of Kahane that lies within the Jewish community comes in this letter from a Rabbi Davis-Cohen of Foster City, California. I believe it is an invaluable sociological document, not only in reference to Meir Kahane but, more important, to an understanding of the mind of a vast segment of American Jewry. I must give you the letter in its entirety (and without corrections of grammar or syntax):

"Rabbi Kahane, It is easy for me to see that you are nuts, absolutely Bananas, a Jewish Hitler. Why don't you do things properly, all Arabs including women and children in the Gas chambers. My Committee are in the process of petitioning President Reagan to withdraw your American citizenship. This is a feasible request and in line with the Constitution of the USA as you have taken the oath of allegiance to the State of Israel. I can only agree that since you were elected to the Israeli Knesset the State of Israel should now be called "the shocking State of Israel." It is very sad that stupid ignorant Jews like yourself should give good inoffensive Jewish people a bad name and cause us to be hated and disliked around the world.

"Not a single member of my congregation believes that you are a rational, sane person. We have written to many Arab organizations apologizing on your behalf and pointing out that you are not representative of decent sincere Jews but most likely a discipline of Satan.

"Most of the Arabs we have written to and have been in touch with do agree with my committee and pray together with us that perhaps in the very near future you will depart from this earth, Please G-d. I do hope that we will soon be saying Kadish [prayer for the dead] for you. I can never forget a Japanese lady who was very pro-Jewish pointing to your picture and saying to me, 'Rabbi Davis, you said that Jews deplore racialism!' My only answer is that, unfortunately, Meir Kahane is not a true Jew."

What can one say concerning the pitiful self-hate and fear of what the gentile will say that is so naked in this tortured letter? The German Jew of 1920 is alive and sick in California.

But, of course, it is the Jewish Establishment, obsessed with its inability to deal with Kahane and the frightening issues he raises, that has mounted a frenzied campaign to defame and silence him.

It began at the beginning. Immediately upon news of Kahane's winning a seat in the Knesset, Arthur Hertzberg—one of the more arrogant doyens of the Jewish Establishment, and its intellectual-in-residence —hysterically inveighed against Kahane, crying out that when he heard the news, he sat down to read Psalms as a balm to his troubled soul. (Chalk up another victory for Kahanism; it is doubtful whether Hertzberg would have, otherwise, opened King David's classic work.) Hyman Bookbinder, the aging liberal of Washington's American Jewish Committee, whose greatest contribution to American Jewish life was his retirement in 1986, called the election of Kahane "a disgrace." Any other reaction by Bookbinder would have led to an immediate reassessment by the Kach Movement over where it had gone astray.

The Jewish Establishment, powerful, wealthy and ruthless, has carefully and methodically followed Kahane and made every possible effort to prevent him from reaching Jews. Let the American Jew understand exactly what a dangerous and ruthless entity the Establishment really is.

On August 7, 1986, Charney V. Bromberg, Associated Director of the National Jewish Community Relations Advisory Council (NJCRAC), the umbrella group for major American Jewish organizations, sent out the following memo to all the group's officers and executives:

"The following message was sent out today to communities on the NJCRAC-CJF Instant Telecommunications Network:

"Yesterday's *New York Times* front page article by Tom Friedman on the apparent growing acceptance of Meir Kahane and 'Kahanism' by segments of Israel's population may be the springboard for additional mass media attention to this deeply disturbing phenomenon. In addition, Kahane is expected to begin a U.S. speaking tour on the 17th or 18th of August....

"Over the past year, I've sent you copies of NJCRAC member agencies' statements, local and national, explicitly condemning and renouncing Kahane and his policies. Under discussion now is whether there would be value to a collective NJCRAC statement. Arguments for such a statement center around the general abhorrence of Kahane by American Jewry and the need to communicate that abhorrence in the most forceful way possible. I would welcome immediate reactions from those on the Instant Communications Network by phone receipt of this message.

"Please call if you know Kahane is scheduled to speak in your community; in the meantime we're trying to ascertain his itinerary."

The fear and obsession with Kahane that leads to a veritable spy network that follows him about is aimed at attempting to pressure news media programs to cancel and to black out all news of his appearance. Incidentally it comes as no surprise that NJCRAC did indeed decide to issue a collective statement of condemnation of Kahane that was sent to the news media throughout the nation. Signed by the American Jewish Committee, the American Jewish Congress, B'nai B'rith, the Anti Defamation League, Hadassah, Jewish Labor Committee, Jewish War Veterans, National Council of Jewish Women, Union of American Hebrew Congregations (Reform), United Synagogue of American (Conservative), Women's American ORT and Women's League for Conservative Judaism, it declared its "abhorrence of his [Kahane's] policies, goals and practices." It went on to declare that "Kahane is not representative of the Israelis. Clearly, he is not representative of American Jewry. More fundamentally, his words and actions are alien to Judaism; we reject them and what they stand for. We reject this affront to our History, to our tradition and beliefs, and to our abiding commitment to our brotherhood and peace." The Jewish leaders' knowledge of Judaism, its tradition and beliefs, would, of course, fill a thimble, and the arrogance of their ignorance is overwhelming. At the last moment the resolution was vetoed by the Union of Orthodox Jewish Congregations, but under pressure, that group's president, Sidney Kwestel, later issued a statement stating that "Meir Kahane's views are anathema to traditional Torah teachings— particularly as they relate to our relationship with non-Jews." Mr. Kwestel, of course, knows better, but the pity is that the non-Orthodox ignoramuses of NJCRAC and the other established groups are joined by the cowardly Modern Orthodox established groups in a common bond of fear of what Kahane is saying—not because it is false, but precisely because it is true. And not one, not one Jewish leader or national organization or Community Relations Council is prepared to even sit and listen to Kahane, debate Kahane, intellectually destroy Kahane before the eyes of the Jewish community. Not one was prepared to do so because not one could. And so, those who cannot debate, defame. Those who cannot intellectually challenge, attempt to destroy. And these are the leaders of the American Jewish Community.

Every appearance by Kahane has been preceded by letters to radio and television news programs asking that they not give him an opportunity to appear. The most vicious smear material has been sent out to them. And every time that the host invited a Jewish leader to appear with Kahane, that leader hastily refused.

The Jewish communities of the United States are, of course, feudal-style baronies, run by a handful of wealthy, powerful people. Jewish leaders in the United States are not chosen for their Judaism, their religiosity, their scholarship. The secular leadership is chosen for its money and its ability to raise the same. The grossest kinds of ignoramuses lead the poor Jewish sheep, the blindest leading the blind. Invariably their interest, narrow and based upon the best way to retain their socio-economic position vis-à-vis the respected, powerful gentile, are at variance with what is best for the Jews. And so, they control what the Jew hears, sees, believes. They decide who is fit to participate in the Jewish community's affairs and events. And who may not. Indeed, they decide who is the Jewish community and who is not.

Thus, once a year the Los Angeles Jewish feudal barons, as do those in every city, hold a "Walk," whose essential purpose is, naturally, to raise money. Every conceivable Jewish group is "allowed" to participate in these Walks. And so when in March, 1986, the Los Angeles group of Kach International applied to participate in the California Jewish event that happily included Jewish Gays, the organization received the following letter from one Ted Kanner, a Jewish functionary who will be little known nor long remembered, the Executive Vice President of the Los Angeles Jewish Federation Council. In his letter, Mr. Kanner wrote:

"The Jewish Federation council does not countenance Kach International. We do not want supporters of Myer [sic] Kahane officially participating in the Walk because we frankly feel he runs counter to everything that we, in the Jewish community, believe."

The "we" and the "Jewish community" in the mind of the well-paid Jewish functionary, are clearly himself and his wealthy employers. The fact that there are a dozen rabbis who differ with the Kanners and their ilk was not important to Kanner, because those rabbis do not threaten him. They do not speak out, do not say what they think. They do not threaten Mr. Kanner or the checks that come from the Federation for their institutions. And so, Kach and Myer (sic) Kahane's supporters are barred by the feudal barons—and the local news media never said a word.

The barring of Kahane is sometimes a quite literal thing. His announced appearance at Jewish Federation's and Community Council's offices have resulted in the doors being frantically locked, barring Kahane and anyone else so unfortunate to have an appointment that day. And yet, there is really nothing new about the ban on Kahane, the fear of Kahane, the obsession with Kahane. Consider the example of the B'nai B'rith, guardian of liberal Jewish values of tolerance and democracy. As early as 1970, B'nai B'rith International issued the following policy guideline (policy #1000.0) concerning Meir Kahane and the Jewish Defense League:

"Lodges and chapters or Hillel Foundations and BBYO groups approached by members of the JDL should, in addition to refusing to provide a B'nai B'rith platform for the organization, report the approach to the nearest Anti-Defamation League Regional Office immediately."

If the ban were not so horrendous, the fearful order to report the approach to the ADL (the B'nai B'rith's private FBI), would be comical. But it *is* horrendous, this fearful, outrageous refusal to allow a Jewish voice to be heard by their own members. And the worst of it is the ban by Hillel. Hillel is the officially recognized Jewish student body on campus and, as such, enjoys university benefits (including funding), that other Jewish groups do not. On a campus, the very essence of academic freedom, to have an officially recognized student group, on the initiative of a non-campus sponsoring group (in this case B'nai B'rith), bar a group or speaker because of opposition to his views by a few feudal barons, is shocking. And yet that is exactly the case.

At the meeting of the B'nai B'rith Board of Governors on August 11, 1981, at Grossinger's Hotel (naturally), the summary of the day's events according to the official summary includes:

"Harry Berman, reiterating the B'nai B'rith policy that we do not provide platforms for the Jewish Defense League or Rabbi Myer [sic] Kahane, asked that this policy be shared [sic] with the Hillel directors and that they implement this policy. Rabbi [Oscar] Groner (International Director of Hillel) stated that the B'nai B'rith policy *re* Rabbi Kahane will be communicated to the field."

And so, Jewish college youth who are already victims of a Hillel that is so bankrupt as to be almost a criminal participant in the spiritual destruction of young Jews, are deprived of an opportunity to hear another view, a truly Jewish view. There is not a campus in the United States in which even five percent of the total Jewish student body are members of Hillel. The campuses are vast wastelands of Jewish apathy and assimilation. They are breeding grounds for intermarriage. Hillel has almost no impact on this with its insipid "Judaism" whose centerpiece is the Friday night meal. Hillel is bankrupt and its impossible directors are so lacking in both scholarship and dedication that it borders on the scandalous. And yet Kahane cannot speak to the Jewish youth because he is dangerous. And that is true. He *is* dangerous. To the Hillels and their directors and the Jewish bankrupt Establishment. For he speaks and exposes their nakedness and their fraud, and that is his real crime in the eyes of the feudal barons.

That is why *The New York Times* (November 29, 1985) carried a story headlined, "Kahane's Rise Troubles Jews in U.S." It is true. Including Establishment rabbis. Every appearance in every city by Kahane brings forth the inevitable censure and condemnation by the local Board of Rabbis or Rabbinic Fellowship. These are, for the most part, made up of the fat and bought pulpiteers, mostly Reform and Conservative, but with a good sprinkling of Moderdox—Modern Orthodox—those moderately pious, moderately moderates who enjoy the best of both worlds, the feeling that they are nearer my Sinai to thee, and yet "moderate" and "flexible" enough to be part of the crowd and never to be lumped together with the "ultra-Orthodox fanatics." Every Kahane visit brings forth condemnation similar to the nonsense put out by the pulpiteers of Pittsburgh's Rabbinic Fellowship (April 25, 1985):

"We reject Rabbi Kahane's racist attitudes toward the Arab residents of Judea and Samaria.... The Rabbinic Fellowship of Greater Pittsburgh lament that a man who holds rabbinic *smicha* [ordination] *and is a duly elected member of Israel's Knesset should espouse policies so inimical to fundamental Jewish values of Tikun Olam* [bettering of the world]: the family of all humanity, the holiness of G-d's creation, Israel's mission as light to the nations and the ultimate redemption of our world in G-d's kingdom of peace."

The overwhelming majority of the rabbis in Pittsburgh's Rabbinic fellowship may, indeed, be jolly good fellows, but that same majority does not believe in Judaism as being G-d's direct word from Sinai and have, therefore, no way of knowing what is "Judaism." More, they have not the slightest moral right to talk *about* Judaism, much less in its name. Every value they spoke about in their declaration is a Jewish value only if Judaism is Divine and exclusive. Otherwise, they are human values, and the setting up of particularistic synagogues and religion is the very antithesis and contradiction of these values. Not a single point raised by the pulpiteers has any relevance to the questions raised by Kahane, and thus it is no surprise that the rabbinic heads of Pittsburgh never mentioned a single one of those issues. Of course they are no better or worse than the Jewish spiritual (heaven help us) leaders of any other American city. All have the very lowest common spiritual denominators.

The fascinating thing is observing reactions when, every so often, a synagogue (always among the least affluent) does decide to allow Kahane to speak. What happens then is reflected in the case of Charleston, South Carolina, where the B'rith Sholom Beth Israel Synagogue decided to invite me to speak so that, in the words of the synagogue's president, Jack P. Brickman, "members of our community who might like to hear Rabbi Meir Kahane should have the opportunity to do so in order to be able to form their own opinion as to the philosophies he espouses." A reasonable, Jewish decision.

But Mr. Brickman was even more decent. Knowing of the furor that the decision had already created among the barons of Charleston, he wrote to the Chairman of the Community Relations Committee of the Jewish Federation stating: "We invite you as Chairman of the Community Relations Committee to present on the evening of May 11, 1982, following Rabbi Kahane's talk, a responsible spokesman to rebut Rabbi Kahane's argument and present the counter view of the established Jewish community."

More than reasonable. An *ultra*-Jewish position. Naturally, that was the last thing in the world the Jewish Establishment wanted. A memo from Steinberg to his Committee on April 27, 1982 was sent out, that read:

"SUBJECT EMERGENCY MEETING
"There will be an emergency meeting of the CRC this Sunday, May 2, at 7:00 PM at the JCC (Jewish Community Center).
"The sole purpose of the meeting will be to discuss the pending visit of Rabbi Meir Kahane to Charleston."
The "emergency" was open only to elected official barons. Of

course, the public was excluded. The following resolution was passed by the Jewish CRC, the spokesperson for Jewish values and tolerance:

"The Community Relations Committee wishes to go on record as being opposed to Rabbi Meir Kahane's pending visit to Charleston. The CRC regrets that B'rith Sholom Beth Israel Synagogue has chosen to provide a forum for Rabbi Kahane and respectfully requests that the Congregation reconsider this action."

This fascinating insight into the democratic mind of the Jewish community is augmented by a letter from the President of Charleston's largest Conservative temple, intended to pressure the inviting synagogue to disinvite Kahane. This is what the feudal barons consider democracy:

"We all recognize fully both the right of free speech and the almost inviolable right of an institution to plan its own programs without external interference. The only time these rights would be challenged would be when there is the potential for harm and damage to the community. We feel that Rabbi Kahane's presence could lead to this.

"Exchange of ideas and healthy discussion of opposing points of view are absolutely necessary in our society. We certainly recognize the existence of multiple opinions. This situation, however, goes beyond the healthy exchange of views."

An extraordinary statement. It is a rich treasure of Jewish Establishment mentality. Of course, diversity and free speech, except when it is controversial and "dangerous" (to us). Of course, the right to listen to all views except those that threaten our positions. And all of this from Jews organizations and feudal barons, whose record is an unblemished one of bankruptcy vis-à-vis the Jewish flock. These are the groups who were deathly silent during the Holocaust, lest their public protests demanding the bombing of the death camps and the bridges and railroad lines that led to them (which would have saved hundreds of thousands of Jewish lives) would lead to anti-Semitism and threaten them. These are the ones who, for half a century, never marched or demonstrated for Soviet Jews. These are the ones whose policy of the "melting pot" led countless young Jews into assimilation and intermarriage. They are the shepherds of whom the prophet spoke:

"Woe be to the shepherds of Israel that feed themselves: should not the shepherds feed the flock? You eat the fat and you clothe you with the wool, you kill them that are fed; but you feed not the flock. The diseases have you not strengthened, neither have you healed the sick, neither have you bound up the broken, neither have you brought against that which was driven away, neither have you sought that which was lost; but with force and with cruelty have you ruled over them..." (Ezekiel 34).

These are the Jewish organizations controlled by ignoramuses whose totality of thoughts and ideas are conceived in gentilization and born in foreign concepts. Can Jewish leaders who are intermarried have anything to say to young Jews who ask why they should not intermarry? Can a Jewish leader who is *not* intermarried but who does not observe Judaism as G-d's total Divine law explain to a Jewish youngster why *he* should not intermarry? Can he explain it to himself? Can empty vessels give drink to a thirsty, parched generation?

And the rabbis. Only they and I know just how bankrupt and fraudulent they are. But all should know and understand the crime that takes place every moment in the American Jewish community run by a religious Mafia dedicated to fat salaries and perks and flight from truth. They destroy you and your children and the question is: will you let them?

These are your leaders, O Children of Israel:

In Chicago there stands a temple. It is a mighty Temple, wealthy and prestigious, awesome in its Establishmentarianism. It is called Kehilath Anshei Maarav, but in deference to the Hebraic linguistic difficulty that this would impose on those who compose its Board of Directors, it is known simply as KAM.

And in this temple there sits a Wolf. Yes, a Wolf. A Rabbi Arnold Jacob Wolf, to be precise. And if you are surprised that a Wolf can be a rabbi, be not dismayed, O Jew. In an era when a homosexual and lesbian can aspire to the rabbinical cloth, why the shock at a Wolf at the temple door?

In 1983, the Wolf, who shepherds the lambs of KAM, wrote a rabbinical message to his sheep. And these are the lupine leavings fed them as the Sabbath meal in the KAM Temple Bulletin, October 19, 1983:

"From the Rabbi's Desk ...

"The Soviet Union brought down an unarmed civilian plane which was apparently over-flying some of the sensitive military installations, causing loss of life and international protest.

"The Soviet Union regularly ships guns to Central America in order to bring civic disorder and revolution.

"The Soviet Union has invaded neighboring nations, occupied and subdued them, annexing whole populations of different convictions and background.

"The Soviet Union permits dissent and debate among elites but no freedom for its occupied or second-class populations.

"The Soviet Union has been repeatedly condemned by the international community but defends its actions by reminding the world that it is surrounded by much larger, hostile enemies who have refused to live with it in peace. In order to defend its right to exist, it has even quietly threatened the world with nuclear destruction.

"NOW GO BACK AND, IN READING THIS PIECE, PLEASE SUBSTITUTE FOR 'THE SOVIET UNION' EACH TIME, THE TERM *'THE STATE OF ISRAEL.'*"

This is the "rabbi's column." Are you still worried, dear Jews, over the seventy gentile wolves who surround us? Not I. I tremble before the Jewish Wolf who eats away at us from inside. I look at a Wolf named Rabbi Arnold Jacob, self-hater and destroyer of Jews and I know that this Wolf in sheepish rabbinical clothing was once Hillel director at Yale. I weep for the Jewish sheep surrounded by gentile wolves from without, but the greater danger by far is from the Wolf within. Because even as they are devoured by him, the pitiful Jewish sheep acclaim him!

And consider this:

In Rockville, Connecticut, a suburb of Hartford, stands a Conservative temple, B'nai Israel. At its helm, skillfully guiding his congregants through the shoals of Connecticut Yankeeism is a rabbi named Marshall Press.

A powerful man is this Press, wrestling with all manner of Jewish problems. A powerful wrestler, a full Press. And in his October, 1883, Temple Bulletin, I was fascinated to note in his calendar of events, a class entitled: "Getting to know your Neighbor's Religion."

Enchanted by a community of Jews that apparently knows so much concerning its own religion that it scholarly delves into the intricacies of Protestantism, Catholicism and what have you, I found to my delight that the rabbi had not merely announced the class but had Pressed on, in a delightful effort to insure that Jews become erudite Christian scholars. His "Rabbi's Message" was dedicated to the class in a clear effort to Marshall rabbinical Pressure on any Jewish ignoramuses who did not see it their duty to delve into the secret of the Eucharist and the extremist of unction.

And thus spake the rabbi to the local Connecticut Jewish press:

"The Greater Rockville Area Clergy Council is presenting a six-part series entitled, "Get to know your Neighbor's Religion." This series is an outgrowth of a series which I developed for teenagers last year [naturally—M.K.]. In this bulletin you will find the following list of presentations and their locations.

"Sunday, October 16, 1983 at: Cong. B'nai Israel, 54 Talcott Ave., Rockville, Conn. 06066, 871-1818; Sunday, October 23, 1983 at: Sacred Heart Catholic Church, 550 Hartford Turnpike, Vernon, Conn. 06066, 875-4563; Sunday, October 30, 1983 at: First Baptist Church of Tolland, 75 Cider Mill Road, Tolland, Conn. 06084, 871-0592; Sunday, November 6, 1983; at First Congregational Church, 695 Hartford Turnpike, Vernon, Conn. 06066, 872-3803; Sunday, November 13, 1983 at: First Lutheran Church, 154 Orchard Street, Ellington, Conn. 06029, 875-5682."

And the grand finale: "Wednesday, Nov. 23, 1983, Thanksgiving Eve Worship Service at St. Luke Catholic Church, 141 Maple Street, Ellington, Connecticut,"

The full Rabbinical Press continues:

"I hope that many of our congregation members will participate in this series. We cannot expect our Christian neighbors to be understanding of us if we are not willing to be more informed about their beliefs and practice.

"One of my mentors, Rabbi Joseph Gold, an Orthodox Rabbi [!] in Worcestor, tells this story: Abe Moskowitz came to America from Russia, changed his name to Arnold Moss, became a wealthy man, lived well to a ripe old age and finally died. When he got to the gates of heaven, he was met by an angel and the dialogue went something like this:

"Abey, tell me, what kind of Jew were you?

"My name is Arnold and to tell you the truth, I wasn't such a good Jew.

"Did you study Talmud? Did you read the Bible? Did you study Jewish Law?

"Um, er, ahem, I was too busy making a living to study much Yiddishkeit.

"Well, listen, you're a Jew. You know what being a Jew is. So you didn't study. I can forgive you that. But tell me, what do you know about Christianity? Have you studied the Gospels?

"Christianity? Are you kidding? I don't know the first thing about Christianity!

"Listen, I could forgive you for not studying Judaism but I can't possibly forgive you for knowing nothing about the religion of most Americans. How could you live as a minority within a majority culture and know nothing about that religion. I'm sorry but down you go!

"We all owe it to ourselves to become better informed about Christianity. Let us make our community a model for others by supporting this educational endeavor. The series will culminate with a community wide Thanksgiving Eve Service in which all the local clergy will participate. I hope to see a large number of our congregation in attendance at this series."

What is one supposed to say about this particular rabbinical sickness? What does one say to a child of the congregation who goes to the local church and finds so much more meaning and piety in a Catholic service than in the pale, vapid, insipid, fraudulent, nonsense that pours forth from the pages of the Marshall Press? What does one tell Jewish youth who say that they have gone to all the lectures and discovered that there is no real difference between Jews and Christians and so they have decided to knock down all barriers and create a universalistic, ecumenical faith called Humanism which is not subject to rabbinical Pressure? What about the young Jew who gets to know his neighbor very well and she is blonde, blue eyed, cute and smart?

What can one say to the poor Jewish sheep being led to the spiritual slaughter by an ignoramus who masquerades under the title "rabbi"? One can only plead with them and cry out: Before you lose your children, Stop the Press!

But the most fascinating in this tragedy is the more than supine position of the sheep. The very same who are being destroyed, understand nothing. Indeed, how often do the sheep turn, remarkably, into donkeys. Some time ago, the sheep-president of a sheep-synagogue in Reading, Pennsylvania, wrote a letter to an Anglo-Jewish newspaper that is, itself, a splendid representation of all that is sheepishly Jewish in our times. The sheep-president wrote to praise his shepherd-rabbi, to count his praises and skills and attributes. I bring this letter for posterity and as a primary document, so that sheep and donkey will forever be enshrined in history and those who follow us will understand what helped destroy the Jewish flock.

"It fell to me, as president of the board of Rabbi Weitzman's congregation, Oheb Sholom, to deliver the sermon on a recent Sabbath when the rabbi was out of town. I took the opportunity to talk about the rabbi because his accomplishments pass largely unnoticed by most of the Reading Jewish Community.

"This man has a dynamic career outside the walls of his temple. He walks into Grossinger's Hotel in the Catskills with a busload of Lutherans following him. They are seeking to find their Jewish roots. Grossinger's is bemused, much to his delight. A year later they are back with him in greater numbers for a second retreat.

"He induces one of the most prominent clergymen in the country, who is his close friend, to lend his person and prestige to head up an Israel Bond testimonial dinner. Over $2 million in bonds is sold, most of the purchases made by members of the Christian community. He is one of the founders of the Berks County Food Bank. He is invited regularly to speak in churches where he effectively delivers the story of Judaism. He counters misinformation wherever he speaks. Once it was to adult Sunday School classes. Now it is almost always at the Christian congregational services.

"He delivers a credit course at Albright College based on the Ethics of the Fathers. It is possible that next year he will be teaching the course in a local Catholic college. In 1979, his social action program at Temple Oheb Sholom, called "Connections" and designed to meet human service needs in our community, received an award from the Union of American Hebrew Congregations at the biennial.

"It was a happy event for me to call some of these things to the attention of our congregation. It continues to be our good fortune, on this his 20th anniversary at Reform Congregation Oheb Sholom, to have Rabbi Weitzman as our spiritual leader.

"Murray Knoblauch, President, Temple Oheb Sholom"

O, let us sing a psalm of joy to the Reading shepherd! He is our shepherd, we shall not want for Christian love. He maketh us to lie down in green Israel Bond testimonials, for that is the job of a shepherd rabbi. He leadeth us beside the still waters of churches where he effectively counters misinformation about Jewish horns and tails, for that is the job of a shepherd rabbi. He restoreth the soul of Albright College and leadeth Lutherans into Grossinger's for his name's sake, and the local Catholic college is his parish.

Surely goodness and mercy shall follow the shepherd all the days of his life for surely no Jews will be left in Reading to do so. For as the donkey-shepherd saves Lutheran and Catholics and Grossinger's, one searches in vain for a word about his utter failure to save young Jews. And so, the intermarriage, assimilation and alienation of the young Jew continue and, like a cancer, eat away at Jewish survival. But for the sheep-president, nothing matters. He is too busy, happily munching away at the grass of Christian love in the green pastures of Reading, as he follows the shepherd-donkey who turns his Jewish sheep into mutton.

And how refrain, in these days of equality of sexes, from including a rebbitzin, a rabbi's spouse, from my collection of Jewish leaders. The truth is that they are not making rebbitzins the way they used to. Consider for example, Rebbitzin Nelly. Nelly, the rebbitzin, is married to Marty, the rabbi, rabbi of the prestigious Hillel group at the University of California at Berkeley. I almost met Marty the rabbi at Berkeley except for the fact that when he heard that I was dropping in, he locked the Hillel doors so that *no one*, Kahane or the students, could enter. No matter. Nelly, the rebbitzin, is married to Marty, the rabbi, who is Martin Ballonoff of Berkeley. And Nelly, the rebbitzin, is angry. Very angry. So angry that, in 1985, she filed a lawsuit against one Dr. H. Joseph W. Lahr charging him with a shocking act. Dr. Lahr is charged with the outrageous performing of an operation on Nelly the rebbitzin's eight-day old child. In a word, Dr. Lahr committed the unpardonable sin of performing a circumcision on the child of Nelly, the rebbitzin.

For those who doubt that the Jewish world is an insane asylum or that we are surely living in the last days of Jewish Pompeii, consider the lawsuit filed by Nelly, the rebbitzin, on March 25 in the Superior Court of California, Alameda County. (The rebbitzin is "the guardian" and "the plaintiff" the eight-day old infant.)

The action is against the doctor who "without consent of the plaintiff (baby), forcibly removed the foreskin from plaintiff's penis," and by reason of this "plaintiff has suffered extreme and severe mental anguish and physical pain and has been injured in mind and body."

"Does now and always in the future will suffer a permanent mutilation." "Does now and always in the future will suffer cosmetically... as abnormal in appearance when compared with persons who have not had their sexual organs altered." And, the final chilling indictment:

"The inhuman act was done ... with defendant knowing full well that removal of the foreskin by defendant has no medical basis and... was done for traditional, cultural and religious reasons unrelated to medicine and for that reason plaintiff ask exemplary and punitive damages."

No, they are not making rebbitzins the way they used to, and let every Jew derive some conclusion from the anarchy and insanity of the "Judaism" of Nelly, the rebbitzin, for it is the necessary logical outgrowth of the rejection of Sinai and the Divine basis for Judaism. For Nelly, the rebbitzin, is so much more logical than all the Reform and Conservative rabbis who condemned her and stood up for circumcision. And any Jewish child will ask: Why is it permissible for certain rabbis to abolish the laws of the Sabbath and yet it is impermissible for Nelly, the rebbitzin, to abolish the law of circumcision? Why is it permissible to abolish kashrut and ritual purity and all the "ancient" Jewish laws that Reform and Conservative rabbis do reject, and why cannot Nelly, the rebbitzin, abolish a primitive rite of circumcision? In short, why can a rabbi stomp on Torah and not a rebbitzin? In the end are they really not equal? Of course they are! In the end, Nelly is not a rebbitzin, nor are the "rabbis" rabbis.

Since I do not possess a television set and do not go to the movies or the theater, I must find my entertainment elsewhere. And for that I am eternally grateful to American rabbis. In them, in the absence of the bard and playwright, producer and comic, I am able to find my pathos, my humor, and my laughter through Jewish tears. American rabbis—a glorious chapter in the American Chelm.

But it is hardly humorous. The American Jew, like his counterpart in Israel, is in the hands of donkeys and shallow-headed creatures, who have nothing to give them. Terrified of meeting me in debate, the most they will do is deal with Kahane in terms of defamation and personal invective. And when they do pathetically attempt to deal with substance, the result is so incredible that one cannot believe that American Jews have been placed in the keeping of such intellectual dullards. Consider the article by one Harold S. Silver, in the *Hartford Courant*, February 20, 1986. The newspaper's description of Silver's expertise on the article's subject, "Kahane's Demagogy: A Perversion of Zionism, Judaism and Democracy," reads as follows: "Harold S. Silver, senior rabbi of Congregation Beth Israel in West Hartford, spent a month in Israel last year."

Praise be! West Hartford Jewry is in the hands of an expert on Israeli affairs, and so let us continue. Silver's piece is typical of all others that have been written on the subject and that is why it is so important to see in it the opponents of Kahane.

Knowing the issues that I have raised—democracy calling for no political distinction between Jew and Arab, with the right of Arabs to peacefully and non-violently become the majority and take over the country; Zionism calling for a Jewish State and thus rejecting the possibility of non-Jews ruling the land; the question being: Do the Arabs have the right to be the majority, yes or no?; the Law of Return of Israel and the Jewishness of Israel being anathema to Israeli Arabs—does Silver deal with any of them? Of course no, because he cannot. Instead we are told by the month-in-Israel-last-year-rabbi:

"What separates the demagogue Kahane mentality from the overwhelming majority of Israelis is Kahane's distortion and perversion of Zionism, Judaism and democracy. The best of historic and contemporary Zionism always has recognized the need and desire to work peaceably, honorably and harmoniously with the Palestinian Arab population." The eternal defamation and *non sequitur*. Of course Zionism called for harmonious working with the Arabs—*if they would accept a Jewish State*. For decades the Arabs made it clear they would not. Silver dishonestly tarnishes history and, above all, refuses to deal with the main issue: Do the Arabs have a right to work peaceably, harmoniously and honorably inside Israel for a majority Arab state?

But the best is yet to come—and how important it is that Jewish leaders do not get involved in public debate with Arabs since the latter would intellectually destroy them.

Silver rides on: "Israelis have tried to make members of the Arab minority population almost complete and equal Israeli citizens. Israeli Arabs enjoy virtually every political, educational and economic right that belongs to Jews. Authentic Zionism never has stood for the racist exclusion that Kahane advocates."

Now it may be that Silver really is not a demagogue or charlatan. He may, indeed, be only retarded. But that is the only choice before us. Look at the inane words again. Israel has tried to make the Arabs "*almost* complete and equal citizens." The Arabs enjoy "*virtually* every right." Dear Jew, how would you like to live in a Palestine with *almost* complete citizenship and *virtually* every right? How would you like that in the United States? This is a rabbi? This is an intellectual? It is certain that he spent no more than a month in Israel.

But the best (worst) is still to come. Having climbed the mountain of respect and honor for Arabs, the tarnished Silver lashes out against the annexation of the "West Bank" (Judea, Samaria and Gaza), saying:

"This would inevitably confront Israel with the prospect of absorbing a million additional Arabs into the present fabric of the Jewish state. Such an infusion would affect the quantity and unique quality of specifically Jewish life in Israel.

"Only with such a majority as exists within Israel's present boundaries—of 81 percent Jewish and 16 percent Arab—can Israeli Jews have complete mastery over their own national and cultural Jewish destiny, something that has been missing from 2,500 years of Jewish exile, homelessness, helplessness and persecution. Were Israel one day to take in an additional one million Arabs, the Jewish-Arab ratio would be radically altered. The Jewish majority control would be significantly imperiled just by the natural peaceful process of vastly higher Arab fertility."

Dear Jew. *Anyone* with a modicum of normal sense! What would an Arab whom Silver so respects, think upon reading this paean to *a Jewish* Israel? Too many Arabs would "affect the quantity and unique quality of specifically Jewish life in Israel." Of course it would, Dear Child Harold, but what difference does that make to your Zionism and Judaism that seek to work peacefully, honorably and harmoniously with their Arab population? What manner of racism do we hear from the Silver mine of West Hartford? What feelings of joy and equality are engendered in the Arab heart upon reading Silver's soothing words "the Jewish majority control"? But that is precisely what the Arab never wanted, does not want, will never want. "Still, I have every confidence that Israelis will make the decisions that lie ahead inspired by the best of Zionism, Judaism and minority-respecting democracy."

Silver is too good. A truly decent chap who years for a minority-respecting democracy. With *the Arabs* the minority, of course. Had he been in Israel longer than a month he would have met some 700,000 Arab citizens who share almost the same dream, with a slight variation. They also yearn for a minority-respecting democracy, but with Long Harold Silver as part of the *Jewish* minority.

The man's ignorance is exceeded only by his courage in exposing it in Macy's window, so to speak. But Silver is typical, all too typical, of the braying spiritual donkeys who run American Jewry. By staying one prayer-page ahead of the congregation, they succeed in persuading the Jews that they see scholars and experts where only ignoramuses and donkeys graze.

Then, of course, there are the deliberate distorters. Thus, one Bernard Avishai, associate professor at MIT and author of a book called *The Tragedy of Zionism*, writes in *The New York Times* in reply to Kahane, and says:

"Let us be clear: Historic Zionism was by no means incompatible with secular democratic goals. The early Zionists, in 19th-century Europe, were as much in revolt against tyranny as against anti- Semitism. The very point of pioneering in Palestine—according to the Labor Zionists at least—was to create an enlightened Jewish majority that would be the vanguard of a Hebrew-speaking social democratic country."

Consider the deliberate fraud. *That* was the purpose of Zionism? *"A Hebrew-speaking social democratic country?"* Fraud! The essential purpose of Zionism was a *Jewish* State! What an outrageous and deliberate fraud to postulate a "Hebrew-speaking state," as if all the Arabs, despite their learning to speak Hebrew and being socially democratic, could ever be the majority in the eyes of Herzl and Nordau and Jabotinsky and Weizman and all the founders of Zionism!

And Avishai continues his fraud. "The Zionist pioneers did, it must be said, evolve a number of institutions that discriminated against non-Jews. But they were intended for a good cause—to prevent Jewish settlers from becoming a colonialist caste among Arab peasants. That was the reason that the Jewish National Fund would not sell land to Arabs. It was also the reason why the Histadrut labor federation hired only Jews to work in its syndicalist enterprises, and why its unions picketed Jewish firms that did otherwise. Similarly, Jews and only Jews were eligible for the development loans, mortgages and relief offered by the Jewish Agency for Palestine."

How good it is to know that the Zionist pioneers discriminated against the Arabs for a "good cause." And even better to know that the good cause was for the Arab's benefit—so that the Jews would not be a colonialist caste. What a pity that the Arabs did not understand all this, did not know what was good for them! What nonsense and what deception and what fraud! But Avishai, yet another Hellenist incapable of dealing with the real issue, continues on his revisionist thesis of Zionism's real purpose and writes:

"Is Mr. Kahane right, then, that Arabs must always be aliens in the state produced by Zionism? Certainly not—so long as 'Zionism' means the classical task of building a Hebrew-speaking democracy. Some Arabs resent having Passover as a national holiday, but most respect Israel's electoral process and civil freedoms, and many have a great affinity for modern Israel culture."

One's heart is filled with gladness. Only *some* Arabs "resent" Passover as a national holiday, instead of the Moslem feast of Ramadan or Id-al-Fide. Of course! Let the bells of joy ring! Arabs have "a great affinity for modern Israel culture." Pray tell which part thereof: Dizengoff Street? Yes. Jewish girls? Indeed. But not one Arab has an affinity for *Jewish* culture and if Avishai's classes at MIT are as fraudulent as this column, woe unto his students. He is right. Arabs need not be aliens if Zionism means building "a Hebrew-speaking democracy." The trouble is it does not. What Jews wanted and needed was *a Jewish state*, and that remains the real aim of Zionism. And that is why, despite all the fraudulent teaching at MIT, the Arab can never accept Zionism or a Jewish state.

This same fraudulent definition of Zionism is brought down by yet another Establishment pervertor and deceiver. This one is known as Susan Satmary Rubin, and she is assistant director of the B'nai B'rith ADL in Los Angeles. Writing in the *Los Angeles Daily News* (September 4, 1985), Rubin states:

"Kahane's view that there is a contradiction between Zionism, Western Judaism and Western democracy completely perverts Zionism and the traditional Jewish way of life." Thus brays the scholarly Ms. Rubin, whose Zionism is measured by her life on the West Coast of the United States and whose Judaism is undoubtedly the product of long years in a Sunday School studying for Bat Mitzvah. She then tells us: "Real Zionists and committed Jews would know that Zionism, as defined by Foreign Minister Yigal Allon, 'is the effort to create a society which tries to implement the highest ideals of democracy for all the inhabitants of Israel, irrespective of religious belief, race or sex.'

"By definition, Kahane's vision of a society which denies such rights to other persons cannot be a Jewish State or a Zionist State, even if it has a majority of Jews in its population."

It may indeed be true that Yigal Allon who, along with Ben Gurion, ordered the Arabs driven out of Ramle and Lydda in the 1948 war, made that inane definition of "Zionism." But if he did, he surely never believed it. He surely made it for assistant directors of the B'nai B'rith ADL. A man who drove out 50,000 Arabs from the country in 1948, out of fear of a large Arab population in the new state, hardly saw democracy as the highest goal of Zionism. Zionism is defined as the movement to create a Jewish state; the movement *of Jews* to go up and live in Israel, the Jewish State. All else is nonsense. What *kind* of Jewish state Israel would be was never the primary concern of Zionism. There were socialist Zionists and capitalist ones. There were religious ones and atheists. There were rightists and leftists. All were Zionists. All had different ideas of what kind of a state the Jewish one would be, but all agreed that Zionism proclaimed: *a Jewish State*. And all knew that this could be achieved only with a Jewish majority. A state without a Jewish majority can never be a Jewish state, no matter how "ethical," and one stands awestruck at the nonsense that emanates from the bells of Susan Satmary. A state with a Jewish majority that is sovereign and independent and master of its Jewish destiny is by *definition* a Jewish State, no matter what its character and no matter how loud the protests from small Establishment Jews who live in Southern California and explain why Kahane, from Israel, "misses the point of Zionism...." The assistant director of the ADL, along with so many other functionaries of the Jewish Establishment, is not only incapable of dealing with the issues raised by Kahane, she goes slowly crazy in attempting to deal with them.

The coolest and most arrogant of the intellectuals, the calmest of the pipe smokers, the most laid-back of the liberal authors, writers, thinkers, all explode in an anger and deception and hate that are remarkable to see. All resort to the lowest and vilest forms of deception and defamation imaginable. *New Republic* is a Zionist-oriented and very Jewish kind of literary magazine for intellectuals of a kind. The editor-in-chief, Martin Peretz, and literary editor, Leon Wieseltier, pride themselves on the intellectual ability to discuss, analyze and dissect issues calmly and dispassionately. Like all superior intellectuals. Until it comes to Kahane. And indeed the November 11, 1985, issue of the magazine was an amazing example of intellectual humiliation for the *New Republic* and a quiet victory for Kahane. The magazine embarrassingly sank to the depths of a gutter rag as a lengthy, hysterical and mud-slinging article on Kahane was slashed across the front page as "Kahane: The Making of a Jewish Monster," no less.

The author was the literary editor himself and never was there a clearer case of a man, Leon Wieseltier, exposing his own particular problems with Judaism and Zionism. Of course, he did not deal with the questions Kahane raised. But the attacks and viciousness would have done justice to the kinds of right-wingers Wieseltier despises. No arguments, but within one intellectual article are such intellectual smears about Kahane as "sinister sectarian," "monster," "national disgrace," "demon," "demagogue," and a drawing by one Vint Lawrence of a truly insane-looking Kahane, in the best manner of the fascist haters, left or right. Of course Wieseltier is a troubled man, and at such moments of truth the intellectual masquerade evaporates.

A similar last resort of the fraudulent, desperate intellectuals could be seen in the February 13, 1986, issue of the hallowed and sanctified *New York Review of Books*, with a grotesque and McCarthyite ugly caricature of Kahane on both the cover and the inside page where an article, by troubled leftist Robert Friedman, exposed yet another inability of the frustrated liberal and left to deal rationally or compete intellectually with the issues at hand. And one need only dismiss, with the contempt it deserves, the editorial in the English-language journal of the Mapam Marxist-fascists (*Israel Horizons*, November-December, 1984), which expressed the hope "that 'someone' would put a bullet into Mr. Kahane and be done with him."

Every confused and soul-troubled article, each inanity and viciously irrational attack on me by the intellectuals only heartens me and convinces me that I am correct. The irrationality of those who arrogantly pride themselves on their intellectual superiority and logic, the babbling by those who see themselves as the *nth* estate, more clearly than anything else would convince objective, normal people of these commentators' intellectual bankruptcy and dishonesty.

In the end, it was a leftist of the school of anarchy in Israel, Dan Ben Amotz, writing in *Hadashot* (August 10, 1984), who was more honest than all the cool and proper middle-class and artistic intellectuals. Ben Amotz is an anti-Zionist, one of the new Israelis or "Hebrews" to whom Jewishness means less than nothing, since he sees in it so much that his decadent soul despises. That is why he can be honest about Kahane, he who so loves to tweak the nose of the hypocritical and terrified Israeli Jewish Establishment. Writes Ben Amotz:

"The Jewish state can allow itself to be democratic as long as its Arab inhabitants are in the minority. The moment they become a majority we will have to choose between a democracy that grants equal citizens to all its inhabitants or a Jewish state that will continue in one stratagem or another to grant full rights only to its Jewish inhabitants.

"Kahane has already chosen. Openly, courageously and loudly he admits and is proud of Zionist racism [sic]. In this sense at least he is an honest man as opposed to the leaders of all the other Zionist parties who hide behind him. Pay attention: Kahane expresses openly the secret yearning of [the] Tchiya [nationalist party].... He, at least, says the truth.

"I accept his basic premise concerning the contradiction between democracy and a Jewish state and differ with his consistent (for him) conclusion. If I would be pushed into a corner and forced to choose between these two options alone, I would not hesitate to give up the Jewish character of the state for democracy.

"And what about you? How do you solve the dilemma that Kahane presents to all of us? What do you choose? Democracy in a bi-national state, tri-national, or pluralistic one as in America, or a Jewish state based on purity of race according to Halacha [an outright lie, of course—MK]? I see no other choice and I plead with you to do me a favor and correct me if I am mistaken before I join the others who are fleeing this madhouse."

But of course there is no other choice and Ben Amotz, despite his fraudulent presentation of Judaism's choice as that of "racial purity" (he knows far better than that, but his hatred for Judaism leads him, like so many others, to create deceitful defamation), mockingly presents the reality of the dilemma. No one will "correct" him because there is nothing to correct about his analysis. Jews will not have enough babies to counter the Arab population growth, most western Jews will sooner move to the safety of Tasmania than come to Israel and giving away the liberated territories of Judea-Samaria-Gaza will bring death to our borders but no more than 20 years of breathing space before the Arab population growth within Israel's narrow pre-1967 borders brings us back to the same threat of Arab majority.

The Jewish leaders in Israel and the west have no answers to this question, just as they have no answers to the greater basic contradiction between Zionism and Judaism on the one hand and the western values they so believe in on the other. They are ideologically schizophrenic, an admixture of two contradictory *Weltanschauungs*. They will continue to babble, equivocate, praise ambiguity. They will agonize in their souls; lie to themselves and the Jewish community; smear, curse, defame and attempt, finally, to kill Kahane. But, in the end, they are both tyrants and victims, and nothing will save them. For the Arab threat and the fate of Israel and of world Jewry are not things that exist in an historical or political vacuum. The Jew, his state, his destiny are part of Creation and there is a destiny for the Jew, whether he likes it or not. There is a G-d in the world and His plan for His people is immutable.

Part VII

CONCLUSION

Chapter 17

Conclusion

I do not hate Arabs; I love Jews. And I feel so terribly sorry for them as they wander blindly and so foolishly away from the path of understanding who they are, where they come from and where they go. As they throw away the glory of being chosen, elevated, special. As their leaders in both Israel and the Exile, leaders who are so ignorant of Jewishness and Judaism, so steeped in foreign, un-Jewish culture and ideas that stand in stark contradiction to Judaism, lead them down the terrible path of gentilization and modern-day Hellenism.

And I am terribly *frightened* for my people. Existence for the Jews is not a sometime thing, an act of change and fortune. There *is* a G-d in the world and He did create it and He does direct it, and the Jews—His chosen people—will not be allowed to escape his chosenness and his directed destiny. And there is reward and punishment, no matter how much the Jew and his leaders refuse to believe it; and I fear, very much, that the Jewish people, today, face an awful and awesome punishment and fate. And so, it is certainly not out of hatred of gentiles that this book was written, but, rather, out of love of the Jews, my people. My foolish people, my blind people, but mine.

There remains only to conclude.

It is clear to all but those who cannot or will not see, that we live today in the final era of a world which the Almighty made for Man, the unique. The rise of a Jewish State, the return of the Jewish people, after two millenia, is not the irrelevancy that both atheist and pious

Jew see in it. The footsteps of the Messiah approach and the redemption comes and there remains only the question: How?

Judaism lays down a firm rule. The final redemption, the coming of the Messiah and the Kingdom of G-d, can come in one of two ways. If we merit it, by doing G-d's will, it can come *today*, instantly, magnificently, gloriously, free of tragedy. But if we do not merit it, though it will surely come, it will be preceded by awesome and terrible and unprecedented suffering and catastrophe. If only we raise our eyes unto heaven and bow our heads beneath the yoke of G-d's kingdom, how beautiful and how magnificent will be our redemption!

Above all, let us know that the choice is ours and that there is precious little time in which to make the decision. Let me share with you a final thought to be pondered carefully and deeply. It may, indeed, be the trumpet to awaken the sleeping Jew.

The idea first entered my head as I sat, one day, in Ramle Prison. It was the eve of Tisha B'Av, the tragic commemoration of the destruction of both Temples, the beginning of both terrible exiles. I sat, reviewing the Book of Jonah, with its message of repentance, on the day of national tragedy. Jonah enters the city of Nineveh, to which he has been sent by the Almighty, to warn them of impending destruction unless they repent. And as I read, the words of Jonah to the people suddenly leaped out at me: "In forty days, Nineveh shall be overturned!"

Forty. The thought suddenly struck me: How many times, again and again, does that number arise in connection with sin and punishment? "And the rain was on the earth *forty* days and *forty* nights" (Genesis 7:12), the punishment of a world flooded for its sin. *Forty*. And centuries later, as the Jews of the desert "despised the pleasant land" and wept over their "home" in Egypt, the Almighty angrily decreed that the generation of the desert would not enter the Holy Land, saying: "And your children will wander in the wilderness *forty* years and bear your faithlessness" (Numbers 14:33). Again, *forty*. And the punishment of stripes, whipping, is one of "*Forty* shall he strike him, he shall not increase." And the atonement for sin and the purification process begins with a study of Torah given *forty* days at Sinai continuing in a *mikveh* (ritualarium), whose waters must be a minimum of *forty se'ah*.

Forty. Again and again, the number forty connected to sin and punishment. Why forty? I do not know except to quote the rabbis in *Bamidbar Rabah* 5:5: "And why does the Torah obligate forty stripes? For he (the sinner) violated a Torah given in *forty* days and brought death unto himself [man] who was created in *forty* days. Let him, therefore, be whipped *forty* times and be relieved of his punishment as was done to Adam who sinned, was deserving of death and was punished with *forty*. For the world was cursed due to his sin, forty curses: Ten for Adam, ten for Eve, ten for the serpent and ten for the land."

And in that tiny cell, in prison, the thought expanded. Not only was the concept "forty" tied to sin and punishment, it was specifically connected to the warning of G-d to the sinner, a warning designed to avert that punishment. Jonah warns Nineveh of impending punishment and this gives them a grace period of forty days during which they might search their souls and change their ways.

And in the case of both Holy Temples, the Almighty gave the Jewish people a period of forty years of grace; time to think and rethink their ways. Time to return to Him and save themselves from that punishment. In the aweful final days of the first Jewish state, the L-rd tells the prophet Ezekiel: "And thou shalt lie again on your right side and bear the iniquity of the house of Judah, *forty* days; each day for a year, each day for a year" (Ezekiel 4:6).

And the Biblical commentator Rashi declares: "We learn that from the time of the exiling of the ten tribes until the destruction of Jerusalem, there was a period of *forty* years." *Forty* years: The Almighty, having brought down His wrath on the ten tribes of Israel, begins the countdown to the terrible day of punishment that is decreed for a House of a Judah that has turned its back on its G-d. But one final opportunity is given them, a grace period. A grace period of forty years. And so a prophet is chosen, a prophet of grace, of final warning—Jeremiah. And in the words of the rabbis: "The book of Lamentations was more effective for Israel than the *forty* years that Jeremiah prophesied unto them" (*Eichah Rabah* 4:27).

And the Second Temple. "*Forty* years prior to the destruction of the Temple, the lot [for the Yom Kippur sacrifice] never was chosen by the High Priest's right hand; and the red slip outside the Holy of Holies never turned white [as sign of Divine forgiveness] and the western candle would not light and the doors of the Sanctuary opened by themselves until Rabbi Yochanan Ben Zakkai admonished them, saying: "Sanctuary, sanctuary... I know that you are destined to be destroyed ..." (*Yuma* 39b).

And again: For *forty* years did the Rabbi Zadok sit in the hopes that Jerusalem not be destroyed" (*Gittin* 56a).

And again: "For *forty* years prior to the destruction of the Temple, the Sanhedrin exiled itself [from the Temple] and sat in the market place" (*Avoda Zara* 8b).

Once again, the period of grace. Forty years. The final hope of the Almighty that, perhaps, His final warning would be heeded. The countdown of forty years. The last chance.

And it was then that the full impact of the thought struck me: If it is true that in the first Jewish State and in the second, the Almighty granted us a grace period of forty years, is it possible that the same could be true with the third state? Our state—the State of Israel?

The thought has become an ongoing one; call it obsessive, if you will. After all, the final redemption is one that our rabbis have explained as coming in one of two ways—and there is no third. "In its time, I will hurry it [the redemption]" (Isaiah 60). And our rabbis explain: "If they, the Jews, merit it I will hurry it. If they do not merit it, it will come 'in its time.'"

The difference is more than chronological. It is a qualitative difference that goes to the very essence of our existence. A "hurried" redemption is one that comes with majestic glory and free of pain and tragedy. But one that is "in its time," by the very fact that it comes despite our unworthiness, is accompanied by terrible destruction and holocaust as the deserved punishment that precedes the final glory and salvation. How important it is for us to avoid this awful and needless suffering! And how convinced I am that the Almighty pleads with us to do just that; to replace a redemption of "in its time" with one that is "hurried"; to search our ways and return to Him. And how convinced I am that, just as twice in the past He gave us a period of grace, so too, today, we have been granted it.

And it becomes clearer and clearer to me that, once again, it is forty years; forty years of warning, admonition, opportunity. The final chance.

The State of Israel, that most incredible of miracles, marked the beginning of the final redemption, a redemption born, not out of the betrothal of Jew to his Maker through faith and return, but rather out of the wedlock of Holocaust that was the depths of desecration of the name of G-d, the "*Hillul Hashem*" that was the mockery, humiliation, and denial of the prowess or very existence of the G-d of Israel. It was that Holocaust which broke the patience of a G-d of Israel who had watched His name mocked and dragged in the gentile dust for 20 centuries. "Not for your sake do I do this, O House of Israel, but rather for My Holy Name that you desecrated by the very fact of being among the nations" (Ezekiel 36).

And so, a Jewish State rose from the crematoria and ashes, not because we deserved it, but because the gentile did. Because the punishment and awesome wrath of G-d were being prepared for a world that had mocked and humiliated the Name of the L-rd, G-d of Israel.

The State of Israel which rose up in the year 1948, I am convinced, is the beginning, not only of the redemption, but of the grace period granted us. In the very marrow of my bones I feel that the almighty, in His infinite mercy and goodness, gives us the final, beseeching opportunity to turn needless suffering into glorious and instant redemption. Not for nothing did Rabbi Eliezer say (Sanhedrin 99a): "The days of the Messiah are *forty* years, as it is said: '*Forty* years did I quarrel with a generation....'" And the rabbis add in *Psikta Rabah* 15:10: "Forty-five days does the Messiah reveal himself and then is concealed from them. In the end, the Holy One Blessed Be He is revealed to them and brings down for them manna."

Forty years. The number may not be exact; it may be a few more, a few less, but the period is clear. Forty years of warning, of heartfelt cry from our Father in Heaven. Forty years of grace, of a last opportunity to reverse needless disaster, to bring the redemption with grandeur and majesty.

For make no mistake. The magnificent miracle of return and rise of a Jewish State is surely the beginning of the Final Redemption, but hardly the end. The true finality, the magnificent era of the Messiah, comes to fruition gloriously and majestically and breathtakingly only if we cleave to the great axiom: "If you walk in my statutes... I will give peace in the land" (Leviticus 26).

This is the immutable law of the People of Israel. There is no escaping it. What will be with the Jew; whether his future will be bright or black; whether he will enjoy peace or horrors, depends only on his cleaving to his role, obligation and mission in this world, upon his bending his neck and will beneath the yoke of Heaven.

"If you walk in my Statutes... I will give you peace."

"But if you will not hearken unto Me... I will appoint terror over you" (Ibid.).

This is the choice; the only choice. All the rest is nonsense. And time ticks away and the decision is in our hands.

How the Almighty pleads with us, His children, to accept all that He so desires to give us! How the Messiah beats on the doors, how his footsteps pound on the street! How the Almighty's voice cries out: "Return unto Me, saith the L-rd of Hosts, and I will return unto you" (Zechariah 1). Swiftly, gloriously, today, this very moment!

"Today, if you but hearken to My voice" (Psalms 95).

Dear Jew, the Almighty gives us this day life or death. Will we not choose life?

Will we have the wisdom to understand, the eyes to see, the desire to wish to see? Will we understand that only the embracing of total faith and trust in the Almighty will bring the redemption, a faith that is symbolized by the manna He once again will feed us? Will we see the Messiah and act and not allow him to be concealed again? Will we manifest and prove our faith in the only possible way—actions, terribly difficult, sometimes terribly dangerous? Actions that stand up to the gentile without the slightest fear for his irrelevance; actions that hold onto the Land of Israel, that drive out the Arab, that cleanse the Temple Mount, that leave the impurity and curse of the Exile and return home. These are the *stuff* of which Jewish faith is made. This is what the Almighty seeks as the forty years tick away.

Consider, Jew. If it is indeed true, what I say, then the refusal to heed is more than mere luxury. It is destruction. And then consider a second thing. If it is true that the forty years began with the rise of the State—how many years are left?

Made in United States
North Haven, CT
26 May 2022

19527104R00173